ANNA

ALSO BY AMY ODELL

Tales from the Back Row

ANNA

The Biography

Amy Odell

ALLEN&UNWIN

First published in Great Britain in 2022 by Allen & Unwin
First published in the United States in 2022 by Gallery Books,
an imprint of Simon & Schuster, Inc.

Allen & Unwin
c/o Atlantic Books
Ormond House
26–27 Boswell Street
London WC1N 3JZ
Phone: 020 7269 1610
Email: UK@allenandunwin.com
Web: www.allenandunwin.com/uk

A CIP catalogue record for this book is available from the British Library.

Interior design by Jaime Putorti

Hardback ISBN 978 1 83895 725 4
Trade paperback ISBN 978 1 83895 726 1
E-book ISBN 978 1 83895 727 8

Printed and bound by CPI Group (UK) Ltd, Croydon CR0 4YY

10 9 8 7 6 5 4 3 2 1

MIX
Paper from
responsible sources
FSC® C171272

For Rick

Contents

"People tend to cast people in clichés."

—Anna Wintour,
New York, October 18, 2018

ANNA

Introduction

O f course, she was wearing the sunglasses.

Anna Wintour walked into the *Vogue* staff meeting and looked at the group that had gathered around the table about ten thirty that morning. Many of them had been working late into the night, coming up with stories attempting to explain the unprecedented. Others had just been up crying, scared, in shock. Anna had extraordinary influence over a great many things, but the outcome of this election was not one of them.

It was November 9, 2016. Despite Hillary Clinton's loss, after *Vogue's* full-throttle support, including an endorsement—the first of its kind in the magazine's 124-year history—Anna started the day as usual. She rose by 5:00 a.m., exercised at 5:30 or 6:00 (depending on whether she played her twice weekly tennis or worked out with her trainer), sat for thirty minutes for professional hair and makeup, and was then chauffeured to her office at 1 World Trade Center, where her three assistants and her usual breakfast—a whole-milk latte and a blueberry muffin from Starbucks, which would mostly go uneaten—were waiting for her.

When she arrived that morning, wearing tall python boots and a printed red dress, Anna told the first assistant to call an all-staff meeting.

Her requests for her assistants were constant—day and night, weekday and weekend, and always delivered in emails with no subject line. Her schedule was meticulously planned, but this meeting was last-minute, and she asked her assistants to attend, which was unusual. No one knew the purpose of the gathering, but they did know that when Anna called for one, if you didn't arrive early, you were late.

Phillip Picardi, the editorial director of *Teen Vogue*'s website, had originally given his team permission to work from home that day. Covering the election live for the first time in the magazine's history, they had all worked late trying to explain Donald Trump's victory to the millions of teenage girls who had expected proof that they too could become anything, the same way Anna had.

At seven thirty that morning, only three hours after Picardi had finally called it a night, his assistant had reached out about Anna's all-hands meeting. He'd called his exhausted, emotionally spent staff, and told them to get to the office.

Seats at the white conference room table filled up, and staff packed into every remaining space behind them, waiting for Anna. The polish associated with *Vogue* employees is legendary, but that morning everyone—except Anna—looked some version of terrible, Picardi recalled.

One of Anna's biggest strengths as a businessperson and a leader has been letting nothing slow her down or stand in her way—not childbirth, not emotion, not corporate bullshit, and not losing—and she had correctly sensed that her team needed a filament of the same hardy fiber at this particular moment.

"There's an article that came out today accusing me of going too far in supporting Hillary Clinton, the first woman to ever win the Democratic presidential bid for president," she said, standing at the front of the room. She was referring to a piece published that morning in the fashion industry newspaper *Women's Wear Daily* (commonly referred to as *WWD*), with the headline "Did Anna Wintour and *Vogue*'s Hillary Clinton Advocacy Go Too Far?"

"With the bitter election now in the rearview mirror, many questions loom for *Vogue*, women's magazines, and the fashion industry," the article went on. "To name a few: Did *Vogue* lose credibility with its readers? Should women's magazines cover stories like news outlets? Anna go too far in her role as editor?"

Anna was believed to have been angling for an ambassadorship, which would have brought an end to her reign at *Vogue*. While Clinton thought Anna would have been a great ambassador, and nominating her was a possibility, she hadn't begun a formal process for filling those positions, an advisor said. It was unclear to both the campaign and Anna's boss that she had serious interest in it. Her then-boyfriend, Shelby Bryan, said, "If she'd been offered the ambassadorship to the UK, I think she would have had to really think hard about that."

Surveying her staff in the conference room, Anna continued, "I would just like to say to everyone gathered here today, who works for me, that if supporting LGBTQ rights, if supporting women's rights, if supporting women running for office, if supporting immigrants, and if supporting people all over the country for equality means going too far, then I hope all of you go too far every single day."

As she spoke, her voice caught. It was something that happened rarely, and noticeable enough that a former employee, Stephanie Winston Wolkoff, had a name for it: "the crackle." The *Vogue* team knew she had to have been hurt by Clinton's loss, but they'd never expected confirmation from Anna herself, a woman who almost never showed her emotions at work and, in fact, was so averse to doing so that she'd habitually placed sunglasses between any hint of sentiment and the rest of the world for most of her life. She once described them in a CNN interview as "incredibly useful" for when she wants to hide what she's really thinking or feeling—"a crutch." But at this moment, the shield slipped and she did something that she hadn't the night before.

She was crying.

Anna's way had always been to move forward rather than dwell on what could have been, and that pattern held. "But he's the president," Anna said. "We have to figure out a way to keep moving forward."

Her statement made, she departed. The staff applauded, and then texted anyone who, for whatever reason—a photo shoot, travel, the usual business of the day—was out of the office: "Oh my god—Anna just cried in front of everyone."

* * *

Before Trump was inaugurated and while her staff were still trying to process their feelings about his win, Anna begrudgingly reached out. Trump had been a welcome guest at many of her events in the past, seemingly as interested in her influence and approval as she was in his checkbook. She arranged to meet with him at Trump Tower, through his daughter Ivanka, a longtime acquaintance. Donald told his wife Melania that Anna was coming to see him. According to Melania's then-friend Stephanie Winston Wolkoff, she had heard nothing from Anna herself about the visit, and was so offended she didn't even say hello when Anna showed up. Melania didn't understand that she had been invited to Anna's events not because she was a friend, but simply because she had appeared on the February 2005 cover of *Vogue*.

Anna arranged to bring Donald to 1 World Trade Center to sit down with Condé Nast's other editors-in-chief. As those around her well knew, while Anna's motives weren't always clear in the moment, there was always an agenda. *Who wouldn't want an audience with the president-elect?* people in the meeting with Trump supposed she reasoned. Her team tried twice, once before Trump's inauguration and once after, to photograph Melania for *Vogue*. But in part since they wouldn't guarantee a cover, Melania wouldn't do it. "I don't give a fuck about *Vogue* or any other magazine," she said.

But, Winston Wolkoff believed, she *did* give a fuck about *Vogue*. She wanted the cover once more.

Anna Wintour has been the editor-in-chief of *Vogue* since 1988, and one of the most powerful figures in media. "I don't know what it is about Anna exactly," said Laurie Schechter, an early assistant, "but if she could bottle it she'd make a million billion dollars because it just was like fairy-tale stuff." Yet the many people interviewed for this book had a hard time explaining why she is so powerful and what her power amounts to.

Across more than three decades' worth of issues of *Vogue* and its spinoffs, she has defined not only fashion trends but also beauty standards, telling millions of people what to buy, how to look, and who to care about. She decides which celebrities and models to photograph and which clothes to dress them in. If she wants a designer to have more influence, she recommends them to lead bigger labels, and she has this power because the owners of those larger labels seek—and follow—her advice. Said Grace Coddington, Anna's former creative director, about the power of her preferences: "She makes it very clear. So obviously it's not a good idea to continue in a track that you know she doesn't like, because then she's probably not going to like the pictures, and if she doesn't like the pictures, they might run, but there'd be many less."

"I haven't ever heard her say, 'Do not do that, do this.' You know somebody loves something by looking at them, and you know if somebody is indifferent by looking at them," said Tonne Goodman, a fashion editor who's worked for Anna since 1999 and attended many collection previews with her. Sally Singer, who worked for Anna for nearly twenty years, elaborated, "There was never an idea that *Vogue* was an editorial project alone. It was an intervention into the fashion world."

That intervention has been largely successful, given the effect of her authority. Tom Ford, a giant in the fashion industry and one of Anna's closest friends, has long enjoyed the distinction of being a "*Vogue* brand." Such favorites have privileged relationships with Anna and her team of editors; she and her staff advise them not only on their clothes, but also on how to run their businesses. In turn, *Vogue* brands are rewarded with coverage in the magazine and, more important, Anna's personal support and advice. And she doesn't wait for the next generation of designers to emerge—she financially supports them, through the Council of Fashion Designers of America (CFDA)/*Vogue* Fashion Fund. That support can be the difference between unimaginable success and bankruptcy. "If I were on her good side, I would be afraid," said André Leon Talley, once one of Anna's closest collaborators, about the danger of falling out of favor. "As much as she loves a person who has talent, if she does not love you, then you're in trouble."

This kind of interventionist strategy isn't limited to the fashion world. She has leveraged the names of her powerful allies to raise money for charitable initiatives, most notably the Metropolitan Museum of Art's Costume Institute, which preserves and displays objects of fashion as art, for which she has amassed more than $250 million. She has organized the fashion industry's efforts to raise money for Democratic candidates, thereby visibly politicizing the business. Her influence extends to Broadway, entertainment, and sports, among other areas. (First-time director Bradley Cooper, who repeatedly sought her advice, sent her a copy of his script for *A Star Is Born* to get her thoughts on whom to cast in the lead role, which went to Lady Gaga.)

Editors of *Vogue* were powerful before Anna had the job, but she has expanded that power remarkably, making the magazine, and herself, a brand that powerful people want to be associated with. "The amazing thing about Anna is the average person knows who she is," said Ford. "You show them a picture and they say, 'That's Anna Wintour from *Vogue*.'" Particularly thanks to the novel and film *The Devil Wears Prada*, how Anna speaks, hires and fires, eats, and shops are topics of both obsession and scrutiny. She is widely perceived as "cold" and "icy," endowed with the rare ability to turn attachments—to both outcomes and people—on and off like a switch. When she walks the halls at Condé Nast, terrified staff press themselves against the wall to stay out of her way and check what's on their computer screens. Yet they are devoted to her—indeed, many former staffers feel the need to protect Anna because working for her was as extraordinary as it was grueling. Certainly she doesn't make it easy for them. Staff responsibilities go beyond running *Vogue*, said Mark Holgate, who joined as senior fashion writer at the end of 2003. "It's also, 'Come up with a list of designers for someone to consider hiring as their new creative director.' It's, 'Can you look at this script because so-and-so's come to Anna with an idea. . . .' There's a ton of other things funneling into *Vogue* on any given day." And when Anna asks for something, she usually wants it done immediately. Despite her work emails to her staff going out before 6 a.m. some days, added Holgate, "It's also kind of addictive." Others praise her directness; you always know where you stand with her, and that's better than working for someone who wants to know about your kid's birthday party but can't make up their mind about a headline.

Those who have worked for Anna often wonder why she has to be involved in *everything*, and how she manages to juggle it all. Anna controls all that she can, right down to the ingredients in the food at the Met Gala. Yet despite her perfectionism, she has made her fair share of mistakes. For someone who has espoused progressive principles like those she mentioned in the postelection staff meeting, her track record is spotty. She has been repeatedly called out for publishing culturally and racially insensitive photos and articles, and for failing to embrace diverse subjects. Years went by in the nineties when only white women appeared on the cover of *Vogue*. Promoting fur was once her cause célèbre. She has publicly body-shamed. Her staff has been mostly white, seemingly picked for their personal style, appearance, and pedigree as much as for their skills and credentials.

For many, Anna has been a source of admiration and envy. (As one of her old friends, Annabel Hodin, concluded, "All you ever wanted to do was to *be* her, really.") Yet it is probably her fearsome reputation that first comes to mind when her name is mentioned. With so few women having attained Anna's level, there's no model for how that should look, just the feeling that such power should be exercised with a warmer touch than she naturally possesses. (Though if a man did her job as well and with similar affectations, his discipline and commitment would likely be celebrated.)

Outside of the office, Anna is said to be different. She is a dog person. She is, friends said, fiercely devoted to her children and grandchildren (yes, she's changed their diapers). At her weekend compound in Mastic on Long Island, they added, she's relaxed. She loves hosting her extended family and serving meals to as many as fifty people. "She's very family-minded," said Emma Soames, a longtime friend. "She's become a matriarch." As her longtime Met Gala planner Stephanie Winston Wolkoff put it, "There is a person there."

Inside the office, some staff view her similarly. Jill Demling, who booked celebrity covers for *Vogue* for twenty years, stated, "Anna played an important role in my life, not only as a mentor, but as almost a mother figure." Yet she remains full of contradiction. Anna doesn't do small talk. Yet she enjoys people who aren't afraid to pop into her office and ask her a question. She is deadly serious about business, yet she likes to joke around with her staff. What she really wants, what she responds better to than anything, is being treated like a human being. Like those famous sunglasses, her icon status has been both an ennobling veneer and an obstacle.

There is debate about how creative Anna is as an editor. Some who have worked closely with her think her strengths are actually twofold: first, managing creative people and the creative process, and second, forming politically savvy alliances to grow her power. Her closest friends said that she absolutely loves fashion, though that wasn't always evident to others who worked closely with her. They wondered if fashion was just her way, as a woman entering the workforce in the era that she did, to attain a position of real power.

Over the course of her reign at *Vogue*, her resignation or dismissal has been a subject of regular speculation. But, despite spates of acute public criticism, her power only expands with time, because she knows the ecosystem in which she operates better than anyone. You might even say she invented it.

Chapter 1

ORIGINS

Born Eleanor Baker to a wealthy Quaker family in 1917 in Harrisburg, Pennsylvania, the future Nonie Wintour was a society girl. Her father, Ralph Baker, was a lawyer who left private practice to become a Harvard Law School professor. He specialized in trusts, and, before his death, established a substantial fund that would support his descendants, including his granddaughter Anna, over the course of many decades.

Nonie had enrolled at the University of Cambridge's Newnham College for women after graduating from Radcliffe in 1938, and was introduced to her future husband, Charles Wintour, also at Cambridge, by their mutual friend Arthur M. Schlesinger, Jr. The son of a major general, Charles was born in 1917 in Dorset in Southwest England. Petite and slim, Nonie styled her hair in short dark waves pinned back from her face. Charles wore glasses and a melancholic expression, and projected an air of professionalism.

Both shared an interest in journalism and writing. At Cambridge, Charles co-edited *Granta*, the prestigious undergraduate literary magazine. Nonie had spent the summer after college working as a reporter at the *Daily Republican* newspaper in Phoenixville, Pennsylvania. The necessary terseness of newspaper journalism might have encouraged her direct and spare use of language, which sometimes drove Charles crazy when they were dating, since he often couldn't tell, particularly in their correspondence, what she was actually thinking.

After graduating with a first for academic achievement, the university's highest possible honor, Charles headed to London to start working at the J. Walter Thompson advertising agency, while Nonie headed back across the ocean—their love was certain, their future anything but.

Among the most minor consequences of Germany's invasion of Poland on September 1, 1939, was Charles being out of a job at J. Walter Thompson barely two months after he'd arrived. Like so many of his peers, Charles promptly enlisted. Before he knew what his assignment would be, he sent a letter to Nonie asking her to come to London and marry him as soon as possible. Weeks later he began officer cadet training, and shortly afterward received word that Nonie accepted and would come in February.

Nonie arrived on the same day the first enemy aircraft was shot down in the UK. Charles was so ecstatic to see her that he nearly fainted. While a bit less euphoric, Nonie was relieved that they still got along so well.

They married on February 13, 1940, at a church in Cambridge, and then celebrated with friends. As thrilled as they were to be together, the war was disheartening and neither of them knew where Charles would be sent now. Soon pregnant, Nonie stayed on a few months before returning to Boston.

Once alone, Charles slid into depression. Terrified of an invasion of Britain, he wondered if an affair might be the antidote. This was only half as shocking as it seemed. Charles felt that being with a woman was a "necessity" for him, and from their earliest weeks together, Nonie had realized that he wasn't the faithful type. Feeling that a ground rule had been established and accepted, he assumed Nonie would agree that an extramarital relationship would benefit him. (Charles's affairs would go on throughout their marriage, becoming painfully apparent to Anna as a teenager.) Nonie—then about six months pregnant—consented to the affair from Boston. Though he worried whether it actually bothered her, Charles started spending his evenings with a twenty-three-year-old divorcée whose new fiancé was conveniently in Rhodesia.

In late November, forty weeks and a day after his wedding, Charles received a cable from Schlesinger announcing the birth of his son Gerald, named for Charles's father. Half a decade would pass before he would meet his son.

For Anna, one of the most difficult periods of her personal and professional life would involve living with a new baby on the other side of the ocean from her spouse. Her parents had to manage this very challenge in the middle of a war, with intense worry that Charles could be killed any day.

Just months after having Gerald, Nonie—after Charles fought with her father about it—sailed back to Europe to be with her husband, leaving their son in safety with her parents. Charles was aware that Nonie came against her will. He had pressured her to come, though she felt deep pain at leaving Gerald behind. Still, Charles was aware that no available course of action would leave either of them entirely happy, and that if they didn't see one another until after the war, their youth would have fled them—that is, if he even lived through the war itself.

While initially homesick and angry, Nonie stayed with Charles for several years, choosing to be present in her marriage, even if that meant estrangement from her child. She moved through the UK following wherever Charles's various posts took him as he ascended in the ranks, both of them grateful when he was assigned to office work after completing a course at the Staff College. She finally sailed home in the middle of 1944, now a stranger to their son. With his wife on the other side of the Atlantic, Charles began another affair. Nonie had left her baby for her husband for several years. Now Charles was willing to abandon his wife through infidelity. Though the circumstances of war were exceptional, Charles and Nonie seemed to share an ability to disregard others' welfare when it might get in the way of their most immediate desires.

In the winter, he was stationed in the Trianon Palace Hotel at Versailles, resplendent with crystal chandeliers, black-and-white-tiled floors, and white columns. Sitting in a garret, Charles and his fellow junior officers discussed what they wanted to do after the war. Charles said he wanted to become a journalist. Arthur Granard, an aide to Air Chief Marshal Arthur Tedder, responded, "If you ever want an introduction to Lord Beaverbrook, let me know."

Lord Beaverbook was a wealthy Canadian who became a millionaire at twenty-seven by merging cement companies before moving to London to pursue business opportunities along with political and cultural influence. He advised Winston Churchill during the war and published a portfolio of newspapers (which just after World War II had the largest combined circulation of any publisher in the world), including the *Daily Express* and the *Evening Standard*. Having failed to become prime minister, Beaverbrook used his papers to promote his friends, attack his enemies, and push for an isolationist Britain.

Once the war ended, Charles wrote Granard to ask about meeting Beaverbrook. To his surprise, Granard followed through on his promise and made an introduction.

Beaverbrook was a known eccentric, but Charles found him disarmingly warm when they met at his apartment on London's upscale Park Lane on Monday, October 1, 1945. He asked Charles to write an article on the differences between British and American work styles, and after filing the story, Charles received an offer to work as an assistant editorial writer at the *Evening Standard* on a trial basis for £14 a week, a job that would change his life.

With his career seemingly sorted, Charles now had to settle. He had one final night out as a bachelor with his lover, then found a place to rent for his family in London's Hampstead neighborhood. He had no idea how short-lived his and Nonie's happiness would be.

Gerald was five years old when Nonie brought him to London in early 1946. Almost immediately, Charles felt Gerald would benefit from living with him, after being brought up "in a predominately feminine environment."

Nonie and Charles had their second son, James (known as Jimmie), in May of 1947, and two years later Nonie was pregnant again. On November 3, 1949, Nonie gave birth to her first daughter, the little girl she'd hoped for when Jimmie was born, named Anna. Aside from the baby's bout of whooping cough the following spring, the Wintour children flourished.

That was until Tuesday, July 3, 1951, four months before Anna's second birthday. Gerald put on his uniform and headed off to school. Now ten years old, he had been riding his bike for years. Tragically, a car hit Gerald while he was riding home that day, fracturing his skull. He was taken to New End Hospital in Hampstead, but could not be saved. At 6 p.m., twenty minutes after he arrived, Gerald Wintour was pronounced dead.

The story that would endure in British journalism circles was that this personal calamity spurred Charles's professional ascent. He had been bored and itching to leave the paper for a magazine job. Still, when notified during a meeting with Beaverbrook that Gerald had been in the accident, rather than rush home, he is said to have gone back into the meeting and carried on with work, making no mention of his son. That dedication in the face of one of life's worst tragedies left an indelible impression on his boss.

Nonetheless, Charles shared Nonie's profound grief, in her case so great that her doctor prescribed her medication to help get her through the worst days early on. Both parents tormented themselves with blame; making it worse, eight days after the accident the man who'd been behind the wheel was charged not with manslaughter, but only dangerous driving. Though he faced a maximum jail sentence of two years, after ultimately being convicted, he was ordered to pay a fine of just £10.

Later that month, the Wintours packed up and sailed to America on the *Queen Elizabeth* to visit Nonie's family. Charles, the sort who never took his full vacation time, departed the States early to return to work, and it would not be until the fall that the family was reunited. The trip, of course, couldn't change their suffering.

Though Anna was twenty months old at the time of Gerald's death—too young to remember the event or grasp the tragedy of the loss—her family was haunted by it for many years to come. No pictures of her brother were displayed in the house, and at one point, Nonie's anxiety was such that she put bars on the windows, fearing that somehow one of her remaining children might fall out.

While his spirit may have been shattered, in the new year Charles got a promotion to political editor of the *Evening Standard*. A profile of Beaverbrook in *Newsweek* that mentioned Charles's elevation called him "brilliant." Though Nonie was proud of her husband's success, she seemed to resent that it resulted from devotion to Beaverbrook, which appeared at times greater than Charles's dedication to her and their children. She especially loathed Beaverbrook's conservative politics.

Charles and Nonie went on to have two more children after Anna, Patrick and Nora. Bored at home raising her four kids, all under the age of ten, Nonie picked up freelance gigs reviewing television shows, reading scripts for Columbia Pictures, and finally writing as a film critic. When she was ready to work full-time again, "she decided that she wanted to work in social issues," Anna later said, and began a whole new career as a social worker helping pregnant teens find adoptive parents for their children, dedicating herself to this effort as much as Charles did the newspaper. "That was very important work to her and I think very inspiring to all of us," Anna said. Though she spoke often in interviews about her father as an inspiration, she almost never, over the course of her entire career, discussed her mother, despite how close they were. She rarely discussed her mother even privately with her friends. Yet her character strongly resembled Nonie's. Anna* may have been more extroverted than Nonie, but, like her mother, Anna was incredibly strong-willed and would adopt equally fierce political convictions.

Anna's professional ambition and ruthlessness, on the other hand, seemed to stem specifically from her father, whose power within the

---

* Friends disagreed on whether Anna is introverted or extroverted herself.

Beaverbrook stable grew with every promotion—from political editor of the *Evening Standard* to assistant editor at the *Sunday Express* to deputy editor of the *Evening Standard* to managing editor at the *Daily Express* and then, in 1959, back, to his relief, to the more upmarket *Evening Standard*.

Being editor of the *Evening Standard* was more than prestigious— it seemed financially advantageous. The Wintours bought a large two-story house in the English countryside, and when she wasn't riding horses or playing tennis, one of Anna's favorite things to do there was curl up on the quintessentially English cabbage-rose chintz upholstery with a book (friends and colleagues later marveled at Anna's voracious reading). The Wintours' vacations, usually during the summer, were along the Mediterranean, likely in Spain or Italy.

Charles kept a strict professional schedule. He rose at 7 a.m. and got to his office at 8, where he was responsible for putting out at least five different editions of the paper each day. If news broke when he wasn't at the office, he dropped what he was doing and dashed back to work, even if the family was out of the country on vacation. "The family all knew that he cared very deeply about us, but we also knew that he cared very deeply about the paper. There wasn't any sense that he was an absent father—on the other side, he taught all of us what a work ethic is, and how important it is to love what you do in life," Anna told a reporter. She witnessed his passion for his work firsthand when she visited his office: meeting writers and seeing the papers getting printed, the smell of fresh ink wafting off the presses.

"There was always this sense of deadlines," Anna told another interviewer. "This excitement about the news." Sunday lunches were often dominated by family conversations about what was in the papers. "The gospel in our house was the newspaper," Anna recalled.

Though Nonie had grown up close to her parents and enjoyed being with them, Anna later said her dad "came from quite a Victorian upbringing. I'm not sure his mother ever spoke to him." But Nonie and Charles wanted to raise their kids more in an American manner, which meant being involved in their lives. In British households of a professional class, the children often ate dinner separately from their parents. In the Wintour household, Anna and her siblings were included in their parents' dinners and social gatherings, which gave her access to Charles's world. This glamorous and intellectual milieu, the excess of those parties, was normalized for Anna from a young age. And when famous journalists weren't dropping by for dinners, the family would engage in their own high-level conversation around the dining table.

Under Charles, the *Evening Standard*'s influence proved that a tabloid could be both populist and sophisticated, and it became known as London's best evening newspaper. ("On the front page you want the headless corpse found by the river," he said, "but inside there must be at least one article that the Permanent Under-secretary at the Treasury cannot afford to miss.") He hired foreign correspondents and ran liberal-leaning political coverage, while giving equal weight to arts and culture. His main goal was to attract a young readership to the paper, and when asked by a colleague about the secret of his success, he replied, "I just recruited young." He valued his inexperienced staff's input and was known to walk across the newsroom simply to ask a young writer which picture they preferred for the front page. It was no surprise that so many journalists wanted to work for him.

For a Fleet Street editor at the time, Charles was unusually good to female talent. "It was the beginning of second-wave feminism, so women's rights were slightly fashionable but still really out there," said Celia Brayfield, who finally got a writing job after applying about four times. Brayfield noticed when she started at the *Evening Standard* after working at the *Daily Mail* that she didn't get wolf-whistled and cat-called when she was walking around the offices—a culture of restraint that could only have originated from on high. When she got pregnant as a freelancer, Charles insisted she take the same maternity leave as a staffer, even though she technically wasn't entitled to the same benefits. That women were cheaper to hire was a given, but unlike many of his peers, Charles valued their talent.

Though Charles was supportive of and respected by his team, he was by no means easy to be around. His staff knew not to bother him before the first edition was set in the morning. In daily interactions, he was quiet, cold, and exacting. Charles had to make decisions constantly and therefore quickly. When he took members of his staff out to lunch once a year, he came with a notebook so he could consult a planned list of conversation topics. His speech, indicative of the British upper class, was clipped as if periods were inserted throughout his sentences: "Now let's. Have. A discussion. About. That. Matter." (The exception was his signature phrase, growled as one word, when someone made a mistake: *"ForChrissakegetitrightnexttime!"*) When a writer came into his huge office to show him a draft, he sat them at a distance from his desk, then put the article down, his forehead in his hand, and read the entire text without a word, making the person about as nervous and uncomfortable as possible. The middle-aged men on staff, who addressed Charles as "sir," cowered in daily meetings where he ripped apart the previous day's issues, demanding to know why one story ended abruptly and another was buried. When he walked by a workstation, Brayfield said, "He was so frightening that people would bend like a field of wheat under a wind as he went past. They would cringe over their typewriters, specifically from sheer authority." Staff were thrilled when he offered a single word of praise—"excellent"—on the bottom of their copy.

Yet as terrifying as Charles was, he commanded respect, and they were eager to please him. "He was fascinating and we were all enthralled by him," said Valerie Grove, who wrote for him. Despite how he came off to others, Anna saw her father as "warm and wonderful," and didn't understand why his work nickname was Chilly Charlie, defending him in a 1999 interview by saying, "It just seemed to have nothing to do with the person he was." Many would later have the same sentiment about her.

Outside of work, he was less forbidding, especially at dinner parties. He loved gossip, and every so often a story about someone he knew would lead him to burst into a surprisingly loud and delightful laugh. Many nights, he and Nonie left their children with a nanny and went out to parties, plays, or the opera, believing appearances were an obligatory part of his job. A successful editor, he thought, must "accept more invitations than he wants and know more people than he likes." Eventually Nonie's attendance ebbed, and Charles went without her.

While Charles's staff thought his success completely deserved, there remained an undercurrent that his rise was in part a reward for his stoicism, a level of militaristic discipline that his staff would recognize as uniquely Wintourian: to suppress a flood of tears, repress the shock, and continue with work as though every parent's most unthinkable nightmare hadn't just occurred. His staff would later notice this same bulletproof discipline in his eldest daughter.

Yet it would be a mistake to claim that Anna's approach was entirely the product of her father. Arthur Schlesinger described Nonie as "bright, witty, and critical" with "a sharp eye for the weaknesses of others," noting her cynical nature as a form of "self-protection, because I think she was extremely vulnerable." Still, he added, "but she also was great fun to be with so long as one wasn't the target." Anna's friends and colleagues would say the same thing about her.

Chapter 2

BEYOND SCHOOL
UNIFORMS

D uring the 1960s, if something was cool, it came out of London. By the time Anna became a teenager, the city was in the throes of a "youthquake," rationing and gloom replaced by hedonism, joy, and, of course, Beatlemania. Anna lived at the doorstep of it all in London's St. John's Wood district, home to Abbey Road Studios. "It was impossible not to be aware and excited, and to feel that the world belonged to the young," Anna said.

Fashion was at the heart of this cultural transformation. Clothes for women who didn't want to dress in stiff midcalf skirts and jackets like their mothers were finally available in boutiques sprouting up everywhere. Nothing more dramatically signified this shift than the miniskirt, which was regarded as scandalous even though the earliest iterations were just inches above the knee. (The *Daily Mail* declared that "a model girl's best friend is a good pair of knees," after designer Mary Quant started selling skirts a shocking "nearly 3 in. above the knee.")

Barbara Hulanicki, a fashion illustrator by training, saw the desperation for new styles firsthand in 1964 when she designed a pink gingham minidress to sell through a newspaper advertisement for just 25 shillings. She received 17,000 orders for the dress, which was advertised as coming in only small and medium sizes. Hulanicki opened a pioneering boutique that she called Biba to sell even more of her affordable designs. She never made more than 500 of each item, and girls lined up outside every Saturday morning to shop before things sold out. Anna had little patience for lines, but managed to get there when the store opened to nab things before they vanished.

As much as fashion fascinated Anna, school did not. Though she "could probably become a sprinter of Olympic standard," her father said, she did what she wanted—and running was not it.

In 1960, she had tested into one of London's best private girls' schools. "Queens College was a school for girls like me and Anna who didn't want to go to university, but whose parents wanted them to," said Emma Soames, a friend who attended separately from Anna. The school had rigorous academics (Anna excelled in English), and an exacting approach to discipline. Among the many things that were not allowed were chatting with friends in the hallway, speaking without being spoken to, asking too many questions, and wearing anything that wasn't part of the uniform to keep warm. "It was so cold in the main hallway where we had prayers every morning that girls would faint. I developed frostbite in my feet as a child because I was so cold," said Stacey Lee, a former classmate who befriended Anna. Anna soon decided to transfer to a new school, seemingly without concern for any friends left behind. "She just moved on," said Lee. "She didn't depend on people, or attach to people."

In 1963, Anna started at the excellent North London Collegiate School. She wasn't warmly welcomed by her new classmates, just about all of whom had attended since first grade, and who were so icy they didn't even help Anna with directions around the school.

Another new girl having a similar problem was Vivienne Lasky. Lasky had moved from Berlin to London, where her New York–born father, Melvin, edited the influential pro-American (later revealed to be CIA-funded) *Encounter* magazine. She found Anna reserved in what Lasky felt was a very "British" sense; her manner of speaking was, like her father's, clipped. But she also sensed that Anna wanted to be noticed on her own terms: she stood like a model in a fashion spread—with her back rounded and shoulders hiked, exhibiting a certain fashionable confidence.

Even though Lasky became her friend, Anna could be brusque. She made unsparing comments to Lasky about other people's appearances—most notably frizzy, natural curls, which she abhorred, and her fellow students who, Anna concluded, having been stuck nearly their entire childhoods in brown uniforms, lacked any "idea of color or style."

Yet such critiques were off-limits when it came to Anna's family. Her dad went to work every day in the typical Fleet Street man's uniform of a white shirt, the sleeves rolled up to the elbow, and a tie. Her sister, Nora, didn't have perfectly straight hair like Anna's, or put much effort into caring for it. Her mom's clothes likely came from a middle-market retailer. (Later, when Anna entered the workforce, she bought her mom a navy skirt from Browns, a designer store in London's upscale Mayfair neighborhood. Nonie only learned that the poorly fitting skirt cost more than £100 when she went to the store to return it.)

Anna, stuck in her school uniform for most of her waking hours, kept up with everything new and trendy by reading voraciously—books, newspapers (as many as eight on Sundays), magazines, literary journals. Anna especially loved *Seventeen,* which Nonie's mom sent her from the US, the covers always featuring a pretty girl, often with flipped hair, in a graphic print or kicky dress. The cover lines touted fashion and beauty, but the issues had more, everything from diet tips to teen correspondents interviewing then–attorney general Robert F. Kennedy. "[*Seventeen*] was just my dream," Anna confessed years later. "I couldn't wait for it to come every month."

For Anna, it wasn't enough to just look good; she wanted to be admired as the best-dressed person in the room, Lasky said. That notice was essential to her, and it spoke of a contradiction. Her life at home was one of culturally elitist comfort and, through Charles, power. As Anna entered adolescence, she would be known wherever she went in London as the daughter of the celebrated newspaper editor Charles Wintour. Yet outside the house she could feel invisible, ignored by her classmates, her individuality suffocated by the sameness of the uniform—not just the wretched ones she had to wear at school, but the general *blah* that had characterized most clothing in Britain. Standing out was more than a tactic for immediate acknowledgment—it was an assertion that some-one could escape not merely the beige and brown but also, in her case, the notions of what it meant to be a Wintour. Her beauty regimen included taking yeast pills from the same trichologist, Philip Kingsley, her father saw to prevent his hair loss, never mind that her hair was perfect all on its own; visits to a dermatologist, even though her skin was nearly flawless; and buying cream by the high-end brand Charles of the Ritz to address her occasional blemish, though she never wore a lot of makeup. While at North London Collegiate, Anna went to Vidal Sassoon, where the bob haircut that became emblematic of the era had originated. She had her thick, naturally straight brown hair cut shorter and got blunt bangs so long they brushed her eyelashes. The whole point of the look was to have perfect, freshly cut ends and bangs—mandating frequent trims, but she had no problem maintaining it with regular trips to Leonard of Mayfair, the salon to which Sassoon stylists defected. The style, though it became her signature, was completely unremarkable in London, where young women everywhere had the same haircut.

Anna usually didn't directly tell someone she disagreed with their choices—of what to wear or eat, or how to act—but she had a way of making people feel they should be a certain way, a way that was, really, more like her. The look of the period was skinny. "We wanted to be Twiggy thin," said Lasky—which is to say, *really* thin. Anna and Lasky ate little more than a Granny Smith apple during the school day. When Anna would invite Lasky over and cook her favorite foods, like cheesecake, but not eat any of it herself, her restraint started to make Lasky feel like she was doing something wrong—something those close to Anna would often experience—and that she needed to do more not so much to keep up the look itself but to maintain Anna's approval. After it came out in 1964, Anna adhered to *The Drinking Man's Diet: How to Lose Weight with a Minimum of Willpower*, which boasted of a one-sentence regimen: "Eat fewer than 60 grams of carbohydrates a day."

Anna loved going over to Lasky's house and talking to her parents. Her mother was a beautiful, slender ex-ballerina who wore designer clothing and fed the girls gourmet food. "Nonie was terribly aware of this crush that Anna had on my mother," recalled Lasky. "They were opposites. My mother never left the house without wearing a couture suit. She wore ropes and ropes of pearls. She never weighed more than eighty-five pounds."

Though Anna's judgments of others were ruthless, she was probably hardest on herself. She once bought an expensive outfit to wear to her cousin's wedding, including a pink skirt with a floral jacket. When she got the pictures back, she was distraught. "Well, I just don't know about my legs," she said." When she found a tape measure and checked the width of both her own and Lasky's knees, she was horrified to learn Lasky's were smaller. It was as if she felt forever doomed by the tiny difference. Lasky pointed out that Anna's weight hasn't appeared to change since she was eighteen years old.

Even once settled at school, Anna never found much of a social circle there beyond Lasky. In interviews, Anna has described her child self as shy, but friends are divided on whether or not she is. They agreed, at least, that she was silent. Lasky didn't see her as shy. "She didn't want to be part of a group that existed. She wanted to be in her own rarefied air," she said, adding, "She wouldn't go out of her way to sort of connect with this one and that one unless it [was] truly necessary. That's part of that mystique."

During Anna's teen years, Charles and Nonie's marriage soured, probably partly because of his affairs, and likely from the irreparable damage to their relationship from the fallout of Gerald's death. The dinner gatherings became increasingly tense, their guests dreading the prospect of the couple arguing. Mary Kenny, who was working for Charles at the time, said their bickering at dinner was so bad that she got the distinct impression that Charles and Nonie were actually trying to embarrass each other. "It was terrible, really, being with them," she said.

But at least the visitors' exposure to their tortured relationship was limited. Anna had to live with it. Lasky and Anna adored their dads and were horrified to come to a realization that their fathers weren't faithful to their mothers. How could their dads—their wonderful dads, whom they idolized—be capable of cheating? Plus, Anna surely recognized that the people who most impressed her venerated dad were not the sort devoted to, say, selflessly helping pregnant teens, but women who were prominent in publishing, just like him.

When Anna was around fifteen, the Wintours moved to a larger house in Kensington where she got the basement apartment with its own entrance, totally separated from the rest of the house. One long wall of the apartment contained a white bookcase (among the furniture her parents had purchased from Habitat, a hip interiors store), stuffed with books. Her large, spare bedroom was done in toile, blue and white, the apartment not only a sanctuary of her own good taste, but also likely sparing her from overhearing her parents.

Anna's academic disinterest was increasingly clear during her second year at North London. She got to study under Peggy Angus, a famous artist with two works in the National Portrait Gallery, further inspiring an interest in art that would influence Anna as a young fashion editor and ultimately help get her a meeting with *Vogue*. But most of the curriculum bored her. Occasionally, without any consequence, she and Lasky forged notes saying they were sick or had to go to the doctor and went to Leicester Square to shop. (They changed out of their loathed uniforms in public bathrooms.) At the end of the school week, Anna couldn't wait to get dressed to go out. She and Lasky took the tube home, washed up, changed into their night looks (usually minis), and watched the live music show *Ready Steady Go!*. (Its slogan was "The weekend starts here!") At 11 p.m., the pair would hail a cab to go to one of their favorite clubs. As Anna described in an article in North London

Collegiate's student magazine, the Garrison's crowd was young blondes trying to impress businessmen (boring); the Scotch of St. James had a better, more mixed patronage, but was too packed (uncomfortable); Dolly's, where "the titled and the rich chat amiably with the famous and the notorious and the debs and the dukes dance side by side with pop stars and their camp followers" had "the most way-out outfits" and "the kinkiest gear. . . . With a Beatle and a Stone or two and Cathy McGowan [the host of *Ready Steady Go!*] thrown in, what more could anyone ask?"

Bouncers didn't check IDs, but Anna and Lasky weren't trying to get drunk—they had a Shirley Temple or a Coke and left in an hour or less, just enough time to see and be seen and still get enough sleep before going to Biba early the next morning. "Both of our families were very trusting. We were not promiscuous girls. We were not crazy girls," said Lasky. And for Anna, going out was never about going wild. Visiting the clubs was more about reconnaissance than excess. Amidst a crowd of the fashionable, she was studying.

Chapter 3

FIRED AND HIRED

A nna's formal education ended when she was sixteen years old, departing North London Collegiate before completing her final year.* University had been an important part of her parents' lives, but she had no reason to go to Oxford or Cambridge (the only real point of spending a fourth year at North London) if she aspired to work in fashion. Years later, Anna told her close friend the playwright David Hare, "I was so desperate to get out in the world and get on with things." She wanted to work.

At the time, it was not unusual for British teenagers to leave school early, with some women going on to finishing school to prepare for domestic life, or to secretarial school.** Unsurprisingly, Nonie and Charles were less than happy about Anna's decision. "I don't think it was snobbishness so much as the Wintours just felt that education was . . . a tool that could absolutely change your life," Lasky said. But Anna's

---

* Her last day was July 27, 1966, but since school records list her as being in the class of 1967, it's possible she quit at the beginning of her last year, as opposed to during the break between third and fourth. Anna herself has never addressed the discrepancy.

** The year before Anna left North London, just a quarter of UK students older than sixteen remained in school.

parents accepted her decision, as far as Lasky could tell. "They never threw it in her face."

On the other hand, her siblings shared her parents' interest in politics and social issues, and all attended prestigious universities. Anna felt like the black sheep of the family. "In the face of my brothers' and sister's academic success, I felt I was rather a failure. They were super-bright so I guess I worked at being decorative. Most of the time, I was hiding behind my hair and I was paralytically shy. I've always been a joke in my family. They've always thought I am deeply unserious. My sister would always ring up and say: 'Where is Anna—is she at the hairdresser or the drycleaner's?' It's not their world," she later recalled. But while her siblings didn't understand her interest in fashion, Charles seemed to appreciate it. Fashion was part of the culture the *Evening Standard* covered, so he had to keep up with it somewhat. But he also cared that fashion exhilarated Anna, who seemed to many to be his favorite child.

Charles denied that he ever pushed Anna into a media career— "Anna said she felt that what I was doing was exciting . . . ," he said— but in fact, she knew that her dad wanted her to go into journalism. (He would sometimes ask her if she'd read certain articles and what she thought of them, almost as if training her for her future responsibilities.)

Yet she was wary, half in and half out. "I certainly grew up knowing that being in publishing was something I wanted to do," she told journalist George Wayne, but "chose to go into magazines because that wasn't so much his world." Still, some twenty years into her *Vogue* editorship, she said Charles was ultimately her primary influence. "I think my father really decided for me that I should work in fashion. I can't remember what form it was I had to fill out, maybe it was an admissions thing, and at the bottom it said 'career objectives' . . . And I said, 'What shall I do, how shall I fill this out?' So he said, 'Well, you write you want to be editor of *Vogue*, of course.' And that was it, it was decided."

Her determination lit up like a match.

A few months after Anna ended her education, her grandfather Ralph Baker died. He left behind an estate for his surviving wife,

Anna Baker; when she passed away in September of 1970, the trust was valued at $2.28 million. Payments started coming out of it for Nonie, her sister, and Anna and her siblings. Many were for specific purposes, such as Patrick's Harvard tuition and Nonie's sister's maid bills. Anna, who didn't need tuition money, began receiving lump sums for unspecified purposes. Over the course of the first six years of her magazine career, she received more than $19,000, which in 2021 currency would be more than $120,000. That money made it possible for her not only to enter the poorly paying publishing field but also to take the risks that would lead to her advancement. It enabled her to buy nice things, like the Mini she drove around London. Still, if Anna wanted a lifetime of designer clothes and luxury, her trust fund would only help—career success would have to buy it for her.

Of course, her father was in a position to help at the beginning. At work one day Charles called Barbara Griggs, the *Evening Standard*'s fashion editor, into his office.

"I want to ask you a favor," he said.

"Sure, Charles. What can I do?" she replied.

"I would be very grateful if you would take my daughter Anna out to lunch. I'll pay, of course," he said. "I think she's very set on a fashion career. Perhaps you could give her a little guidance."

Griggs took Anna to lunch and was immediately impressed by how confident, stylish, and put-together she was. This girl was just a child, but with an adult's poise, grooming, and sense of purpose.

"All she wanted from me was some information, not terribly important information. What she didn't want at all was any guidance or tips on how to manage her career," recalled Griggs, who concluded the teenager in front of her had a brilliant future in fashion, and whatever she wanted to do, she would do.

Griggs then called Barbara Hulanicki and asked if Anna could get some experience working in the shop. Hulanicki didn't know Charles Wintour, but did know that his newspaper was hugely influential and had a large circulation. Plus Griggs had written kindly about Biba in the paper. Of course she would hire his daughter.

*   *   *

As Charles Wintour's daughter, Anna got the job without even a formal interview. In a sense, that wasn't too surprising: working at Biba required no qualifications except being pretty and fashionable. The young women who ran the stores in the sixties were among London's "It girls." Stylish and brash, they appeared in newspapers and magazines and were about as cool as you could be. But Anna never became one of them. "She wasn't gloriously gorgeous. She was very plain and very ordinary so she wouldn't have been a typical girl that we would have hired, realistically," said Kim Willott, an assistant manager. And personality-wise, she was the opposite of the extroverted staff members—quiet and sweet. "I'm sure she was terrified," said Hulanicki. Staff said they were told to treat her delicately since she was the daughter of the influential Charles Wintour, so she could not even be given anything hard to do.

Biba buzzed like the backstage of a rock concert. Celebrities like Brigitte Bardot and Barbra Streisand came in and out along with customers looking for the shortest possible skirts. If there wasn't a line outside, there were nose marks on the window to wipe off every day. Though Hulanicki used her staff to model in Biba's catalogues (shot by famous fashion photographers like Helmut Newton) she never asked Anna to do it because she seemed too reserved.

Part of the craziness of Biba was its rampant theft. The absence of a security system, along with the low lighting and busy communal changing room, made it easy for customers to steal clothes, and steal they did. In a 2002 *Independent* profile, Alexandra Shulman, then the editor of British *Vogue*, bonded with the interviewer over recollections of all the shoplifting that went on at Biba. Shulman recalled that when the police came to her school to discuss it, "We all sat there listening, in our stolen Biba scarves."

Anna had been working there just a few weeks when Rosie Young, one of her managers, recalled receiving orders from the higher-ups to let her go because they believed that Anna too had been taking clothes. Stealing was so common, she might not have thought anything of it.

Young certainly didn't get the impression that Anna cared about being fired, but now Anna had to find something else to do. In the summer of 1967, hoping to capitalize on the boutique movement, Harrods had opened a 20,000-square-foot department on its fourth floor called the Way In. Decorated in deep blue with low lighting and a blue-and-black-striped floor, the area had a DJ and resembled a nightclub. The staff all wore white minidresses.

The vibe resonated with Anna and she got a job on the sales floor, where her colleagues included debutantes and out-of-work actors. To Lasky, working a retail job never seemed beneath Anna. That's not to say Anna was *excited* about starting at the bottom. "Because of our backgrounds at North London, I think we all thought we wouldn't have to work so hard at things that weren't so great, but go straight to the top," said Lasky. But being at the bottom created opportunities too.

Around the time Anna was working at Harrods, Lasky found an internship at *Petticoat*, a weekly teen girls' magazine founded by Audrey Slaughter, who had already successfully launched *Honey*, which targeted a slightly older audience. Lasky's job was to borrow samples of clothing and accessories from designers and retailers for fashion shoots, then pack them up and send them back. At one point, however, the editors were short on models. "Vivienne, you do it," her boss said. "Bring a friend." Lasky asked Anna.

Fortuitously, Anna happened to be available for the day. Predictably, she had little idea of what a fashion editor did, and perhaps her greatest takeaway from the shoot was how much work it was to pull it together.

Along with a few other young women, they posed in micromini pink and gray coatdresses and too-big sample shoes that gaped in the back. The pictures were published in an exciting double-page spread, Anna Wintour's debut in the world that she would eventually rule over. The two friends looked like they were playing dress-up in a grown woman's closet.

*   *   *

For someone who would later be so closely linked to political power brokers and foreign leaders, the social unrest of the 1960s didn't seem like Anna's primary concern. Fashion was her obsession. She once had a date at a big anti–Vietnam War protest in London, in which eight thousand mostly young people marched the mile and a half from Trafalgar Square to Grosvenor Square. But the antiwar cause may not have been the attraction: the march was *the* thing for young people to do in London that day, so of course she wanted to be there. Her big dilemma had been what to wear. (After trying on countless outfits, she settled on something leather.)

In a joint interview almost twenty years later, Charles teased his daughter about that day. "Having spent two hours wondering what you wore to a demo, I heard her patter down the steps, turn, and run up again. I opened the door and she said: 'Daddy, am I for or against Cambodia?' I think things have changed. I am almost sure she is aware that there are two parties in American politics," he said.

Anna, the lone apolitical family member, may have taken her dad's comments as a challenge. She would work her whole career to prove she could be the world's best fashion editor as well as a serious political person. After she started running *Vogue*, she insisted on publishing political stories in every issue, firmly believing that a love of expensive clothing didn't mean her readers were intellectually limited. "Just because you like to put on a beautiful Carolina Herrera dress or a pair of J Brand blue jeans instead of something basic from Kmart, it doesn't mean that you're a dumb person," she said. Her father had put the headless corpse on his front page and something for the permanent undersecretary at the Treasury inside, and at *Vogue* she would follow her own version of that formula. But for now, her focus was less on the revolution than on what was trending.

Anna made one final attempt at a formal education when she enrolled in fashion classes. She hardly talked to Lasky about her classes, and on the rare occasions that she did, it didn't sound like she was having fun.

During one of those infrequent discussions, she explained that one of her classes seemed a lot like chemistry, a subject neither of them had studied at North London. "I didn't do very well," she told Lasky. "We were testing fabrics and I set a sample on fire."

But the classes weren't a complete waste: they gave her an opportunity to research the fashion scene in America to write a thesis on trends in retailers' buying methods. Anna planned to visit all the major department stores in New York City, and also wanted to go to Dallas to visit Neiman Marcus, which worried Nonie, who didn't want her staying there by herself. Anna had visited the US many times growing up, but never on her own. In April of 1968, when Anna was eighteen, she went to New York for a few weeks, staying with Nonie's cousin in her Park Avenue apartment, walking distance from the upscale boutiques and restaurants on Madison Avenue.

Charles wrote to Arthur Schlesinger to make sure Anna would be looked after and to ask, per Anna's explicit request, that he show her New York nightlife. Schlesinger, a prominent New Yorker who had served as special assistant to President John F. Kennedy in the early sixties before becoming a humanities professor at the City University of New York, was happy to oblige, sweeping Anna into his glamorous Manhattan social circle. Little did either know that in seven years Anna would decide to make New York City her home.

As the sixties neared their end, Anna started a relationship back in London with Steve Bobroff, a fashion photographer whose family money had allowed him to set up his own photo studio and live in a spacious carriage house with a swimming pool.

Even then Anna was drawn to creative people, especially successful ones, but as far as Lasky could tell, Anna was genuinely crazy about him. Their relationship brought out a whole new side to her friend, an Anna who enjoyed a grown-up domestic life, including decorating a shared living space and inviting her parents over for dinner.

Bobroff had privilege but also talent, and his photos were appearing in major magazines like *Queen*, which covered fashion in Swinging

London. The two of them collaborated on a moody black-and-white shoot for *Student* magazine, founded by future tycoon Richard Branson, that ran in the Summer 1969 issue. The two-page spread featured a black-and-white photo of Anna in a sleeveless crocheted minidress, lying on her side as though asleep, hands clutched to her chest. In one inset photo, she wears a trouser suit; in another, she kneels in knitted high-waisted briefs and a matching triangle top, midriff exposed. The short text extolls the season's "sleek" and simple designs.

There was more: Anna, with the last name "Winter," appeared on the *Student* masthead under the title "Fashion Editor and Model." She would never model again, but her career as an editor had begun.

Chapter 4

ANNA WINTOUR, FASHION ASSISTANT

As before, being a Wintour helped.

When Anna showed up for an interview at *Harper's Bazaar*, the magazine was preparing to merge with *Queen* to become *Harpers & Queen*. Sitting down with editor Jennifer Hocking, a former model, Anna made a point of exaggerating her limited experience with fashion shoots. Whether Hocking realized this or not, it didn't matter: her boss, Willie Landels, who was both editor-in-chief and art director, didn't care.

Landels, an artist who'd moved to England from his native Italy almost two decades prior, knew Anna's father and, more important, that the *Evening Standard* was a great newspaper. Those were good enough reasons for Landels to try out twenty-year-old Anna as an entry-level assistant in the fashion department.

After dead-end stints with fashion classes and retail jobs, it was the *Harpers* job that would provide the foundation for Anna's entire career. Here, finally, was something she loved and did well, which also placed her in her father's dazzling element.

One of the first things Landels noticed about Anna was that she was quiet, like Charles, always hiding behind her hair and sunglasses. The glasses, which seemed like an eccentricity, may have had a purpose beyond fashion. Her father suffered from macular degeneration—a hereditary condition in which the macula in the center of the retina deteriorates, causing vision problems. Anna claimed that her nearsightedness was paired with acute light sensitivity, hence her need for sunglasses, but her close friend and *Vogue*'s longtime West Coast editor Lisa Love said she just preferred the appearance of sunglasses (which she would constantly misplace), which defined her iconic look and added to her mystique. Lasky remembered Anna unhappily having to wear glasses when they were in school together, but didn't recall her wearing sunglasses. "I thought it started because if you're wearing sunglasses, people don't know they're prescription," she said.

Both Anna and her dad were thrilled when she was hired and, in the March 1970 issue, debuted on the masthed as a fashion assistant. Here, her last name hardly made her stand out. "We also had other members of the magazine at the time who were daughters of dukes and lords," recalled advertisement manager Terence Mansfield. "It came with the affluent market." She would remain at the magazine for five years, her longest tenure outside of Condé Nast.

Since the fashion pages were run on small budgets by a team of three, Anna never felt like the kind of assistant who would later serve her, an easily replaced subordinate who would suffer in the coffee-fetching, receipt-collecting trenches. "I learned how to go into the market and choose clothes. I learned how to choose talent. I learned how to collaborate. I learned how to do a layout. I learned how to write a caption. I was thrown into my career, frankly, with ignorance. I knew nothing," she said. "You had to learn everything, you had to do everything. You had to know how to multitask. I think this also gives you a certain strength that you're not stuck in one box. I just started as an editor, they told me to go on a shoot."

Of all the entry-level jobs Anna could have held in fashion or media, there was perhaps none she was better suited to than this one. A successful fashion shoot depends on taste, creativity, and organization. In collaboration with the art department, models are cast, a photographer is hired, and a location chosen. The editor, who goes to fashion shows and designer showrooms to keep up with the latest collections, decides which clothes to photograph and how. An assistant borrows the clothes and accessories for the shoot. When they arrive, the assistant unpacks and organizes everything so the editor can breeze through and make selections.

The job is creative, but also tedious. Shots are planned in advance, so that when everyone gets to the set, time isn't wasted on decisions. The model may have ideas about how to pose, the photographer may have ideas about how to shoot, but the editor is ultimately responsible for going back to the office with the set of pictures that the boss wants, so she must command her set.

Anna was a perfectionist, not the type to forget a dress or lose some jewelry, and knew how to select clothes. She was also good at putting the right talent together. She didn't second-guess herself, so people weren't left wondering what to do.

Ironically, unlike most people who passed through Anna's post-tween orbit, Landels didn't like how she dressed. In fact, he thought she badly *over*dressed. But this he was willing to overlook because her job—informing the public about fashion—wouldn't be done by way of her own example. Anna seemed to agree with him in a 1986 interview, describing as a mistake how she used "to go out and buy a complete outfit—Bill Gibb or Missoni—hat, leg-warmers, skirt, everything."

Landels was impressed with shoots she did with the young illustrator Eric Boman, who was trying to break into photography when Anna, who covered the lingerie market, first hired him in 1971 to photograph swimwear. "Anna was rather in the background," recalled Boman, who went on to have a successful photography career and shoot for *Vogue* well before Anna started working there. "She was good at finding people who are gifted," said Landels.

In addition to sparing Anna the more demeaning aspects of assistanthood, the job allowed her to start developing an editorial point of view. In a late November 1971 spread featuring gifts the *Harpers & Queen* staff wanted for Christmas, Anna's high-low taste—which would become her signature at *Vogue*—was on full display. Portrayed by a professional model, "Anna" wore nothing but diamonds and a long fluffy white fur coat casually slipping off her bare shoulders, a matching Great Pyrenees dog (available then at Harrods) lying at her feet. "Anna Wintour, fashion assistant, 21, would like to taste St. Moritz living next year . . . wearing this ankle-length white fox coat, £1,930 from Harrods," reads the caption on what is one of the earliest published examples of Anna's work as a stylist. The price of the model's diamond ring and hair accessory were too high to disclose, but the wicker chair from Biba was listed at only £29. As fancy as her life and taste would become, Anna never seemed to forget that she was one of the girls waiting in line on Saturday mornings to buy dresses for a few pounds at Biba.

Charles and Nonie left Anna alone when it came to her personal life. That's not to say that Charles failed to notice that Anna had many boyfriends, and that she had a type, which he described as "unusually appealing but highly unstable" characters. Many of the men she dated were older, and many were writers; she seemed attracted to people with life experience, intellect, and ambition.

After her relationship with Bobroff ended, Anna moved back into the basement apartment at her parents' house. Charles's interest in Anna's personal life was piqued when Richard Neville came along.

Neville, a hippie with a dark moptop, moved to London in 1966 from Sydney, Australia, where he'd launched the counterculture magazine *Oz*. The debut issue had included an interview with an abortion doctor and an article on chastity belts; by the fourth issue, newsstands were refusing to sell the magazine and printers refusing to print it. Neville was charged with obscenity twice, avoiding jail the second time by posting bail. After reading about "Swinging London" in *Time* magazine, Neville decided to move and publish *Oz* from there.

Writer Anthony Haden-Guest introduced Neville to Anna at a party in 1969, when she was around twenty. They kept bumping into each other at social gatherings and he and Anna fell into an affair, often disappearing to her basement apartment at her parents' house after they'd all dined together.

Neville continued using *Oz* to attract press through controversy and shock value. The cover of an issue guest-edited by teenagers featuring two naked women led to another obscenity charge, as well as one for conspiracy to corrupt public morals, the penalty for which was life in prison.

In the end, the *Oz* team was acquitted of public corruption but guilty of obscenity. After almost a week in prison, Neville was released on appeal. Charles asked Anna to bring him over. Many years later, she would allude to the encounter as one of the worst dates of her life. "We had an extremely uncomfortable exchange, but at the end of it, my dad said to the young man, 'I know you're interested in politics—would you like to go to America and cover the upcoming election campaigns?'" she said. "And he, of course, was stunned, and immediately said yes. And he left the next day and I never saw him again. So, my dad was quite cunning."

Clare Hastings landed as Anna's assistant at *Harpers & Queen* in late 1971 after Anna was promoted to assistant fashion editor, thanks to the departure of her immediate superior. It didn't matter to Hastings that Anna wasn't easy to talk to and didn't give detailed explanations about how to do things; she learned fast and somehow just "got" Anna. And Hastings got the feeling, though they never explicitly discussed her performance, that Anna was invested in her success. "It was just the way that she would treat me or talk to me or include me that I imagined I wasn't completely hopeless," she said.

Hastings found Anna impressive on many levels. She showed enormous respect for the fashion pieces loaned to the magazine—everything they borrowed had to be sent back in the precise condition it arrived in, down to the tissue paper wrapping—and to those who lent them. Then there was Anna's own style and grooming, attended to as if she were constantly starring in a fashion editorial. She got blowouts and bang trims three times a week and wore clothes by cool designers, some of which she bought and some of which she received as gifts from labels, which was pro forma for the industry. Like the magazine, Anna's wardrobe featured a lot of fur, which wasn't taboo then. ("Anna loved fur. Anna dripped fur. We all dripped fur," recalled Hastings.) She often brought her castoffs into work for the other young women on staff, but she reserved extra kindness for the fashion team. One day the houseboat where Hastings lived with her boyfriend went up in flames along with everything she owned. The next day, Anna showed up to work with a whole new wardrobe for her.

Hastings saw that Anna was meticulous about everything, from what she kept in her purse to what she ate. She never ate much, but what she did had to be the best. Sometimes she would send her steak back repeatedly until it was rare enough, and then only take a couple of bites. (For a while, she paid Hastings to bring her the yogurt that she was making at home because Anna thought it was better than anything else she could buy.)

There was something else about her boss that impressed Hastings, something she couldn't quite put her finger on. Anna had the power to get people to do what she wanted with a look or a sentence. "Even at that point, she would control the whole lunch table. If there were eight people around, and everyone was thinking, 'Oh, I'll have a glass of wine'—because everybody drank in those days—and 'I'll have a cigarette,' there'd be Anna at the end who'd say, 'Just a yogurt for me, please.' Everyone would look around and go, 'Oh god. We're not supposed to be eating.' 'Oh my goodness, we're not supposed to be drinking.'"

And there was Anna's busy social life. She wasn't famous at the time, but she was attractive and interesting, and conveyed an air of mystery. In addition to the usual business calls, Anna got daily calls from men. They were fascinated by her and wanted to take her out (among them the actor Terence Stamp), but she only called some back; she sometimes told Hastings to lie that she was out of the office.

When not at work, she regularly went out to hot spots like Tramp and Club Dell'Aretusa. ("Are you one of the beautiful people?" the *Evening Standard* once asked. "Simple test: Can you get in to the Dell'Aretusa?")

At dinner, Anna sat silently, her bob in her face. Emma Soames was working in fashion PR when she met and became friends with Anna in the early seventies. "Anna's power in those days, such as it was as a fashion assistant, lay in her silence," she said. Her crew included gossip columnist Nigel Dempster, nearly a decade older, whom she dated (though she later denied it), and his journalist friends Jon Bradshaw and Anthony Haden-Guest. The latter never saw Anna as shy. Anna's "was a kind of Cheshire Cat silence," he said. "You knew there was a lot going on in her head. But she just wasn't sharing it."

"I know there was a lot of drinking," said Anna, who never much liked alcohol and only ever was seen drinking white wine, usually no more than half a glass. "But I was always the first to leave. I had to get up and go to work in the mornings. Because they were freelancers, they could wake up later." She was always home by eleven thirty.

P art of Anna's job was to always be on the lookout for the best people to work with; photographers, models, and designers constantly streamed through the *Harpers & Queen* office for "go-sees." Manolo Blahnik, the shoe designer who later became a household name partly thanks to being Carrie Bradshaw's favorite on *Sex and the City*, was one of them, and one of the first designers to receive Anna's endorsement. "I just remember this sort of madman coming in and putting all these shoes down and going, 'Here's my new collection, it's my new collection,'" said Hastings.

Anna didn't bother with niceties if a photographer came in with a portfolio she didn't like. There was no pretending that she would think about it so as to spare someone's feelings—she'd just look the other way, close the book, and say, "Thank you."

One photographer who did appeal to Anna was James Wedge, a former milliner who got his start at the Royal College of Art. He was able to switch to a photography career thanks to Anna booking him repeatedly. They began a romantic relationship, and extensively discussed not only their shoots but also goals for the future. And Anna was frank about her ambition, even as a lowly junior fashion editor. "American *Vogue* was the job that she really, really wanted," said Wedge.

As Anna developed a reputation, photographers sought work with her at *Harpers & Queen*. One was Jim Lee, a rising talent who liked the freedom that came with shooting outside of a studio.

Anna was experimental at the time, and suggested that instead of following the trend for soft-focus romanticism, he should do a shoot of sailor-inspired clothes on a stark gray battleship she liked, which was anchored in the Thames.

Lee thought the whole conceit was silly and had a hard time getting into it, especially since the boat was a difficult place to shoot. Unsurprisingly, he shuddered at the resulting pictures. Insisting they couldn't be published, he offered Anna a free reshoot.

"Do them again, wherever you want, however you want. That's fine," she said. "I understand." Lee decided to take the clothes to Brighton Beach with the same models, but without Anna. Anna liked the new photos, and they were published. Given that she was just starting out and had very little power, Anna may have felt she couldn't afford to alienate a photographer like Lee, and it was best to give him freedom to do as he thought best. This wasn't an approach she would use forever.

Anna's job also now mandated that she attend fashion shows. For the industry, these are biannual gatherings of editors, stylists, retailers, photographers, models, and designers—a well-heeled herd converging on an exclusive watering hole. If the various attendees don't know each other, they know *about* each other. Anna, always dressed immaculately, attended the shows with Jennifer Hocking, trailing just behind her around the runways, clearly her support staff.

That said, the media back then weren't interested in the editors or what they wore. Plus, photographers had to lug their film around and didn't want to waste it on spectators. But something about Anna struck Monty Coles, a newspaper photographer, at one couture show. Fair-skinned, small, always hiding behind her hair—Coles never saw her speak to anyone or anyone speak to her—Anna was strangely captivating, and he snapped a couple of photos of her as she walked past him on the way to her seat. Tucked under her arm was a bag large enough to carry a sketch pad because, although she couldn't really draw, she'd figured out how to sketch the clothes she liked as they came down the runway, which was how top fashion editors noted which pieces they wanted to photograph.

By the early seventies, Anna's name and photo were appearing not only occasionally in *WWD* but in newspapers and magazines in small items about London parties. This didn't make her a celebrity, but her name was out there.

In 1972, Anna started a five-year relationship with Jon Bradshaw—always simply Bradshaw to his friends—an American journalist who had recently divorced his first wife. Bradshaw was swashbuckling, drank a lot, and loved to gamble. Twelve years older than Anna, he'd moved to London from the US and was writing for *Harpers & Queen* while she was working there. Anna fell for him. "There just weren't many people like Bradshaw," she said. "He stood out. He would walk into a room and own that room. Living in London and being American—which added to his aura. The polar opposite of the upper-class English world that I knew when I was growing up. He was not so polite and not so careful, wore jeans, had that great smile, and was just much more open. And yeah, a little bit dangerous. He caused a stir." They moved in together, and, just as Anna had with Bobroff, she decorated the new apartment beautifully.

Like her father, Bradshaw was someone who could teach the much less experienced Anna about magazine publishing, and who could tap his connections when she needed help, which was exactly what he did down the line.

While covering the lingerie market, Anna often bumped into British *Vogue*'s young lingerie editor, Liz Tilberis, who would many years later become one of Anna's biggest rivals. "We quickly recognized each other as fellow foot soldiers in fashion (although she was always better dressed than I was), sitting together at tedious industry lunches and meeting up at showrooms to peruse racks of Maidenform bras and flannel robes, two ambitious neophytes glad to have each other's company and conversation," Tilberis later wrote. "She was serious but not humorless, determined but not devious, obviously as frustrated as I was . . ."

In fact, Anna had quickly tired of doing shoots, recognizing early on that she didn't want to be the person out in the field creating content, but the person in the office making decisions, like her father. "I was terrible on shoots. I was bad. I was so happy to give it up. It was just not my strong suit. But it did help me understand what went into them and how you needed to be so much more patient than I ever was," she said.

In 1974, a more senior role at *Harpers & Queen* opened up when Landels fired Jennifer Hocking in order to bring in someone with a writing background. Anna decided she should take Hocking's job— after all, by then she and Hocking had been splitting the big fashion spreads, including the cover shoots. Anna's assistant, Clare Hastings, also felt that a promotion was deserved.

To help her case, Charles called Landels to lobby for his daughter, but this time Landels took offense. "I will never tell you how to run the *Evening Standard*, so don't tell me how to run my magazine," he said. Landels worried that Anna's silence—the very thing that seemed to empower her socially—prevented her from connecting with others on staff. In retrospect, Hastings wondered if Landels's real issue was feeling threatened by her.

The job went to Min Hogg*, who had been contributing feature stories to the magazine, and Anna got a consolation title bump to deputy fashion editor. ("Over five years, I rose by gradual degrees from fashion assistant to deputy fashion editor, which wasn't what you would call a meteoric promotion," she later said.)

Hogg was dramatically different from her predecessor, Hocking, who went on to a second phase of her modeling career. Hogg's expertise was in textiles and interior design. (Later in her career she would help start the highly respected home décor title *World of Interiors*.) Though Landels had justified the hire by saying he wanted a writer in the fash

---

*   Hogg died in 2019.

ion editor position, Anna and Hastings didn't understand why they suddenly had to report to someone who didn't seem to care that much about fashion.

Being passed over made her resent Hogg intensely, but it wasn't Anna's style to have an outright disagreement with somebody—she hasn't ever been confrontational and would continue to avoid direct confrontation throughout her career. Still, she made her feelings known. "Min would have realized pretty soon that Anna didn't think much of her work," Hastings noted. "Anna wasn't going to stay around, being subservient to somebody that she perceived as not being as good as she was."

As Michael Hodgson, who worked in the art department and laid out Anna's pages, recalled, Hogg could also be a difficult person to get along with: "They're very different characters. Anna was kind of young and go-gettish. Min was kind of old and, to a certain extent, stuck in her ways." Those two approaches were not particularly convivial. Anna "could be vile to people that she didn't like," said Hastings. Once, things got so bad between them that Landels was called to the shows in Paris, which Anna and Hogg were attending together, to defuse the situation and "tell Anna to behave properly," he said.

After several months under Hogg, Anna had had enough. One day, she pulled Hastings aside.

"It's outrageous I haven't been made fashion editor. I'm resigning. Are you going to stay?" she said.

"Mm, no," said Hastings, who felt loyal to her boss. She followed through on her promise to quit in solidarity, even though she hadn't given any thought to what she'd do next. *

Anna had no master plan for her career at that point, but she had more options than most since, thanks to her mother, Anna had an American passport. She set her sights across the Atlantic and was the driving force behind her and Bradshaw's move to the States.

---

* "You'll never work in this business again," the editor told Hastings. The editor turned out to be wrong. Hastings became a freelance stylist, a career she had for the next thirty years, which she credits to Anna, who got her to leave the magazine in the first place.

After considering San Francisco, Anna decided on New York, planning to stay there if she could find a job. "She regarded New York as a center of the universe," recalled Emma Soames. On Thursday, March 13, 1975, her family gave her a farewell dinner in London. Charles supported her decision but was sad to see his daughter move so far away.

Anna wouldn't miss London, but she had no idea how difficult working in New York would be.

Chapter 5

A NEW START
IN NEW YORK CITY

Moving to New York at age twenty-five without a job lined up, Anna started out with freelance gigs, including one for American *Vogue*, which may have sounded more impressive than it actually turned out to be.

Anna was hired to oversee a reshoot of a single photo for the November 1975 issue. Grace Mirabella, *Vogue*'s editor-in-chief, didn't like the earrings model Rosie Vela had been wearing, so she sent a whole crew back out to the very same Hamptons sand dune to take the photo again.

Anna showed up for the hundred-mile drive looking chic and cool as always, carrying a tiny bag with the replacement earrings in them. When the van reached the designated dune, everyone got out, snapped the photo, packed up, and drove the hundred miles home. It was terribly inefficient and wasteful, but it was how *Vogue* could afford to operate, which must have stunned an editor like Anna, coming from a London magazine with a fraction of the budget. And after all that, the photo was never even published.

Despite what her father called "a rather depressing start" as a freelancer, Anna began to enjoy her new city. She and Bradshaw moved into an apartment on the Upper East Side and went out to hot spots like Maxwell's Plum and the jazz clubs on Fifty-Second Street. Here, no one knew her as Charles Wintour's daughter or said anything to her about her father at all. "I felt quite isolated growing up in England, not because of family but with it being such a class-driven culture, and one of the things I like here is that it is not all about class and where you went to school and what your parents do, and everyone in New York is from somewhere else, and that creates a very positive force," she said. Yet Anna would, many years later, seem to place outsize weight on family and educational background when hiring at *Vogue*.

After interviewing with one of America's top fashion editors, Carrie Donovan, she got a job at *Harper's Bazaar* (which had the same parent company as *Harpers & Queen*). As a junior sittings editor, Anna's job was to organize and oversee shoots but with almost no editorial say in the photos. It was the best magazine she could have worked at in New York other than *Vogue*, but, she would learn, the position would also come at the cost of creative freedom.

*H*ave we hired the wrong person? Michele Mazzola, *Harper's Bazaar's* special projects editor, wondered as she observed her new twenty-six-year-old junior editor on set. The staff was at the five-star Jamaica Inn resort in Ocho Rios for a shoot featuring supermodel Cheryl Tiegs in bathing suits and caftans for the May 1976 issue. Michele was there with her husband, Tony Mazzola, the magazine's editor-in-chief, on what she later described as business but what the crew figured was vacation.

This particular crew had worked together many times before, making Anna the new girl, and they liked her a lot for the very same reason her bosses worried about her—she didn't meddle in what they were doing. Still, Michele was a bit disconcerted: Anna was on a trip with a whole crew and photo shoot to manage, supposed to hold the whole thing together with authority, and she just hung in the background, the same way she did during meetings at the office, quiet.

This was unusual in American fashion, where flamboyance and power trips were taken as proof of competence—*Vogue's* Polly Mellen cried when she loved a shot. *Bazaar*'s Gloria Moncur once threw a shoe at a staffer and said, "Are you trying to make me sick bringing me these terrible-looking shoes?"

Working at an American fashion magazine was a huge adjustment for Anna. Back in London, her creativity and ideas had mattered at *Harpers & Queen*, but here she had to fight the Mazzolas for the same influence over her shoots. The fashion editor decided, with Tony's approval, on the clothes; the bookings editor and art director decided on the models and photographers. As a junior sittings editor, Anna wasn't meant to stamp her vision on *Bazaar*'s pages. The magazine's aesthetic was dictated by Mazzola, and his vision wasn't artistic or fashion-forward. He had previously edited *Town & Country*, a magazine that featured socialites. But Anna and her young colleagues thought *Bazaar* should hew more closely to the Paris runways than to Park Avenue.

Mazzola's primary concern was finances. "All he did was capitulate to the bean counters in Hearst," said Alida Morgan, a fashion editor who worked alongside Anna, and whose family—unlike Anna's—was against her doing the poorly paid job. Mazzola micromanaged budgets, which routinely add up fast during photo shoots, and would only allow select photographers to expense anything at all. There wasn't always money to bring an assistant on shoots in far-flung locales. And shoots could be grueling: shoot days in a studio could last from 9:30 a.m. until 2 or 3 the next morning. Meanwhile, at their number-one competitor, *Vogue*, no expense was too great—including hiring a crew to spend a day reshooting a photo simply because of earrings.

Though Tony had approved Anna's hiring, those at the magazine thought he never really liked her. They, however, did. Anna might have been quiet and hard to get to know, but she was nice and hardworking. Also, she was *so* stylish. She came to work every day much more dressed up than everyone else in elegant European clothes—Missoni knits and shorts suits by Kenzo and flirty dresses by Sonia Rykiel. Wendy Goodman, whom Donovan hired to assist Anna and another fashion editor, Jun Kanai, said she never saw Anna dress down. She went to a shoot with Anna in the Hamptons, and was struck by Anna's lace eyelet Sonia Rykiel dress and heels. Anna liked clothes that showed off her legs, toned at Lotte Berk—the eponymous studio of a trained ballet dancer who devised a barre-style workout for everyone. When she was done with her clothes, she brought them into the office for the other girls on the staff. Goodman once snatched up a Sonia Rykiel shirt with armholes that were too small for her. She said, "I was like a little sort of Flipper. I couldn't even move my arms in this shirt. I thought, *I'm going to wear Anna Wintour's shirt. I don't care. I'm wearing it.*"

And then there was Anna's British accent, which made the whole staff jealous. Brits weren't common at the time in the New York publishing industry, and Anna's posh intonation may have eclipsed even her wardrobe in making her seem chic.

In the office, Anna developed a long-standing friendship with her first American boss, Carrie Donovan, a highly respected editor who'd been passed over to be editor-in-chief of *Vogue* before joining Tony's team. Donovan had a big personality and the statement accessories to match, including turbans, round black-framed glasses that extended past the sides of her face, and gold cuffs on each wrist. She was known for developing young talent and would go on to champion Anna for decades. Anna "is a fashion person if there ever was one," she said, adding, "She may not take the time to be polite about it." Indeed, Anna had one concern when she was on the job, and it wasn't adopting friendly American manners. Zazel Lovén, another fashion editor, said her focus was singular: "She was very clear-minded about wanting to do work that she thought was the best."

That was made harder as the Mazzolas "were against any new models. They were against any new photographers. They were against anything that diverted in any way from the pages that they'd been doing, basically, at *Town & Country*," said Morgan. Fashion editors would get stuck with one photographer over and over and over, which meant they eventually ran out of ideas of what to do with them. Complicating things was Tony's wife, Michele, who, while influencing the pages through her role as special projects editor, dressed casually and clearly wasn't a fashion person—her colleagues never forgot their mortification when she attended couture shows in Paris in a white T-shirt. Goodman thought her attire came from intention rather than cluelessness. "I think that was a real sort of choice, like, *I'm not a fashion person. I'm a serious working girl. . . . I have better things to do than worry about fashion.*" (Michele noted that she often wore Halston, and "looked perfectly respectable . . . just not couture.")

Anna's taste was edgier. She loved Hiro, the legendary surrealist fashion photographer who had defined *Harper's Bazaar's* innovative look under editor-in-chief Nancy White the decade before. (His memorable images include a fish decked in fine jewelry and standing models shot directly from above.)

By the time Anna arrived in 1975, the Hiro days were long gone. The covers of all the issues Anna worked on were tightly cropped head shots, with Tiegs—a Mazzola favorite—appearing on more than half of them. Mazzola and his art department threw text all over photos to plug advertisers, which editors felt destroyed the presentation and beauty of the clothing. To better control the outcome of their spreads, Anna and Morgan devised a work-around: when the film came back, Anna met with photographers in the lobby to select their favorite pictures, and that was all she turned in. If the Mazzolas asked where the rest were, she'd say, "I'm sorry, there aren't any more." Explained Morgan, "So either they were going to have to pay for a reshoot or they had to accept what you had to give." And since budgets were so tight, that often meant Anna got what she wanted.

Goodman was in awe of Anna's work ethic. "She really had no qualms about being completely focused, and to the point of being very abrupt, seemingly rude, to people because she just didn't have time. She just was on her path to what she needed to do, period, the end," she said. "In an office people kind of clown around, and they take breaks, and they gossip. She never did any of that. She wasn't in it for fun and games. She was in it to work."

But Anna and Tony were never going to get along. As colleague Marilyn Kirschner said, "Tony was the boss and Anna has a bossy personality, and she doesn't just take orders." Yet when Anna and Tony clashed and Tony berated her, she didn't fight back. In fact, being nonconfrontational by nature, she didn't argue at all. Morgan believed part of it was Anna's shyness, but also, she said, "There's a point where fighting back doesn't feel like it's worth it, because I think she knew she could go on to other things. And she knew damn well she wanted to run *Vogue*."

Bradshaw and Anna seemed to have a good relationship in New York. The craziness of working at *Bazaar* led Anna to develop friendships with a small group of her fellow fashion editors, and sometimes they'd all go out to dinner together with their boyfriends. They liked Bradshaw, who was affable and always supportive of Anna. "Do it, Anna," he would say when she had an idea about her work. He had a glow around her.

Bradshaw occasionally went to the office to see Anna, who sat in a small but busy room with Goodman, Morgan, and their colleagues. "We all had crushes on him, and he'd come to the office, and we'd all flirt with him," Goodman recalled. The attention was one reason for him to drop by, but he had a greater purpose than ego-boosting: Bradshaw was a gambler and Anna controlled their finances, so he was visiting Anna, Goodman recalled, to get his cash allowance. Goodman just thought, *Oh my god, she just has control over everything*.

In the spring of 1976, he invited her to see one of Bob Marley's four sold-out shows at the Beacon Theatre. Not one to miss something cool, Anna went with him. The next morning, she came to work talking about the concert like it was a transcendent experience. "I feel like I've met God," she told Morgan, which was unusually high praise coming from Anna. (This story would later get misconstrued into reports that Anna disappeared for two weeks to have an affair with Marley; she later called the rumors "fake news" and said she never met him.)

Despite how well they got on, Bradshaw was away a lot on assignment for *New York* magazine, where he was a contributing editor. Meanwhile, Anna was assigned to collaborate with the photographer James Moore, who had shot for *Bazaar* during its glory days in the sixties. Anna started working with him a few months into the job, and after the Mazzolas liked their first shoot together, she was frequently paired with him going forward. This meant Anna regularly found herself locked in a studio for hours and hours with Moore. Their working relationship evolved into a romance, leading to an off period with Bradshaw. (Another person Anna dated around this time was the writer Christopher Hitchens, whom she said she was "mad about.")

"She just was very suave in juggling attention," Goodman said. Goodman was dating someone when another guy became romantically interested in her and she didn't know what to do. Anna laughed and said, "You really just don't know how to do it, do you?"

"She wasn't being mean," Goodman explained. "She was just being like, *Oh, Wendy, boy, could I teach you a thing or two*. Not that she ever did."

Ultimately, the relationship with Moore would also end up having a serious effect on Anna's work.

Mazzola liked themed issues because advertisers liked them. January was the health issue, February was the "independent woman" issue, and for March, Donovan said, "Let's gather all the pretty single women at the magazine, and let's do a single women's issue." She rounded up the single women on the staff and sent them off to a studio to sit for a group photo with Bill King, one of *Bazaar*'s most frequent contributors.

The newly deputized models, wearing matching black long-sleeved T-shirts with the *Harper's Bazaar* logo in white across the chest, were excited to be on set getting hair and makeup done—but not Anna. She was the only one who put a vest on over her logo shirt. After some cajoling, Anna's colleagues managed to get her somewhat into the mood. King turned on a big fan, blowing Anna's bob off her face. She smiled with her teeth, but crossed her arms. The only one purposefully obscuring her employer's logo in the final picture, Anna made clear that she was not a shill for *Bazaar*.

In mid-1976, not even a year into her tenure, Anna's friction with Tony reached its apex. He had soured on her shoots with James Moore, which Morgan thought were starting to look too sexy for Tony's taste.

It didn't appear that things were going to improve for her. First, the magazine showed no signs of going in the fashion-forward, zeitgeist-y direction Anna preferred. Former department store executive William Fine had just started at Hearst as publishing director of *Bazaar* and two other titles, and he boasted about editing "fashion" out of his magazines.

Then Donovan—Anna's champion—left the magazine for the department store Bloomingdale's. Her replacement was Elsa Klensch, who had a background as a journalist (and would years later go on to host *Style with Elsa Klensch* on CNN). Right away, Klensch and Anna clashed. "Elsa, I think, completely resented Anna for every possible reason. That she was young, that she was pretty, that she was upper class, from a better background—everything," Morgan said. Under Klensch, Morgan believed, Anna had little if any protection from the Mazzolas. (Though, in an interview many years later for the biography about Anna called *Front Row*, Klensch described Anna as "very conscientious" and said she "tried very hard to please. But Tony was a very difficult man who ran a tight ship and was a control freak who really didn't want anybody's ideas.")

The end for Anna came after she was sent to Paris for a shoot with Moore. She came back with a set of pictures featuring models with, as Morgan remembered it, cornrows in their hair, instead of the sanctioned Farrah Fawcett waves. Objectionable today, at the time the style was more accepted for white models. (Bo Derek famously wore her blond hair similarly in the 1979 movie *10*. Also, it was nearly impossible for fashion editors, including Anna, to convince Tony to feature models of color in the magazine.) As Morgan remembered it, the Mazzolas' issue with the shoot was mostly its sexuality. "We all thought it was beautiful," she said. "It was too much for them. They just didn't get what it was about. And it was very erotic and quite sexy. Not erotic in a vulgar way, but just the light and the shadows."

Tony was furious when he saw the photos. As he had done before, he called Anna into his office, only this time it felt more ominous. When Anna got back to her shared office, she was slumped over and said, "That's it." Tony had fired her. "She was very upset," Goodman said. She and Morgan took her across the street to the St. Regis for drinks in the middle of the day.

"I was fired by the editor-in-chief, who told me that I was too

'European,'" Anna later said. "At the time I didn't know what he meant, but in retrospect I think it meant that I was obstinate, that I wouldn't take direction, and that I totally ignored my editor's need for credits. In his eyes I was neither commercial nor professional," she said in a 1997 interview, nine years into her editorship of *Vogue*. "Thinking about that chapter in my life, what I find most interesting is to realize how little things have changed: talented, but totally self-absorbed, young English girls now come to see me with some regularity, and with some regularity they tend, not unlike myself way back, to have an almost total disregard for readers. With a bit of regret, I also realize that I have moved closer to the position of the editor who fired me."

Many years later, Tony denied firing Anna, blaming it instead on Carrie Donovan, who wasn't even on the staff at the time. Perhaps he forgot the details. It's also possible he was embarrassed because, by then, Anna had established herself as one of the most successful fashion editors of all time. Tony Mazzola would go down as one of the few people who failed to see it coming.

Chapter 6

VIVA LA VIDA

Anna felt like New York made her even more ambitious. Work at magazines in London was fairly laid-back, but here audiences were bigger, more money was at stake, and editors took everything more seriously. It was a better work environment for Anna, who was intense herself. But her first opportunity in the capital of fashion media had been, by her own admission, "a disaster." Once more, she'd failed to get along with management. And once more, she'd failed to advance, her first New York job ending without her proving herself.

Back in London, her parents' tumultuous marriage was finally ending. Charles had found Nonie increasingly difficult to live with, and she had dealt, for their whole thirty-six-year relationship, with his perpetually wandering eye. Though their breakup was a long time coming, when they finally split in December 1976, Nonie grieved. Charles tried to rally support for her through family and friends and was pleased, especially, with how his children came to her side.

Their divorce seemed difficult for Anna too, according to friends, and can't have been made any easier by losing her job around the same time. But, true to her stiff-upper-lip attitude about most things, she accepted it. Close though she was with her parents, she could see that they were better off apart.

Charles, now fifty-nine, moved right into the Islington home of his girlfriend, Audrey Slaughter, an editor a decade younger than him. She was exactly the kind of woman he admired, having founded a number of magazines (including *Petticoat*, which Anna had modeled for years earlier). Anna never liked her, but knew she could do nothing about it.

While Charles was starting a new life with a new partner, Nonie moved into a modest house of her own. She refused to take any money from Charles, and she never remarried.

Viva, the sister publication to *Penthouse*, was founded by Bob Guccione, who bragged that the latter was the first "to expose the clitoris completely." Guccione saw himself not as a pornographer, but as an artist. After failing to make a living with his art, he decided to copy Hugh Hefner's formula for *Playboy*. *Penthouse* made him hundreds of millions of dollars, and he moved into in a 22,000-square-foot mansion in the middle of Manhattan with a pool in the basement, and launched a media company that would publish more than fifteen magazines.

Guccione, whose daily uniform consisted of printed man blouses unbuttoned halfway down his chest and white socks with sandals, was bothered that *Viva*'s photos of male nudes had attracted a larger audience of gay men than of women. In order to broaden his female readership and attract better advertisers (who, it turned out, weren't keen on the porn either), he needed a legitimate fashion editor.

Thus, Jon Bradshaw's timing was perfect when he called Peter Bloch, an editor he knew at *Penthouse*, to see if *Viva* had any openings for Anna. Their relationship had ended, but they remained on good terms, so Bradshaw, now enjoying the apex of his career success in New York, helped her. Bloch asked Alma Moore, *Viva*'s editor, if she needed a fashion person. As it turned out, Moore had just let go of her fashion editor and was looking for a replacement. Male nudity had been absent from *Viva*'s pages for six months, but the magazine still hadn't turned around.

The minute Anna walked into Moore's office to interview for the job, Moore had a good feeling about her. She loved both the jodhpurs Anna wore to the interview and her attitude. "She was cheeky. She was spunky," recalled Moore.

Moore could tell that Anna, unlike many candidates, had looked at the magazine, and liked that her taste seemed edgy. She too had done her research before meeting with Anna and knew she had been fired from *Harper's Bazaar*, supposing it had to do with her being a junior editor who wanted to run the whole magazine.

Moore knew bringing Anna on was a risk. *This woman knows what she wants, but she's going to be difficult*, she thought. She offered her the job anyway. When Anna accepted, she was amazed.

"I needed a job, and *Viva* offered me an enormous amount of freedom," Anna later said. And though her time at *Viva* would become a source of personal embarrassment, the autonomy she would enjoy there was what allowed her to thrive.

Viva was a peculiar publication and a peculiar place to work. Part of the weirdness was trying to produce an ostensibly feminist magazine with *Penthouse* profits. Yet despite running articles about serious women's issues, including the inadequacies of the American legal system for women when it came to rape or domestic abuse, the magazine would never overcome the stigma of its pornographic origins.

For Anna, the other odd aspect of *Viva* was working for Guccione's girlfriend, Kathy Keeton, whom he assigned to run the magazine, though she didn't understand fashion or magazine editing. It was an echo of the management structure that had been challenging at *Bazaar*. Keeton wanted *Viva* to compete with *Vogue* and *Glamour*, but it was still often banned from supermarkets and drugstores, and consigned at newsstands to the top shelf with other porn titles, which wasn't where the target female audience usually looked for magazines.

A former dancer, Keeton was soft-spoken with long blond hair, heavy makeup, and, like her boyfriend, shirts unbuttoned to display her chest (his: hairy; hers: pushed-up; both: laden with jewelry). Other memorable fashion statements included a "chain mail headpiece that looked like it came out of *Monty Python*," said Joe Brooks, who worked in the *Penthouse* art department for many years. The staff got the impression that Keeton respected Anna's fashion taste, but was, like most everyone else, intimidated by her. Anna, who surely didn't want to lose another job, figured out a way to manage her through just the right amount of deference.

The first thing Anna did when she got to *Viva* was set up her office, a no-frills space with a desk right next to Keeton's. (Keeton brought two Rhodesian Ridgebacks to the office, so it wasn't always the quietest spot on the floor.) Anna was given, as all staffers were, company stationery with the *Penthouse* logo. She rolled in a rack for clothing and started buying stacks of French *Elle* and *Vogue*, and Italian *Vogue*, which cost as much as $20 an issue, to look for ideas. She wanted to emulate a European look, and here, unlike at her last job, she could do just that, because no one else at *Viva* was a fashion person and Alma Moore left her alone.

The freedom suited Anna. Her work involved being out of the office for appointments and shoots, so no one thought much about where she was. On days she came in, she fast-walked through the office to her desk, where she propped up her chunky boots, long floral skirts dangling, chatting on the phone.

Wanda DiBenedetto, a receptionist who sat outside her office, said, "She was always her own person. Didn't really listen to any structure. Because, whether she was or not, she was the boss."

Guccione, as Anna would later do as editor-in-chief, edited everything from captions to cover lines. Though *Viva*'s masthead credited him as a staff photographer and the publisher, as owner Guccione's reach was total and his word final. He liked to work through the night and sleep through the day and made his staff, including Anna, fit into his schedule. People often waited forty minutes at his mansion to see him at 10 p.m. Meetings were held around a huge marble table in his library. His own pack of (seven) Rhodesian Ridgebacks ate filet mignon as though it were dog food, next to paintings by Degas and Toulouse-Lautrec stacked on the floor.

His son, Bob Guccione Jr., would sit in meetings about the maga-zine late into the night with Keeton and his dad, who wanted him to run the company one day. Bob Jr. could tell his dad respected Anna. "She got her way a lot. I think if she said we should do something, he probably did it," he said. And Guccione needed to rely on Anna, because while he had lots of money, taste wasn't something he could buy (evi-denced by the column in his house with his face carved into it). Though he wasn't always sure about Anna's more avant-garde shoots, her work was probably the closest thing to art he was publishing.

With limited oversight, Anna became an expert at manipulating situations to her favor. To get clothes for her shoots, she sent her assis-tant to pull from the upscale Dianne B. boutique in Manhattan. To ensure they'd loan, she instructed her to say they would use the clothing in cover shoots and credit the store on the first page of the magazine. Often none of the ten or twenty items borrowed were actually shot, but this never got in the way of Anna's ability to continue borrowing. Per-haps emboldened in her job, she was less careful than she had been as a new editor in London five years earlier; sometimes she returned pants with dirty hemlines that she had quite possibly worn herself.

Anna also understood how to curry favor with fashion advertisers: photograph their clothes and they'd buy a page or two. She knew that, given *Viva*'s budget problems, if she could help the magazine grow its fashion ad business, she'd be seen as indispensable, and with that would come both more power and more reason for a place like *Vogue* to take her on. This didn't mean that everything that was shot was accurately credited; while there's usually no mistaking one item of clothing for another, with makeup, even today editors often just credit products by their advertisers when they aren't used, which is what Anna did.

She also took advantage of not having a set budget. Said Moore, "I didn't think about money, which is probably the same thing she was thinking. I knew that to turn the magazine around, money had to be spent."

So Anna ran her department the way most fashion magazines did: she paid for messengers to pick up and return clothing, she expensed cabs to and from her appointments, and if she felt her story would look best photographed on a tropical beach, she'd pack up her crew and fly to one.

One shoot with particularly contentious expenses took place in Ocho Rios with photographer Arthur Elgort, a favorite into Anna's *Vogue* years. Attempting a better version of the sterile Jamaica shoot Anna had done for *Harper's Bazaar* with Cheryl Tiegs about a year earlier, Elgort's photos intended to juxtapose real-world settings with high-end styling and a mix of designer items (including, predictably, *Penthouse* and *Viva*'s own tennis clothing line). Two women and a man modeled in lustful entanglements. In one shot the girls strutted through thigh-high surf; in another, one feigned an orgasm in a white caftan underneath an outdoor shower. A photo at night showed them sipping drinks by the pool in bathing suits and open bathrobes. A Black tour boat operator appeared as though a prop in one shot.

Moore, though a fan of Anna's, thought the photos were "ridiculous." The polish normally evident in Anna's stories—the seamless transition of scenes, cohesion of the clothing, and sense that it would be better to be the girl in the photo than whoever you really were—wasn't quite there.

That may have been because Anna had gone to a cosmetics convention in Florida with Keeton instead of the shoot (part of her job was indeed to schmooze with brands and try to help attract advertisers). But even though she hadn't been there to direct Elgort, Anna still got in trouble with Keeton for the cost of the weeklong trip. (Among other expenses, the makeup artist Anna hired refused to leave her room for meals because she didn't want to eat in front of other people, racking up a huge room service bill.) Anna blamed her assistant for how much it cost.

That issue marked the assistant's last appearance on the masthead.

Stephanie Brush started at *Viva* in the unglamorous role of editorial assistant. One of her first days in the office, "this kind of strange creature wafts into the room," Brush recalled.

"Oh, that's the fashion editor. That's Anna," a colleague told her.

Anna often came to work draped in Yves Saint Laurent, fur hats and all. "We're talking, like, full Siberian peasant kind of outfits," said Brush. Anna was quiet and kept to herself, avoiding eye contact with people she passed in the halls, using her hair to hide. And though Moore didn't love Anna's refusal to be in the office and do the same things the other staffers had to do, she didn't push her on it because her work was good and she got it done on time.

Recalled Brush, "There were all these little details about her that were just like, *Oh, be careful. She's not really one of us, she's special.* I don't mean it one bit sarcastically. She had a talent for, I don't know what—people just always believed she was special. If you told me she was born in a truck stop somewhere, I wouldn't be surprised, because maybe she just invented herself."

Anna took a liking to Brush, which was unusual because "she mixed with the men," said Moore. Anna would frequent the local bar, P.J. Clarke's, after work with men from the office, wearing her sunglasses even though it was dark, and sat there giggling and peeling the paper off sugar cubes. But she started inviting Brush to her office to chat, took her out to parties, and introduced her to her British friends. When Brush went to London, she gave her a long list of people to call there, but Brush was too intimidated to do it.

While Anna didn't casually stroll the office, she would regularly speed down the halls to Rowan Johnson's area. *Viva*'s art director, Johnson was a talented mess, his drinking and drug use an obvious and tragic problem. Once he spray-painted his entire office black—walls, desk, pencils, everything in sight—with the door closed. But Keeton adored him, and paid for him to go to rehab repeatedly.

Johnson was a lucky break for Anna. He was respected by the best fashion photographers. Even if they were loath to shoot for the magazine because of its association with Guccione and *Penthouse*, they trusted Johnson—and, by extension, the little-known Anna Wintour.

After cycling through at least two assistants at *Viva* in less than a year, Anna hired Georgia Gunn, a fellow Brit, who would serve her faithfully for years at three of her magazine jobs. Gunn worked hard and was friendly with the entire staff. When free clothes and beauty products piled up in the fashion department, she organized giveaways for coworkers. Gunn "was very nice. If you went into [Anna's] office, she would be in there, and you would talk to her because Anna didn't talk to any of us, really," said Patricia Lynden, who worked as articles editor and wrote copy on a few of Anna's fashion spreads.

Alma Moore liked Gunn a lot, but not what she observed about Anna's treatment of her. Sometimes Anna blamed Gunn for things that went wrong on shoots or trips. It didn't seem, to Moore, like the best way to treat the person who always had her back. When Anna was out and Moore didn't know where she was, Gunn was the one who gave excuses, true or false. Gunn went to meetings and shoots when Anna wasn't around or didn't want to go herself. Their colleagues speculated that Gunn actually did a lot of Anna's styling work behind the scenes. "She always seemed to be her sidekick, even if they had their own personal issues, maybe her not giving Georgia credit for what she did," said DiBenedetto. "But they seemed to get along." Indeed, from what the staff could tell, Gunn became more than an assistant to Anna. Anna listened to her feedback on stories, and Gunn got a few bylines of her own. For her part, Gunn never complained about Anna.

A number of things bothered Anna about Keeton, including how she muscled her own fashion ideas into the magazine. As a budding talent with increasing industry recognition outside the office, Anna rebuffed Keeton's ideas. Keeton also assigned stories that Anna had no interest in doing, such as the cliché idea to make over members of the *Viva* staff. But of all their disputes—over messengers, travel expenses, stories—those over the staff models may have been the most heated. These women worked on a $176 weekly retainer for all of Guccione's publications, posing in everything from centerfolds to promotional ads for *Penthouse*-branded lingerie, and Keeton really wanted them to work for *Viva* too.

When Keeton looked at the staff models, she saw money saved. But when Anna looked at them, she saw women who were not high-fashion models and therefore unsuitable for her stories. When Keeton implored her to cast the staff girls, Anna simply said, "No," and huffed off. The head of the promotions department would joke with the models, "Stay away from that end of the floor, because Anna and Kathy are having a fight over the girls." But they sat close enough that they could hear the clashing, punctuated by Anna stomping in and out of Keeton's office.

Working with centerfolds "didn't serve her ambition," said Cheryl Rixon, one staff model Anna deigned to cast. "We all knew she wanted to be fashion editor of *Vogue*, and was looking to bigger things."

Anna liked Rixon because she had fashion modeling experience and didn't look out of place with models from agencies like Ford. Plus, she had the work ethic Anna expected: she showed up early, stayed late, worked through lunch, and followed instructions. She was also the rare person who wasn't afraid of Anna. "She was never in good humor, and everybody approached on tiptoes. She rarely smiled, unless it was gleeful sarcasm. But I'd grown up Australian, so I was used to a British, glum personality," she said.

When Rixon met with Anna to try on clothes before shoots, she always found Anna standing near her long desk against the wall, ready to move through the fitting with the same rapid pace of an assembly line. She had all the looks planned in advance and hanging on her rack, ready for try-ons. Rixon tried on whatever Anna told her to, and the fittings were quick because Anna was decisive. She never said, "That looks great," or got excited over how Rixon looked in anything. Rixon put on the outfits; Anna looked at them and said "Okay." Then Rixon was dismissed. And on set, Anna had almost nothing to do with Rixon; having planned everything in advance, she often didn't even show up, sending her assistant instead.

Anna's fashion spreads tended to be both clever and glamorous, naughty and sweet. Her pages were developing a signature look. There were the country scenes that looked just like her later *Vogue* spreads, where models posed in dune grass or on old farms, with wispy hair and chunky sweaters and props (a bow and arrow, a motorized scooter, just-caught dead fish) that only seem bizarre if you stop to think about them.

There was also edge. The October 1977 issue included an S&M-inspired collection of photo illustrations by Jean-Paul Goude, a respected fashion photographer known for the stylized album covers and music videos he created with Grace Jones. The series featured a model on her hands and knees in a baby-doll dress and bonnet being fed a bottle of milk by a man standing above her, the liquid splashing into a puddle on the hardwood floor beneath her chest. Said Patricia Lynden of Anna's work broadly, "It's all very suggestive. Nobody did anything like that. Now this looks very tame, but it wasn't. Then, it was way out there."

While at *Viva*, Moore took a meeting with Condé Nast's editorial director, Alexander Liberman, one of the most important people in magazine publishing, who would years later hire Anna at *Vogue*. "I love *Viva*. I noticed you have an Englishwoman on the masthead," he said, referring to Anna. Clearly, the job was doing exactly what she needed it to do—making her a name.

That was more important now than ever. Anna had been at *Viva* for three years, about half its life, but it had never shed its pornographic reputation. "The writing was on the wall that the magazine wasn't going to last forever," recalled Deborah Dichter, the managing editor. "The magazine was losing so much money, they didn't know what to do. The only thing they wanted to do was get rid of her," Moore said.

But it would have been hard to let Anna go. Her fashion pages were valuable real estate against which to place ads, and also gave the magazine currency in the world of New York media. Editors at *Vogue* and *Harper's Bazaar* looked at *Viva* just to see what Anna was doing. Anna was also protected by the same person as Keeton—Bob Guccione.

At that point, Vivienne Lasky was also living in New York, and she once asked Anna how she could stand working for Guccione, whether he was as gross as some people said. "She thought he was sort of interesting," Lasky remembered. Said Bob Jr., "Anna was not squeamish about it. That wouldn't be politically savvy."

In early 1978, Gunn went with Anna to meet her friend Michael Zilkha at the Plaza Hotel for lunch. Zilkha was interested in Gunn and asked his friend Michel Esteban, with whom he had just founded ZE Records, to come along. Esteban was instantly attracted to Anna. He invited her for lunch the next day, and Anna confessed she'd thought Esteban was gay because of his clothes. "She said no men in New York dressed like that," Esteban recalled. "I took it as a compliment."

They began a relationship, and Anna invited him to move into her apartment in a classic brownstone she shared with a roommate, the restaurateur Brian McNally, who subsequently moved out. Together they loved going out to restaurants, art galleries, and museums. Though they went to concerts of Esteban's artists, "this was not really her cup of tea."

She remained busy at work. Despite *Viva*'s financial troubles, Anna managed to shoot all around the world—Japan, Jamaica, Guadeloupe, Puerto Rico. And despite all the company's faults, it was a great job for Anna at a time when she needed it. However, the magazine never found a large enough audience, and by the second half of 1978, *Viva*'s circulation had dropped from 700,000 in 1976 to just about half that. Keeton blamed prejudicial treatment by newsstands, which still buried it like a dirty picture magazine.

On Thursday, November 17, 1978, an announcement was made to the staff that the magazine would cease operations the next day. Anna immediately started sobbing, tears streaming down her face. Lynden was shocked by her reaction. Her flippant attitude and frequent absences had led the staff to believe she didn't really care for the place. Her expensive clothes suggested she didn't need the salary. But she was probably mourning not for the magazine, but for the job itself—the flexibility, the first place she had been able to carve out a kingdom, all of it now gone.

Her career wasn't the only deeply altered area of her life. Just a week before *Viva* announced its closure, Anna's father had married his girlfriend, Audrey Slaughter, and celebrated in London with a dinner party.

It would be a year and a half before Anna found herself at another magazine job.

Chapter 7

A SAVVY MOVE

After *Viva* closed, Anna threw herself into jet-setting with Esteban. They traveled the world, from the South of France to Jamaica to London, but spent most of their time together in Paris. There, Anna became closer with Anne McNally, a ballet dancer and occasional model. They'd met when Anna was at *Harpers & Queen* and sometimes worked with McNally's then-boyfriend, photographer André Carrara. "It's like when you like chocolate. I can't explain it," McNally said. "We just liked each other." Once they turned up to the premiere of a Baryshnikov ballet performance wearing the same Thierry Mugler tunic and leggings, but in different colors. (Though this happened frequently when they got together, Anna was always just "cool," said McNally.)

For Anna, this period was her only true break from work since being a teenager, but it didn't dampen her ambition, Esteban recalled. "In French we say *reculer pour mieux sauter*," which translates to "to make a strategic withdrawal."

In the spring of 1980, she was ready to get back to New York and back to work. There, she found a job at a magazine called *Savvy*.

Anna and Esteban broke up shortly thereafter because he didn't want to stay in New York, though they remained friends. Meanwhile,

McNally moved to New York, and her bond with Anna only grew stronger. Shortly after she moved, she and Anna were on Lexington Avenue near Bloomingdale's, wearing fur coats and high heels, when a mugger snatched Anna's purse. Still possessed of the sprinting talent of her youth, even in her heels, she took off after him and grabbed the bag. "The guy didn't stand a chance," McNally said.

She was about to run just as hard at her career.

In early 1980, *Savvy* magazine launched with the tagline "The Magazine for Executive Women."

"Other magazines, like *Cosmo*, were always saying it's O.K. to be excited about men. What I wanted to do was to release women and say it's O.K. to be excited about your work," said founder and editor-in-chief Judith Daniels, formerly of *New York* and the *Village Voice*, who was born Judy but started going by Judith as an adult, which she considered more serious. It sounded like a good match for Anna, then thirty years old and in need of employment. Without much leverage, she accepted the paltry offer of around $1,000 per monthly issue (and during her tenure, she didn't even work on every issue).

But there was friction between Anna's worldview and *Savvy*'s, which was meant to speak to women who had fought throughout the seventies to ascend to management roles at law firms and banks. Ambition aside, Anna couldn't relate to them. Unlike the target *Savvy* reader, she had entered an industry where her femininity was an asset rather than a handicap. The fashion needs of a lawyer were vastly different from those of an ascendant "It girl" like Anna. In early editorial meetings, *Savvy*'s staff debated whether or not to cover fashion at all, and even whether or not to take advertisements from beauty brands. Banning fashion coverage and beauty advertising was unheard of for women's magazines, which relied on such income to survive.

Daniels had spent years trying to launch *Savvy*, and she knew she couldn't afford to be so high-minded. Executives with disposable income would be interested in clothing, and good for them if they were. Still, she felt the kinds of fashion stories Anna had previously done wouldn't work.

Daniels wanted to see "real people" instead of models, wearable office clothes instead of stuff no one wore off a runway, and reasonable prices—a précis for C-suite-striving women reading stories like "What Your Business Card Says about You" and "Picking the Next Hot Computer Stocks."

But Anna wasn't at *Savvy* to support its mission to propel women to the great heights of corporate America. She was there to continue her own mission: filling her portfolio with the kinds of stories she liked, which would propel her to her next, better job, be it at *Vogue* or one that would get her to *Vogue*. "Anna was very strong-minded, and she just did whatever she wanted," said Susan Edmiston, *Savvy*'s executive editor.

Daniels would become the third boss in a row who wanted to fire Anna.

W hen Anna got to *Savvy*, she was a mysterious presence in the office, just like at *Viva*.

She'd brought Georgia Gunn along to assist her, but it was unclear how she afforded her; she either used money from the pittance of a fashion budget or paid her out of her own pocket (Anna was still receiving trust fund payments around once a year; one in 1980 totaled $4,000, equivalent to around $13,500 in 2021).

Gunn, as she had at *Viva*, interfaced with the staff, who found her friendly and Anna inaccessible. She and Gunn came and went as needed and worked out of a back room, to which drifted a steady stream of photographers and models with portfolios to show Anna. Anna mostly spoke with her boss, Daniels; the art director, Carol Devine Carson; and Carson's assistant, Dan Taylor. Anna adored Taylor, one of the few men in the office, and called him "the thin man" after the 1934 film because he reminded her of its star, William Powell. He also did his own photography and wanted Anna's pages to be beautiful. It was clear to the staff that Anna worked hard, though she only went to them when she needed something, like text for her stories.

While at *Savvy*, Anna moved into the Upper West Side loft of her new boyfriend, the writer Michael Stone, who was well-off and about her same age. There she set up a big white desk and, when not in the office, put in eighteen-hour workdays—though part of what she was likely working on was looking for another job. When she was at the office, she always looked glamorous in her shades, jeans, Liberty of London blouses, and balloon pants (it was the eighties). But why, some wondered, was Anna working for *Savvy* for almost no money, maybe even *losing* money? Why would this clearly talented, self-important European with her own assistant want to cover fashion for women whose day started with nude pantyhose and shoulder pads?

As a startup, *Savvy* had tight budgets, which meant everyone had to be scrappy, including Anna. She pushed her own racks of clothing down the office's city-block-long hallways and called in favors to get her shoots done. For one shoot in Jamaica, she cast Anne McNally as a model. "We just got the pictures. She handled the whole thing. It wasn't like I was an art director for her. She was her own light and spirit," said Carson, who loved Anna's pages even when Daniels or other editors questioned them.

Unsurprisingly, Anna's expenses were, just like at *Viva*, a point of contention. But unlike at *Viva*, so was her creative approach. A story she did for the February 1981 issue featured six women fashion entrepreneurs, including Norma Kamali and shoe designer Maud Frizon, who also appeared on the cover. Anna shot their pieces on a model whose face appeared in full in only one of the seven photos; the rest of the time, she was shot from the back or the nose down. For one cover shoot, Anna obscured a model's face with a dark rose–colored hat, and Daniels refused to publish it.

For another shoot, she photographed Tina Chow, who was exactly the kind of businessperson Anna liked because she was actually part of the fashion world—a model and jewelry designer and fellow "It girl." Along with her sister, Adelle Lutz, she was pictured lounging in her husband's swanky Chinese restaurant Mr. Chow, wearing a $650 Ron Leal suede jacket while her sister wore a $300 Issey Miyake cardigan. Guy Le Baube, a fashion photographer who had shot for Anna at *Viva*, took the pictures. Though the fee was a fraction of his usual rate and he thought the shoot was conceptually simple (and therefore a waste of his time), he liked working with Anna, who struck him as smarter than most people in fashion. Plus, Le Baube didn't know anything about fashion itself; he was mostly concerned with the light and trusted her entirely with the clothing. "Anna was extremely sophisticated, she had that beautiful, exotic accent, and she knew what she wanted," he said. And Le Baube recognized something beyond that: Anna was evolving from someone who "had the faculty to know" celebrities, to someone who could also "invent" them.

Though Anna's pages were right for Anna, they upset the magazine's readers, prompting letters saying, "I would never be able to afford this," or "I would never wear this in a million years." Daniels became so concerned that she considered getting rid of Anna, not only because of her fashion preferences but because she did whatever she wanted, no matter the costs to budget and readership. But, with the same fearlessness she brought to her creative work, Anna talked Daniels into letting her stay. *

Claire Gruppo, the managing editor, said, "It was a good gig for her. Was it fancy enough or prestigious enough? Of course not. So she did it just as long as she needed to."

Staying bought her time, ideally enough to look for a better job while she was still employed. On Wednesday, March 18, 1981, she stopped by the office of *Interview*, Andy Warhol's magazine, to show editor Bob Colacello an idea she had worked on for three months. "He just looked at it for one second and said it was trash and she started crying. And she's such a tough cookie that I could never even imagine her crying," Warhol wrote in his diaries, "but I guess it was her femininity coming out." **

---

*   Predictably, years later Daniels would be among those who denied ever wanting to fire Anna, in an interview with Jerry Oppenheimer for his biography on Anna, *Front Row*.

**   A month after this rejection, on Sunday, April 26, 1981, Warhol saw Anna out to dinner at the hip downtown Italian restaurant Da Silvano with Michael Stone and wondered if he had made a mistake. "Maybe we should have [hired her]," Warhol wrote, "we do need a fashion person but—I don't think she knows how to dress. She's actually a terrible dresser."

But when she believed in something—even if, at this moment, that something was simply herself—nothing would stop her from making it happen. She was still trying to prove herself to her intellectual and academic family, perhaps most especially her father. She left the *Interview* offices and moved on to her next interview.

Chapter 8

IN VOGUE

The first time Laurie Jones saw her, Anna was sitting on the floor of the *New York* magazine office. She wore a hat and was so slight that at first Jones thought she was a boy. At the time Anna was dating the magazine's writer Jon Bradshaw, who was on deadline, and she had nowhere else to wait.

About five years later in early 1981 while Anna was at *Savvy*, Jones, *New York*'s managing editor, called Anna in to interview for a new fashion editor position.

It had been a tough job to fill. The editor had to create the fashion spreads without a team, going to fashion shows, selecting the clothes, booking the photographers and hair stylists, models and makeup artists—all mostly on her own. Also, the stories had to run in almost every weekly issue and be culturally relevant to New York City, not just showcasing the trendiest items.

Jones had interviewed people from *Vogue*, but none of them seemed like they'd be able to handle the job. She was so desperate that she called Grace Coddington in London. Coddington was the lead fashion editor at British *Vogue* and already a legend in the business, but she wasn't interested. Then one of *New York*'s writers, Anthony Haden-

Guest, known for chronicling Manhattan's upper crust, recommended his friend Anna.

Jones immediately liked Anna, whom she found animated, enthusiastic, and clearly knowledgeable about fashion. Jones asked her to come back with story ideas. Anna left and prepared boards with page layouts, including Polaroid pictures of the clothes. The ideas were varied and unique and exceedingly well-planned. "Anna, this is fabulous," Jones said when she saw them. "I like every one of these story ideas." She promptly took Anna's boards to editor-in-chief Edward Kosner, who had been running the magazine for about a year, after editing *Newsweek*. "Ed, this woman is amazing. We're all going to be working for her someday," she told him. Kosner laughed, then hired Anna.

Anna's job at *New York* was the one that brought an end to her string of unstable jobs in America, and finally earned her the industry stardom she sought.

Anna was again a bizarrely glamorous presence in a newsroom staffed by journalists. She was in a phase of wearing mostly Japanese designers, and came to work in an outfit by Kenzo that she owned in two different colors because, she told a coworker, "I can't help it, I just can't help it." Her bob obscured her face and her clothes hung in layers of fabric on her skinny figure. She wore high heels by Susan Bennis/ Warren Edwards every day, which didn't bother her because, she said, "It's not that far from the front door to the limo."

Anna brought in her own big white Parsons table instead of working at the same crappy desks as everyone else. ("I prefer to have a large white surface with which to view clothes and accessories against," she said.) She also brought along a clothing rack, and a chic chair with a bungee cord back. She asked for whiteboards on which to post pictures, creating a perfect sanctuary, distinct from the rest of the newspaper-littered office, even though she worked out of a cubicle with just a tiny separate coat closet to store the clothes she borrowed.

While Anna aspired to live the life she was photographing, she was actually living the life of the executive she planned to become. Despite her mismatch with *Savvy*'s mission, she was singularly driven by professional advancement. She was now one of New York City's top rising fashion editors, slim and beautiful and delicate, but also capable of projecting the demeanor of an army general or CEO, and was described by her colleagues as "businesslike" and "professional," if not warm.

The *New York* team were friends who worked hard, but also liked to have happy hour in the office and joke around with one another. Anna was never fully part of the clique, but befriended the men's fashion editor, Henry Post. After he came down with AIDS, Anna went to visit him at the hospital and rubbed his feet. Another friend on the staff was Haden-Guest, but their relationship ceased shortly after he helped Anna get the job. He said, "I don't think she's selfish or anything like that, I think that's just her nature. She just moves on."

Though others may have found her distant, Anna felt like the outcast just by virtue of being the fashion editor. "*New York* magazine didn't think very highly of fashion at the time, so I think I was basically working out of the ladies' room," she said. Yet, as had been the case before and would be the case after, Anna didn't reach out to her colleagues to cultivate relationships that would have eased that sense of ostracism. Jokes intended to be playful struck her as venomous. Occasionally she would put her bob up into a tiny samurai-style bun on the top of her head with a rubber band. The first time the staff noticed it, one by one they started putting their hair up in rubber bands, even the men, even if they had barely any hair. When Anna looked around the room and saw what was happening, she burst into tears and left.

The joking around may have made her feel even less likely to engage. Once Anna asked Nancy McKeon, a senior editor who worked on *New York*'s service pages, to accompany her to a meeting with an editor at the book publisher Clarkson Potter. Anna was interested in turning an interiors issue she had worked on into a coffee table book. On the walk there, Anna was silent.

"Don't you chat?" McKeon asked.

"I chat to my friends," Anna replied, ending the conversation.

Her closest friends were European ex-pats, like Anne McNally and writer Joan Juliet Buck, and British journalists Gully Wells and her husband, Peter Foges. She stayed close with Emma Soames, who came to New York with her fiancé around the time Anna started at *New York*. They went out to dinner, and the fiancé left early. Immediately, Anna turned to Soames and said, "You can't marry that man."

"Oh, Anna, I know," said Soames, who was having doubts anyway, and somehow sent a glass of red wine flying across the table and spilling down the front of Anna's new white Yves Saint Laurent blouse. Recalled Soames, "I never heard another word about the shirt, and she was right about the man."

New York was high-profile, known for stories like the 1976 feature that became the movie *Saturday Night Fever*. It was, like the *Evening Standard* under Charles, the publication journalists read with rapture, and the place many of them wanted to work. But most of the fashion advertising was going to the competition, the *New York Times Magazine*, where Anna's former boss Carrie Donovan was fashion editor. Anna was supposed to help change that. She convinced Kosner that in order to make the magazine more high-end (and thus fashionable), she had to use only the best photographers and models for her stories. It was more expensive than anything the magazine had been doing, but, unlike her past bosses, Kosner, who fetishized the notion of *New York* being perceived as the crème de la crème, let her do it. (That said, he did once complain to Haden-Guest about Anna's preference for photographers he found weird.)

"He thought the world of her," said Patricia Bradbury, an associate art director. "He also, I think, adored her because she was beautiful and charming. I think he had a little crush on her. I had a little crush on her. Everybody did."

Kosner saw her as a great talent right away, and set her up for success, even when doing so seemed to defy his own logic. Bradbury sat in meetings where Anna pitched Kosner. "She did her homework. She didn't come in with something that would be easy to turn down," she said. Anna specifically wanted to blend New York's burgeoning downtown art scene with her fashion shoots, and commissioned Michael

Boodro, who had worked at the Museum of Modern Art and the Grey Art Gallery, to help her identify artists to collaborate with. "She didn't want to just have models in a studio," Boodro said. "She wanted to do something different."

For her first *New York* story, Anna worked with Guy Le Baube on a shoot of summer dresses with Andie MacDowell and another model. Le Baube wanted them to look like they were on a New York City rooftop on a hot night with the Empire State Building slanted, as though "dancing," behind them against a deep-blue night sky. Creating a shoot like this at the time was difficult because there was no way to manipulate the look in postproduction. Le Baube found a building with a view of the Empire State Building from its roof and, using wooden shelves, created a slanted platform for the models to pose on so that when he leveled his camera with the platform, the buildings tilted behind them. Anna posed MacDowell on the platform in a $1,750 brightly colored deck chair. The photos ran under the headline "In the Heat of the Night."

Though she worked with him often, Le Baube didn't feel they were particularly great collaborators. When they were on set together, Anna was "like a hawk, like a bird of prey," he recalled. "She could see any details and intervene right away with courage and authority."

That wasn't always appreciated. On set they had "a continuous disagreement," he said, defused by Georgia Gunn. Gunn once again worked for Anna at *New York* after Melanie Skrzek, the first assistant she hired, left less than a year into the job.

It helped that Gunn was good-natured and "wanted everything to be fine," said Le Baube, "since Anna and myself, we never bothered to please each another."

But Le Baube was fine with their tension on set. He liked shooting for Anna because it was a lot better than shooting for other editors. When he shot for *Vogue*, there was no guarantee his photos would be published. Anna, he felt, didn't waste his time like that, and it was obvious that she disdained when anyone wasted hers.

Kosner understood that if the magazine was going to stretch for the high end, that meant occasional ostentation. In the fourth issue she contributed to, Anna did a spread on furs, including a $20,000 sable and an $8,000 beaver coat. In one 1982 issue, she did a two-page spread on goatskin luggage. "Prices range from $750 for a vanity case to $9,000 for a steamer trunk," it read. Editor Nancy McKeon thought the trunk was beautiful, but expensive for a *New York* magazine recommendation for luggage. But in a subsequent desserts story, Kosner became disturbed by a chocolate-covered cake from Sylvia Weinstock that cost $600. He called staff into his office one by one, including McKeon, who had nothing to do with the story, to ask how a $600 cake ended up in the magazine.

"Didn't you think that this was odd? Why didn't you bring this to my attention?" he said.

"But, Ed," McKeon said, "you want the $9,000 goatskin trunk."

"Well, that's different," Kosner replied. "You don't eat that."

Thick as her skin was—and Anna certainly had developed some to survive fashion media for as long as she had—she still had feelings, and on rare occasions revealed them. One spring Friday night Anna stayed late in the office with photo editor Jordan Schaps, an opera fanatic who oversaw the magazine's covers, to meet with photographer Oliviero Toscani. Toscani was flying in from London and wanted to come to the office to see Anna's rack of clothing before their spring fashion cover shoot the following week. Anna had picked designer clothes for models to wear posing alongside real-life New York City archetypes, like a taxi driver, a bike messenger, and waiters from the upscale Le Cirque restaurant.

Schaps recalled that no matter what Anna had chosen, Toscani would have said it was trash. The meeting wasn't really about seeing the clothes; it was about his ego, a power move. Though predictable, Toscani's disparagement left Anna in tears. "I thought it was a goddamn generous thing of Anna to pave the way so thoroughly and to allow this prima don to fly in and come in the office at nine o'clock at night and review the clothes," Schaps said. "He was a pig. . . . There was no reason to make her cry." Toscani said he didn't remember this run-through, but that he "probably" did make her cry. Yet when they did the shoot, everyone was so busy that there was no time for power moves, and things went fine. Toscani admired Anna's efficiency, intellect, and sense of humor. Anna worked with Toscani a number of times again.

Professional resentment was not always as easily smoothed over. Anna's first assistant at *New York*, Melanie Skrzek, had attended Parsons and was just starting her career. She kept her head down and did what she had to do—getting Anna's fashion show seats, picking up her yogurt and banana for lunch—and seemed fine with the job. Once she'd proven herself, Anna allowed Skrzek to style and plan a shoot. They agreed to cast up-and-coming comedienne Sandra Bernhard, and to commission Steven Meisel, a young fashion illustrator who was transitioning to photography. When the photos came back, Anna killed the story without explanation. It didn't matter that this was her assistant's first shoot or that they had cast someone notable as the model.

This was something she would do again and again over the course of her career, and once she decided, there was usually no way to get her to change her mind. Also, she knew that killing stories, which *Vogue* did then all the time, was necessary to let people know that you had standards, regarding both the final outcome and what happened on set. Killing a story let the victim know who had the power, and what they should do the next time if they wanted to see their work in the magazine.

Meisel, who was about as exacting in his vision as Anna, was not happy. He would go on to become one of the greatest fashion photographers of all time, but it would be years before he worked again with Anna Wintour.

No matter what happened on set, Anna never seemed to turn in a bad set of photos, and before she had been at *New York* a year, she got a promotion to senior editor. Kosner expanded her purview with a new column called In Style that allowed her to cover interiors and influencers as well as clothing. With every issue, she was attracting more attention in the industry—not only among designers and models, but from editors. She wouldn't end up going to *Vogue* for another year, but conversations were starting.

Grace Mirabella had been editing *Vogue* since 1971. She was known for her love of the color beige, made evident by her wardrobe and the décor in her office. While Anna was innovating at *New York*, one of *Vogue's* highest-ranking fashion editors, Polly Mellen, began to feel *Vogue* was becoming "boring"—the last adjective anyone would apply to Mellen herself. To save a shoot in 1981 that she felt was turning out to be lackluster, Mellen found an animal trainer. She hired him at the last minute to bring a massive boa constrictor to the set and pose with model Nastassja Kinski. Photographer Richard Avedon asked Kinski to lie down naked on the floor with the snake, which slithered up to her face and tickled her ear with its tongue, at which point "the shoot was over and I was crying," Mellen said. The result was one of *Vogue's* most famous pictures.

Mellen wondered if Anna, whose personal style she'd admired since she started seeing her at fashion shows beginning in the early seventies when Anna was at *Harpers & Queen*, could, in her own serpentine way, liven up *Vogue*. Impressed with Anna's work at *New York*, she arranged a meeting with Mirabella. Mirabella asked Anna what job she would like at *Vogue*, and Anna replied, in what she later described as "a sudden fit of candor" that was unlike her, "Yours."

That ended the meeting.

As spring became summer in 1982, Anna's relationship with live-in boyfriend Michael Stone was eroding. Anna had traveled to the Hamptons for a shoot with Stone in tow. The crew stayed at a house that Stone had been renting from model China Machado. It was obvious that Anna and Stone weren't getting along. Guy Le Baube's assistant thought it stemmed from what he perceived as Anna's romantic interest in Le Baube. However, Anna professed disgust with Le Baube, who she believed was having a romantic relationship with the model on the shoot. ("He thinks he's Helmut Newton," the edgy and influential photographer known for erotically charged imagery, Anna quipped at one point.) She had no tolerance for his unprofessional behavior. (Le Baube said he didn't remember this shoot.)

When it came time to shoot, the day was dominated by frustration on all sides: Le Baube didn't like the positioning of the model; Anna, usually so decisive, didn't seem to know what she wanted, and criticized every attempt by her assistant to help out. The whole thing was so exasperating that they decided to end it abruptly and go home. The pictures came out fine in the end, but it was the last time Anna and Le Baube's bylines appeared together.

Though Anna expected flawless judgment and behavior from her collaborators, she sometimes faltered herself. For the 1982 "Summer Pleasures" double issue, Schaps wanted to put a "bathing beauty" on the cover, inspired by Alberto Vargas's *Esquire* illustrations. In a meeting, Anna said, "Why don't we do Rachel Ward?"—an English-born actress who would become best known as the lead in *The Thorn Birds* in 1983—"I know her and she would pose for us."

Schaps loved it. Anna was staying in Machado's Southampton house again, and they decided to do the shoot out there, outdoors in the summer sunlight. Since photographer Patrick Demarchelier had a house close by, Schaps booked him to save money on travel. They got a hotel for Ward and some of the crew, and Schaps and Anna stayed at her rental.

The shoot began badly. It rained and rained with no break in sight. With time running out, Schaps suggested clearing the furniture off the covered porch and setting up a makeshift studio there. The shoot finally started, and Ward posed in her bathing suit against the thunder-gray backdrop, looking gorgeous. Schaps was thrilled. He asked his assistant to get her to sign the standard model release form during a break. But, after he'd asked three or four times, the clipboard never came back to him. "We're not leaving without her signature on the model release," Schaps said. The next time he asked, his assistant said, "Anna took care of it."

Back at the office, Schaps was putting the selected photos up on a board when Anna came by to ask for copies to send to Ward for approval.

"Anna, we don't do that," Schaps said. This was a matter of journalistic principle—Kosner did not allow subjects to sign off on how they are portrayed.

Anna went to her desk and came back with the signed release, which said, "We hereby give Rachel Ward picture approval."

"Anna, I think you better show that to Ed," Schaps said.

Anna went into Kosner's office and closed the doors behind her ("When the doors were closed, you either came out with one ball or three balls," Schaps reflected). When she came out, she was crying.

"I'm flying to Los Angeles to get Rachel's approval," she told Schaps. He gave her photos to take and she bought her own ticket.

When Ward saw the photos, she cried. She said she looked fat, terrible, that the cover would ruin her career. Schaps couldn't have disagreed more, but told Ward on the phone it was fine, he would scrap the cover. Now he had to come up with something else at the last minute. He recalled that Anna had recently done a shoot on bathing suits, so he met with the two models she'd used and cast one to photograph for the new cover. Anna couldn't help with the shoot because she was flying back from her disastrous meeting with Ward in LA, so Schaps took over. He thought the bathing suits the substitute stylist had picked out weren't working and asked the model to weigh in on the shot. "Well, I have a bikini in my purse," she said. She put it on, and Schaps had another idea. He said to his assistant, "Run out and get a shitload of peonies." He shot the model with an armful of pink peonies gushing from her bosom. And finally, he had his cover.

Back in the office, Anna stopped by after she returned from California. "I love your cover," she said. Like her father, she rarely offered compliments at the office, so when she lavished one on your work, you knew she really meant it—and it felt wonderful.

Schaps looked at her and, in his only time ever addressing the Ward catastrophe with her, said, "It's our cover."

As she did in previous jobs, Anna relied on a dutiful assistant to get her assignments done. After Skrzek left and Anna brought on Georgia

Gunn to assist her, she wound up promoting Gunn after a few months. To replace her, she hired Laurie Schechter, who would work for her for the next decade. Schechter had gotten her start in fashion working for Dianne Benson, who started the boutique Dianne B, where Anna bought her Comme des Garçons clothes and often borrowed pieces for shoots. Before she landed at *New York*, Schechter would see her shopping in the store on Saturdays.

On her first day, Anna said, "I'm not very organized, so you'll have to take care of everything." Since, as she quickly learned, Anna was extremely organized, Schechter came to realize this was a management tactic to ensure she wouldn't slack off. (The only thing Anna seemed unable to keep track of was her prescription Wayfarer sunglasses. She had them custom-made at Better Vision Optical in Soho to fit her small face, and Schechter went there repeatedly to get replacement pairs.)

Vogue employees later described being "hazed" by Anna, who nitpicked their work when they started—whether it was arranging a photo shoot or selecting collars for her dogs. They believed this served the purpose of asserting her dominance. People who had gotten used to working with her would tell new employees, "That's just how she works, don't take it personally."

Schechter lost eight pounds in her first two weeks working for Anna at *New York*. The first one in and the last to leave, she was constantly busy with shoots and sometimes personal errands for her boss. She drank "too much coffee," but still easily fell asleep when she got home, sometimes as late as eleven thirty at night. One errand was to the loft apartment Anna shared with Stone, where she had to get something out of the closet. Schechter was amazed because, like a dry cleaner, Anna had an automated clothing rack.

The first shoot Schechter worked on took place in the fall of 1982. The concept was "clothes for a country weekend," and Anna planned to go to the dune grass of Bridgehampton to photograph models in chunky layers and boots with soft, wispy hair.

"Call Bryan Bantry and tell him I want Sam McKnight for this shoot," Anna told Schechter. She didn't explain that McKnight was the hair stylist and Bantry was his agent, nor did she offer a Rolodex with his phone number. Schechter found the number and called Bantry. "Hi, my name is Laurie Schechter and I'm calling for Anna Wintour. She'd like Sam McKnight for these dates."

"No," Bantry said, and hung up the phone.

Schechter was mortified, and told Anna that McKnight wasn't available.

"Call Bryan back, tell him I really need him. You've got to get him for me," she told Schechter, reminding her that Skrzek used to do that sort of thing. Schechter, who didn't want to fail where her predecessor had succeeded, called Bantry back and convinced him to book McKnight. Anna also told Schechter that she and the crew needed a van to get out to Bridgehampton. Schechter called a car service company and booked a van with a driver. When Anna called from the road declaring the tires on the van dangerously worn, Schechter panicked and called the car service. "You have to send a new van with a new driver. You're about to get me fired from my new job," she told them. Anna and the crew got their new van.

Alex Chatelain had been hired to take the pictures. He had shot a spread for Anna when she was at *Harpers & Queen*, and they got along well. Unfortunately, their previous chemistry didn't translate to Bridgehampton's cold beaches and pleasantly decaying barns.

The weather was freezing, and the models were exhausted from driving three hours from the city. So they took a break in a diner called Bridgehampton Candy Kitchen.

"They have five minutes," Anna said.

"No, they're cold. They need to warm up," said Chatelain, who got them soup.

"We don't have time—we have to get back to work," said Anna, who still never ate much herself, and would later regiment her business lunches so that they ended after exactly forty-five minutes no matter what food had yet to be served. Chatelain was used to joking around on set, but now they just sat there in awkward silence. The rest of the shoot was tense and terrible. Chatelain just got it over with so he could go home.

Several years later, when Anna became editor-in-chief of British *Vogue*, he was one of two photographers she decided she wanted to cut from the magazine. "She destroyed my career," he said.

Anna's personal life was no less dramatic. The "Flower Wars" began after she met David Shaffer, a child psychiatrist. Shaffer, thirteen years older than Anna, had moved to New York from London in 1977 with his wife, Serena Bass, to become the chair of child psychiatry at Columbia University. Anna met Shaffer—and his wife—in the West Village home of Peter Foges and Gully Wells, who invited her along with Stone for a get-together. In London, Shaffer and Bass had regularly held cultural salons, painters and writers and prominent people like Daniel Day-Lewis gathering over a traditional English Sunday lunch. They brought the tradition to New York with them, and Anna became one of their frequent guests.

Though Anna was still with Stone, that didn't stop Shaffer, whose marriage with Bass fell apart after she left him for someone else. He was single, but Anna wasn't when overtures began. "Michael would send flowers, David would send flowers. Daily. *Daily*," said Schechter. The mixed bouquets never included freesia or narcissus, which Anna disliked. There were also phone calls from Shaffer, followed by Anna heading "out for lunch" only to return "starving," with her hair a mess.

Finally Anna left Stone, who had always resented feeling second fiddle to her career, for Shaffer. Schaps was glad to see Anna moving on from Stone. "I thought he was a piece of shit. I thought he was a male chauvinist. I thought he put her down and I didn't like that," he said. (Laurie Jones also deemed him and Anna "an odd combo.")

A native South African, Shaffer was slightly hunchbacked and not handsome. A father and child psychiatrist with certain convictions about how to raise kids, he was different from the playboy types Anna had previously dated, of whom her father never approved. Anna, now in her early thirties, knew she wanted children. When Laurie Jones got pregnant, Anna stopped by her office at *New York* to tell her how happy she was for her and how she wished that she could have children one day. In Shaffer, she may have seen that future.

Despite his occupation, Shaffer wasn't alien to Anna's world. While studying for his PhD at Yale, he had befriended the artists Jennifer Bartlett and Brice Marden, inspiring in him the same interest Anna had in modern art. But he also had an interest in fashion that long predated that: he had been squirreling away, for twenty years before meeting Anna, issues of British and American *Vogue*. The appeal of being attached to someone in the *Vogue* world had probably occurred to him long before he even met Anna. Unlike Stone, his relationship with Anna would be driven by her career, not hurt by it.

For Anna, the relationship provided not only adoration but fortification. Shaffer put her on a pedestal. Being the fashion girl in both the newsroom and within her family had left her feeling like she always had to prove herself. With Shaffer, she didn't have to worry about that. He was an intellectual and academic, a leader in his field, who took her and her work as seriously as she did. But some friends saw something sinister in his support of Anna. Perhaps stemming from his psychiatric training, he seemed to enjoy pitting people against one another, playing mind games as only a professional could. Two of their friends independently described Shaffer as Anna's "Svengali."

Yet with him, Anna finally had nothing to prove. Shaffer, though self-conscious about how he looked compared to her, seemed just as dedicated to her rise as she was. It was their alliance that spun Anna's talent and already unwavering determination into pure force.

For the February 28, 1983, issue, she styled a spread of models in different locations around New York City. Toscani took the pictures. In one, the model gets her hair cut at the famous Astor Place barbershop. Toscani loved a shot with Anna and her piercing expression reflected in the mirror behind the model, but when he selected it and showed it to Anna at the office, she reacted strongly. She said she didn't want to appear in the picture. Toscani pushed for it, arguing that it worked with the story. Anna got so upset that she cried.

"Listen, Anna. I think you need a shrink," he said, and left the office. The photo ran with Anna cropped out.

A few weeks later, she called him. "I found a shrink," she said. "And I'm going to marry him."

However, while Shaffer may have aided her success, he wasn't responsible for it. Anna was, above all things, *driven*. And her work ethic came from one person: herself.

To grow her power at the magazine, Anna needed to grow her page count. The logical section for her to take on was *New York*'s popular Best Bets, which recommended things to buy, see, and do in New York City, everything from banking services to underwear to lamps, and intersected with her fashion beat. The most popular items featured in Best Bets—run by McKeon and Anna's desk neighbor Corky Pollan—sold out with such regularity that if McKeon wanted to buy something after the issue came out, she asked stores in advance to set one aside for her.

Anna's favorite word for Best Bets was "rubbish." It was the word she used for much of what she disliked, including many of the gifts she was sent. She once sat at her desk, opening gift after gift, calling each item "rubbish" and throwing it out. After she left, her coworkers went through her trash can. (Anna also had a habit of throwing away her pennies, which were retrieved by the guys who worked in the mail room after she left.) One rare exception to such treatment was a crocodile Susan Bennis/Warren Edwards personal organizer, about which she commented, "Oh well, I guess this is acceptable."

Anna's dismissive attitude regarding Best Bets was unsurprising: it aimed to feature things that might actually be purchased by the *New York* reader, while her spreads were less driven by practicality.

As direct as Anna could be about her preferences, this was only with certain people. Despite sitting on the other side of a cubicle wall from Pollan, she never shared her thoughts about her coworker's pages with her. Instead, if she thought something in Best Bets was "rubbish," she told Kosner, who then called Pollan into his office to say Anna didn't like her ideas, which wasn't the sort of thing her colleagues generally appreciated.

Once she created a memo containing her thoughts on the ugliness of Best Bets, which she tried to influence even though Kosner didn't officially give it to her. She was about to take a vacation, and told her assistant before leaving, "Would you please keep an eye on it and see if you can make it look better?" The memo was left in the copier by mistake, and one of Pollan's colleagues told her about it.

Later, Pollan laughed the whole thing off. "She was very opinionated," she said. Despite Anna's interference, Pollan preserved the sanctity of Best Bets.

A lot contributed to Anna finally getting her first job at *Vogue*. She had spent more than half her life developing a personal brand—the hair, the sunglasses, the polished designer wardrobe, moving through the world like the star of her own never-ending photo shoot. As Schechter put it, "She's not loud and she's not theatrical. She's always commanded the room. Even when the hair was in the face . . . just sitting on the sofa, you never didn't notice her."

And having been fired from *Harper's Bazaar* and nearly fired from *Savvy*, Anna had learned how to commercialize her taste and appease management. That could be why her relationship with Kosner was the healthiest she had had with any editor-in-chief up until that point, allowing her to produce some of her most noteworthy work. And she made an academic effort to learn about art and train her eye. She collected art show catalogues and visited exhibits in her spare time. By incorporating illustrations into her fashion pages and posing models alongside artworks, she appealed to Alexander Liberman, *Vogue's* former art director, who became the editorial director of *Vogue's* parent company, Condé Nast, the creative genius behind the whole operation.

Liberman was a Condé Nast company man by day, and a fine artist on weekends. On Friday afternoons, he changed out of his suit (gray if it was fall, winter, or spring, tan for summers), dark knit tie, and blue shirt, and into overalls, then headed from his Manhattan townhouse to his Warren, Connecticut, home in Litchfield County, where, like a posh welder, he sculpted steel into large-scale artworks. He was so devoted to his art that he had begun spending $360,000 a year—half his salary in 1978—on the materials and labor required to produce it.

Born in Russia, Liberman had escaped to London with his family during the famine of 1921, and later started his career at a magazine in Paris. After arriving in New York in 1941, he landed at *Vogue*'s art department. Though creating and studying art was his passion, he took the job for the money to support his wife, Tatiana, who became a hat designer at Saks Fifth Avenue (and increasingly fond of finery). Liberman's mother, on the other hand, had always wanted him to excel in the arts. While in theory he thus lived between these seemingly opposed goals, Liberman seemed to enjoy luxury as much as his wife, telling an interviewer in 1981, "I admire everything that smacks of megalomania!" This made him perfect for Condé Nast.

In 1962, a few years after newspaper magnate Sam Newhouse bought Condé Nast (in part because his wife liked *Vogue*), Liberman was promoted to editorial director of the whole company, giving him influence over the entire portfolio of magazines, which then included *Vogue*, *Glamour*, *House & Garden*, and *Bride's*. And while friends thought working at a commercial entity like *Vogue* perverted Liberman's artistic sensibilities, he actually used the magazine to indulge his interest in art, publishing photos of his favorite European artists and fashion against backdrops of modern paintings.

So when, in the August 29, 1983, issue of *New York*, Anna published a story in which a dozen artists created paintings inspired by the fall fashion collections and posed her models in front of their work, Liberman noticed. It was this story, Anna has said, that finally got his attention and moved him to open the door for her.

Anna has said she can't remember which of them first made contact. (Though according to another account, they spoke well before Anna even published the famous art story. Toscani also remembered Liberman asking him about working with Anna when he was thinking about hiring her: "I said she was very pleasant and effective as an editor, intelligent. She has a sense of humor and she was not as boring as all the average American fashion editors at the time.") Liberman brought in talent regularly, explained Rochelle Udell, who assisted him at the time after first working for him as *Vogue*'s art director in 1971. He'd ask them about their "hopes and dreams," then try to place them at Condé Nast.

At age seventy, Liberman, a natural seducer, was taken with the thirty-three-year-old Anna, a seductress in her own right. Here was a sophisticated, young European, beautiful and impeccably groomed and styled, the physical embodiment of fashion, who shared his studious interest in art and a devotion to bringing it to the printed page.

But they had something else in common. Each had cultivated a certain mystique, which made it easier to act purely in their own self-interest, even at the expense of people who supposedly mattered to them. Anna was honest with Liberman: she wanted to be editor-in-chief of *Vogue*. Liberman later said he felt "an absolute certitude I needed this presence."

Things moved quickly in the summer of 1983. Shaffer picked Anna up at work one morning and together they drove to the Libermans' Connecticut home. They stopped at a motel along the way so Anna could change into "a wonderfully simple gray tunic," Liberman said, and miniskirt. "I was absolutely enchanted with her." (Tatiana, however, disapproved of both the brevity of Anna's skirt and the zinnias—not even roses, the horror!—she brought as a gift instead of a plant. But Anna preferred cut flowers.)

Liberman had a problem. He wanted Anna at *Vogue* but there was no obvious place for her. Mirabella had been, judging by her circulation figures, successfully running the title now for twelve years. What's more, he had been a witness at Mirabella's wedding (to the famous thoracic surgeon and antismoking activist Dr. William Cahan, in 1974) and one of her closest friends for more than a decade. Furthermore, Anna was the young editor who'd had the gall to tell Mirabella to her face that she wanted to be the one keeping the throne warm at *Vogue*. Yet here she was, adeptly pecking her way into Liberman's inner circle.

Liberman, who claimed he couldn't bear to fire anyone, resorted to his usual solution. "I'm often accused of hiring two people for the same job and letting them compete for it," he said. "I certainly have done that, but very often they both stay." In fact, his start at Condé Nast in 1941 had been similar. Liberman said, "I came in on Monday. On Friday, Dr. [Mehemed] Agha, the great [*Vogue*] art director, called me in and said, 'I don't think you're good enough for us. Good-bye.' But [company founder] Condé Nast hadn't had time to see me that week, so the appointment had been made for the following Monday. I brought the only thing that was easy to carry—an award for design I'd won at the Paris exhibition of 1937. Nast said, 'A man like you must be on *Vogue*,' and he called Agha and told him to hire me." Soon, Liberman ended up in Agha's job.

Mirabella couldn't override Liberman, not just because of his rank but also because he was deeply involved in the day-to-day operations of the magazine, so much so that some on staff saw him as the true editor-in-chief and Mirabella as its public face. While Mirabella selected clothes to feature and maintained relationships within the fashion industry, Liberman did almost everything else, from laying out the pages to editing the nonfashion features to hiring photographers. He was responsible, one staffer said, for any creativity that got into the magazine. So Mirabella was powerless to fight any intention of bringing on Anna.

Liberman's boss, S. I. Newhouse Jr.—known as Si—was the chairman of Condé Nast. When his father sent him to work at the company in 1961, Si Newhouse, short and socially awkward, was wealthy but not naturally glamorous or artistic. Liberman, then art director of *Vogue*, was his entrée into the sophisticated, expensive world that existed for most people only in the pages of Condé Nast's magazines, and hadn't existed for Newhouse previously because no one had invited him in. Together the two went to parties, hip restaurants, and cultural salons. Newhouse adored both the attention and his new milieu. Unsurprisingly, when it came to both his obsessive acquiring of art and Condé Nast, Newhouse almost always went along with Liberman's suggestions, later referring to their relationship as "the most meaningful experience of my life."

Now Liberman and Newhouse felt *Vogue* needed a shake-up and perhaps saw Anna as a kindred spirit who could rattle the leaves from the tree, which would be a useful test and training exercise before she became a Condé Nast editor-in-chief herself. Though it wasn't clear how Anna and Mirabella would fit within the same magazine, Newhouse gave the okay. "Alex's mind is quite subtle and complex. I won't dare to say what was in his mind. Everything I heard was, 'Here is a great talent,'" said Newhouse.

Those who saw Anna and Newhouse together said he loved her glamour and her charm, which she could ignite as needed, particularly with powerful men. But to assume his attraction to Anna was just about the clothes, the beauty, and the drive would be to slight Newhouse, who was surrounded by those things all the time. He was a billionaire with seemingly no vices who appeared to derive pleasure from two things: running magazines and controlling the people he hired to run them.

There was something else about Anna that made Newhouse comfortable with her: she had no interest in interpersonal norms, such as small talk and long discussions. This alacrity and aversion to having a second of her time wasted by a pleasantry, which made other people deeply uncomfortable around her, aligned with Newhouse's style of communication.

Approval given, Liberman offered Anna the title of creative director, which had never been used before, and carried a vague scope of responsibility later described to the *Vogue* staff as "working to enrich the looks of the pages and bringing to the pages other aspects of a woman's interests." It was a cunning move, an example of why, around the office, Liberman was known as the Silver Fox. His personality—sweet but also devious—was a microcosm of the whole company, and an extension of Newhouse himself. Perhaps Anna learned to succeed under Newhouse and Liberman because she was so good at the same games.

Anna had to make a decision. She was being offered the number-two position at *Vogue*. But Anna wasn't a number-two sort of person.

As she was making up her mind, she called Bruce Wolf, a photographer she had worked with at *New York* and who had done a lot of work for various Condé Nast magazines.

"What's it like? What do you think? Do you think I should do this?" she asked.

Wolf had the feeling she had already made up her mind, but he told her, "Yeah, you've got to do it, but you've got to be really careful, because there are a lot of sharks."

Anna and Shaffer went to the Algonquin Hotel to meet a friend of his, Grace Coddington, the legendary fashion director of British *Vogue*, for a drink. "She's just been offered a job as creative director of *Vogue*," he told her when she arrived. "What do you think?"

"I haven't a clue what that means," Coddington said, "but it sounds amazing."

Anna also went to Kosner with Liberman's offer. Kosner didn't want to lose her, and enlisted his wife, Julie Baumgold, who was a contributor for *New York*, to convince her to stay. Shaffer also thought she should remain at *New York*. And they were temporarily successful—Anna did at first decide to stay. But Liberman came for her again weeks later, and at that point, Shaffer chose to remove himself from Anna's decision-making. She decided to go.

Kosner was terribly upset to lose her, but to the rest of the staff, Anna Wintour and *Vogue* made perfect sense together, like bouclé and Chanel. Of course Condé Nast was going to snap her up—what was an exotic bird like her doing in this grimy newsroom anyway?

Once she had made up her mind to go to *Vogue*, Anna called her dad from her desk in the *New York* office. She excitedly told him about the job, but it sounded to Pollan, who overheard their conversation, like his response was negative.

"Well, they think I can do it," Anna said into the phone. As she spoke, it sounded as if she was on the verge of tears.

Laurie Schechter was upset too, albeit for other reasons. She had been working for Anna for just about a year and didn't want to lose her as a boss and mentor. She decided she had nothing to lose by asking Anna to keep her.

Anna liked the idea right away. "Well, you'll have to interview. I'll talk to them," she said. Schechter then went to meet with a woman in Condé Nast human resources. The interview felt pretty standard, until the woman told Schechter, "You know you're not going to have any power here, don't you?" Of course Schechter knew that—she was an assistant, the definition of which was not having any power. But she had a feeling the statement wasn't exactly directed at her—but at Anna.

Chapter 9

SECOND BEST

With Anna in at *Vogue*, she and Shaffer took the next step in their relationship when they jointly took out a $280,000 mortgage to buy a townhouse on MacDougal Street. It wasn't up to Anna's standards, so they set about renovating it.

Her approach was similar at her new job. Aside from an appreciation for twenties-inspired fashion spreads and an office mode of polite professionalism, Grace Mirabella and Anna Wintour didn't have a whole lot in common.

Anna's earliest *Vogue* colleagues use words like "cordial" and "professional" and "polite" to describe her first days at the magazine under Mirabella.. Though her stint as creative director has been characterized as a reign of terror, not everyone who was there saw it that way. First of all, she was hardly reigning and therefore could hardly terrorize. *Vogue* had been running solidly under Mirabella and Liberman for nearly a dozen years by the time she showed up to work at 350 Madison Avenue. Mirabella's staff was loyal to Mirabella, both because they liked her and because it would be unwise not to be. Second, Anna exacted her influence with subtlety and manners.

As *Vogue*'s creative director, Anna appeared on the second line of the masthead, right under Mirabella, a few strokes of the delete key from the very top. But while Anna was a deputy as far as optics were concerned, she was a perplexing presence to many on the *Vogue* staff. *Why is she here? Is she a plant to unseat the art director? What exactly is her job?* While she wanted—and was well on her way to having—Mirabella's job, it wasn't immediately obvious to the staff, Mirabella included. Part of the confusion stemmed from the vague nature of her role, but also from Anna not having the reputation of being a star stylist, like Polly Mellen, the fashion director behind some of Vogue's most famous pictures. She was clearly comfortable making decisions from her desk in her corner office, which had an antechamber where Schechter sat, and the staff got the sense she would have chosen to always be there instead of spending the day in a location van, unlike other fashion editors who loved directing shoots. This was her chance to manage the content instead of generate it, something she had been longing for, and she was going to take it. She intended to be a creative director—of her own ascent.

What *was* clear when Anna arrived was that she represented change. "As shy as she's sometimes described, she's not shy about her thoughts," said Schechter. "So if she's there to do something, she's not going to be shy about doing it." That said, entering the court of *Vogue* was a big change for Anna too. She hadn't worked at a high-fashion magazine in America since *Harper's Bazaar*, which was seven years earlier, and *New York*'s newsroom had been an entirely different atmosphere.

First, there was the office vernacular. Editors talked as though in cover lines—"It's new, it's now!" "The new dazzle!"—which struck Schechter as ridiculous. Then there was the hierarchy, denoted by who was addressed as "Miss" or "Mister," and how one staffer would deign to speak to another. Maggie Buckley, a fellow Brit who assisted Mirabella when Anna started before being promoted to fashion coordinator, said the organization oozed with theatrical showings of rank. "Once somebody dropped something, and one of the assistants who'd just become an editor went to pick it up. Polly [Mellen] goes, 'No, dearie, don't do that. You're an editor now.' We were all kept in our places, and when you went to that next level, it was a big deal. But it was very sort of old-fashioned. And Anna wasn't about that," Buckley said. Lesley Jane Seymour, a junior copywriter when Anna started, said, "She was cool as a cucumber. A lot of those women at *Vogue* were terrifying. I don't remember her being terrifying."

Just like her father, Anna was actually interested in the opinions of the office's youngest assistants—she wanted to know what the young staff were into, the best way to tap into the zeitgeist. She never demanded that subordinates call her "Miss Wintour," and while everyone in the office called their editor-in-chief "*Miss* Mirabella," Anna just called her "Grace." (That said, she was quick to correct Schechter if she ever slipped and called Mirabella by her first name alone.) "She got the work done and she was pleasant," added Seymour, pointing out that there were other female bosses who were truly "mean," adding, "There were always assistants crying in the hallways and crying in the bathrooms."

Seymour sat in a room with a handful of other copywriters. Once Mellen, the most senior fashion editor, came in to yell at her for writing "white ermine" instead of "yellow ermine." Seymour said, "I remember we turned to each other and somebody said, 'You know, so at least we just get yelled at.' We'd heard that across town at *Harper's Bazaar*, [one editor] grabbed the copywriters. We thought we were doing great. At least they weren't physically assaulting us."

Mirabella's management style was antithetical to Anna's. Run-throughs, the meetings where clothing was selected to be photographed, could last eight or ten hours, and Mirabella had a habit of starting them late in the day knowing they would drag on. Editors brought extra chairs into Mirabella's beige-and-white office, to settle in for these anguished caucuses.

The sessions began with the arrival of two models. Editors brought their favorite looks and made a case for them. The models changed into the clothes worthy of further discussion in Mirabella's en suite office bathroom, separated by a mirrored vestibule. "And then everyone would sort of say, 'Oh, we love it. We hate it.' It was a belabored conversation, actually," said Maggie Buckley. Mirabella wanted to analyze; she didn't just look at something and say yes or no. She wanted to know *why* a woman would want that, *why* an editor brought it in, what the *motivation* was to feature it in the magazine. One of her favorite comments was, "This needs more. I need more." What "more" meant was often anyone's guess. Mirabella's fashion editors didn't need to obsess over photos of the shows to decide what the day's ten best looks were—it was obvious to them which dresses in a given runway show would make the best pictures, that's why they were fashion editors—but Mirabella analyzed the looks to death. "Well, do you think that really serves any purpose, that jacket? Is it a new proportion? What is the meaning of it?" she'd press her team, leaning over the light box, sometimes until 2 or 3 in the morning if a show had ended at 10 p.m.

Even Anna, who would sit there with her legs crossed, couldn't hide how stunning she found this process. "The first time I could just see the look on her face of like, *God, is this ever going to end?*" said Buckley.

In this way, Liberman had a lot more in common with Anna than with his friend, Mirabella. He liked quick decisions, encouraged editors to trust their first instinct, and didn't dally over anything. All of this made him a useful foil to Mirabella for Anna.

Mirabella had started at *Vogue* as an assistant in 1952, following jobs at Macy's and Saks Fifth Avenue. She worked her way up to editor, and was appointed editor-in-chief in 1971. She was seen as the antidote to her predecessor Diana Vreeland's wild, artistic, and business-destroying genius.

In 1962, Vreeland had arrived at *Vogue* as an associate editor—lured from *Harper's Bazaar* by Newhouse and Liberman with a huge raise and limitless expense account. (They both always worried about *Vogue* losing readers to *Bazaar* and enjoyed upsetting their competition by poaching top talent.) After Vreeland became editor-in-chief in 1963, she would famously arrive each day at noon and work in a haze of incense and Rigaud candles. Her daily lunch of a peanut butter sandwich and half-melted bowl of vanilla ice cream ended with a nurse giving her a vitamin B_{12} shot. She remains known for the memos she dictated for her staff every morning before leaving bed, pronouncements like, "Today let's think pig white! Wouldn't it be wonderful to have stockings that were pig white! The color of baby pigs, not quite white and not quite pink!"

Vreeland was right for the sixties, the era during which fashion loosened up like the bell bottoms of a pair of pants, when Anna discovered her own love of miniskirts. Vreeland asked Mirabella to be her second-in-command when she became editor-in-chief, and Mirabella reluctantly agreed, eventually coming to see Vreeland's flightiness as methodical genius. At the beginning of the seventies, though, the magazine was suffering. Vreeland might have brilliantly captured the flower-child mood of the sixties, but now women baby boomers were demanding parity with men in the workplace, having careers for the first time in history. And they wanted practical clothes to wear to work, like the Yves Saint Laurent pantsuit that, when it debuted in 1966, revolutionized how women dressed. With the pages of Vreeland's *Vogue* devoid of office-appropriate fashion, circulation dipped to a low of 428,000. In the first three months of 1971, ad pages were down 38 percent. "Under the great Diana Vreeland, *Vogue*"—the crown jewel of the Condé Nast portfolio—"almost went out of business," observed Mark Clements, who conducted research for Newhouse, in an interview for Thomas Maier's 1994 book *Newhouse*.

The struggle of editing *Vogue* was balancing the interests of three primary stakeholders: those of readers, those of designers, and those of corporate management. Early in the seventies Newhouse began to conduct copious research on how audiences responded to covers and content within the magazines, and then make editorial decisions accordingly. It was an approach that treated magazines like toothpaste or sneakers or any other product. Vreeland had no interest in Newhouse's new methodology. Meanwhile, Liberman was getting increasingly fed up with Vreeland's fantastical attitude and began, despite their friendship, to distance himself from her.

Mirabella was in California on a shoot for *Vogue* with *M*A*S*H* actress Sally Kellerman when she was abruptly called back to New York by Condé Nast president Perry Ruston, who wanted to see her at nine the next morning. She canceled her dinner plans, caught a red-eye, and got to Ruston's office, where she was surprised to find him with

Liberman. Ruston said, "It's been decided we'd like you to be the next editor-in-chief of *Vogue*."

Mirabella's appointment drew an onslaught of criticism, she recalled in her memoir. Andy Warhol said it meant "*Vogue* wanted to go middle class." She was cast disparagingly as a "nine-to-five girl." Nonetheless, she did away with the leopard-skin rugs, slathered her adored beige over Vreeland's famously crimson office walls, and committed to remaking *Vogue* in the image of beautiful and functional American sportswear for the—yes—"nine-to-five" woman. She featured advertisers and edited according to research. Circulation rose to 1.2 million in the mid-eighties with a commensurate increase in ad business. And Liberman remained more involved with *Vogue* than with any other magazine in the company.

But though the *Vogue* business was strong by the eighties, Mirabella has admitted in retrospect that this had not been her moment. To her, the decade was nothing but gauche displays of affluence and bad taste—"more costumes than clothes." She was especially annoyed when women snapped up the embroidered, flamenco-inspired fashion of Christian Lacroix even when it cost $45,000 per piece. "[The] Lacroix moment was so totalizing and so widespread within the fashion industry that it was impossible to ignore. And the sensibility that created it, reflected it—the wealth worship, the elitism, the disdain for the real lives of working women—was so thick that in the mid-1980s it was virtually impossible to find anyone willing to create images on a page that suggested other values," she wrote in her memoir.

It was in this era that Liberman brought in Anna, who reported to him and not to Mirabella. Though Mirabella would later write that Anna was "foisted upon me," what staff observed in the office was respectful professionalism. They weren't friends, but it wasn't rivalry—outwardly, anyway.

"I don't think Grace got her. I never heard her making any disparaging comments," said Buckley. "It wasn't bad-feeling, it was just like parallel lines, in a funny way."

Mirabella saved the disparaging comments for her book, where she described Anna's tenure under her as "a very bizarre three years . . . during which Anna created a kind of office within the office, working with Alex [Liberman], with fashion editor Polly Mellen, with Jade Hobson, and *against* me."

W hen Anna joined *Vogue*, the magazine had two distinct fiefdoms: there was fashion (the pictures, run by Mirabella), and features (that is, the words, run by features editor Amy Gross), divided physically on the *Vogue* floor by the elevator bank. The features staff joked that the IQ level dropped several points when they traveled to the other (fashion) side of the office. Both departments produced excellent work. But the true sovereign at *Vogue* was Liberman, and he moved through it like a royal court, where his editors (usually women) vied for his attention. New favorites could materialize suddenly, and those falling out of favor were only sometimes sent signals of their devaluation.

Floating amidst the kingdom, not loyal to anyone but Liberman and Newhouse, was Anna. Liberman didn't involve himself with the selection of the clothes but entered the workflow when it came time to decide how to photograph them. Mirabella would call Liberman over to get his opinion on a shoot. Liberman, enamored with his new hire, would come in and then call in Anna to get *her* opinion.

To most on the staff, Anna's presence felt more curious than threatening. She suggested photographers, and brought in big names like Sheila Metzner and Paolo Roversi. She suggested that fashion shoots be done against backdrops of art, the way she had at *New York*. She occasionally popped into shoots to talk to the photographers and check on things. She looked at Polaroids or slides from her desk and called the studios to provide feedback like, "We got the first shots in. They're great, so keep doing them," or, "Do something a little less moody."

In the January 1984 issue, just the second in which she appeared on the masthead, Anna got a story into the magazine about new designers in London, styled by Vera Wang (who would go on to become one of America's most famous designers). It was an unusual story for Mirabella's *Vogue*, which focused on established American labels. That she let it sail through may have been Anna's "beginner's luck," said Schechter. "It was too early [for Mirabella] to be so adversarial."

"In terms of fashion photography, the girl running down the street has been exhausted. One of my concerns at *Vogue* is to bring in other aspects, to mix fashion with anything that's cultural. That's the direction I think things are going," Anna told *Adweek* in a March 1984 feature about "up-and-coming magazine people" who "promise to shake things up in the magazine establishment." Anna's next story did just that, displaying colorful clothes from the New York collections against similarly vibrant abstract paintings inspired by "Russian Constructivist theater sets . . . created especially for *Vogue* by Dennis Ashbaugh."

All of this was in line with Anna's determination to place fashion within the context of culture, in order to push fashion onto a higher plane of significance, the same way she sought to elevate herself. "Developing a creative eye or developing taste, I think that's something that you have within you from a very early age but it is also something that you can develop through exposure to culture, to the arts, through reading, visiting museums, looking at what's going on in the world around you," she said. "Creative exposure, cultural exposure, I think [it] is so important to spend as much time on that as you possibly can."

As Anna told *Adweek*, "I'm working on every aspect of the magazine from the choice of photographers to the overall design. There hasn't been someone who can stand back a bit and say, 'What can we do with this fashion sitting to make it different? Maybe there's a new photographer we should try. Maybe we can mix painting and illustration to add dimension to the pages.'" Still, despite her ambition, Anna felt that Mirabella, who excluded her from meetings, didn't want her there, and that the team didn't want her to succeed.

The fashion team, previously accustomed to dealing only with Mirabella and Liberman, now had to deal with Anna too. When photos came in from a shoot, announced with the photographer's last name

("The Meisels are in!"), the trio plus the fashion editor responsible would scurry to the art room and review them. Anna sometimes recommended a reshoot, which everyone hated, but which Liberman and Mirabella requested all the time anyway. But the real authority, staff felt, resided with Liberman and Mirabella.

This was not how Mirabella characterized things in her memoir. Of Anna, she wrote:

> She'd sit in on editorial board meetings, shaking her head, obviously disagreeing with everything I said or did, and biting her lip to keep from saying so. Then, she'd go behind my back and redo layouts, bringing new art, circumvent me and my fashion editors, and take charge of planning fashion sittings with photographers.
>
> When she couldn't bypass my editors, she'd harass and criticize them: demanding Polaroids, dropping into sittings, and ordering them redone from scratch. [Hobson] and [Mellen] eventually got so angry that they came to Alex and me and threatened they'd stop working if Anna stayed on the scene. "Keep that woman out of the studio; we can't stand her," they said, and they began, as much as they could, to shut her out of their work.

Jade Hobson, one of Mirabella's senior fashion editors, actually liked Anna's idea to use paintings as backdrops. "Some of them were kind of terrific, but she tried to get into the workings of the magazine that had been working really well, and change them," she said. "I tried to have as little to do with her as possible, because I didn't really want to shake the boat."

The fashion team's vocal resistance to her input prompted Liberman to tell Anna within her first months on the job that she would no longer work on those pages; she would now work on features alongside Amy Gross. Anna put on a good face around the office. "I feel she was probably really upset when she was told she couldn't work on the fashion," said Schechter. But it didn't really matter, because Liberman told Anna he would protect her and they would work through it. And he continued making his favoritism of Anna known, aggravating Mirabella. She wrote that Liberman would "often show up in my office and, with all the pride of a cat presenting a dead mouse to its owner, show me samples of art that Anna Wintour had brought in. 'Isn't this wonderful,' he'd say, breathlessly. 'Look at what Anna has done.'"

Mirabella, by that point in her tenure, had learned to tune out rumors about her possible successors, so she went along with Liberman when he gushed about his latest protégé. "I know how you feel about talent," Liberman would tell her. "*Harper's Bazaar* feels that way too. I'm quite sure they're about to make Anna an offer. Don't you think that we should keep her here?" And all Mirabella could think to reply was, "We can't survive without talent."

All the while, Anna took mental notes on what she would change once in command. At night, she took a dummy copy of the magazine home—later immortalized in *The Devil Wears Prada* as The Book—to review it with David Shaffer. Mostly they were concerned with the visual flow of the magazine. But Anna would read articles and make comments like "deadly" in the margins regarding copy she didn't like.

The process was yet one more example of the influence Shaffer had on Anna as an editor. He called the office multiple times every day to talk to her. Though she tried to hide her frustration at being shut out of the editorial process by Mirabella and her generals, she wasn't always successful. Once Schechter saw her in the office on the verge of tears, but Anna just said she had broken a tooth. Shaffer also continued keeping the florists busy with weekly flower deliveries. Unlike at *New York* magazine, Anna now had space to display the large arrangements of fragrant white Casablanca lilies on her mostly empty desk, which usually contained just a magazine, pencil holder, and telephone. The flowers arrived with the pollen, which badly stains anything it touches, removed from the stamens. Shaffer would pick up Anna from work in his navy Volvo station wagon, which friends called "the shrinkmobile." They sometimes gave Schechter a ride home, and she saw, from the comfortable leather backseat, how "loving and supportive and communicative" their relationship was.

Despite Anna's desire to innovate, there was no meaningful change to the look or feel of the magazine while she was creative director. But her impact went beyond the page. She had been following André Leon Talley, who had covered fashion for *Interview*, *WWD*, and *Ebony*, and who was friends with Karl Lagerfeld. Anna called him repeatedly to try to get him into *Vogue*. At first Talley didn't return her messages, but when Mirabella called him in for a meeting, per Anna's recommendation, he went. Talley wondered why Mirabella had called after not hiring him when he interviewed with her back in 1980. He had no idea Anna had recommended him.

But now Mirabella hired him right away as fashion news editor. Talley later speculated it was because she liked a video interview he had conducted with Lagerfeld in the backseat of a car going to a fashion show (Arthur Elgort showed it to her).* As he left *Vogue*, he passed Anna's office, and noticed her at her desk, two assistants sitting just outside.** Talley took the subway home to his apartment off Astor Place, and there, under his door, was a handwritten note from Anna that read, "Welcome to *Vogue*. I look forward to working with you."

Though he admired both Mirabella and Anna, Talley quickly joined Team AW, though he still didn't know Anna was a crucial force behind him getting hired. (Anna, who didn't talk about what she was doing behind the scenes, wouldn't have advertised that fact.) He had seen her out at parties and found her terribly intimidating—in fact, too scary to speak to. Now his job was to fill two pages of each issue with fashion news, and he would be relying on Anna to get it done.

---

* Mirabella had recommended Lagerfeld for his new job as creative director of Chanel, one of the fashion industry's most significant appointments in the last century, according to Talley.

** After Schechter became too busy, Anna hired Isabella Blow as her second assistant, but she was so disorganized she mostly just made things harder instead of easier.

For the December 1984 issue, she suggested he commission a portrait of Vreeland by Andy Warhol for an article on the exhibit Vreeland had curated at the Metropolitan Museum of Art's Costume Institute, where she worked after *Vogue* (in fact, Talley got his start in fashion working there under Vreeland). Warhol said yes, and Anna loved his idea to impose Vreeland's head onto Jacques-Louis David's painting *Napoleon Crossing the Alps*, but didn't trust him to finish on time, so she sent Talley to Warhol's Factory every day to take Polaroids of his progress. (It wasn't terribly efficient, but it wasn't as bad as another situation Talley heard about, where Mirabella and Mellen sent a skirt back to Calvin Klein seventeen times requesting modifications. As Talley later remarked, "How can you be enthusiastic about a skirt after seventeen send-backs?")

Talley believed Anna had "intuition" that they would be "fast friends"—emphasis on the "fast." When he started at *Vogue*, he and Anna went to lunch at BiCE Cucina. Anna ordered a starter of prosciutto and avocado, and before Talley could bite into his main course, she said, "Okay, we're done, let's go back to the office." He wrote in his memoir, "We never really spoke about our friendship or worked to develop some long-lasting bond. It was just perfectly understood between us, like a silent language." Maybe it was born out of an implied mutual understanding—they were the young, with-it editors who were perplexed by Mirabella's agonizing meetings and her disdain for the "underground influence" of Warhol. (To Talley and Anna, Warhol wasn't "the underground.") Mirabella "didn't quite get me," said Talley, who felt that Anna, however, did. Naturally, their shared taste would bring them together, but so too would their status as floaters in this dysfunctional hierarchy, a house of cards they would, in time, topple. For now, there was no way to know that their relationship would be long and complicated, both comforting and turbulent, important until it wasn't.

When Anna was in Paris to see the collections with the *Vogue* team, she met her father at the bar in the Ritz. They hadn't been seeing much of each other, but started arranging visits when she was in Paris for the shows. He noticed she was wearing a nice ring, and she told him it was for her engagement. Shaffer had given the ring to Anna earlier, and she'd told him, "I'll start wearing it when I'm ready to marry you." It was characteristic Anna—getting proposed to but still dictating terms.

Before the wedding, she got a call from her ex Michel Esteban. He would be in New York and asked her to grab lunch or a drink, and she said that she was getting married a couple of days later and invited him to come. So on Friday, September 7, 1984, he was among the ex-boyfriends, family, and just two *Vogue* colleagues, Schechter and Talley, whom Anna hosted at her renovated MacDougal Street townhouse for her wedding. Working with architect Alan Buchsbaum, Anna had decided to tear down walls, leaving the main two floors completely open, in the style of a loft. Shaffer's teenage sons lived on the bottom floor, while Anna's master suite, formerly four small rooms, occupied the entire top floor. The bed was made with a simple white down comforter. The suite's few accessories comprised family photos and Anna's small ivory objects collection, including a comb and a brush. The master bathroom had been expanded in the large English style Anna was used to and included not only a freestanding antique claw-foot bathtub but a fireplace.

The nineteenth-century furniture and décor were spare with an English flavor. "She's an edited person. So, same with her townhouse. True English, it would be overwrought with stuff everywhere. That's not her thing," said Schechter.

The wedding took place during the day and was, like her home (aside from the fact that it was a Manhattan townhouse), low-key and unfussy. Despite living her life in the spotlight, Anna has never cared to be the center of attention.

For the wedding, Anna wore a tea-length cream Chanel dress, and her dad walked her down the stairs to the ground floor where the event was held, daylight streaming in through the windows. Joan Juliet Buck, a friend from London, was her only attendant. She had gone to Bergdorf Goodman with Anna to help choose her wedding and honeymoon dresses—the latter also Chanel, ankle-length, in blue-and-white-striped silk—off the sale rack. Talley was stunned that he was one of only two people from *Vogue* invited, signifying something it wasn't in Anna's nature to verbalize: that she considered him close.

Anna changed into the second dress and came down the steps holding her bouquet, a mix of flowers including hyacinth, but instead of throwing it as the crowd at the bottom of the stairs expected, she thrust it at Talley. "Here, take care of this," she said.

About six months after the wedding, two major things happened while Anna was toiling away at *Vogue*. First, she found out she was pregnant.

Then, on Tuesday, April 23, 1985, Beatrix Miller, who had served as editor of British *Vogue* for twenty-one years, told her staff she was stepping down, having led the magazine to an era of "soaring" profits and a readership of nearly two million.

Anna Wintour was expected to replace her.

Chapter 10

A TALE OF TWO *VOGUE*S

"Oh my god, I'm back in England," Anna said to Liz Tilberis, the very same woman she used to bump into in her early twenties when, as a lowly *Harpers & Queen* editor, she had to slog through racks of Maidenform bras. Tilberis was now executive fashion editor at British *Vogue* and Anna's employee.

It was Anna's first day as editor-in-chief in the magazine's London offices in Hanover Square, appropriately named, as though a private club, Vogue House. Tilberis was showing her black-and-white photos of young women wearing head bandages, looking, Anna said, "as if they'd dropped in from Mars."

Her reaction was one indication among many that things were about to change—and fast. Anna had inherited a commercially successful magazine, but she thought the visuals were outdated, silly, and at times absurdly "British": models posing with horses at country castles, in full riding regalia—even if the riding regalia was made by Hermès, it had little to do with the modern woman. Anna wanted the magazine to appeal, just as Mirabella's *Vogue* did, to working women, to provide practical information about how to dress, not just showcase the whimsy of fashion editors who had been left to their own devices for nearly twenty years.

The experience of working for Anna at British *Vogue* is a tale of two cities. For the veteran staffers, like Tilberis, it was the winter of despair. ("She wanted saneness and sameness," Tilberis wrote in her memoir. "It was the end of life as we knew it.")

For the new ones, it was the spring of hope.

Anna had no choice but to act quickly and boldly if she wanted to turn the magazine around and get back to a bigger, better job in New York. But the unhappiness among those she pushed aside dictated a tabloid narrative that branded Anna as fashion's indomitable and bitchy new ice queen—a characterization that, for better or worse, would stick.

Editing British *Vogue* would put Anna on the other side of the velvet rope separating editors from editors-in-chief. It was an exclusive club you didn't leave unless you left the industry entirely. Still, though it offered her that coveted leap in status, Anna had a hard time accepting the job.

Bernard Leser, the managing director of Condé Nast's London office, had tried to lure Anna away from Liberman's inner sanctum shortly after Beatrix Miller announced her resignation, but she turned him down. She was early in her pregnancy but worried about being with a newborn so far from Shaffer, entrenched in his job at Columbia University.

On June 5, 1985, two months before Anna accepted the job, she had lunch at the Four Seasons with Tina Brown, a fellow Brit who was also relatively new at Condé Nast's New York headquarters as the buzzy editor-in-chief of *Vanity Fair*. As a new Condé Nast editor-in-chief herself, Brown (who had been the buzzy editor-in-chief of *Tatler* magazine in London when Condé Nast bought it in 1982) was perhaps one of the few people who could truly understand Anna's frustrations at the time. "She's clearly bored with being the second chair at *Vogue*, waiting for the sainted Grace Mirabella to go," Brown wrote in her diary. Anna confided in her that she did want to take the job in London, and that her husband supported it so long as it wasn't more than a couple of years.

Brown thought Anna would have difficulty replacing the beloved and legendary Miller, and would find Condé's London offices "very damp and debby after New York," but also saw that "her talents here are enabling Grace to keep her job, whereas in London she can show off her flair and prove executive chops."

The next month, Anna was in the press as a front-runner. Brown told Newhouse, who was struggling to find an editor to replace Miller, that he should give Anna the British *Vogue* job. True to form, Newhouse simply "looked thoughtful at that." Part of the problem, Brown learned, was that Liberman didn't want Anna to leave *Vogue*, claiming to think that she and Mirabella could work through their differences. But Mirabella, though still dismissing rumors that Anna was being warehoused for her job, was eager to fling what she saw as a disruptive hazard across the ocean.

Finally, after months of thought and speculation, Anna accepted, and on September 18, 1985, was announced as British *Vogue*'s new editor-in-chief. She arranged to defer her start date so that she could have her baby in New York in January, then start the job in London in April.

Before Anna left for London, she wanted to find an assistant. Both Tina Brown and Shaffer's friend Michael Roberts, former art and style director for *Tatler*, knew Gabé Doppelt, who was working at *Tatler* in London. At first Doppelt thought she was being asked to simply recommend people to Anna, which she did. But then a fax came through from Anna asking, "Well, what about you?"

Doppelt had never thought of working at British *Vogue* because the place seemed like a joke. It was known as a resting place for stuffy debutantes who had been there for thirty years as a hobby. Employees drove BMWs to work instead of slumming it on public transit. But Anna offered Doppelt the possibility of tripling her current salary, which made refusing impossible. A day after accepting, she got another fax from Anna. "We've never met. What are you doing tomorrow? We'll send you a ticket," she wrote. Doppelt, used to the sleepy speed of London magazines, where no one felt urgency about anything and certainly no one instantly dispatched transatlantic plane tickets, was stunned.

She flew to New York within days. When Doppelt got to the Condé Nast office, Anna wasn't there because she was having early labor contractions and had stayed home, so Doppelt spent the day training with the *Vogue* staff. That night she dropped by Anna's house. When she arrived, there was Anna at the door, more than eight months pregnant, in a tight white Azzedine Alaïa dress and high Manolo Blahnik heels. She was holding a glass of red wine.

Doppelt thought they would spend an hour or two going over Anna's needs and expectations. Instead, they talked for just a few minutes. When Doppelt got back to her hotel, there was a message from Condé Nast human resources saying Anna had decided to hire her and to plan to report to work in about six weeks.

Anna's appointment to British *Vogue* was instantly controversial.

Beatrix Miller was said to have run her magazine like the headmistress of a girls' boarding school. She loved a beautiful duchess or a princess in her pages, especially Princess Diana, especially against the backdrop of a castle. She had a country house in Wiltshire named Pig. She liked sensible heels and never tried to dress fashionably, but kept her long nails painted a glossy red, all the better for pointing out mistakes or sloppy writing in a page of text, which she cared much more about than the clothes, leaving the fashion team to mostly do whatever they wanted.

Anna, on the other hand, had left Britain for America eleven years ago, and was parachuting back with, one reporter noticed, "a slight twang in her accent" and the hard-charging manner stereotypically associated with indurate New Yorkers. "I want *Vogue* to be pacy, sharp, and sexy," Anna said. "I'm not interested in the super-rich or infinitely leisured. I want our readers to be energetic, executive women, with money of their own and a wide range of interests."

Two of Miller's deputies, Tilberis and Grace Coddington, had been given perfunctory interviews to be editor-in-chief. Tilberis didn't feel qualified, and Coddington, who liked being on shoots and didn't want to be the boss, told management in her interview to hire Anna because "I thought she would be amazing," said Coddington, who started her fashion career as a model a decade before Anna, and used to bump into her socially in London. Nonetheless, it appeared to the press as though a woman who had happily severed her British roots had elbowed aside two well-liked, respected, thoroughly British editors for the role.

Anna had tried to bring people over from New York to work with her, but it was frustratingly hard to get anyone to accept; she did convince Shaffer's friend Michael Roberts, who hated New York, to leave Tina Brown's *Vanity Fair* and join as a part-time design director. She offered Laurie Schechter a job but, within the month Anna gave her to decide, her former assistant found a spot at *Rolling Stone*. Anna asked *Vogue* fashion editor Robert Turner to go with her, but he didn't want to move. And she asked Talley, but he worried about both being far from his aging grandmother and logistics—British *Vogue* didn't have the budget to rent him an apartment—so he decided to stay at Condé Nast in New York and work for Brown at *Vanity Fair*. Anna did, however, manage to hire her old friend Emma Soames as features editor.

Despite bringing in so few of her own people initially, Anna proceeded to fire almost everyone at British *Vogue* who predated her, which didn't help her reputation. She also let go of freelance drama critic Milton Shulman and film critic Alexander Walker, who had worked for her father.

"Get rid of them," she told Soames.

Soames replied, "Anna, you've got to do that yourself." They didn't stick around much longer. This was additionally shocking given that the magazine had barely changed in decades. She did decide to keep Tilberis and Coddington for the simple reason that she admired them. "She was civilized and polite and reassuring about wanting us to stay on," Tilberis later wrote, but it was hard to feel at ease, maybe because Anna wasn't someone who worried about putting anyone else at ease.

Vivienne Lasky reached out to Anna after she moved, upon Nonie's urging, when she was visiting London with her family. Anna invited her for tea, but Lasky didn't get the impression Anna had any interest—

despite her professed feeling of isolation—in reconnecting with an old friend. The meeting was icy; Anna, who wore all-black, didn't offer Lasky anything to eat or drink until her mom showed up later and told her to. When Lasky looked at Anna that day, she didn't see her friend from childhood. That person, Lasky felt, was no longer there.

That meeting marked the end of their friendship. Anna had moved on.

On a Friday night in April, Beatrix Miller left her office for the last time. Over the weekend, the room was painted soft white, one wall was knocked down for a new entrance, and bookshelves were installed for storing back issues of the magazine. Up came the carpet, and down went polish on the bare wood floors. In came Anna's desk, designed by Alan Buchsbaum, the architect who had renovated her New York townhouse. It was "a long, lean affair with playful legs reminiscent of the fins of a 1950's Cadillac . . . made of sandblasted ebonized mahogany with an inset panel of black patinated steel," the New York Times reported in a profile of the desk in 2003 (at which time Anna had become so famous that individual pieces of her furniture warranted their own articles). The final touch was a large NO SMOKING sign.

Anna ran the magazine with unprecedented, iron-fisted discipline. She wanted the staff to be on time, work hard, and run everything by her for approval, a stark departure from Miller, who allowed photographers to come into the office and select their photos and approve their layouts. Emma Soames, who'd worked for Miller, had seen Antony Armstrong-Jones, Lord Snowdon—the photographer who'd married Princess Margaret—do just this. But then Anna came in and reduced a shoot of his to a photo the size of a postage stamp. Soames told Anna she couldn't do that because it was Snowdon. "And she just ignored me," she said. "So it was a radical, radical change."

Anna started her own workday shockingly early compared to the previous administration, leaving her house shortly after seven, having gotten up at five thirty to spend time with her infant son, Charlie, named for her father. (After eighteen years under Miller, Coddington was, by her own admission, becoming "lazy." With Anna there, Coddington felt much greater pressure to work in Anna's hyperefficient style. Still, Coddington was habitually late.) But Anna also got her staff raises—something nearly impossible under Miller.

Overall the pay was low with few perks. Tilberis was covering shows in New York when Anna called her from London to say she was getting a "significant" raise. It turned out to be all of £4,000, taking her from £23,000 to £27,000 (about $115,000 in 2021).

"I don't know what to say," Tilberis said.

"You could say thank you," Anna replied.

W anting to be especially involved in fashion coverage, Anna started having weekly planning meetings. ("I think just the sheer fact that they had to wheel clothes into her office before any shoots was wildly different and unheard of," said Doppelt.) Anna would sit there in her sunglasses, tapping her pencil on the desk if she didn't like an idea. Reflecting in her memoir, Coddington noted she had a hard time adjusting to Anna's work style, cribbed from Mirabella's *Vogue*. "We had to go through so many hours of run-throughs, it was awful," she wrote. "[I]t simply isn't possible to simulate the mood one hopes to achieve in a beautiful photograph taken on location by putting the same clothes on the wrong girl in a grimly lit office. Besides, no decent-looking model ever wanted to come in and try on the clothes just so we could see how they looked, because how far was that going to advance her career?"

Anna reviewed every photo from every shoot herself, which also stunned the staff. As soon as the film came in, Anna would go into a room with a projector and examine all of the shots one by one. It was in there, with the door closed, that she would put on her thick, round eyeglasses, only to suddenly move them off her face if certain staff members unexpectedly walked into the room.

She also demanded "endless reshooting," Tilberis said. For her very first cover, Anna wanted to feature the English actress Amanda Pays in a bright-orange coat with wide, architectural lapels and the exaggerated shoulders of the period, designed by Jean Muir. "I can't tell you how many cover tries of that coat we shot and reshot until we arrived at the ultra-simple image on a stark white background that she wanted," wrote Coddington.

Having said just a couple of years earlier that she was tired of fashion photos of girls running down the street, that's exactly what Anna now asked for—"motion, models in the streets, looking as if they were off to work," Tilberis recalled. It was an image of womanhood cast very much in the mold of Anna, always moving, never slowing down, thoroughly devoted to her career and her own appearance.

Anna later admitted that this approach was directly inspired by Grace Mirabella, though she also picked it up at *Savvy* and *New York*. "There was certainly an eccentric side to London I thought was great," she said, "but women also wanted reality. Maybe I put too much stress on it at the time, but I was new and I wanted to put my stamp on it."

Not everyone could handle Anna's new way of working, and their radiated discontent was difficult to be around all the time, especially for Anna's new hires. Doppelt found it all so exhausting that, when Anna went to lunch, she sometimes went up to the top floor to lie down on the cold stone floor to rest.

"I was really wiped out from the sort of pressure of the job and the tension, and the animosity toward Anna that kind of leaked off onto me," Doppelt said. "It must have been a thousand times worse for Anna."

Even though she hadn't managed to hire André Leon Talley, Anna consulted with him when he was in London. "I could stop by Anna's offices," he later recalled, "and she would tell people to let me use their desks. . . . She would show me layouts and we would review designs, as though we still worked together." She also wanted to know what he thought of certain fashion shows. The conversations were always brief because "we almost spoke the same language," said Talley, who once visited her at home, where he found her breastfeeding baby Charlie. That he worked for another magazine was irrelevant.

The staff was confused by and possibly jealous of Anna's attachment to Talley. He seemed the antithesis to her—as Tilberis wrote, a "Southerner who tends to dress in riotous excess—striped stretch pants and red snakeskin backpacks, patent leather pumps with grosgrain bows, faux-fur muffs." Coddington wrote that she also found it strange: "For a time it almost seemed he was running the whole show because Anna kept deferring to him, telling us things like, 'André thinks we should be doing a story on so-and-so' or 'André feels such-and-such is really important.'" Talley was oblivious to his effect on the atmosphere.

As hard as it was for Anna to recruit those in New York, her growing reputation as a visionary was an incentive for others to join. Sarajane Hoare was working as fashion director at the *Observer* newspaper when Anna asked her to come in for an interview.

"I want you to start next week," Anna told her.

"Oh, I can't. I've got to give the *Observer* three months' notice," Hoare said.

Anna pushed her to start sooner, Hoare suspected, because she needed to turn the magazine around as quickly as possible.

She suggested Hoare speak with Grace Coddington, assuming that Coddington would convince her it was worth it. Because she actually had plans to make a job change herself, Coddington, Hoare recalled, was less than encouraging. But working for Anna was just too enticing. Hoare took the job.

Even before she got to London, Anna had a reputation for being icy and scary and fabulous. Part of it was the sunglasses. Part of it was probably being descended from Chilly Charlie. There was also her last name, which seemed to have been formulated simply to drape a pun around it.

Of course, dismissing goings-on at the magazine as silly ladies' stuff and casting Anna as "Nuclear Wintour" and her tenure as "Wintour of Our Discontent" was largely sexist, and the scrutiny of her merciless methods far outstripped that bestowed on male executives. So were some of the other accusations, such as the rumor (later called a "fabrication" by her brother Patrick) that she was induced in order to give birth on a timeline that would allow her to attend the couture shows. Her father's old paper described "her habit of crashing through editorships as though they were brick walls, leaving behind a ragged hole and a whiff of Chanel." *Private Eye* reported details of her contract: a salary equivalent to nearly $330,000 in 2021 and perks including a full-time nanny, a car and driver, and two round-trip airfares on the Concorde each month to visit Shaffer. *Private Eye* also delighted in items about staff quitting and the news that, because of her indecision, Anna had turned in the September issue of *Vogue* (traditionally the biggest and most lucrative issue of the year) late.

Though she never revealed to her staff how she felt about the nastiness, the *Private Eye* item about her "late" September issue was a breaking point. Anna sued, forcing them to print an apology and pay her legal fees. She weathered the negative press, as she would over the course of decades, unflinchingly, but those she's close with outside of work said it does bother her.

Emma Soames was stunned by these stories. "People misinterpret her focus for coldness. But she's not cold, she's generous to a fault," she said. "If it did not involve editing *Vogue*, she didn't address it. So she had no small talk."

But quickly Anna's British *Vogue* was successful, its circulation rising to 170,000, up from Miller's 164,000, with annual profits of more than $6 million. More important, she developed relationships with British designers, who were eager for the connection, Coddington said, because she represented American *Vogue*, and everyone in London looked to American *Vogue*. "She always saw English fashion as very long skirts, droopy, flat shoes and things. And she felt this was the time when everybody should be much more sexy," said Coddington.

Part of that was shorter skirts. She'd ask designers to take six inches off a hemline, and, just as designers did for American *Vogue*, they would do it. "She was always there for them. I think she inspired them. She advised them. And I think their businesses probably did very well because of it," said Coddington. Part of the disconnect between Anna's vision and the city around her was that London was hardly the same launchpad for career-hungry women that New York was. During her first features meeting, Anna suggested a piece about women judges in England, only to be told there weren't any.

Still, while Tilberis claimed that Anna demanding shorter skirts "infuriated" designers, she acknowledged that "soon everyone from fashion editors to corporate vice-presidents owned a padded-shouldered red-jacketed power suit with a short skirt, and we were all running to catch taxis in our black opaque tights and high-heeled pumps."

Not every insider was on board. Photographer Bruce Weber, whom Anna's predecessor had hired and nurtured, refused to shoot for her, declaring, "I don't really believe that a photographer should be told what kind of film he should use. And also, I think a woman deserves more than to think that she should be photographed running across the street hailing a taxicab." Jewelry designer Tom Binns made a pin attacking Anna's vision that read "Vague Vogue Vomit."

Anna didn't seem to care. "Any reaction is better than none," she told the *New York Times*. "A new editor is going to change a magazine. People resist change. British fashion was a little insular. One had to open it up."

Coddington only stayed at British *Vogue* nine more months. Her departure was prompted not by discontent, but by a financially attractive offer from Calvin Klein in New York, where her boyfriend, hair stylist Didier Malige, lived, and the timing seemed right to move.

Coddington, whom Anna later called "very much the queen of fashion in London," had been central at the magazine and her exit was a huge loss. Tilberis, who was also struggling under Anna, cried when she learned of the departure, but pulled herself together and asked Anna for the fashion director job. Though she was next in line for it, Anna put her off at first.

"You have to stop complaining," Anna told her at lunch. "I'm tired of hearing about the good old, bad old days. You know how to do what I want—the question is, will you? If you want to stay, then back me up."

Tilberis realized that Anna had a point—she wouldn't want a number two who wasn't fully supporting her either. She also wasn't interested in squandering her career over her own stubbornness. Tilberis moved into the role, did what Anna wanted, and, in time, felt that her boss started trusting her.

* * *

About a year into the job, Anna was seriously unhappy, though she kept this from her staff. She now had a one-year-old child and was pregnant with her second, wearing the same Yves Saint Laurent suits and high heels she always did, hiding her stomach with beautiful long scarves that flopped between the lapels of her jackets. Living away from her husband was hard. She didn't have a big social circle in London, and would go every Saturday morning to visit her favorite shoe designer, Manolo Blahnik, at his shop with Charlie, who knocked over all the displays. (This wasn't the only quality time she had with her son; she told an interviewer in 1986, "Sundays I spend the whole day with him.") Anna was also the one flying to New York with her son as often as she could since Shaffer usually couldn't leave work to come to her. "The logistics are terrible," she said at the beginning of her tenure at British *Vogue*. "I wake up at night in a cold sweat. Endlessly, parts of one think: 'I'm crazy. I should stay home, look after my baby, have a nice quiet life.' But I didn't think I wanted to have a kid in New York. I've worked so hard for 15 years here [in New York]—and British *Vogue* was always the magazine I wanted to edit." That last claim was not entirely true, of course; Anna knew that London publishing was the minor leagues, and it's hard to imagine that she didn't worry about being so removed from New York, the apex of media. This may have been one reason she worked so hard to remain connected to Liberman and Newhouse. But Liberman also seemed to be making an effort to keep tabs on her as both his mentee and the future fashion leader of Condé Nast. When Anna struggled designing the magazine, she flew to New York and worked with Liberman on fixing it. When Coddington was in New York for shoots, Anna had her deliver the film to Liberman so he could give his input.

By April 1987, Anna was vigorously denying speculation that she wouldn't return to British *Vogue* after the birth of her second child in July. In May, the *New York Times* reported she was a contender for both

Mirabella's job editing *Vogue* and Tony Mazzola's job editing *Harper's Bazaar* (the very same Mazzola who, more than ten years earlier, had fired her). In the same story, Liberman denied the rumors, but slyly offered, "It is possible Anna Wintour will come to the United States within a certain period of time." She was also rumored to be in talks to run *Elle* as well as with the makeup brand Clinique.

Though Anna later described receiving offers, she said she never seriously considered them. But she did fully intend to move back to New York after having her baby, and it's possible she planted rumors of her relocation in the press to make Newhouse consider the risk of losing her to a rival—in turn, prompting him to take drastic measures to make her happy.

This is exactly what happened: afraid of losing her, Newhouse got on a plane to London to meet with Anna, then so pregnant she said she was "practically on the delivery table." But while she was hoping for American *Vogue*, over breakfast he offered her something else entirely: the editorship of *House & Garden*.

Anna was stunned. Not knowing what to say to Newhouse, she went to her office and called Liberman right away.

"Absolutely, you have to come," he told her. Newhouse claimed he needed Anna at *House & Garden* because the magazine was "having problems." It wasn't exactly what she wanted, but it was her ticket out of London, so she accepted.

Newhouse denied he was giving Anna the job as a practice run for *Vogue*—"You don't park somebody," he said. "That's the worst kind of publishing management—and no way to treat a lady." In fact, that was exactly what he was doing.

Chapter 11

HOUSE & GARMENT

O nce again, Anna needed to assemble a team to work on the other side of the ocean, and childbirth wasn't going to slow her down. On the way to the hospital to give birth to her daughter, she called Doppelt and asked her if she wanted to go to New York in two weeks.

"What's this about?" Doppelt asked.

"I'm going to take over *House & Garden*. We'll talk about it after I've had the baby."

After Anna gave birth to Katherine (who would go by Bee), Doppelt went to visit her at home. Doppelt had just spent six months renovating a new apartment and couldn't imagine leaving her London life behind to move to New York, but once again, Anna made it impossible to say no.

"We'll take care of you," she told Doppelt. Condé Nast, she said, would put her up in a hotel and help her find an apartment.

Anna had left work at the end of the week to have her daughter, and by the middle of the next was back in the office. She wore a slinky, slim-cut striped dress and high heels, shocking her staff, who couldn't believe this was the very same woman who'd given birth less than a week ago and didn't show it at all. In fact, her physicality in that moment was more surprising than what Anna then told them.

"I have an announcement to make," she said. "I'm leaving, and your new boss will be Mark Boxer," the editor of *Tatler* who had encouraged Doppelt to work for Anna.

Before Anna departed, she wanted to take care of Liz Tilberis. Tilberis had just resigned to take a job at Ralph Lauren, which was offering her the staggering salary of $250,000. (Anna had received her resignation by saying, "That's ridiculous. Don't you realize you won't be able to change one shirt button at Ralph Lauren?") Two days later, once Anna knew she was on her way out, she called Tilberis into her office and closed the door. It was in her interest to set British *Vogue* up for success after she left—she didn't want the changes she'd made to appear to have failed.

"I'm leaving," she said. "Do you want to be the editor?" Tilberis said yes right away. The caveat was she had to work with the title of editor under the new editor-in-chief, Boxer—who tragically died suddenly of a brain tumor shortly after Anna left, leaving Tilberis in charge on her own.

A week after she told the staff she was leaving for *House & Garden*, Anna was gone. A couple of weeks after that, her appointment was announced in the press, along with rampant speculation that she was now just waiting for Mirabella's job.

The *House & Garden* transition began with one of those classic Condé Nast stories that showed just how cruel and capricious Newhouse firings could be.

Louis Oliver Gropp, whom Anna was succeeding, had been editing the magazine, founded in 1901, for six years (previously, he had spent thirteen years editing the newsstand offshoot *House & Garden Guides*, which Newhouse closed when Gropp took over *House & Garden*). His *House & Garden* attracted a loyal readership who loved the how-to approach. Gropp had no idea he was out of a job until after news of Anna's appointment appeared in the August 12, 1987, edition of *WWD*. He was on vacation in California when it came out, and Newhouse didn't reach him by phone until a few days later, their exchange reported in the book *Citizen Newhouse*:

"Lou, have you been reading *WWD* while you've been on vacation?" he asked.

"No," said Gropp, who didn't even read it when he was in the office.

"There have been a lot of stories in *WWD* that Anna Wintour is going to become the editor of *House & Garden*," said Newhouse.

"Well, is that true?" replied Gropp.

"Yes," Newhouse said.*

Gropp stayed on until September 9, 1987. Before he left, however, Anna began putting together her team, planning to do exactly what she had done at British *Vogue* eighteen months earlier—clean house, wipe out the existing editorial vision, and start from scratch.

Though she hadn't officially started yet on September 1, she called *Vanity Fair*'s Tina Brown, beginning with some pleasantries, asking Brown how her husband, Harry Evans, was, as well as their baby. That out of the way, she said, "Just one thing, I'm taking André." And she did, making him her creative director.

Talley recalled that he made no mistake about what Anna—and he—were doing at a home décor magazine: "She didn't tell me how or why she made the move, but she didn't have to. I wasn't stupid; it was clear where all this was going. It was a well-known secret that Anna was working her way up to Grace Mirabella's job," he admitted.

The "problems" Newhouse was having with *House & Garden* seemed, to some of Gropp's staff, more of an excuse to give Anna an editor-in-chief job than anything else. But Newhouse's professed fears may

---

* Gropp later told *Newhouse* author Thomas Maier he felt Newhouse was tortured by the awkwardness of having to deliver the bad news. Perhaps that's why his firings were so terribly orchestrated.

not have been entirely without merit. Since the 1970s, the magazine had been second to *Architectural Digest*, which was considered the most upscale home magazine. Condé Nast had spent $8 million on market research, advertising promotion, and other prepublication expenses in 1983, just a few years before Anna's appointment, to make the magazine tonier in an attempt to usurp *AD* as the number-one ritzy home title. Other competing home magazines, like *Metropolitan Home* and *House Beautiful*, tried to do the same thing. Yet in 1987, *House & Garden*'s ad pages grew less than 1 percent and ad revenue was up just $1.5 million, compared to *Metropolitan Home*'s 18.1 percent ad page growth, with corresponding ad revenues up 46 percent.

Though most criticism of Anna has been based on her terse personality and intimidating decisiveness, those very qualities were what enabled her success at this point. To change what she was put in charge of, she had to go about the unpleasant business of firing people, killing work, and not apologizing for any of it. This was her way of signifying her standards for the magazine—and signifying to Newhouse that she was moving faster than his mind could change about her. She knew she would have to be unyielding despite relentless disapproval.

As expected, Anna worked hard to make over *House & Garden* in her image. Her company town car deposited her at the office at seven thirty each morning, and whenever she had time during the day, she would clear old, unpublished portfolios out of the art department filing cabinets. She, Doppelt, and Talley went through drawer after drawer, reviewing images that looked creepily devoid of any human touch, such as dining tables perfectly set but with no indication that anyone would be eating at them. In about three days Anna reportedly threw out $2 million worth of contracted articles and photos. Spending this time with Anna, Doppelt started seeing her in a new way. "She's incredibly funny, very dry British sense of humor, really self-deprecating. And that was the person I discovered, and it is shocking to me that I'd missed all of that in England. But maybe I didn't see it because she was under so much pressure," she said.

Anna also began sorting through the existing staff with what others felt was the same frigidity she applied to the photos she killed. Apprehensive employees hurriedly bought short skirts, designer clothes, and high heels, fearing if they didn't cast themselves in Anna's image they'd be cast right out the door. Elaine Greene Weisburg, an editor who had worked at the magazine for twenty-two years when Anna started, invested in a better wardrobe out of fear, but after her first meeting with Anna, she felt there was nothing she would be able to do to win her over. A week after Anna's official start date, Weisburg was fired.

"You made up your mind the minute you saw me. You don't know that age is inside the head, not outside on the skin," Weisburg told Anna on her way out.

Anna said she was sorry Weisburg was taking it this way.

They ended up shouting at one another as Anna rushed to open the door to show her out. Weisburg's final words to her were: "I hope you fall on your face."

The new *House & Garden* tended to feature celebrities like Bette Midler and Steve Martin and socialites like Baron Eric de Rothschild and Gloria von Thurn und Taxis (whose daughter Elisabeth became a *Vogue* contributor in 2012). Fashion, previously absent from the magazine, became a prominent element: for Anna's first cover she had Talley style a model wearing a $2,300 floral dress by Karl Lagerfeld, photographed by Arthur Elgort in the Bagatelle Gardens of Paris. To further telegraph to the world that this was a new era, Anna changed the name to simply *HG*. Condé Nast said the new title was meant to distinguish the magazine from the twenty-five or so other home titles containing the words *house* or *home* or *garden*. Liberman and Newhouse supported the change of direction, not just of title but of content. Liberman, who looked at every layout and every photo in the art department every single day, said, "I personally questioned the introduction of fashion, but she was so innovative and daring about it, and Si loved what she was doing. We were both stimulated and excited by the idea of a total magazine of style."

One February night in 1988, Condé Nast threw a black-tie coming-out party for the new *HG* at the New York Public Library. Attendees included fashion designer luminaries like Bill Blass and Calvin Klein, and, most welcome, Anna's father. Once arrived, Anna seemed over-whelmed by the event, but part of it was probably sheer exhaustion. She was always thin, but now looked especially so—her sparkly jacket could only deflect so much—and Shaffer confided to Rochelle Udell, Liberman's assistant, that he was worried about how hard Anna had been working. (In later years, Anna would go on "the diet of cream," said friend Miranda Brooks, which involved drinking chocolate milkshakes, so she wouldn't get too thin.)

Inspired by Parisian gardens, Anna had hired Robert Isabell, a bril-liantly creative and wildly expensive party planner. She said, "You know you have a successful party when the guests never have to wonder where they're supposed to be or what they're supposed to be doing next." So scattered throughout the space were Anna's beautiful new staff, meant to usher guests down the stairs to the dinner area and, like the models in her made-over magazine, serve as ornamentation. It was, said Nancy Novogrod, the editor from Clarkson Potter who had been recruited by Anna to be her deputy at *HG*, what Liberman expected; when Novo-grod later hired someone he didn't find attractive, he scolded her for it.

Newhouse gave a speech praising his fabulous new editor, speak-ing in what guest Tina Brown described in her diary as "a slow, halting interior monologue." Anna then stood up and, Brown said, "threw bou-quets at everyone who might be dangerous," including *HG* contributor Graydon Carter, then editing the satirical *Spy* magazine, and her former boss from *New York*, Ed Kosner.

The thinly veiled truth was that Anna was much more interested in fashion than in home interiors. She featured so much fashion and so many fashion people in the magazine (Diana Vreeland, Manolo Blahnik) that people started calling it *House & Garment* and *Vanity Chair*. But while New York media people were merely sneering and snickering, readers were offended. A special 800 number had to be set up for complaints and subscription cancellations. A Condé Nast execu-tive told the *New York Times*, "we cheerfully refund their money." The publisher of *Architectural Digest* boasted that Anna's March relaunch drove ten to twenty advertisers to run in *AD* exclusively.

But some people thought Anna's *HG* was simply ahead of its time. "She really would do things that people had never done before, and that alienated some people," said Michael Boodro, who became features editor. Boodro interviewed the decorator Albert Hadley in his Connecticut cottage, and the photos included an image of his basement laundry room with a box of detergent on the washing machine. "People were horrified at that," recalled Boodro. Every day working under Anna, he woke up and thought, *Today's the day she's going to fire me*. Anna didn't offer higher praise than simple approval, and when she didn't like something it had to be scrapped and redone. Still, he said, "I recall it being one of the most fun jobs I ever had."

In later years décor magazines became, like Anna's *HG*, a voyeuristic look at the private spaces of the rich and famous, rather than instruction booklets for arranging living room furniture. The difficulty she faced may have been that *House & Garden* wasn't, like other titles Condé Nast had turned around, such as *Vanity Fair*, a magazine in hospice. Its readers liked it as it was, and the changes Anna made were too drastic for them to accept. The good news for Anna was that by the time criticism of her *HG* was peaking, the moment she had been waiting for had come: Newhouse decided to give her Mirabella's job.

Chapter 12

ANNA WINTOUR,
EDITOR-IN-CHIEF

One June morning, Anna went to visit Nancy Novogrod.
"I'm going to *Vogue* and I'm starting today," she said. Novogrod was in shock. She had only been at *HG* a few months; she'd known Anna wouldn't stay long, but had no idea it would happen this quickly. Anna told Novogrod that Newhouse and Liberman were pretty convinced Novogrod should succeed her, but that she should go make her case. One of their biggest concerns was the loss of advertising under Anna.

What then unfolded was one of the ugliest episodes in Condé Nast history, a stormy collision of Anna's crusade for power, Liberman's deviousness, and Newhouse's deep aversion to confrontation.

Grace Mirabella was sitting in her office on June 28, 1988, when her secretary patched through a call from her husband, Bill Cahan.

He had just watched gossip columnist Liz Smith deliver this report on WNBC:

Ever since Anna Wintour, the editor of British *Vogue*, was brought to New York by Condé Nast to take over the remake of

their *House & Garden* there have been rumors that Miss Wintour would become the editor of American *Vogue*, replacing the
veteran Grace Mirabella. Well, now the hot publishing story is
that this probably will happen on September 1. Don't ask me
why Condé Nast would want to replace Grace Mirabella. *Vogue*
is one of the healthiest, heftiest magazines in the Condé Nast
chain. You know, if it ain't broke, don't fix it, but they're going
to anyway.

"Grace, this is ludicrous," he said. "What's it all about?"

Mirabella didn't know. She told her husband she'd call him back
when she knew more. After thinking for a moment, she went upstairs
to Liberman's office, where she found him just sitting there idle at his
big black desk, apparently waiting, most likely for her.

"Grace," he said. "I'm afraid it's true."

The story commonly told about why Mirabella lost her job to Anna
that summer of 1988 is that Newhouse and Liberman were worried
about the threat posed by the American edition of *Elle* magazine. By
1988, *Elle* had surpassed *Vogue*'s old rival, *Harper's Bazaar*, in both
circulation and ad revenue: *Harper's Bazaar* had a 1987 circulation of
700,000, while *Elle* had leaped to 850,000 after debuting in September
1985, and unsurprisingly ad dollars were flowing to the publication with
more readers. *Vogue*'s circulation, meanwhile, dipped in 1987 and the
first half of 1988, though it still reached 1.2 million people.

But the downfall of Mirabella and the ascension of Anna was about
more than *Elle* and the numbers. Mirabella's weaknesses had become
prominent in recent years. Early in the spring of 1987, Liberman was
out of the office for an extended period with prostate cancer and heart
problems. He kept the seriousness of his illness from his colleagues,
instead telling them that he had acute pneumonia. However, without
his usual involvement, *Vogue* became rudderless. Staff filtered through
the human resources department, exhausted by Mirabella's indecisive-
ness, complaining that the magazine had no direction. Phyllis Posnick,

who became beauty and health editor in 1987, remembered the chaos: "I didn't see how much longer Grace could stay there. It was like Kafka. You just did not know what was going on." And that was not likely to change, as Liberman, who was seventy-five years old in the summer of 1988, was simply unable to give *Vogue* the attention he had before—from attending fashion and beauty meetings to managing staffing to overseeing art direction and article assignments. When Liberman reviewed layouts with Mirabella in the art department, where the pages of the issue were put up on a board, Mirabella often didn't know the names of famous people and artists featured in her own magazine. Linda Rice worked as Liberman's deputy then and was sometimes the only other person in the room with them. "I was always shocked at what Grace didn't know," she recalled. "And I like Grace, but she was not the woman for the job."

Mirabella had another problem that Anna did not: a nearly nonexistent relationship with Si Newhouse. From their first meeting in the sixties, when she was introduced to him at the 21 Club not long after his father had bought Condé Nast, and onward, she never grew any more comfortable with him and intentionally avoided him, despite Liberman telling her this was a bad idea. And if Mirabella wasn't in his ear as the singular voice and authority on *Vogue*, who would be? There was really just one woman who could deal with the pressures of running *Vogue*—working with Newhouse, keeping Liberman involved but not depending on him, cutting Liberman's bloated staff, updating the magazine to compete with *Elle*, and not doubting herself along the way. That woman was Anna Wintour.

So when Newhouse decided to go ahead that summer and give her the job—something Liberman wanted to delay—it was in fact a full month before the news leaked to Liz Smith in late June 1988. Yet Newhouse couldn't bear to fire Mirabella any more than he could bear to fire anybody. And Liberman, because of his long-standing friendship with Mirabella, especially didn't want to tell her and be the face of the decision (that, he claimed, was all Si). What's more, when Mirabella did ask him about rumors that Anna would replace her, he'd said, "Don't worry darling, there's nothing to these."

But Liberman wasn't as incapable of firing people as he claimed, and this was hardly the first time he had done so to a close friend; as Mirabella knew well, he'd done it to Vreeland. Leo Lerman, who edited *Vanity Fair*, was one of Liberman's closest friends when Lerman was fired in the early eighties to make way for Tina Brown. (Noted Brown, "There did not seem to be a trace of sentiment in the way Alex turned on Leo, it struck me as deeply scary that he had no conscience about it.") He went along with Newhouse's push to remove Mirabella, and that was that.

After the news of Mirabella's firing broke, the *Vogue* floor was in shock. Office doors that were usually open were now shut and the lowly staff who sat outside them pressed their ears against doors to find out what was going on. Though many had assumed Anna would eventually get Mirabella's job, it was still hard to believe it was actually happening.

That Mirabella could be let go so quickly and so cruelly, after thirty-seven years working at *Vogue*, was both stunning and heartbreaking. "It was like regicide," said Lesley Jane Seymour, the copywriter.

The news was earth-shattering even beyond the halls of *Vogue*. Jade Hobson, a senior fashion editor, got a call from a designer asking if it was really true. When she went to Mirabella to find out what was going on, Mirabella was just on the phone finding out the news from her husband.

Newhouse asked Mirabella to make an announcement to her staff after they met the next day. She called her editors into her office, took a deep breath, and told them that Anna Wintour would, in fact, be the new editor-in-chief of *Vogue*. Later that day, Newhouse issued two memos, the first announcing Mirabella's "retirement" and the second announcing that Anna would replace her "effective immediately."

All of this was an effort to move things along: while Newhouse and Liberman had made their decision more than a month before, they'd held back the announcement because they couldn't decide when. After Anna learned she was getting the job, she'd sat in "endless meetings with Si and Alex," she said, "at which we mostly talked about dates and timing because Alex was so undecided. Sometimes it was going to be September, and sometimes the following January. The whole thing was unfair to Grace, who had not been told, and unfair to me, because I had to come back from the meetings and try to do a magazine that I knew I wasn't going to be at for very long, and lie to all my people. It was awful, really awful."

A number of Mirabella's generals decided not to stay. Amy Gross, who ran the features department for five years, including while Anna was creative director, went briefly to *HG* before leaving the company. Hobson, who hadn't wanted anything to do with Anna when she was creative director, took a job at Revlon. With such brush cleared, Anna moved to build her own world-class fashion team. Polly Mellen stayed on, along with a fashion editor Liberman had previously brought over from *Elle*, Carlyne Cerf de Dudzeele. (The latter had been so frustrated working for Mirabella that she almost quit, but Anna had convinced her to stay on and wait for her to become editor-in-chief.)

Perhaps most important, Grace Coddington, who had left Anna at British *Vogue* for a job at Calvin Klein, called Doppelt when she saw the news and said, "Do you think Anna would ever consider having me back?"

Anna and Coddington had been seeing each other regularly since Anna's return. Living in New York had helped Coddington understand why Anna worked the way she did. Plus, she really missed magazines.

Anna called her back. "Come meet with me and let's talk about it," she told Coddington.

It was Thursday. Coddington met her for dinner, and at the end of it, Anna said, "I formally start on Monday, why don't you start with me?" Coddington, moving at Anna speed, had a day to give her notice and leave her job. (She and Calvin Klein remained friends.)

Anna brought in other favorites: Michael Boodro became features editor, Gabé Doppelt associate editor, and Laurie Schechter style editor. André Leon Talley became creative director, making him, he said, "the highest-ranking Black man in the history of fashion journalism."

While Mirabella finished out her last two weeks, Anna called the *Vogue* staff to her *HG* office one by one, where she briefly interviewed them to decide if she would keep them on.

Waiting for the meeting with Anna was, for many of Mirabella's people, horrible. Anna wanted to know what everyone was doing in their jobs, and see if they had the connections or talent or work ethic or some combination thereof to be able to work for her—all in a few minutes. After these meetings over the course of three days, Anna reduced the staff from around 120 to fewer than 90.

Phyllis Posnick was among those who got good news; she would end up being one of Anna's longest-serving editors. Anna combined two copy roles and gave a thrilled Seymour a promotion. She kept Maggie Buckley as bookings editor. And she kept Linda Rice, Liberman's deputy who was running finance and operations for *Vogue*, as associate business manager. She told Rice, "Your job is to control André Leon Talley."

Rice almost fell on the floor. Yes, Talley's expenses had grown completely out of control, and reining him in didn't seem like it would be easy. But it was Anna asking. She said yes.

Chapter 13

CALCULATED RISK

A nna's first day as editor-in-chief of *Vogue*, on Monday, August 1, 1988, began with a nasty gossip item by Liz Smith in the *New York Daily News*:

WINTOUR CHILL pervades the Condé Nast offices. From high to low, people are afraid to speak on the phone. All wait for the other shoe to drop. There is gossip over coffee and people holding bated breath for Wintour's next action. Many expect a reign of terror. . . . So—people are talking about Wintour and Newhouse and the exactitude of their relationship. The rumors are wild.

Smith also wrote that Anna had merely "fail[ed] upwards" to *Vogue*, a desperate attempt by Newhouse to stem *HG*'s bleeding of audience and ad dollars.

To squash the speculation about an affair, Newhouse told Smith the rumors of him being romantically linked to Anna "are probably the most flattering thing ever said about me. But I am very much in love with my wife and my wife's dog. There is absolutely no truth to the whole thing."

By this point in Anna's career, she had long been the subject of gossip. She hardly ever denied what was printed. But that morning, when she got to work, she assembled her staff and told them that anyone who believed she had gotten to where she was by sleeping with her boss "is still living in the era when a woman could only make it to the top by pleasing a man. This is the 1980s. You don't have to do that anymore."

The affair rumors tarnished what should have been a celebratory summer for Anna. Colleagues around the office could tell when the gossip was getting to her because, steely as she was, she occasionally looked quite distressed. Anna later admitted that the Smith allegation had put a terrible strain on her marriage. Still, each time it seemed she might crack, Anna would just put her sunglasses back on and move forward.

Anna told her staff she wanted the new *Vogue* to be younger, more accessible, and more energetic. But she also made clear that the changes would be more of an evolution than a revolution. Still, Doppelt remembered that putting together the first issue "felt very much like doing an issue of British *Vogue* on acid."

For starters, *Vogue*'s covers badly needed updating. Richard Avedon had been shooting them since 1965, when Liberman enticed him away from *Harper's Bazaar* with an unprecedented $1 million contract. But Avedon's covers hardly varied from one month to the next: tightly cropped studio head shots of perfectly made-up models were mostly distinguishable by the color of the girl's hair and whatever eighties statement earrings she wore.

Rather than fire Avedon immediately, Anna made him audition, though she didn't state it so bluntly. She wanted to try a cover with models photographed out on the street, and asked Avedon to do just that, which created immediate tension. Begrudgingly, he followed instructions, only to be asked to reshoot twice—a great indignity to a photographer who had only ever been asked by one other editor over the course of his career to reshoot anything. Insulted, he severed ties with *Vogue*, and got Condé Nast to buy out the remaining two years on his contract for a reported $480,000.

Anna's legendary first cover, for the November 1988 issue, starred the Israeli model Michaela Bercu, photographed by Peter Lindbergh and styled by Carlyne Cerf de Dudzeele. The eighties were the ideal era for Cerf de Dudzeele, a flashy French fashion icon in her own right who summed up her styling approach as, "I love to make shit look like gold, capisce?"

The shoot, which would become one of the most famous fashion magazine covers of all time, was first assigned as just an inside story. Cerf de Dudzeele (who loved mixing designer pieces with basics, like a Chanel jacket with a Hanes T-shirt) dressed Bercu in a $10,000 couture black silk Christian Lacroix jacket bejeweled with a colorful cross—and paired it with $50 Guess jeans. "The jacket was actually part of a suit, but the skirt didn't fit Michaela; she had been on vacation back home in Israel and had gained a little weight," Anna later wrote about the cover. Bercu walks down a street in Paris, her long blond waves cascading over her shoulders, looking off in the distance with a big grin, a slice of her lower stomach exposed. It was the first time jeans appeared on the cover of *Vogue*.

"The powers that be were a little bit surprised, the printers even questioned this picture, but it made a statement. It made a statement that it was a different time—we had a different view on fashion that we wanted to be much more accessible, much more free," Anna explained. It was unprecedented—and with it, everything *Vogue* had been doing was suddenly blown up.

Newhouse sent her a note, which she proudly displayed on her desk: "You knocked it out of the park, Anna. I'm so proud."

Vogue staff hadn't been afraid of Anna when she was creative director, but as editor-in-chief, she was scary. To some extent, it was grandfathered into the role: Mirabella, and Vreeland before her, had the same effect. And of course, during Anna's first year, she let go of so many people that it was hard for employees to feel safe. Some days, it felt like every hour someone was being shown the door. Mirabella had a bathroom in her office; while Anna was having it renovated, she walked down the hall every day to use the staff bathroom, often wearing her sunglasses, usually not responding to young staff who greeted her along the way.

But her manner didn't bother Gail Pincus, a senior market editor: "This was not my first job. And so for many people, if it was their first job, they could get very insulted that she could be so clipped." Anna got things done much faster than her predecessors—though sometimes she moved too fast. Anna would ask Pincus and other market editors to meet her at designer showrooms in the morning. Only she would get there at 8 for a 9 a.m. appointment and be gone before anyone else on her team showed up.

In one of her earliest features meetings, Anna gathered staff and contributors into her office, where everyone sat in the shape of a V pointing toward her desk, three chairs in the first row and five in the second. Only two people brought ideas, William Norwich and Graydon Carter, both of whom she had given contracts to be contributing editors at *Vogue*. The rest of the staff seemed too paralyzed to pitch anything. Another editor described something similar when attending their first features meeting during Anna's early years. "This is our new editor. Why don't you start?" she said. The person then went through twenty ideas. When they were done, Anna said, "Anyone else?" And no one else spoke. People went to her privately, rather than dragging out meetings by speaking.

In run-throughs, where editors showed Anna clothes for her to approve for shoots, she had a habit of looking down, flicking her bangs, and saying, "No, no, no," usually with no explanation. Once she did just this regarding a pink floral minidress with a flared skirt that one editor thought would be fabulous for a May cover. Shortly thereafter Anna was in the office wearing the very same dress with, as expected, no explanation.

Anna did ask questions. "You can have a hundred answers, and Anna would ask you the hundred and first thing you didn't have the answer to," said Maggie Buckley, the editor who became responsible for booking celebrities. "When I was really new at the celebrity thing, she said, 'Oh, what did well at the box office this weekend?' And I didn't have a clue. So you can bet that next time I knew what was happening at the box office."

Anna always believed there was a way to get what she wanted, and pushed her team until she got it. With celebrities, she often tasked Buckley with finding out if, say, Madonna would do a one-page beauty story. "It was like, 'Can you do this? Can you do that? Yes. No. I want an answer,'" said Buckley. If Anna didn't get what she wanted, her approach was to keep calling until she got the answer she sought. Dealing with Hollywood was particularly annoying because in her mind the industry was so inefficient. "Why do those agents have their assistant call your assistant to call you back when the agent is free to call you back? Why can't they just pick up the phone?" she said.

"She would want you to keep calling, and I just didn't do it. Because I'm not going to make everyone crazy," said Buckley. Once Buckley told her, "I've actually been avoiding your office, because I know you're going to ask me this." And Anna just laughed.

Now that she had her hands on the very thing she'd wanted since she was a young girl, Anna's work ethic went into overdrive. While editing her first six issues, she stayed until eleven or twelve at night with Liberman and Seymour, the copywriter. They met in the art department every night to review layouts and make edits. "I would follow along and take notes of what she and Alex agreed to. Change this, fix that, change that. Don't use this word. Better headline here," said Seymour. "It was brutal."

It was clear when Anna liked or disliked something. She also had a way, Seymour thought, of picking out the things that made fashion exciting. Whereas Seymour struggled to write about things Mirabella loved that didn't resonate with her as a twentysomething, Anna would pick out things that were just cool, including up-and-coming designers. "It wasn't the same old five Armani and Geoffrey Beene people again and again and again," said Seymour.

Said Coddington, "She really brought a breath of fresh air into the magazine world. Anything was possible at American *Vogue*. They did have huge budgets to play with and she could have any photographer she wanted. And everybody wanted to be a part of it."

Unlike Mirabella, who liked being in her office, Anna also spent a lot of time with designers. "Designers that she felt most close to, she would express what she wanted them to add or to do," said Gail Pincus. But she also needed to ingratiate herself with those she did not know because *Vogue* needed their advertising dollars. She had strong relationships with European designers, but the same wasn't true for the giants of American fashion, like Oscar de la Renta and Ralph Lauren, all of whom wanted to know her as well.

"It was a mutual business interest, but they didn't have the flair of the European designers that she was so friendly with for all those years," said Pincus. "So it took a little bit to get her to understand simple, less-detailed clothes"—in other words, American sportswear. She didn't appreciate Ralph Lauren, for instance, until her team got her to visit him in the Hamptons.

Everything about Anna was fast, including her office rounds. She walked so fast that Seymour regularly slammed into her when she was coming around the corner because, being a Brit, she used the other lane. The infamous hours-long run-throughs were now over in minutes. Seymour said, "Anna would just go, 'Yes, no, yes, no, yes, no. Good-bye.' I remember thinking, 'Well, she comes from a newspaper family. And newspapers in England, remember, no matter how much time you spent on them, next day they were wrapping fish.'"

In fact, the office did start to feel more like a newsroom, albeit one with plentiful floral arrangements. Anna had replaced the beige walls, butter-colored director's chairs, and soft seats with white walls, glass offices, and hard metal seats—not that anyone was in those seats for long. Under Mirabella, every request had to be written down, but Anna complained of "drowning in paper," so she wanted editors to just come into her office, stand, ask their question, and then get out. It was almost as if the seats were for show. With Anna, people say, "You get two minutes, the second is a courtesy." Being late meant you would not only likely receive a look of death but also probably miss a lot of the meeting.

Anna always had her office door open, but the new glass walls were a huge adjustment for editors who were used to shutting their doors and having privacy. Now she could look up from her desk, catch someone's eye, and think to ask them to do something. Seymour felt the only reason Anna asked for her so much was because her office happened to be in her sight line.

She also wanted to bring great writing into *Vogue*, and hired many of her friends to contribute. "She's not a writer per se, but she knows good writing," said Boodro. "She loved humor in writing. Some people say she has no sense of humor. I know that is not true. She laughs and everything."

But not everyone was privy to her sense of humor. When staffers stood before Anna, they received The Look—Anna's way of quickly yet obviously (and daily) assessing someone's outfit. "She would do that automatically. You would walk into her office, and she would start at your shoes and work the way up," said Maggie Buckley, who, this in mind, started living in Manolo Blahnik heels, Anna's favorite.

Whereas magazine editors decades later would conscientiously devote themselves to "personal brands" to flaunt on social media, Anna tacitly demanded it. Under Mirabella, editors came to the office wearing comfortable clothing. Those clothes were out as soon as Anna was in. With the new boss came high heels and even higher expectations.

People interviewing for jobs at *Vogue* didn't get very far if they didn't look good, and Anna screened every single person before hiring them. During one search for a writer, a human resources manager was having a horrible time finding somebody. The fashion people who desperately wanted the job couldn't write, but the people who could write looked down on *Vogue*. When they found the perfect person, who was about twenty-five pounds overweight, human resources knew not to send her to Anna without a warning; otherwise Anna would see her, almost instantly make up her mind, and end the interview. So Anna was asked to give the woman at least two and a half minutes. Anna did, and the person was hired.

In another instance, Seymour, in need of help, got a great copy test in from a candidate who'd worked in both women's magazines and the beauty industry. Seymour was nervous to send her to meet Anna because, for Anna's taste, she overdressed with a matching pearl necklace and earrings. *She's going to like her copy, but not her look*, Seymour thought, but didn't feel she could tell the woman not to wear her pearls. After the meeting, Seymour said, "So, Anna, what did you think?"

Anna looked at her and said, "Too matchy-matchy."

Seymour said, "I knew you were going to say that." She would have to find someone else.

David Shaffer had always advised Anna about work, and running *Vogue* was no different.

Once, spotting the San Francisco–based health magazine *Hippocrates* at the airport, he told Anna she should hire someone from there. Peggy Northrop, a senior editor at *Hippocrates*, got a call to come to New York and meet with Anna for a role at *Vogue*.

After their meeting, Northrop went back to San Francisco, and they sent her a job offer. Northrop was unsure if she wanted to move to the East Coast. She deliberated with her husband, making lists of pros and cons, before deciding against the job.

"I'm not seeing anything in the magazine that I really am loving," she told Anna.

"Well, neither am I. Come and help me fix it," said Anna, who didn't naturally attract a lot of forthright opinions and probably appreciated Northrop's honesty. She offered Northrop $20,000 more, doubling her salary, and she accepted. Anna then sent Northrop a "totally stunning" flower arrangement that was "the kind of spray that would go on top of a coffin," along with a note that said, "I'm thrilled." Northrop just thought, *Oh my god, this is the new life I'm leading*.

Northrop arrived in New York with a wardrobe that included bowling shirts, a vintage tuxedo jacket, and a single knee-length black skirt. She did not own one pair of high heels. Her first day at *Vogue*, the fashion editors all came in wearing fitted hip-length jackets and leggings. Her third week, sittings editor Phyllis Posnick* invited Northrop to lunch at 44 at the nearby Royalton Hotel, run by Anna's former roommate Brian McNally and so commonly frequented by Condé editors that it was referred to as the Condé Nast Canteen. (Anna, too, ate there often because McNally got her out in under an hour and as soon as she threw her coat on the lime-green banquette, a waiter bestowed an espresso upon her.) They both ordered tuna niçoise, which only Northrop ate.

"Do you have a place to get your hair cut?" asked Posnick. "Would you like to go to a showroom and pick out some clothes?" Northrop thought this was a nice gesture, that they were beginning a friendship. Following up, she went to Oribe, one of the city's upscale salons, and got her permed, purplish hair dyed brown and cut short. She allowed the stylist to wax the back of her neck to even out her hairline. She had her single black skirt shortened to the "regulation nineteen inches." Posnick then took her to the Donna Karan showroom, where she tried on a gathered-front jacket, a skirt, and a chocolate-brown pantsuit. Posnick said she "wished the suit had more interesting buttons, perhaps of horn," but Northrop bought it all wholesale for $1,723.

Northrop understood the rationale for all this. "It's like, if you're going to be out in public as a *Vogue* editor, you should be looking like a *Vogue* editor. . . . I could not go all the way because I didn't have the money to spend. But I was certainly willing to take a stab at it," she said.

At the office, Anna was pleased. "How do you like your new haircut?" she asked. "I'm glad to see we got you into a short skirt."

Northrop and Posnick never had lunch again.

In Anna's first year as *Vogue* editor-in-chief, she made a decision that was as remarkable then as it would be unremarkable a dozen years later: she put Madonna on the cover—all because of a random encounter.

On a flight during that period, the man next to Anna asked her what she did. When she told him, he said, "That's the most incredible publication, it's so chic, it's so elegant, it represents everything I think of

---

*   Posnick said she did not remember this exchange.

as being very classic and beautiful. It's Katharine Hepburn, it's Audrey Hepburn, it's Grace Kelly—it would *never* be Madonna." So Anna took it as a challenge.

Madonna was, in early 1989, more controversial than she'd ever been. Her single "Like a Prayer," which had come out that March, concerned the spiritual ecstasy of sex, and its music video featured burning crosses and romantic love with a Black saint. A month after its release, Pepsi canceled its Madonna commercial because of objections from religious groups.

Anna seemed to dislike Los Angeles, and herself had little interest in celebrities. But, like Liberman, she liked defying expectations.

Any doubt she had about putting Madonna on the cover vanished after talking it over with Tina Brown, who had revived *Vanity Fair* with a splashy mix of stories about celebrities, politicians, and society people. "She said, 'You should do it,' and she was absolutely right," Anna said.

Maggie Buckley booked Madonna for a shoot in Los Angeles with Patrick Demarchelier (a second photographer, Oberto Gili, was hired just to photograph Madonna's house). Celebrities at that time weren't clamoring—as they later would—for Anna's approval and the *Vogue* cover that affirmed it. ("I'm sure [Madonna] thought she was honoring us as well," said Buckley.) Talley went to Madonna's house with a suitcase full of clothes to style her, all approved by Anna, who'd received Polaroids of the dresses from Paris. "You didn't show up to a shoot with clothes that Anna had not seen, that was never done," said Talley, who dressed Madonna in Patrick Kelly.

As it ended up, the cover was a minimalist image of Madonna in her pool—Anna didn't want anything "bombastic," Talley said—hair wet and combed back from her face, with red lipstick but no jewelry, in a simple white bathing suit. The photograph took the image of Madonna—big hair, fishnets, corsets—and turned it on its head.

"The fact that that very nice man that I sat next to on the plane thought that it would be completely wrong to put Madonna on the cover and completely out of keeping with the tradition of *Vogue* being this very classically correct publication pushed me to break the rules and had people talking about us in a way that was culturally relevant, important, and controversial, all of which you need to do from time to time," Anna said.

Her instinct paid off. When the Madonna issue came out, it sold 200,000 more copies than the previous May issue edited by Mirabella. It foreshadowed a sea change in fashion, which soon would replace models with celebrities as the faces of the industry.

A year later, Anna doubted her instinct about another controversial May cover idea. She said to Boodro, "Michael, do you think it's too tacky to put Ivana Trump on the cover?" Boodro encouraged her to do it—but it was, of his decade working for Anna at *Vogue*, one of the most scandalous stories they published. However, Anna was a savvy marketer, and while this wasn't something she would do every month, the issue's newsstand sales of nearly 750,000 and media attention seemed to easily justify the choice.

Killing the cover with Cindy Crawford in a bathing suit seemed like the beginning of the end of the supermodel era, to Laurie Jones. Having hired Anna at *New York* magazine over a decade earlier, Jones found the dynamic reversed when she started in November 1992 at *Vogue* as Anna's managing editor. Anna had lured her away from *New York*, fulfilling Jones's prediction that she would one day be working for Anna. It was the same year that *Vogue* ran an iconic cover featuring ten supermodels in white tied-up shirts and white jeans, climbing and leaning against white ladders. Grace Coddington had styled that shoot for *Vogue*'s hundredth anniversary issue after Anna had the idea to use a group of supermodels on the cover and, working with photographer Patrick Demarchelier, arrived at the idea to re-create an iconic 1950s Irving Penn photo. "They were such a part of *Vogue*, so there was no one girl that you wanted to single out and put on the cover," said Coddington.

But now in 1993, a few months after Jones had started, she was looking with Anna at a shoot that had come in of Crawford wearing a bathing suit. Anna put a bathing suit on the May cover every year from 1995 to 2001, but now she looked at the photos of Crawford, one of her favorite models, and said, "We just can't run it." (The May 1993 cover instead ran a photo of Princess Diana on a tour of Nepal, from a photo agency.)

Supermodels had been significant in popular culture. But interest in them was being replaced by a celebrity tabloid–fueled fascination with actresses like Winona Ryder. Anna held occasional off-site meetings with her team to discuss what was working or not in the magazine. Jones recalled that model covers were among things discussed as needing to be phased out. Having the same rotation of models on the cover didn't allow for rich features, month to month, but actresses could be both profiled pegged to a film and photographed beautifully.

Los Angeles–averse Anna reluctantly came around to celebrity covers because culture seemed to demand it. "She realized that she couldn't stay behind," said Coddington.

Newsstand sales indicated the audience liked it. And Anna's success as an editor was telegraphed through numbers. Though editorial excellence was always an important and intangible success metric for her at *Vogue*, she also knew that she had to make the magazine popular with advertisers and keep her bosses happy. If she didn't sell magazines and her magazines didn't sell ads, she could lose her job. After her first year, *Vogue*'s revenue was up 16.7 percent. But job security for any editor-in-chief was usually fleeting. And as she had seen, Newhouse and Liberman could drop anyone on a whim.

Chapter 14

"IN" VERSUS "OUT"

The power of *Vogue*, and the power of Anna as the editor of *Vogue*, was to decide who and what was in or out. But this only connoted power and influence if being "in" truly meant something. So being "in" could never be easy, and Anna, with her exacting taste and obsession with details, made sure it wasn't. Just like her father, Anna viewed her social life as part of her work. While working in London early in her career she had been a regular at parties for Harrods and Selfridges and Fortnum & Mason and all the other labels that mattered, either to curry favor because they advertised in *Harpers & Queen* or because the magazine needed to borrow their clothes. When she took over *Vogue*, she made hosting duties as much a part of her work as reviewing magazine layouts.

Anna's parties were a way to bring the world that existed in the pages of the magazine to life, and a party's currency was its people. The people had to both impress one another and feel special in one another's presence. No matter what or who the party was for, Anna controlled the guest list. She'd invite thirty-five people over to her house for dinner, a mix of designers and *Vogue* staff and anyone else she found interesting.

Gabé Doppelt helped plan these events using the same methods that would apply to organizing the Met Gala many years later, by supervising seating as if the wrong pairing posed a national security risk. "We'd sit there with Post-its, putting uptown together with downtown, and it was just the most bizarre thing but we did it, and it worked," said Doppelt.

"She likes conversation. People say, 'Oh, she breaks up couples at dinners and everything,'" said friend Lisa Love. "It's an old-school mixing of cultures and stories that is more amusing than being next to the same person." At one party, Anna sat Susanne Bartsch, a party promoter known as "Mother Teresa in a glittering G-string," next to Henry Kissinger.

By focusing so much on the social side, Anna was asserting herself as more than a magazine editor. By virtue of editing *Vogue*, she was necessarily a leader in the fashion industry, but she also seemed intent on using her position to become the leader *of* the fashion industry. To get there, she had to impart a very clear idea of what *Vogue* meant to the world and what *Vogue*, as a brand beyond a magazine, could become.

A few months into Peggy Northrop's new job as health editor of *Vogue* in 1990, Anna called her into her office. "Peggy, I want to do something called Seventh on Sale, where we are going to have a big sample sale getting all the designers together. And I want you to figure out where to give the proceeds. We're going to raise a million dollars," she said. (The name referred to New York's fashion hub, Seventh Avenue.)

Northrop initially felt overwhelmed by the directive. She had just arrived in New York and didn't know the city very well or that many people in it. But one of the things she liked about Anna as a manager was that she gave her an order and just wanted her to figure it out.

Anna and Northrop decided to donate the proceeds to the New York City AIDS Fund. The fashion industry, which employed many gay men, had faced criticism for years for its lack of response to the AIDS epidemic, which took a horrific human toll on those who made it run. Anna had been devastated by the loss of friends like her *New York* colleague Henry Post.

Anna got Newhouse to underwrite the costs of the event at the end of November 1990, where 148 designers donated merchandise to sell at discount prices in booths set up in the 69th Regiment Armory on Twenty-Sixth Street and Lexington Avenue. *Vogue*'s partners were Donna Karan and the Council of Fashion Designers of America, along with its president, designer Carolyne Roehm.

As she did in the pages of *Vogue*, Anna brought together fashion's establishment and up-and-comers, Ralph Lauren and Oscar de la Renta plus Marc Jacobs and Anna Sui. Michael Kors donated gray flannel suits made from extra fabric. De la Renta sold spring samples. Gianni Versace printed $2,500 T-shirts, one of which Anna wore to the Emanuel Ungaro show in Paris prior to the event. Betsey Johnson contributed one of her favorite recipes, for pickled Polish potato salad, to a cookbook created just for Seventh on Sale (it also featured meatloaf by Bill Blass). And *Vogue* offered what *Vogue* uniquely could: makeovers and portraits by top photographers.

Robert Isabell, who had been behind Anna's *HG* event at the New York Public Library, trucked in dozens of white birch trees from New Jersey and created booths in the cavernous space with 12,000 yards of white voile. Like Anna, Isabell's primary concern was aesthetics. When Karan saw his work, she said, "I hope this is fireproof," and held a lighter to one of the curtains. "Of course," said Doppelt, "nothing was fireproof."

On opening night, Anna hosted a $1,000-a-plate dinner in the armory and a "champagne shopping preview." Chanel designer Karl Lagerfeld flew in from Paris for the evening just to attend the party and, as a sign of his devotion, wore a pin on his lapel with a photo of Anna. Jean Paul Gaultier also flew in because "it was very important to come to this." They all did it for the cause—the fashion industry wanted to fight AIDS—but they also did it for Anna.

Anna attended the party looking glamorous as ever in a silver sequined minidress from Marc Jacobs's spring 1991 Perry Ellis collection and sunglasses. She had spent so much time working on the event that, she joked, "There may be no February issue of *Vogue*."

But Anna was also terribly nervous. Everything needed to be perfect because AIDS was a controversial cause. And while the Karl Lagerfelds of the world were enthusiastic, *Vogue*'s other highly valuable mass market advertisers didn't necessarily approve of the magazine taking a stance, in a homophobic world, supporting the fight against a disease then identified with gay men.

The event grew so much from Anna's original ambitions that she decided to increase the fund-raising goal from $1 million to $3 million. Seventh on Sale ended up raising more than $4.7 million, all of which went to the New York City AIDS Fund. There was no ostensible business purpose to Seventh on Sale. No sponsorships were sold, no magazine coverage was sold to an advertiser. Anna's staff thought that she viewed giving back as part of what she and *Vogue* should do. But in an article about magazines raising money for charity, the *Wall Street Journal* suggested otherwise: "On the charity ball circuit, there's a new catchword: 'cause marketing.' In a difficult advertising environment, with many traditional forms of promotion exhausted, publishers are adopting causes ranging from AIDS to homelessness and breast cancer as their favorite charities." If *Vogue* wasn't sending a message to readers by waving the *Vogue* banner over fashion's first big and long-awaited AIDS fundraiser, it certainly sent a message to the industry that *Vogue*—and Anna—cared more and did the most.

But while Anna had proven she could pull in money for a cause, could she do the same for *Vogue*?

Anna had brought unquestionable buzz and intrigue to *Vogue*, and, if you could see through the gossip that clouded every mention of her name, reams of praise. In February of 1990, *Adweek* named her editor of the year, declaring that at *Vogue*, "she's certainly thrown open the windows and let in the fresh air."

But in 1990, the country was in a recession, and over the first seven months of the year *Vogue*'s ad pages decreased 10 percent compared with the previous year, while its number-one competitor, *Elle*, rose slightly. Thus, the idea of her stumbling was both a legitimate news story and catnip to the press. *Elle*'s publisher, Anne Sutherland Fuchs, jumped at the chance to criticize a rival, telling the *Wall Street Journal* that *Vogue* had "gone more mass" after putting Madonna on the cover along with the headline "Dress for Less" ("less" meaning under $500).

Newhouse decided to do what he loved to do: hire the competition before they became more of a threat. On December 4, 1990, Fuchs was named publisher of *Vogue*. She had a lot of work to do—but so did Anna.

Anna was able to set the standards for *Vogue* that she did in part because Newhouse gave her so much money to do so. Similar to when she was at British *Vogue*, Anna had a clothing allowance, a car and driver, and an expense account that seemed to cover everything she might need for work and then some. Since iconic hair wasn't going to do itself, she even started getting her hair professionally done every morning at home before work. But though she and *Vogue* cost a lot, Anna was perceived within the company as being good with money. When she was told to keep her staff's salaries at a certain level, she did it (though she paid salaries that were around 30 percent higher than at other Condé titles). When she had a budget, she stuck to it. Still, shoots could cost six figures, and Anna didn't feel that she had to publish the results just because they were expensive. She still killed entire shoots to drive home the understanding that editors and photographers who wanted to have their work in the magazine had to do an extraordinary job and surprise her each time (without, of course, surprising her too much). She knew killing shoots would anger photographers, hurt editors' feelings, and cause celebrities to balk. She knew reshooting would be difficult and stressful. But this was exactly how Anna built up *Vogue*: by insisting on getting what she judged as excellent, and making sure no one who worked for her ever got lazy. She expected as much from her team as she expected from herself.

As the editor-in-chief, deciding on the cover subject and cover image were the most difficult decisions she faced each month. The cover subject "has to connect with readers," she wrote in her editor's note.

"She can't come across as snooty or aloof or sad or dour. She must be simultaneously chic, accessible, natural, friendly, and warm." And while cover shoots were killed the most seldom, they were still discarded if they didn't meet her standards.

As a perfectionist, Anna had many checks in place to ensure that photographs came out the way she wanted them to. But ultimately, the only way for that to happen was for her to be the one looking at the pictures, not leaving final judgment calls up to anyone else. Anna was never on the set, but for cover shoots, she'd check in with twenty other people who were. She also reviewed photos somewhat in real time. If a cover shoot was in New York, a Polaroid of the subject would be rushed to her via taxi. If it was somewhere else, a Polaroid would be photocopied, sealed in a pouch, and overnighted to her in New York so she could provide feedback before the second day of shooting.

While editors came to know what she liked (gardens, happiness, smiles, sunlight! —which is why a lot of cover shoots happened in Los Angeles), anything could be tossed in the trash. After actress Uma Thurman divorced Gary Oldman in 1992, a *Vogue* writer spent more than three hours interviewing her, and their conversation was reportedly epic. But, after the first shoot wasn't up to Anna's standards and neither was a reshoot, Anna killed the whole story. The writer wondered how anyone could take a bad picture of Uma Thurman, but it didn't matter—Anna's decision was final, so there was no point even transcribing the tape.

Anna decided to put Gwyneth Paltrow on the August 1996 cover at twenty-three years old, when she was the star of the movie *Emma* and Brad Pitt's girlfriend. "Even for Gwyneth, the road to the cover of *Vogue* has been bumpy," Anna wrote in her editor's letter that ran in the front of each issue, explaining that she had been photographed for the magazine four times in the last three years. "At the time of Gwyneth's first *Vogue* photo session—with a promising young photographer—the regrettable 'trailer trash' look was at its peak, and the pictures made her look like someone in the late stages of drug addiction. The second time around, a distinguished photographer decided to try out his fish-eye lens, which made poor Gwyneth look like she had a very rare disease. Our third time, the weather refused to cooperate, and at the last minute we had to move into the studio. Alas, Gwyneth came out looking like, as she said, 'a girl in an old Ivory-soap commercial.'"

Each time Anna killed one of Paltrow's shoots, Buckley, who booked them, had to call Paltrow's publicist and "be shouted at." Anna "knew it was difficult and awkward," Buckley said. Paltrow kept doing the shoots because she was early in her career and needed the publicity—and the validation of a *Vogue* cover and, by extension, Anna's approval.

Anna's judgments of women in the nineties were exacting in a way she wasn't with men. She was fine with putting the Coen brothers or Steve Buscemi inside, but thought Susan Sarandon in her midforties was too old for the magazine. In the April 1993 issue, she featured a scruffy group of young, mostly male film directors in casual clothing, looking nothing like supermodels, because she liked that *Vogue* could crown them as the up-and-coming directors who mattered.

While Anna valued good writing and wanted *Vogue* to publish the best journalism, the text people felt that her primary concern was visuals; writers and text editors who were royalty at other magazines and went to work at *Vogue* had to accept that they were now second-class citizens. Knowing she was more of a visual editor than a text editor, she sought outside help. Though this complicated things for her editorial team, who now had to worry about appealing to Anna plus her out-of-office whisperers, they respected her process. Staff printed out drafts for Anna to read, and she scrawled feedback in her difficult-to-read handwriting, often in the form of a single word, like "dreadful" or "wonderful" or even just "no." Sometimes she made more specific comments, like that she wanted to hear more about a certain person mentioned in a story. Boodro said Anna killed articles, all of which she read several times, less often than photo shoots. "If she didn't like the article, she didn't care if it was [written by] a friend of hers," he explained. Anna simply said, "Not every idea works," and that was that. "It's not about, *Why didn't this work? Whose fault is it?* It was saying, 'It didn't work. Let's move on.'"

At home, she would show articles to Shaffer. Laurie Jones said, "He read things, and there were times that she would come back with a manuscript and there were words that were not in her vocabulary that she used to discuss the article. And then if you wanted to question it, she shut you down."

Said André Leon Talley, "We all knew that Dr. Shaffer was the shadow editor of *Vogue*. The book went home with her every night. So of course she's going to discuss that with her husband, who's a psychiatrist. And of course she's going to take his assessment of the personalities in the magazine, because he's a psychiatrist. I suffered from anxiety and depression—I did not know it then, I know it now. And he probably had given her coping skills to cope with me and many other fantastic, talented, gifted, mercurial, neurotic editors."

The final mark of approval on stories, her initials plus OK— "AWOK"—became a verb in the office. "Is it AWOK'd? Is it AWOK'd yet?" editors would parrot in frustration. Once Anna decided she was over something—a dress, a trend, a story—that was it.

However, sometimes she changed her mind about smaller matters. In the eighties, billboards advertising *Forbes* magazine with the slogan "Capitalist Tool" were all around New York City. For a profile of the designer Arnold Scaasi, Boodro wanted to call it "Capitalist Tulle." Anna initially rejected it, but Boodro, crestfallen, pitched the headline to her again, and Anna accepted it. He recalled, "If you were passionate about something, she respected that. The thing that she couldn't stand was if you didn't give a crap."

Again and again, Anna showed that more than anyone else she knew what trends were coming (or going), and which designers were up-and-coming. But in other ways, her obsession with fashion itself limited her field of vision, and her best intentions could lead to problematic outcomes.

In one features meeting in early 1994, Anna shared an idea inspired by what she had been seeing on the runways. "I want to do something about Asians. They're everywhere," she said. *Vogue*'s covers featured only white faces in 1995 and 1996. Most actresses and models featured in the issues were white. A lack of diversity in fashion magazines broadly received only scant attention in the press. "Woke" was decades away from entering the lexicon. In this case, Anna had noticed that Asian models had been appearing in a lot of runway shows, which was a new development in the predominantly white fashion industry. But the way Anna brought it up, it was as if an entire race of people was now "in" because fashion had decided it so, the way it might next season decide on chartreuse.

"What are you going to call it?" asked someone in the meeting who was stunned to hear this idea coming out of her mouth.

As a matter of fact, under the heading "*Vogue* Beauty," a story in this vein ran as "Eyeing the East." "No longer willing to be regarded as either docile and demure or exotic and dangerous, Asian women are shaping their own identities and telling their own stories," read the subhead. Treating Asian women as a previously mostly invisible and easily stereotyped bloc was offensive, and would be far from the only time Anna's attitudes about people of color would strike some as deeply hurtful.

Though it would many years later seem perilously unwise, Condé Nast was fine with the cost of a certain amount of excess. Writers, even those doing what were just short pieces for the front of the magazine, could fly business class to places like Australia, stay in a nice hotel, eat at the finest restaurants, and take cars everywhere while they reported their stories.

Some editors, however, were known for taking advantage of the company's generosity. André Leon Talley had a reputation for spending extravagantly. In the beginning of Anna's editorship, he would go to the cashier's office when he was traveling to Paris and take out $15,000, no questions asked, then go off to his prepaid room at the Ritz. All he had to do was bring back his receipts. In 1990, he moved to Paris to work out of Condé Nast's headquarters there; his apartment on the Boulevard de la Tour-Maubourg, a rented television, restaurant "accounts," a full-time assistant/driver, Karl Lagerfeld's hand-wash laundry service, and dry cleaning for his sheets and shirts were all expensed. He remarked in his memoir, "This was Condé Nast! This was *Vogue*!" Talley said later that he was unaware that his expenses were a concern, and Anna never addressed them with him. But that was typical of Anna, who avoided confrontation. "That's what makes her tricky for everyone who works for her. You didn't know where you were sometimes. And that's cause of frustration. Because Anna did not like to explain," said Talley.

But back in New York, eyes were rolling and a coterie of Talley nay-sayers was forming. Freddy Gamble, who worked in the human resources department, said Talley was an example of Anna's loyalty to certain people: "She felt that in spite of his excesses, which were plentiful then, he brought something that was valuable to her and so she was willing to overlook certain things." As Jones put it, "She indulged him all the time."

Talley wrote in his memoir that he thought his value to Anna was really just his close friendship with Karl Lagerfeld. But Jones saw it as more than that. Anna trusted his taste, both when it came to what to feature in the magazine and when she had fittings for her personal clothing, much of which was custom-made by the world's best designers. "Anna does not use people," said Jones.

Yet the special allowances Anna made—enabling him to expense his Paris apartment and dry cleaning, taking him to Si Newhouse for an interest-free loan to buy a house for his grandmother—were insufficient for Talley. In 1995, fed up with what he saw as being inappropriately recognized for his work, he walked into Anna's office and quit. (He later wrote that he felt he was no longer being assigned to run photo shoots, but said in an interview his breaking point was probably Anna killing a shoot of his.) Anna's closest colleagues were stunned by his rudeness and lack of gratitude, after she had made it possible for him to have the glamorous, expensive, *Vogue* life he had enjoyed. But despite him slamming a door in her face, she would keep doing him favors.

"Anna had her pets and she was blind to her pets. And she was not always good at rewarding hard work," Seymour, the copywriter, said of Anna's management style. "She fell for a lot of people who were blowing smoke."

On Monday, February 25, 1991, Anna was honored at the Council of Fashion Designers of America's annual awards with a special prize for her contribution to fashion. *Vogue*, and Anna as its editor, were embraced by an industry that wanted a queen to whom everyone looked for direction.

Anna chose Carrie Donovan, her first boss at *Harper's Bazaar* (and *New York Times Magazine* style editor at the time), to introduce her at the ceremony, which was sponsored by *Bazaar* parent company Hearst. In the crowd sat Tony Mazzola, still *Bazaar*'s editor-in-chief, as Donovan took the stage and delivered a twenty-two-minute speech about Anna, covering everything from her time at *Bazaar* in the mid-seventies when she was twenty-six to the birth of her two children. Donovan said that Mazzola had fired Anna for being "too fashionable or something." She rattled off a long list of her accomplishments as Mazzola slumped in his seat.

In the audience sat Anna, wearing a beautiful, fitted, dark lace dress with long sleeves, clutching her notecards, looking away, her hand cupped over her nose and mouth. When she got to the stage, she said, "I'm mortified," then thanked Liberman, Diana Vreeland, and Grace Mirabella, which—perhaps accent more than slip—came out as "Grease."

In the audience, Anna's former *Bazaar* colleagues were cheering.

In December, Hearst announced Mazzola's retirement.

Chapter 15

FIRST ASSISTANT,
SECOND ASSISTANT

In the summer of 1991, three years into Anna's editorship of *Vogue*, she took a vacation with Shaffer and her children to France. She rented a house with a swimming pool near Mont Ventoux, and hosted her dad and stepmother, her sister Nora and her husband and daughter, and her brother Patrick and his partner. Her two stepsons came for part of the time. Housekeepers came just about every day. "I am still amazed at her lifestyle," her dad remarked.

But Anna, despite coming this far and working as hard as she had, wasn't really ever on vacation. A nearby sausage factory received "a constant stream of faxes" for her from *Vogue*, Charles said, "giving the proprietor a belief that he was at last in close touch with the world of haute couture." When Anna was younger, it had been Charles who interrupted family vacations to work; now Anna was the distracted one.

In 1992, with a $1.64 million interest-free loan from Condé Nast, Anna purchased—in her name only—a townhouse on Sullivan Street. Just a block away from her MacDougal Street home, the new Greek Revival–style house was cheaply constructed, but had something special: access to a lush patch of land in the back, shared by twenty houses surrounding it. Beyond Anna's private garden and an English-style hedge was the communal courtyard. "You could go across the garden to your friends' house in a way that's so, so rare in New York," her daughter Bee later told the *New York Times*. Homes on this block attracted artists, musicians, and filmmakers—the creative set Anna adored.

Just before they moved in, Anna hired Miranda Brooks to design their private garden as a birthday gift for Shaffer. She used beach pebbles as cobbling and planted it. Right after Anna and Shaffer moved in, they got a golden retriever puppy for the kids named Sandy, who promptly dug everything up. (Anna had dogs from then on.)

Anna seemed to come most alive when she talked about her young children, which Lesley Jane Seymour noticed when she got pregnant. "She really became much warmer, much less the fashion icon that you are terrified of," she said. "When I was pregnant, she was very animated."

Anna fitted in time with her children around her job. She took them to school each morning in her car at seven fifteen after having her hair done. After she got her first issues of *Vogue* out of the way, she started leaving the office at six. In a 1998 *Telegraph* interview, a decade into her editorship, she called herself "religious" about not staying late at work so she could go home and have dinner with her kids and her staff could do the same, and said she "[tried] not to go out more than two or three nights a week" and avoided commitments on weekends. (Though Anna herself sometimes went to the office on a Saturday, always calling an assistant in to be with her.) She also described instituting rules for her children, including no television whatsoever. "I'm ruthless!" she said. "American television is just too awful. They read a lot instead. Or I take them to the theatre or the movies or the ballet. When they are older they can do what they want. Of course, they're probably watching it all the time behind my back already!"

Like Anna growing up, her kids spent a lot of time with nannies. One, Lori Feldt, who lived in their home in 1997, said it was her responsibility to get the kids ready for their chauffeured ride to school each morning, at which point they'd see Anna and Shaffer. Contradicting what Anna had said in the 1998 interview, Feldt said the kids then often wouldn't see their parents again until the next morning since they went to so many events at night. Feldt didn't see much of the couple either, mostly communicating with them by writing notes in a notebook left in the kitchen, to which she would receive printed, typed replies. Anna and Shaffer also used her as a personal assistant and household manager. "Essentially, I was a gofer," said Feldt, who was tasked with taking Sandy out, picking up medication from the pharmacy, and ferrying forgotten items to Anna's driver, in days that began at 5:30 a.m. and ended at 9 or 10 at night.

That said, no matter what Anna was doing at work, if her kids ever called, she answered the phone. And she showed up physically whenever she could. Charlie and Bee attended the private St. Luke's School in the West Village in their early years (they later transferred to different private schools, Charlie to Collegiate and Bee to Spence). Lots of the parents were affluent and had high-powered jobs, so Anna didn't stand out as the mom who was the editor-in-chief of *Vogue*. One Halloween, she and the parents of Charlie's friends gathered in her kitchen as the kids trick-or-treated through the courtyard in back. One of Anna's stepsons came over, and she made him a pot of coffee and unloaded the dishwasher while she chatted with the other parents. She struck Susan Bidel, a mom who was there and had a son who played with Charlie, as shy but in many ways remarkably normal. "She's a busy woman, but she showed up and did her level best as a mom. Our sons had playdates. She took my son to the theater. She invited kids for sleepovers," said Bidel. "She went the whole nine yards as an active mom, as much as her job would allow."

Even so, Charlie's and Bee's childhoods were, like Anna's, hardly normal. Anna took them to work events—glamorous fashion parties—whenever it was appropriate in order to fit in more time with them. On bring your daughter to work day, Anna brought Bee, who colored on the floor of her office, and expressed to Laurie Jones that she was sympathetic to her son, who had wanted to go too.

Some Fridays, Jones saw Shaffer pick her up from 350 Madison Avenue with their children in the backseat. Anna would slip into the front seat without looking back or greeting her children at all. Jones said, "Anna was an incredibly efficient woman."

*   *   *

Anna's preference for efficiency over politesse, for control over abandon, made her the subject of endless gossip and rumors inside and outside of Condé Nast. It was said you couldn't get in the elevator with her (false, but most people were too afraid to), or that poinsettias were banned from the *Vogue* office ("you never knew where that came from," said Buckley), or that she couldn't stand chewing gum (true, actually, and she once had Jones, her managing editor, tell a staff member never to chew gum in a features meeting again).

However, there were some indisputable and idiosyncratic guidelines, and by making them known, Anna managed to erect a bubble around her so she never had to be subjected to one of her dislikes. New Yorkers love all-black, fashion people love all-black, fashion designers love all-black. But Anna got to a point early in her tenure at *Vogue* when, along with polka dots, it became something that she just couldn't stand. "I wouldn't have any staff if I told them what to wear," she told the *Chicago Tribune* in July 1990—which was untrue: she actually *did* tell her staff what to wear. Sarah Van Sicklen, a copywriter at *Vogue* starting in January 1994, said that when certain guests were coming to the *Vogue* office, Anna issued memos to the staff that said, "No all-black," but among the staff the command was generally considered as binding, visitors or not. And there were cases like Peggy Northrop getting fashion advice from Phyllis Posnick, where Anna made sure her staff dressed as she felt appropriate.

Anna wanted Laurie Jones to help her build a solid editorial staff outside fashion. Part of her job was screening assistants for Anna.

She has had at any one time, over the course of her career, anywhere from one to three assistants, but most years as *Vogue* editor-in-chief, she had two or three. In the 2010s, this is how her office ran: The first assistant managed the other two, handled her schedule, and was the primary assistant Anna communicated with. The second assistant liaised with the caretakers and chef at her homes in Manhattan and Long Island, coordinated her film screenings, and took care of her dogs (three goldendoodles at this time, all named for characters in *To Kill a Mockingbird*). Once when her dogs went missing out on Long Island, she told an assistant to go find them.* The third assistant ran errands, picked up theater tickets, helped with fashion week, and ordered Anna's clothes directly from designers, usually a customized runway look. (Tom Ford said, "Usually someone in her office sends an email and says, 'Anna loved this and this and this and this'"—then he makes it in her size and sends it over.) The second and third assistants alternated being on call on weekends.

Anna sent all three assistants constant emails, all with no subject, asking for things: "Get me on the phone with this person." "I need to see that person." "Coffee please." On weekends, she often asked them to remind her to do various tasks the following week, but sometimes there were errands, like finding hard copies of old newspaper articles or fetching a book left in the *Vogue* offices that she needed to have in London immediately. Her assistants didn't know why she asked for some of the things that she did, but they knew there was a reason, even if it was just that they were new and perhaps being "hazed." (Others, however, disputed that Anna hazes, saying her behavior is not about testing people, it's just the way she operates.) Her needs dominated their lives.

When second assistants started, they received a twenty-one-page manual reviewing everything from how to handle expenses to maintenance of Anna's home. It noted that, while detailed, the guide is not comprehensive.

Their jobs were highly ritualized. They arrived at the office between 7 and 7:30 a.m. to prepare for Anna's arrival. They fetched the whole-milk Starbucks latte and her blueberry muffin. They pulled up a blank Word document or email draft to furiously type everything she said once she walked in. Because as soon as she arrived, she just started talking, issuing to-dos without periods or pauses. (This was why her assis-

---

* The assistants printed fliers to post around Mastic, but the dogs turned up before Anna's driver got them out there. Afterward, the dogs got tracking devices, for which the second assistant became responsible.

tants didn't want to ride the elevator with her—if they did, she'd issue demands the entire time and they'd have to remember everything she said if they didn't have a way to write it down.)

The second or third assistant greeted her at her car to pick up the "AW bag," a monogrammed L.L.Bean canvas tote with navy handles containing the book, papers she had brought home to look at the night before, and her burgundy crocodile designer planner, which her assistants custom-ordered whenever she filled it up and needed a new one. Her assistants understood why she didn't want to carry this up herself—it was heavy and it was a functional tote bag and everyone was always staring at her.

Even the way Anna was supposed to be addressed was specified. Her assistants used to communicate with her primarily through notes. They had to write: "Note; please advise" and then the question—"please advise that we are able to go to Sullivan today." They never wrote: "Can we go to Sullivan Street today?" The process was so inefficient that it was eventually done away with.

Not everyone endured. Days could easily last twelve hours or more, and assistants woke up in the middle of the night thinking about Anna and feeling they ought to check their email and do things for her. When one assistant quit because the job was too stressful, Anna offered to set her up with a therapist, and followed up with her to make sure she knew she was allowed to leave the office for the appointment during her final days on the job.

Being an assistant to Anna—then and now—means being her *personal* assistant: doing everything that's not work so that she can spend all of her waking seconds on the work that does need doing. Despite the difficulty and stress of the job, the young women who lasted did so because they respect Anna and saw working for her as an incredible opportunity. The job was hard because when she needed things she needed them *right away*, no matter that they weren't curing cancer. Whenever an assistant disappointed her, she made sure the first assistant knew. She didn't yell, but her tone, both when speaking and in emails, radiated

displeasure. The constant reminders that these young women were failing her were difficult for many of them to handle. One recalled Anna
being so frustrated over an assistant's mistake reading her handwriting
that they could hear her banging her hands on her desk. They saw her
power as a result of her personality, which is informed first and foremost
by her work ethic. They were impressed by her knowledge of fashion,
her taste, her ability to manage advertisers, her ability to manage a chaotic office. Most of the negativity, they said, doesn't come from Anna,
but from the people around her. Some saw critiques of her controlling
nature as something that men with power don't have to endure, a view
shared by many on her staff. Still, finding the right person among those
who aspired to the job of Anna's assistant was not always easy. Many
were too slow and too stressed and quickly flamed out. "Most of her
assistants were loyal and sophisticated and smart, but they had to be
discreet as well," said Jones.

Anna's instinct, Jones said, had been to hire friends of friends or
certain people's children—"girls of privilege." Preference was given to
those with degrees from certain colleges. The problem, Jones said, was
that these young women didn't always have the necessary work ethic.
Jones was supposed to help her find people "who had experience and
could really contribute."

Meredith Asplundh started as an intern at Condé Nast in 1993,
and a month into the job was hired to be Anna's second assistant. Her
boss was Anna's first assistant, a "nervous Nellie" who laid out the rules.
Asplundh saw that most of the directives and the scariness of the job
came not from Anna, but from the first assistant. One of the most
important rules was not leaving her desk, not even to go to the bathroom, while the first assistant was away. "It's not like Anna told me I
couldn't leave my desk and go to the bathroom," said Asplundh. "It was
kind of like lore, passed on from generation to generation."

To be successful as Anna's junior assistant, Asplundh realized, you
had to accept that the job was not about getting editorial experience
at *Vogue*. Before Anna arrived each morning, she called the office from
her car to warn them of her approach. (Though she had a phone in
her car, the assistants were chained to the office landline.) "I'm fifteen

minutes away," she'd say, which was Asplundh's cue to go downstairs at 350 Madison Avenue to get her latte, praying the elevator wouldn't be slow because if the coffee wasn't there when she arrived, Anna would seem "testy." (Asplundh understood—she would also be annoyed if her coffee was late.)

In the beginning, Anna addressed Asplundh using the first assistant's name, not her own, seldom making eye contact because she was wearing her sunglasses or was in the middle of doing something else. So many young women flunked out of the job—either because they gave up or because Anna gave up on them—that Asplundh figured that if you do as much in a day as Anna does, why bother learning someone's name when she might not be there next week? "She didn't torture any of us on purpose. We needed to get the job done, and so if you were able to put up with what the job required, I think she would start calling you by your name, and you were like, *Oh my god, oh my god. I made it.*" Not learning the second assistant's name seemed to fly in the face of Anna's high executive functioning—of course she could make an effort to remember their names—however, the assistants who lasted had to accept this: either as a forgivable eccentricity or as normal behavior. But some in the office saw it as just one of many demeaning aspects of the job.

By the end of her first week, Asplundh was hired at an annual salary of around $25,000. For the next two years that she had the job, she felt exhausted most of the time. The hours were long and the job was as intense as Anna, who had something scheduled every minute of her day: meetings with her team, meetings with heads of fashion houses, meetings with advertising partners. "If she had Karl Lagerfeld on the phone and she needed something, you can't spend ten minutes rifling through paperwork to get it. She wants it right away. So you had to move quickly and you had to think really fast. I knew what was expected, so I was like, *Okay, you either sink or swim,*" Asplundh said. She got in before 8 a.m. and often worked until 8 p.m. Each day was a hamster wheel of errands—getting coffee, lunch, answering the phone, setting up chairs for minutes-long meetings in Anna's huge office, which could fit a dozen people at a time. At the end of each day Asplundh, as second assistant, had to wait at the office for the book, and then take a car to drop it off at Anna's house where Anna would sometimes greet her after dinner, wearing her slippers. Then Anna would review it for the visuals, to see how one photo flowed to the next, adorning the pages with Post-its of her handwritten notes, before packing it up and bringing it back the next morning.

Appearance was as important for the assistants as for the rest of the staff. Asplundh didn't have the money to buy an all-designer wardrobe, but her fashion-forward mom gave her some hand-me-downs. Anna generally approved. Still, Asplundh said, there were times when "she would glare at whatever I was wearing. It wasn't a glare like approval. It was sort of, *What the hell is that?* You could definitely tell when she was like, *Why would you put those pants with that top?*"

But the hardest part of the job was handling the requests from Anna that were delivered with almost no background information. Many of these directives came with the tacit understanding—or explicit instruction from the first assistant—that you could not ask Anna for clarification or help. Assistants were afraid even to ask Anna what she had written in her illegible scrawl on a piece of paper.

Anna was particular about everything, from the flowers in her office (she never liked orchids) to the wrapping paper for Christmas presents (popping into the drugstore to pick some up was definitely not okay) to her lunch. When she didn't have lunch meetings out of the office, she ate the same thing every day from the Royalton, served to her on a plate instead of a takeout container: a rare steak and mashed potatoes, with a silver fork. She'd take a few bites and then say, "Take my plate, I'm done." Asplundh rinsed it in the sink in the bathroom across from her office, which only Anna used. Sometimes Anna said thank you, but the times she didn't it didn't strike Asplundh as a sign of rudeness—just that her mind was already on to the next task.

The best part of the job was helping with parties at Anna's house, a rare opportunity to experience the glamour of her world in the flesh instead of through a phone at a desk. Anna liked when the assistants attended; in case anyone needed anything, it was an insurance policy that any last-minute to-do would be taken care of immediately. Sometimes an editor from the fashion team would tell the assistant, "I have something you might like to wear tonight," perhaps because Anna had told them their office attire wasn't sufficient.

Hamish Bowles first met Anna in 1986 in London, when he interviewed for the job André Leon Talley had declined at British *Vogue*. Since Talley continued advising Anna, she never ended up filling the job, but Bowles, self-described as a "somewhat eccentric and flamboyant figure" on the British fashion scene, must have made an impression. Fascinated by fashion since childhood, he attended London's prestigious art and design college Central Saint Martins, where he became friends with another student, designer John Galliano, and then got a job as fashion director of *Harpers & Queen*.

In 1992, Bowles got a call asking if *Vogue* could feature his small but colorful Notting Hill apartment, which he'd decorated eclectically with fashionable vintage furniture and art. Bowles was working for Condé Nast rival Hearst, but did the story anyway. After Anna saw the pictures, she surprised him with a phone call.

"This is Anna. I'm looking at these pictures of your apartment. I can see you have an interest in interiors," she said. She told Bowles her style editor was leaving and asked if he'd take the job. "Fascinated" by Anna, he accepted "with alacrity," and quickly thereafter moved to New York.

American *Vogue* was an alien environment. At *Harpers & Queen*, Bowles had worked autonomously on shoots, sometimes not telling his boss anything about what he was doing until the photos came back. But here, Anna was involved in everything. Bowles said, "Suddenly to have an editor who was keenly interested in understanding every element that was going to go into the finished image—so, the choice of photographer and the location and the subjects and hair and makeup, and then every detail of clothing and accessories, what jewelry was going to be put with what outfit, the shoes—nothing in my previous working environment had prepared me for that degree of, I suppose some might call it today micromanagement."

Bowles was "amazed" by run-throughs, and how Anna approved

everything and caught every mistake. "She was looking at text, captions, images that had gone through countless layers of editorial intervention to get to that point, and she would say, 'This directional should say left, not right.' No one had noticed it, but she never missed it," he said. Though none deny Anna is controlling, a few of her most trusted and longest-serving editors were able to sidestep some oversight.

Phyllis Posnick, who worked on photos for beauty and food stories, said nothing was too edgy for Anna. In 2003, she needed Posnick to do a photo for an article on roast chicken. She called Posnick, who was on her way to another shoot in Monte Carlo with Helmut Newton, and said, "Do you think Helmut would take a picture of a chicken?" Posnick called Anna back and told her Newton would do the picture. "What's he going to do?" she asked.

"I'm not telling you," Posnick said. "You're either going to love it or hate it." Newton took a photo of a lightly roasted chicken, loosely trussed, legs akimbo, with plastic doll's high heels on the ends of its legs. When Anna saw it, she laughed and said, "Okay." Which was just about the highest praise anyone on her staff could expect to receive.

Anna's flat affect coupled with her taste and vision made her good at managing internal clashes, foremost among them the tendency of fashion editors to steal pieces from one another's racks when they weren't assigned to shoot the clothes they wanted. Anna had editors make boards of Polaroids of clothes they planned to shoot, which she approved. It was her way of making sure that clothes and shoes weren't smuggled onto a set without her knowing. But Carlyne Cerf de Dudzeele, who styled Anna's first cover, never seemed to play by the rules. She filled her boards with pieces "that had nothing whatsoever to do with what she was actually shooting," Coddington recalled. Talley described an altercation with Cerf de Dudzeele over who would get to feature a Bill Blass dress: "There was a big fight in the fashion closet about that dress, and Anna ended up giving it to me and not Carlyne. Carlyne and I didn't speak to each other for five years because of that dress"—which ultimately appeared alongside Talley's column instead of in Cerf de Dudzeele's shoot.

Anna seemed to dislike the chaos, keeping a physical distance from the fashion department. However, it may have been Anna's leadership that inspired it. Editors weren't nearly as competitive under Mirabella, but under Anna, competition for certain items was fierce. Coddington said that complaining to Anna was "pointless" because Anna would just say, "This is not a girls' boarding school. Deal with it yourself." But according to Coddington, "a girls' boarding school—with its sulky outbursts, tears, and schoolgirlish tantrums—was exactly what it occasionally resembled."

Anna liked over-the-top personalities, attracted not only to their talent but also to their distinctiveness. As Talley put it, Anna "surrounded herself with strong independent thinkers, which could sometimes lead to differences of opinion." Or as Lisa Love, *Vogue*'s West Coast editor, said, "They were vicious, horrible people, some of them." Working out of LA, Love assumed none of them saw her as a threat. "I survived *Vogue* because I was away from the madd[ing] crowd—editors vying for favor, and backstabbing and competitive and catty and mean."

Just a few years into her job as *Vogue* editor-in-chief, Anna's name started surfacing in the press as a potential replacement for her champion and mentor, Alex Liberman. In February 1991, the seventy-eight-year-old Liberman had been admitted to the hospital after suffering a heart attack, made worse by severe diabetes and prostate cancer. He survived, but his health would remain poor until his death in late 1999. His ailments made it impossible to continue working as he had for the past three decades, but he remained connected to Condé Nast, seemingly unable to give up the material perks it offered him and the work that was his identity. For many cast-off Condé Nast editors, losing such gratuities was the harshest blow of termination, but Liberman was one of the few people who would never have to worry about losing it all in an instant because of his unique relationship to Newhouse.

Unlike Grace Mirabella, Anna was never dependent on Liberman. If she had been, she would never have become truly powerful. Besides, Newhouse wanted to empower her. When she started editing *Vogue*, Newhouse told Liberman, who loved *Vogue* more than any other magazine, that Anna should have "total control" over it. Initially, Liberman was offended at being shut out, but ultimately had no choice in the matter. After Newhouse let her know of his order, Anna started showing Liberman layouts and asking his advice, but she did so for the remainder of his life only as a courtesy.

Anna said that her replacing Liberman was "never discussed," but people who worked with her believed she indeed wanted more than to just edit *Vogue*. After all, only a few years into editing *Vogue*, she was functioning in an executive capacity that was above her pay grade. In 1992, Graydon Carter received a job offer to become editor-in-chief of the *New Yorker*. The day it was supposed to be announced, Anna called him.

"It's going to be *Vanity Fair*," she said.

Carter was stunned—as the editor of *Spy*, he had spent five years making fun of *Vanity Fair*. Anna told him: "Act surprised when Si calls you." Anna, who had been employing Carter as a *Vogue* contributor, was getting scintillating information within Condé Nast before other people—and if people at the company were talking to her, they were probably listening to her as well.

Gabé Doppelt, who had faithfully worked for Anna through three editorships, had the impression it was Anna who recommended her to Newhouse to edit *Mademoiselle*. Doppelt didn't know why—she loved her job at *Vogue* and hadn't been gunning for another one. Some figured that Anna's coordinating the move was a sign she would become the next Alex. Doppelt agreed with *WWD*'s declaration that "The Doppelt appointment demonstrates once again the ever-increasing influence of Anna Wintour at Condé Nast."

But Doppelt's tenure at *Mademoiselle* turned out to be something of a disaster. Anna gave her guidance, the most important of which—to let Liberman choose her art director—she ignored. Trying to run the magazine the way Anna had run hers, Doppelt fired the staff within days. She totally overhauled the editorial to reflect early nineties grunge culture, the opposite of Anna's gorgeous, happy, smiling, vivacious direction. Anna had hired Grace Coddington—a legend in the business—for her fashion department, but Doppelt chose for her editorial staff "kids who looked like street urchins from England." She also brought in a whole new slate of photographers.

Working at a company like Condé Nast demanded political acuity as much as editorial acuity, and Doppelt failed at both. Her extremely skinny models offended feminine hygiene advertisers. Being shut out offended Liberman, who in this case, unlike at Anna's *Vogue*, most definitely had Newhouse's ear. And the November 1993 issue, featuring Kate Moss with braided pigtails on the cover, especially offended her publisher, who called it "'the ugliest girl in eighth grade' cover." (Doppelt said the last issue she worked on was October.) With readers and advertisers fleeing the ship, she resigned in late September 1993. With Anna's encouragement, she accepted another job at MTV.

By this point, Anna told Liberman's stepdaughter Francine du Plessix Gray for her book *Them* about her parents that Newhouse "distinctly felt that [Liberman] was disengaged." For months he had barely been at the office. His wife had died and he was spending time in Miami with his new partner, Melinda, who had been one of his wife's nurses. Liberman was able to retain the title of deputy chairman, his four-person office staff, a chauffeured white limousine, and Condé Nast–funded domestic staff. When he tired of Miami, Newhouse loaned him $1 million to buy a house on Long Island.

Anna was upset by the way Liberman was treated. Despite the cruel firings she'd witnessed under Newhouse, she never expected him to push out Liberman and didn't like the way he did it, despite the golden parachute.

But Anna wouldn't become the next Alexander Liberman. On January 26, 1994, Si Newhouse announced that James Truman, the thirty-six-year-old editor-in-chief of *Details* magazine, would be the next editorial director of the company.

Truman had entered Condé Nast thanks to Anna, who hired him

in 1988 as one of *Vogue*'s features editors. His ascension—over Anna and over Tina Brown, the company's most famous and intriguing figureheads—was stunning to editors inside the company, as well as its observers from outside the building.*

Some thought Anna (or Brown) not getting the job was sexist. But Doppelt thought it was a typical Newhouse move. "He would always do these things to sort of pit people against each other," she said. Liberman felt similarly, telling Truman that the biggest pieces of advice he could offer were: "'Be extremely Machiavellian at all times.' 'Act as if you're the only proprietor and your colleagues are the hired help.' 'Flattery is the only way of getting *your* way.' 'Don't worry if people oppose you, sit it out and they'll fall by the wayside.' And 'Don't make this job the center of the world or you'll go mad.'"

Eventually, Anna would in fact be promoted to a job like Liberman's, but not for two more decades. In the meantime, she would have to expand her power in other ways.

In 1994, only a year after the introduction of Mosaic, the very first web browser to seamlessly integrate text and images, Condé Nast hired Rochelle Udell, Liberman's former assistant, to launch an online division called CondéNet. Udell hired Joan Feeney, who had interviewed with Anna to be *Vogue*'s managing editor in 1992 but didn't get the job. (Anna's world was both big and small.) Udell and Feeney had to figure out what websites should be like for Condé Nast magazines, and how they could benefit the company's business.

Udell believed the internet was the future, but she had a hard time convincing Newhouse. Even though he had a sense that the internet

---

* The three had something in common: they were all British. In late 1992, the *New York Times* reported on American publishing's "British Invasion," citing Anna, Brown, Truman, and Doppelt, who is South African but was educated in England, along with Elizabeth Tilberis, who went on to run *Harper's Bazaar* after British *Vogue*. British editors were praised for their willingness to experiment with a high-low mix of content endemic to British publications including Anna's dad's *Evening Standard*, where serious political news ran alongside that about pop culture and headless corpses.

was going to be important, he was comfortable with his business, which made money from selling printed advertisements, and anything that suggested a future where that wasn't the most important thing was, frankly, unthinkable.

Udell and Feeney decided to start with food, because all they had the rights to publish online was a cache of five thousand recipes from *Gourmet* magazine. They didn't call it Gourmet.com, however, because Newhouse believed it would undermine the print product. Instead, they named the site Epicurious.com. It had no pictures, because in the age of dial-up modems, they would take too long to load. Such technical challenges were moot, however, as the team also didn't have the rights to run the magazine's photo archive online.

Anna wasn't necessarily a tech-oriented person at that point. (Joe Dolce, a features editor, sent an email to the entire staff on his first day in 1994 to introduce himself, only to receive a fax from Anna from Europe that said, "Joe, this is *Vogue*. We don't email. It's so impersonal.") Still, from the beginning of the Epicurious.com project, Anna started calling Feeney. "When can *Vogue* go online?" she'd ask. "It's starting to get embarrassing that Vogue.com is not online. Why aren't we online?" But Feeney knew that she would be unhappy with the technology. "The images will look like the dog's dinner," she said. "You'll be embarrassed by anything we can do."

"Okay. Let me know when it's time," Anna said.

"The entire purpose of fashion is to be a reflection of the times," said Feeney. "I think that's why it really bugged her, because she did not want *Vogue* to feel antiquated or out-of-date." She also recognized that print and digital could be mutually beneficial. "What made her such a good partner was she understood what we were trying to do immediately," Feeney said. "Many, many, many of the editors had no idea. They only were able to think of it in terms of a threat or a competition."

Anna's calls to Feeney were persistent, but she'd have to wait years for her website.

Chapter 16

A NEW PROJECT,
AN OLD FRIEND

The evening of December 4, 1995, was an unseasonable forty-eight degrees, a tolerable temperature in which to ascend the famous granite steps of the Metropolitan Museum of Art in a sleeveless gown. As the night's hostess and first-time chair of the "Party of the Year," which celebrated the opening of the museum's new exhibit by its fashion department, the Costume Institute, Anna wore a white satin column dress by Oscar de la Renta, with matching white gloves that extended to just below her toned biceps. The event's sponsors were Chanel and Versace, who at Anna's request jointly put down $500,000 for the honor.

After Anna, Naomi Campbell sparkled her way inside wearing a slim, strapless, glittering silver Versace gown. Kate Moss climbed the steps in a simple pale-yellow Calvin Klein apron dress. Along with fellow models Christy Turlington and Shalom Harlow and designers Tom Ford, John Galliano, Calvin Klein, Ralph Lauren, Bill Blass, Marc Jacobs, and Diane von Furstenberg, they mingled around a Christmas tree made of roses in the Great Hall. Dinner was served at tables decorated with even more roses and epergne centerpieces filled with fruit.

The Met's exhibit offered the public the chance to bask in the limelight of a hundred bona fide couture gowns. But most people there that night, who'd purchased a $1,000 ticket to the dinner, weren't terribly interested in museum displays—they just wanted to party. (Anna would, in later years, ensure that every guest walked through the exhibit.)

Historically, the museum's staff had worked such events, but Anna, as with past parties, wanted her people working it which, in 1995, included *Vogue* copywriter Sarah Van Sicklen. "God forbid if they're fat, if they are unsightly, they have to go. That was absolutely a thing," she said. To guarantee acceptability, Anna ordered apron dresses from Calvin Klein for her staff to wear. The women were stationed throughout the space, their job to direct guests to the bar or bathroom.

Following the dinner was a dance party in the museum's Temple of Dendur, a cavernous glass-walled space housing an Egyptian temple dated to around 15 BC. At this point the younger crowd were admitted with $150 tickets. They smoked and drank, and drank some more, until the hour came when people were puking right there in the temple (at one gala years later, the after party got so big and out of control that a Met staffer witnessed women peeing in the Great Hall).

If Anna was going to keep hosting this party and turn it into the red-carpet fashion event to end all red-carpet fashion events—the flashiest, most unmissable possible signifier of who was in and who was out according to her judgment—she had her work cut out for her.

The Costume Institute, founded in 1937 as the Museum of Costume Art, is a hugely important resource to the fashion and entertainment industries, its collection routinely used for research.* In 1995, Richard Martin was the institute's chief curator, a position famously held before

---

* High-profile research visits have been paid by the world's most famous designers, such as John Galliano, and celebrities like Beyoncé and Madonna, and it is available for academic research as well.

him by Diana Vreeland after she was fired from *Vogue* and needed a job. Beloved by his staff, Martin had been the editor of *Arts Magazine*, and brought that same art-world knowledge and flair to his exhibits. He was over six feet tall and, aware of his image as a leader, had a habit of adjusting his posture and tie before he walked through the doors of the Costume Institute. He started work at seven thirty in the morning and regularly stayed until after ten at night. He rarely turned down an invitation to write an article or speak.

Martin had started at the Costume Institute in 1993 with his long-time collaborator Harold Koda, with whom he had previously curated widely admired shows at New York's Fashion Institute of Technology. Without Vreeland, who worked there until her death in 1989, a critic for the *New York Times* concluded, the Met's 1992 show *Fashion and History: A Dialogue* had "no razzle-dazzle." Martin's charge was to reignite the department's buzz.

The shows under Martin's leadership included *Orientalism: Visions of the East in Western Dress* and *Cubism and Fashion*. But a big part of reinstating said razzle-dazzle was reviving excitement about the so-called Party of the Year. The Costume Institute is unique within the museum because it must raise all of its own funds, rather than dipping into the museum's coffers. The money raised by the party went toward maintaining and growing its extraordinary collection, in addition to funding the exhibits.

In 1995, Anna got a call from Oscar de la Renta and his wife, Annette, asking if *Vogue* would help them with the Party of the Year. Anna knew that Vreeland had been a huge loss for the Costume Institute. "There was no one spearheading it, so it had slightly fallen off the fashion map and the social map, and was no longer talked about or raised the money that was needed for the museum," she later said. However, part of the reason the Met needed her was that the socialite Pat Buckley was ready to move on from planning it; the museum thought it made sense to put someone from the industry in charge of raising the funds, but knew it would be a conflict of interest if it were a designer.

Obviously, if Anna was going to cohost the event, she was going to make it as spectacular as her previous parties and fund-raisers, and raise more money than anyone ever had before. Plus, one of the ways she prevented boredom in her job was regularly finding new projects— such as this one—within it. Still, she said, "I think I was quite naïve when I said to Oscar and Annette how much I would enjoy taking that on."

Martin, the chief curator, was as dedicated to his job as Anna was to hers, and was not receptive to feedback from Anna or anyone else outside the department on his exhibitions. One way he kept Anna in check was by rotating who would chair the party. After Anna hosted in 1995, the baton passed to her rival Liz Tilberis, now editor-in-chief of *Harper's Bazaar*. (Her replacement as editor-in-chief of British *Vogue* was Alexandra Shulman, previously editor of British *GQ*; Anna took Shulman to lunch when she started, but American and British *Vogue* operated as separate entities.)

Anna had been competitive since childhood, and the arrival of Tilberis on her shores forced Anna to up her game even more. Her attitude was: "Great competitors make you work harder." And she had no intention, now that she was no longer the hot new editor, of ceding territory to anybody. Tilberis had taken the *Bazaar* job on the condition that she could put three of her favorite photographers on contract. Hearst agreed to let her have two, and she signed Patrick Demarchelier and Peter Lindbergh for contracts rumored to be upwards of $1 million each, which meant they couldn't also work for Anna at *Vogue*.

In response, Anna signed Steven Meisel to an exclusive contract. She also started having her cover stars agree that they would appear on no other covers while their issue of *Vogue* was on the newsstand. She counter-offered to keep editors Tilberis tried to poach with "very big salaries." And Newhouse, who was just as competitive as Anna, had her back.

In 1996, Tilberis hosted the party for an exhibition on Dior. Her guest of honor was Princess Diana, then at the very height of her fame. Martin, a control freak himself, seemed to enjoy working with Tilberis more than with Anna because she didn't seem to expect that she'd be able to tell him what to do, which led to an easier rapport.

One of the things Martin took great pride in was the text he wrote to go with the pieces in his shows. His writing was confidently intellectual; just because he was concerning himself with dresses and not antiquities or seventeenth-century paintings didn't mean it needed dumbing down, he felt. Anna was back to hosting the 1997 party promoting the institute's Versace exhibition. One piece of text Martin wrote explained how one of Versace's early influences was prostitutes. Anna told Donatella, Gianni's sister, she thought the text should be changed. But Martin, buttressed by his own personal relationship with Gianni, refused. The text stayed. That was not how things usually went for Anna.

On January 5, 1996, a month after Anna hosted her first Party of the Year, her mother died at age seventy-eight. Nonie had been suffering from osteoporosis before contracting pneumonia. When she was nearly recovered from the pneumonia, a blood problem surfaced. Tests revealed the blood problem had gone undetected for months. It was Nonie's osteoporosis that inspired Anna to take up tennis as weight-bearing endurance exercise after her mother's death.

Anna's great strength at work was her containment, any true feelings seemingly tucked away behind a padlock to which only she had the key. But after losing her mom, "she was very emotional about it," said Laurie Jones, the managing editor. She would credit her mom with instilling her social conscience.

When Anna was in London for the funeral, she called André Leon Talley. Talley had relocated to Durham, North Carolina, and was living in the house formerly occupied by his beloved and recently deceased grandmother. He wrote in his memoir that Karl Lagerfeld had urged him to get back in Anna's good graces after his dramatic resignation ten months earlier.

"Probably at the time, his role was just not clearly defined for him," Jones said. "Also, he was not a nine-to-fiver by any means. And

Anna wants people to be there in the morning when she gets there, and she wants people to work on her schedule. . . . He gets in and he's got a whole lot of ideas and he wants to do something, and then it's just real hard for him to stay on schedule and do exactly what you expect him to do." Talley had spoken out publicly when he quit, calling his situation at *Vogue* a "creative Chernobyl" in the *New York Times*. "I am something that is associated with the old school, and I mean it in the best sense. I would like to be in a pure environment of elegance. Advertising does not create fashion excitement." (In the same article, Anna responded, "What we on the editorial side of *Vogue* think about is editorial.")

Nevertheless, Anna considered Talley "one of my oldest friends," which would explain why she thought to reach out to him in her state of mourning.* When she called, Talley could tell, even though it was snowing and the connection was bad, that something was wrong. Anna told him that her mother had died, and then the line went dead. The next call that came through was from David Shaffer, who was in New York with their children. "Anna shouldn't be alone right now," he said. He told Talley that planes had been grounded across the entire Northeast. Newhouse had offered him a private jet, but it couldn't take off until conditions improved. Since Talley was farther south, Shaffer was hoping he'd be able to find a flight to England to be with Anna. Talley managed to get on a plane to Miami; as soon as he landed in London, he changed and went straight to the crematorium, where he found Anna along with her dad and siblings.

At the funeral, Anna's brother Patrick "couldn't trust himself to speak," Charles recalled, "so Anna had to do it." Talley sat in the back as Anna delivered her eulogy. "She was close to her mother, though she didn't talk about her that much," he said. At the end of her speech, tears filled Anna's eyes and she "broke down, in front of everyone, and ran out." Talley rushed to her side and held her as she exited.

---

* While Talley has said he and Anna did not reconnect until after her mother's death, according to a December 8, 1995, *WWD* article, he was seen around the *Vogue* office, and they were regularly eating out together.

Adding to her stress, just before Nonie died, Charles, then seventy-eight, had gone to the doctor after experiencing nagging pain in his chest. On being sent to the hospital, he was surprised to learn he had suffered a heart attack. He spent five days there, some of it in intensive care. Also, his eyesight was failing, a damaged left retina making it "useless for reading," he said, while the right eye was "dodgy in the mornings."

The lone improvement for her, it seemed, was reuniting with Talley. As cold and removed as she is said to be, Anna's relationship with him revealed a side invisible to most—the human being that exists outside the bizarre and merciless worlds of fashion and media, that supports people in the way that she herself sometimes needs support, and that has the heart to forgive. Her closest friends say that no amount of power can shake that core, even if she has attained so much power that revealing that part of herself widely might be seen as a weakness (not that, Jones said, Anna would ever worry about seeming weak).

Despite their reconciliation, Talley did not go back to work at *Vogue* right away. He continued living in Durham, still processing his feelings after his grandmother's passing, and traveling between there, New York, and Paris, where, in keeping with the lifestyle to which he was accustomed, he stayed in suites at either the Royalton New York or the Ritz Paris. He became style editor for *Vanity Fair* under editor-in-chief Graydon Carter, and got back to doing photo shoots. Meanwhile, Anna gave Grace Coddington, her faithful fashion editor, the title of creative director.

In 1997, Talley told Anna he wanted to come back to *Vogue* because, he said, "my heart was still with the magazine." Anna decided to take him back at a salary of $350,000, with the title of editor-at-large and the official duty of writing a monthly column, as well as the unofficial duty of going with Anna to fittings for many of her clothes.

The coterie of Talley naysayers back at the Condé Nast offices in New York didn't know what Anna was thinking. "Sometimes he would be very obliging, and other times he would be just rude to her, and she would always look the other way. She would just say, 'Oh, that's Andre.' She was so forgiving of him for all those years," said Jones. "It was not that she just felt sorry for him and brought him back. She trusted him. He was of service to her, and she provided an income and hours and he had a great job."

A manager in human resources was perplexed by Anna's decision to rehire Talley, even in a lesser role than before. "Why in the name of God did you do that?" she asked Anna.

She replied, "It is better to have André where you can see him."

Chapter 17

FOLLOW THE MONEY

In fashion, Anna was queen. But at work, she was merely a subject in the Kingdom of Si Newhouse. And what an incredible place that kingdom was. In the nineties, it was *lush*. Employees luxuriated in Big Apple town cars and business class airplane tickets and five-star hotel rooms and $29 hamburgers. The vast majority couldn't afford this stuff on their own, making them serfs with corporate credit cards. Newhouse expected his people to run hard for him every day, making money for his magazines. The company's most senior editors and executives never knew when they walked into his office, to find him sitting there in his uniform of an old *New Yorker* sweatshirt, khakis, and loafers, whether he was going to promote them or fire them. Not even Anna.

The early nineties were challenging for *Vogue*. In Newhouse's eyes, the magazine never really attained a position of unquestionable dominance after the 1990 recession. Ad pages were down in the first quarter of 1994 by 4.5 percent compared with the first quarter of 1993. Meanwhile, Tilberis's *Harper's Bazaar*, boasting fashion layouts that struck even Anna's *Vogue* staff as gorgeous and modern, saw pages up 11 percent for the period; *Elle*, where former *Vogue* features editor Amy Gross was editorial director, was known for its great look and even better writing, and saw an increase of 14.5 percent. And while *Vogue*'s revenue was $112.2 million in 1993, *Bazaar* had nearly doubled its to $57.3 million.

If Newhouse's people didn't hit their numbers, typically he made changes. So it was with *Vogue*. Anne Sutherland Fuchs, whom he had hired away from *Elle* to be *Vogue*'s publisher and solve this very problem for him years ago, transitioned to a corporate role as senior vice president and director, international. Newhouse hired her replacement from Hearst, *Bazaar*'s parent company and Condé Nast's biggest rival.

The only reason Ron Galotti was at Hearst publishing *Esquire* was that Newhouse had fired him ten months earlier from *Vanity Fair*, where he had been publisher. He had now been hired back at a seven-figure salary six weeks into his *Esquire* job out of fear that he would move over to *Harper's Bazaar* and crush *Vogue*. It was the Newhouse way. In March of 1994, Galotti was announced as the new publisher of *Vogue*.

The stories about Galotti's temper were legendary—that he threw chairs, that he yelled. Some loved him, and others thought he was just a giant ego with a loud New York accent, a red Ferrari, and the minimum necessary amount of charm. Around the time he was at *Vogue*, Galotti dated the writer Candace Bushnell, who based her character of Mr. Big in *Sex and the City* on him because Galotti seemed "like a big man on campus." Unlike Anna, Galotti didn't self-censor in the office, and he made known his views of Bernard Leser, who had become Condé Nast's president. While Galotti was publisher of *Vanity Fair*, a camera crew came to his office to interview him for what he called "a corporate film." Of the encounter, he recalled in a *New York* magazine profile: "They ask me what I want to see for the company's future. I said, 'I want to see Bernie Leser walk out of the building and get hit by a bus. I don't want him killed, just hurt so he has to go back to Australia or New Zealand or wherever the hell he came from.'" A few months later, Galotti was fired.

Galotti was as ruthless as the Kingdom of Si Newhouse demanded. He wasn't afraid to tell Newhouse when he wasn't getting what he needed from his editors. He knew he wasn't going to earn that seven-figure salary just minding the store. He was there to make *Vogue* the most dominant fashion publication in the world. Before long rumors surfaced in the press that Galotti coming in spelled trouble for Anna, and that she would soon be out of a job.

Buzz about Anna leaving *Vogue*—of her own volition or at Newhouse's choosing—would surface cyclically over the course of her career as editor-in-chief. Like all rumors about her, it was hard to know if they were based in reality or just another instance of the press shooting arrows at a powerful woman.

This time, however, there was some truth to them.

Initially, Anna and Galotti seemed to align. The September 1994 issue of *Vogue* was an homage to glamour, meant to obliterate the grunge trend—the same one that had helped submarine Doppelt's *Mademoiselle*.

"The granny slip dress with sneakers is too difficult," Anna told the *New York Times*. "And no makeup and dirty hair is not what the Leonard Lauders of the world want to see," referring to the president of Estée Lauder, one of her key advertisers.

"From a purely business standpoint, the waif thing affected us across the board," Galotti added. "Retailers weren't moving product, designers were trying to identify themselves with grunge, the waif look and absence of color and shape, and there's not a lot you can sell people. If you can't sell it, you can't advertise it."

But according to Grace Coddington, Anna mainly wanted to kill grunge simply because she didn't like it. "I think she just felt strongly that women should be chicer than that," she said. "Look at her, she's very groomed, no matter what." That said, one of Coddington's most famous *Vogue* shoots was a grunge spread photographed by Steven Meisel, published in 1992, in which models wore floral dresses (albeit a $760 one by Calvin Klein), plaid shirts, and black Dr. Martens boots (Meisel even added a nose ring). "She didn't love it, but she printed it, and people talked about it," said Coddington.

Still, even as she reluctantly featured grunge, Anna's choices of which clothes to photograph were not dictated by ad dollars. Galotti respected Anna as an editor—there was no question in his mind that she was talented. But he didn't understand her persona, her regal aura, and the way others indulged it. To him, she wasn't in the role to be Anna Wintour; she was there—just like he was—to make money for the company.

So it was perplexing to Galotti when she didn't photograph pieces by advertisers when there was an obvious opportunity to do so. He didn't want to tell her which dresses to feature in a couture story— but why, if she needed a white shirt, wouldn't she choose Anne Klein, or another brand that was buying pages? His team provided hers with detailed lists of all the credits for every advertiser; how hard was it? To Galotti, Anna's taste was not more precious than the business. Having been fired by Newhouse, Galotti knew firsthand that he relished making unpredictable decisions and destabilizing his magazines. So he never took Anna's employment for granted, and always suspected that she was smart enough to view herself the very same way.

Before Galotti raised this with Anna and Newhouse, he had to bring the magazine back to a position of strength. By early 1997, business was finally looking up. *Vogue* had its biggest March issue since 1990, with ad pages up 5.9 percent. The first quarter was up 7 percent; April was up 22 percent. Galotti declared, "Everything looks pretty damn good."

And it stayed that way. For 1997, the magazine's ad pages were up 10 percent overall. But no issue was more important to Newhouse than September. And that year, he had to have been both thrilled and relieved. Packed with ads, its 734 total pages weighed 4.3 pounds. (The cover featured Linda Evangelista, wearing, to the horror of animal rights activists, a light-blue Birger Christensen Mongolian lamb coat.)

Ad pages were up 9.7 percent, with the fashion category alone up 20 percent. It was the biggest issue in nine years—since before Anna started—and the fifth-biggest of all time, in terms of ad pages.

Yet Anna couldn't help but push back at times. A 1997 ad for the shoe brand Candie's featured Jenny McCarthy on the toilet with her underwear around her calves. Galotti accepted the ad, but then Anna rejected it. Galotti later told *WWD*, "We felt that the ad was not exactly a reflection of what we wanted *Vogue* to say. Taste is something very subtle, and a decision was made."

But what Galotti really wanted was for Anna to feature advertisers' clothing in editorial spreads. With *Vogue* performing well, he brought this up to Newhouse, who agreed: Anna's taste was not more precious than the business. They both felt that she needed to play the game better, and the game wasn't just about credits for clothes, it was about the relationships with the people who ran companies who bought ads.

To make this clear, Galotti and Newhouse and Anna all went to lunch at Da Silvano, one of her and Newhouse's favorite restaurants. Newhouse's message to Anna, now about ten years into her editorship, at that lunch was that if she didn't help Galotti, she would be out of a job.

He and Galotti had in mind a list of people who could replace her.

"I suggest," Newhouse told her, "you follow the money."

Anna hadn't reacted at that lunch, but afterward she knew that she had to make some changes. She was more deliberate about shooting advertisers' clothing—the very thing that had offended Talley and contributed to his quitting, but which also made both his and Anna's jobs possible. She made herself more available for meetings with advertisers, everyone from Revlon to Versace. Despite any annoyance she may have felt with Galotti for taking his concerns to Newhouse, she seemed to like him. It's possible that being Newhouse's favorite earned her this stern and clear reminder instead of the sack.

But she also had an ally in company president and CEO Steve Florio, who firmly shut down the idea of replacing her.

Anna's tendency toward controversial positions within the company translated to consumer-facing issues as well.

There was a time in New York when pretty much anyone could

walk into the lobby of most upscale office buildings and ride the eleva-
tors without confronting security. So, on September 30, 1993, there was
nothing stopping protestors from PETA (People for the Ethical Treatment of Animals) from popping into Condé Nast's headquarters at 350
Madison Avenue. Kate Pierson, a member of the B-52's, was among the
group of eight of them who took the elevator to the thirteenth floor,
which belonged to *Vogue*, to stage a protest against the magazine's coverage of fur.

The PETA contingent marched through the office blaring bull-
horns and sticking antifur slogans to the walls. Norman Waterman, who
worked on the publishing staff, came down to try to stop them, yelling,
"Get out of here!" Editor-at-large William Norwich watched from his
glass-walled office as a protestor kicked Waterman in the groin so hard
that he fell to the floor. Anna's assistant closed her door and stood outside her office, while the staff waited for security to come. Eventually
the police took the protestors to the Midtown South precinct, where
they were charged with criminal mischief and criminal trespass.

This would hardly be the first or last time Anna and *Vogue* were
aggressively targeted by antifur protestors. A lot of the big fashion
houses in the nineties, known for the stuff or not, sold fur or put it on
pieces from time to time. Anna, who had worn fur for decades, still
regularly indulged in wearing it.

Each year the racks lining the *Vogue* office would be filled with it,
some items retailing for as much as $250,000, and *Vogue* published an
annual fur story, the same way it would reliably publish a story about
coats every August. Although the magazine carried ads by furriers like
Fendi, fur wasn't a must-photograph for business purposes. Nevertheless,
banning it would have led to a cascade of concerns. Does *Vogue* then ban
leather? How would it affect ads from brands who had licensed fur lines?

Anna's assistants felt that part of their job was to shield her from
antifur hate mail, but these intrusions on paper or in person never
seemed to bother her too much. So what if the PETA people were
traipsing around her office? If her closest and most trusted *Vogue* confi-
dantes could seldom change her decisions when it came to running the
magazine, a mob with stickers certainly wasn't going to do it.

In fact, Anna kept featuring fur in her pages unapologetically. It was like her to see the fur-related provocations as a challenge, the same way she did when her airplane seatmate told her he liked *Vogue* because Madonna would never appear on its cover. In her September 1996 editor's letter, when the issue had hardly died down, she wrote, "Perhaps this is the moment for me to confess that, yes, I wear fur. I also eat juicy steaks. If you are appalled at my political incorrectness, you should know that I, for one, don't see any difference between raising animals for hamburgers and farming mink for coats."

It was these very words that, on December 19, 1996, reportedly inspired a woman to take a dead raccoon from the trash pile of an upstate New York fur farm and ferry it in a trendy black nylon Prada tote bag to the Grill Room at the Four Seasons, where Anna was having Christmas lunch with senior members of her team. The woman—who wore black—got the maître d' to escort her to Anna's table. "Excuse me. Are you Miss Wintour?" she asked.

"Yes," Anna replied.

She then whipped out the raccoon carcass, which Grace Coddington, who was at the table, noticed was "frozen solid, stiff as a board, and flattened, rather like roadkill." Whacking it down on the table, the woman shouted something—"Fur hag! Fur hag!" according to *WWD*, and "Anna wears fur hats!" according to the *New York Times*, before running out and evading apprehension. Anna threw a napkin over the raccoon, and it was quickly whisked away. With her typical dry sense of humor, she turned to CEO Steve Florio, sitting at a nearby table, and said, "Merry Christmas." To her team seated around her, she smiled and said, "Well, that certainly broke the ice." The Four Seasons later joked that they were holding the raccoon in their freezer, in case the woman returned.

The following year, in 1997, Anna made an acquisition that would become a significant part of her nonwork life. Her friend Miranda Brooks, who would develop the reputation of being the only person who could tell Anna what to do, learned of a house for sale in Mastic,

Long Island. She couldn't buy it for herself, but told Anna, who had a weekend home in nearby Bellport, to go take a look at it.

Anna's Bellport house was small. It had a pool and a garden, which had been designed by Brooks, plus the advantage of being near Newhouse's home in the same town. Mastic was geographically close to the ritzy Hamptons, but, as a working-class area, also a world away. But the Hamptons, being a scene, weren't Anna's scene. On the weekends, she didn't want her life to be like the Met Gala; she wanted to get away from all that (even if she occasionally later hosted celebrities like film director Baz Luhrmann and *The Wire*'s Dominic West there). Aside from trips to the Tortuga Bay Puntacana Resort & Club in the Dominican Republic—an elegant hotel decorated by Oscar de la Renta where Anna, who actually dislikes cold weather, stayed many times in her own beachfront villa—she preferred to staycation in a paradise of her own making.

This eighteenth-century homestead in Mastic was, to Brooks, the best of American clapboard architecture. Situated at the end of a private gravel road in the middle of woods roamed by deer, the house and barns were "derelict," Brooks said, bursting with errant wisteria. The lot extended to the riverfront, and Brooks thought it was ideal for a pony (though Anna never got one).

Friends told Anna not to buy it. It would be a ton of work to renovate—plus it was *Mastic*. Anna would later describe the town as "white trash" in an interview with Kelly McMasters for her book *Welcome to Shirley: A Memoir from an Atomic Town* about growing up in Mastic and witnessing the horrific effects on public health of toxic waste leaking from a federal nuclear facility into the drinking water. Anna took on cleaning up the local Forge River as a charitable cause, and met with McMasters to discuss it. She made donations to Save the Forge River, hosted blue-collar locals at her Mastic house for an elegant fund-raiser, and marched in a parade. But McMasters wondered if her impetus for helping was simply that the pollution in the river caused her property to stink.

While Anna may have been bothered by the smell, she didn't care about who lived nearby. Once she was in the compound, she didn't often mix with the locals. As with the magazines she'd edited, she took on the work of transforming it—this time with Brooks's help.

Also English, Brooks had a feeling that Anna, though they never discussed it, shared a homesickness for the British countryside, and wanted the Mastic gardens to feel like being "lost in meadows and not pretentious and long grass." That landscape went with the English country interiors, done in a colorful Bloomsbury style by Carrier and Company, the husband and wife team Anna later credited with "turn[ing] a series of broken-down barns into a wonderful compound for my family."

Brooks convinced Anna and Shaffer to clear a wide path down to the beach at the riverfront. Seeing the bulldozers and the trees coming down, Shaffer "was irate and thought I'd ruined it," recalled Brooks. But once it was done, he said it was his favorite thing she did.

Anna also had her frustrations. Landscaping rarely delivers instant gratification; the hornbeam hedges were wisps when they were planted, and for years, when Anna did her walk-through with Brooks every weekend to look at the plants and make notes on what had been eaten by deer and needed to be replaced, she'd just say, "Are these hedges going to grow?"

But she indulged in carefree moments, like when she played baseball for hours with her children, or British Bulldog, a game of tag. She was still a lightning-fast sprinter. "No one could catch Anna," said Brooks. They developed a close friendship, which Anna would call "one of the great joys of my life," that largely played out in scenes like this at Mastic. Anna became the godmother to Brooks's daughter, who enjoyed packing Anna's suitcase for work trips to Paris.

For the most part, Anna deferred to her friend's suggestions. However, there was the instance when Brooks was designing the circle garden, so named for its shape, and said, "You could lie on the grass and look at the moon here."

Anna replied, "I am *never* going to lie on the grass and look at a full moon."

Anna was the rare exception who didn't seem to need such an escape to deal with the pressure of her work.

*   *   *

The fur-related attacks against Anna continued aggressively leading up to Christmas in 1997. On December 2, Anna, having exercised and wearing a bathrobe, answered the front door of her townhouse at 6 a.m., as she always did, to let in her hairdresser. But on this morning, she greeted not just her hair stylist, but also a rash of red graffiti—her townhouse stoop and façade were covered in paw prints and paint splatters. Before leaving to take her kids to school, Anna called Condé Nast human resources, and asked them to remove the paint before any reporters got wind of it. The crew that removed the paint—before 9 a.m.—used a substance that Anna's live-in nanny Lori Feldt said gave her a brain injury, causing her to sue. Condé Nast, having provided the cleanup crew, was liable, and settled with the nanny seven years later, in 2004, for $2.1 million. Anna was angry about the incident, but mostly because it resulted in Feldt's injury.

On Wednesday, December 17, just two weeks after the vandalism at Anna's house, PETA protesters returned to the Condé Nast building, but now there was security so they couldn't go inside. Instead they spent the afternoon lying down in front of the building. At night, they moved outside the hot new restaurant Balthazar, where *Vogue* was holding its Christmas party. They stood behind a police barrier with an electric sign displaying antifur slogans, facing a lucky member of the *Vogue* team stationed at the door wearing a coat trimmed with fur.

Inside the tastefully lit restaurant, it was business as usual. The champagne flowed as Anna and Galotti celebrated the year with their teams. However, with the graffiti incident fresh on everyone's mind, Galotti decided to issue a sassy rebuke to the protesters, and instructed security to present them with a platter of rare roast beef (though the security team declined, fearing it would escalate the situation).

But Anna simply carried on. Jones said, "It's just business as usual in Anna's mind that these things happen."

In the late nineties, *Vogue*'s covers underwent a sea change, perhaps foreshadowed by Anna's famous 1989 cover featuring Madonna. Out went supermodels and in came celebrities. In 1997, *Vogue* photographed actresses—Cameron Diaz and Uma Thurman—for two out of twelve covers. In 1998, celebrities appeared on seven out of twelve, starting with the Spice Girls in January. Anna knew this cover would be controversial. *WWD* called them "those very un-*Vogue*-like Spice Girls." Unconvincingly (and, if you were the Spice Girls, somewhat cruelly), Anna explained that she felt the cover acknowledged the "naysayers" because "that issue was taking a look back at the best and worst of 1997. Whatever you may think of them, 1997 was their year. It seemed the perfect cover to illustrate that point."*

Shooting celebrities with *Vogue* standards was difficult. "The celebrities weren't always the size that you wanted them to be to photograph in the clothes perfectly," said Jones, the managing editor. Noted Coddington, "They're not really model size. They're very often much smaller than model size. Models are six foot tall and actresses are usually five foot six or something, max."

Charles Churchward, *Vogue*'s art director, said, "There was a lot more work on the editor's part. A lot of the editors were so familiar with using models that fit the clothes. Models wouldn't talk back about clothes or anything else, and they didn't have agents there on the shoot trying to mess with the camera." But *Vogue* was able to on occasion have clothing custom-made for celebrities. And then there was Oprah.

The year 1998 marked Anna's tenth as editor-in-chief of *Vogue*. She had long ago believed, when she was just starting out at *Vogue* as creative director, that an editor had a life-span of five years, which meant she had outlasted her own prediction by twofold. And here she was, a decade into the job, producing better numbers than she ever had.

Vogue's October 1998 issue featured Oprah Winfrey on the cover. "Every now and then we encounter a personality who, like many of our

---

* Anna ultimately decided they weren't the most *Vogue*-like choice. In a 2011 *Wall Street Journal* interview, she said, "I'm not terribly proud of putting the Spice Girls on the cover."

readers, wants to do more than just turn the pages, she wants to live the fantasy. She wants a '*Vogue* makeover,'" Anna said in her editor's letter, citing other celebrities who got the *Vogue* treatment, like Courtney Love, who was de-grunged for her feature shoot. "The biggest thrill of all, however, came when we heard that Oprah Winfrey wanted to be made glamorous. She knew she had to lose weight, but she has done that before, and she promised she would lose 20 pounds by our deadline. She did, and I think that, as you will see in this month's issue, together we have more than succeeded."

Anna was open about her belief that larger bodies did not sync with her vision of *Vogue*. In a November 1998 profile in *Newsweek*, she said, "I just felt [Oprah] would look more beautiful 20 pounds lighter." And regarding the subject of her staff having to be thin, she said, "If these young women are going out to represent the magazine, I obviously expect that they should look a certain way." Asked how she would feel about an ingenious fashion editor who happened to be 250 pounds, she said, "I would have a problem with that." In 2009, when Morley Safer asked her about the Oprah cover during an interview for *60 Minutes*, she characterized telling her to lose weight as "a gentle suggestion," going on to say, "I had just been on a trip to Minnesota where I can only kindly describe most of the people that I saw as little houses." She continued, "I just felt like there's such an epidemic of obesity in the United States. And for some reason everyone focuses on anorexia. . . . We need to spend money, time, and education on teaching people to eat, exercise, and take care of themselves in a healthier way."

Anna personally spoke to designers about making custom clothing for Oprah's shoot. Paul Cavaco, the sittings editor, said the designers submitted sketches after getting Anna's directions, and then Anna picked the looks. "She was the one who said to them, 'Maybe you should do this,' and they would. I did not have a say in it. She really, really commandeered the whole thing," said Cavaco.

Oprah called Cavaco personally to talk to him about her hair. She wanted to use her own hairdresser, but *Vogue* wouldn't allow it. "Look, I think if you're going to do the *Vogue* experience, you need the *Vogue* experience," Cavaco told her. "You've got to go all-in."

She did, and Garren, the famous hair stylist, did her hair, though she brought her hairdresser, Andre Walker, along for the day.

For the accompanying profile of Winfrey, pegged to her role in the film *Beloved*, writer Jonathan Van Meter went to her house in Telluride, Colorado, where she was staying "for a week of hiking and dieting" with her friend Gayle King and her trainer to lose weight for her photo shoot. Van Meter asked if she'd dreamed of being in *Vogue* as a young girl. "Dreamed to be in *Vogue*? I'm a black woman from Mississippi. Why would I be thinking I was gonna be in *Vogue*? I would never have even thought of it as a possibility. That's why it's so extraordinary," she said.

That issue was the biggest in Anna's editorship, selling 816,000 copies at newsstand, outselling the September issue (typically the biggest seller) the month prior featuring Renée Zellweger on the cover.

Magazines that hadn't switched from models to celebrities got on the bandwagon in 1999. Linda Wells, who edited Condé Nast's *Allure* magazine and only put two celebrities on covers in 1998, told her staff at the end of the year that celebrities would be the magazine's new direction, and, "Nobody cares about models anymore."

Oprah's appearance on the cover was remarkable not just because she was a one-name celebrity with unprecedented star power, but because she was one of a small proportion of *Vogue*'s cover models up to that point who were Black. From May 1994 through June 1997, only white women appeared on the cover. In 1998, Oprah was only the second Black woman to appear on a *Vogue* cover, following Spice Girl Mel B who shared the cover with her white bandmates for the January issue.

Vogue had lacked diversity since debuting in 1892, featuring women of color on just twenty-seven covers through 1997. In 1989, Anna had been the magazine's first editor-in-chief to put a Black model, Naomi Campbell, on the cover of *Vogue*'s September issue (the year's most important edition) surprising male Condé Nast executives in her monthly boardroom presentation of the issue. "And at the end of my presentation after I had shown the whole issue and proudly shown my September cover, one of the people present looked at me with great surprise and said, 'Are you putting an African American girl on the September issue? Are you not concerned about sales?' And to be completely honest, that had not even crossed my mind. I had felt that Naomi was the right choice for all the right reasons regardless of the color of her skin," she later said.

Yet in her editor's letter for the July 1997 issue, which featured Black model Kiara Kabukuru, Anna acknowledged that *Vogue*'s covers had lacked diversity:

> . . . America is a country of people with varied backgrounds, many of whom are not above exposing their racial biases. In terms of fashion magazines, for example, it is a fact of life that the color of a cover model's skin (or hair, for that matter) dramatically affects newsstand sales. Although it is rare for an issue of Vogue to go to the printer without one or more black models featured prominently inside, black models appear less often than I, and many of you, would like on *Vogue*'s covers—which, no one will be shocked to hear, are designed to appeal to as large a group of potential readers as possible. This month, we feature a young, fresh-faced black model named Kiara Kabukuru on our cover, and I am crossing my fingers that Kiara will be embraced by magazine buyers everywhere—not because she's black but because she's beautiful.

André Leon Talley regularly sent Anna memos urging her to make *Vogue*'s pages more diverse. He specifically encouraged Anna to feature on covers and inside pages Jennifer Hudson and Serena Williams— women who would go on to appear repeatedly in *Vogue*—but Anna covered stars in the magazine only when she sensed their celebrity had reached a certain threshold, and the timing felt right to her. So while she valued Talley's suggestions, she didn't always take them. According to two people familiar with the incident, her off-handed response following one of his entreaties in the early aughts that she feature more Black women was to say to another *Vogue* editor, "Could somebody tell André that not every month is Black History Month?"

Two people familiar with Anna's thinking in the late nineties and aughts said her decisions about casting models and cover subjects for *Vogue* stemmed mostly from instinct about what would resonate with her audience, rather than feeling she should make special effort to spotlight people from underrepresented groups.

Many years later, Anna would—as she did when switching from model to celebrity covers—take a completely different approach to diversity in *Vogue*.

After Tonne Goodman started in 1999 as fashion director—accepting her job on the spot in her interview with Anna, who wanted an immediate replacement for Paul Cavaco, who went to *Allure*—her job ended up being to style celebrity covers. "What you have to do for a cover of *Vogue* is to present two elements that come together seamlessly. Which is the reputation and the personality of this celebrity, and the reputation and the personality of *Vogue* magazine," she said. "And sometimes they're not equal."

Goodman quickly earned Anna's trust through her directness, instead of treating her like an intimidating superior. "That whole thing you get over very quickly," she recalled. Still, she was too nervous to tell Anna she wouldn't shoot fur, feathers, or animal skins other than leather until she had been on the job for a couple of years. "When I stopped shooting fur, Anna would say, *'Tonne'*—because Anna was always wearing fur," she said. But Anna never forced her to shoot it.

Very early in her job, Goodman had run-throughs with Anna for a shoot with Heather Graham where she pitched a Dolce & Gabbana dress. "I don't think you should take that dress, it's not right," Anna told her. Goodman, who liked to have room to figure out some styling on set, hesitated, but left the dress behind. Once on set with Graham, however, she realized she needed that dress. "From then on . . . if she didn't want something on the rack, I would say, 'Anna, I'm just going to keep it in my back pocket. I'm going to keep it on the rack just in case,'" Goodman said. She also didn't send Anna photos from her set for approval. "If they say, 'Oh, look, I don't like the color of that lipstick,' you may be looking at it ten seconds later and say, 'You know what? I think we should change—' you cannot interrupt the process with somebody else's opinion who is not there to know what is going on," she said.

Anna's decision to feature celebrities on the cover of *Vogue* had impact beyond magazines. It inextricably linked the fashion industry with a whole new group of people who would become the stars of fashion and cosmetics ads, paparazzi-hounded presences on the front rows of fashion shows, and the general faces of fashion to the masses. It furthered the movement to ask celebrities on red carpets, "Who are you wearing?" And they would in turn court Anna, for *Vogue* covers, and for Met Gala seats eventually, but ultimately and overall for her approval.

While celebrities made overtures to Anna, she and her team made overtures to them too. British *Vogue* had set the precedent for a magazine having such a role; its staff advised Princess Diana on what to wear beginning in the eighties. Anna didn't personally style people, but her staff at *Vogue* could.

One such offer went to Hillary Clinton after her husband was inaugurated as president in 1993. Anna sent her a note asking if *Vogue* could help her dress. "This was just a way to offer informal assistance," *Vogue* publicist Paul Wilmot told the *New York Times*. "We read that she was getting barraged from designers sending in sketches and people calling. We ourselves were getting called daily about what she was wearing and what our opinion was. We simply offered to sift through all of the fashion for her." Clinton accepted the help.

Part of Anna's power was existing at the center of a network of people with public lives, and she maintained her position at that center by always having an agenda. In 2001, *Vogue* did a story about Rudy Giuliani and Judith Nathan's wedding. The magazine offered to help Nathan with her wedding look, and brought her some jewelry to choose from, but she wanted to wear all of it, which, to *Vogue* editors, "was sort of embarrassing," said Laurie Jones. Nevertheless, pairing people with designers had the effect of making both the people and the designers indebted to Anna, swelling her favor bank, and in 1998 she would ask for a very big one.

The cherry on top of Anna's spectacular 1998 was a cover featuring Hillary Clinton. Never before had a first lady appeared on *Vogue*, and her presence was made all the more extraordinary in that it was in the wake of the revelation of her husband's affair with Monica Lewinsky. Reported the *New York Times*, "By sitting for the cover of *Vogue*, Mrs. Clinton generated a storm of international press so thick that the *Vogue* publicity department sent it out in a binder."*

Like the Oprah shoot, all the clothes were custom. Anna called designers and talked about what they should make for Clinton, all based on their collections but also considering Clinton herself and what might be appropriate for her to wear as first lady. She'd say, "You know the dress that you did? Wouldn't Hillary look beautiful if it was in burgundy? And maybe let's do it in satin instead of velvet." In the end, Clinton wore a dark velvet Oscar de la Renta dress, to beautiful effect.

The week after the cover came out, Clinton toured New York "with her *Vogue* makeover," the *New York Times* reported, mixing with editors at various magazines and talking up her favorite causes. One night she attended the premiere of the Miramax film *Shakespeare in Love*, entering on the arm of Harvey Weinstein, who besides co-running Miramax had become a major Democratic fund-raiser. In a speech before the screening, Clinton lavished praise on Miramax, and told the crowd of a thousand who had given her a standing ovation how much she and Bill enjoyed watching Weinstein's films at the White House. As Anna would learn, being a political fund-raiser could be a very powerful thing.

---

* In fact, the cover story had originally been assigned as just an inside feature. As the scandal unfolded, Ann Douglas, the historian assigned to write the article, thought it would be killed. Instead, it took on even more urgency in Anna's mind, and she put Clinton on the cover.

*   *   *

Approval from people like Hillary Clinton was also part of Harvey Weinstein's agenda. But while he could donate his way into her good graces, winning favor from Anna Wintour wasn't quite so straightforward.

When Miramax started producing costume dramas such as *The English Patient* in the mid-nineties, Weinstein became obsessed with getting Anna to his screenings. Weinstein was desperate to win awards, and he thought coverage of his films in *Vogue*—ideally, covers for his actresses—would help. He also wanted magazine editors, but most especially Anna, to personally host screenings for his films, believing that would improve his Oscars chances. Miramax's head of publicity began calling people who knew Anna asking them to convince her to show up, and when she did, "it was a very, very big deal," said Rachel Pine, who worked in Miramax's publicity department. "Harvey would be really, really excited." Anna would get a plum seat, somewhere in the middle of the screening room, partly so that there could be enough distance between her and the three or four Miramax publicity staff assigned to monitor her reactions and report back to Weinstein.

Except that Anna was famous for never reacting to anything. She sat there and watched entire films with her sunglasses on, which made any flicker of a reaction impossible to detect. Rumors went around the Miramax office that the sunglasses actually hid that she was sleeping.

Weinstein got so frustrated at one point that he told a publicist to ask Anna to take her sunglasses off. Another publicist set him straight: "Harvey, you just don't ask Anna Wintour to take off her sunglasses."

In the summer of 1998, four years after Galotti started at *Vogue*, he resigned. He left for a new venture with the backing of Miramax and Weinstein: to start a magazine called *Talk* with Tina Brown, with whom he had previously worked at *Vanity Fair*. Brown had gone from editing *Vanity Fair* to being the only woman ever to edit—to mixed reviews—Newhouse's beloved *New Yorker* beginning in 1992. Galotti's replacement at *Vogue* was Richard Beckman, who had been a successful publisher at the Condé Nast title *GQ*.

Anna and Beckman didn't click as she had with Galotti. In fact, many on the *Vogue* staff weren't looking forward to him coming on. When he first arrived on *Vogue*'s floor to meet with Anna, "she kept him sitting in the waiting room for a very long time," Jones recalled.

Galotti had turned the *Vogue* business around. In 1998, it earned $149 million in ad revenue. The magazine charged the highest possible rates and sold the most ads of any magazine in its category. For 1997, *Vogue* finished the year with 2,800 ad pages. *Elle* sold the second most, at 2,100. The once threatening *Bazaar* sold 1,525. *Vogue*'s dominance was then unquestionable. But, of course, not unshakable.

In the spring of 1998, CondéNet editorial director Joan Feeney called Anna with some good news. "I think it's time," she said. "Let's put *Vogue* online." Feeney had the idea for the magazine's website to post images of all the runway shows and make them searchable, so users could find, for example, all the skirts from the Milan runways from the spring of 1998. Anna liked this right away.

But before they did it, Feeney had a very important question for Anna: Why do you want a website? Feeney asked stakeholders this question at various titles, and got a range of responses. Some wanted to use websites to give away ads to big print advertisers. An editor at *GQ* told her, "To show titties."

Anna's response was simple: "To make money."

But monetizing the website became a problem that dogged *Vogue*—and the entire media industry—for decades. Originally Feeney wanted to charge for content, even if it was a small sum, like $12 a year, much like a magazine subscription, but she couldn't find support within the company for this idea. Ad sales helped determined executive bonuses, and they didn't want to do anything that would depress the audience of their print edition and therefore ad rates. Also, the executives weren't exactly digital people. Newhouse hadn't used the internet until he visited Feeney in her office and she'd showed him how it worked.

Given that she couldn't charge for content, Feeney thought Vogue .com could make money through a combination of advertising, circulation, and e-commerce (taking a cut from any clothing sold through the site). Feeney and her boss, Rochelle Udell, had ambitious plans for Condé Nast's digital future. Udell had envisioned Epicurious as much more than a website. She drew up a business plan that included television, a print magazine, and a store, but it sat on the back burner and never happened.

To start *Vogue*'s site, Feeney and Anna proceeded with plans to publish all the runway shows. To further delineate the online content, Anna sent her a memo that said: "Joan, here's a list of designers we would never cover." Noted Talley, "The big designers got in, but I'm sure there were some designers that, it was just unspoken, they were not going to make the grade."

Publishing images of runway shows came with two sets of challenges. Just finding digital photographers, as the medium was in its infancy, was hard. Also, in the late nineties, images couldn't just be transmitted from a camera to a human being in an office who could easily publish them—people had to run the cameras between the photographers and computers, where each image was individually uploaded and then tagged according to what items were in the photos.

The second challenge was convincing fashion labels to acquiesce to having every image from their runway shows published to a website, which was where Anna came in. With the help of lawyers, she drafted a letter on Vogue.com letterhead, dated September 3, 1999, to send to designers asking them to allow the website to publish images of their shows.

The ask was extraordinary at the time. Many designers had never used the internet. When Feeney embarked on a tour of fashion houses to present Vogue.com and convince them to go along with her plans, she discovered that many of their offices didn't even have the internet. Also, access to fashion shows was strictly controlled, designers being understandably concerned about copycats, and magazines were only allowed to publish a handful of looks (usually fewer than ten) after a ninety-day embargo.

Despite constantly obsessing about what's new fashion-wise, the industry itself can be remarkably resistant to change. Roughly half the designers said no that first season. New York designers were the most receptive, and those in Paris and Milan the least. But Feeney proceeded anyway, with Anna providing *Vogue* staff to contribute reviews of shows—all of which she approved—and her public relations team to help with the website launch. Making her endorsement clear, she invited Feeney to present the website to the press before the spring 2000 shows in New York.

At the time, *Vogue* had a marketing campaign running on buses that said, "Before it's in fashion, it's in *Vogue*." Feeney, now officially the editor of the website, told Anna she wanted to do a campaign with the tagline "Before it's in *Vogue*, it's on Vogue.com." She thought Anna would reject the idea because it could be seen to undermine print *Vogue*.

"I love it," said Anna. She liked that it made her brand more modern.

As part of the launch, Feeney had T-shirts made to give away with the Vogue.com logo. She was told (not by Anna, but by another member of the *Vogue* team) to use the most chic and expensive brand, which was then Three Dots, and that it was "policy" to order only extra-small and small sizes, because that's who *Vogue* wanted to wear the name. Feeney said, "Considering and controlling every detail of the message was very much the *Vogue* way."

After that first season, designers started to see the benefits, beyond the publicity, of allowing Vogue.com to publish their shows, and access became much easier. The slide shows were, among other things, a digital look book of entire collections that labels could send to buyers. "We saved them a lot of money," Feeney explained. "We were taking better shots and tagging them and storing them at much, much higher resolution. And it was a very antiquated business by the year 2000. Vogue.com really opened that up."

Chanel was one of the brands that wanted, like Anna, to be modern and current, and readily signed on. For their resort show on June 7, 2000, Anna helped get the company to partner with Vogue.com on what may have been high fashion's first "livestream." The site showed the collection live, and as soon as items exited the runway, Feeney's team photographed and posted them so Chanel customers could preorder what they wanted. In 2013, Burberry would receive accolades for doing the very same thing—then called "see-now-buy-now"—everyone seemingly forgetting that *Vogue* and Chanel had done it more than a decade earlier.

In Vogue.com's infancy, Anna also helped orchestrate a deal with Neiman Marcus that would become routine, but was then unheard of, giving Condé Nast a cut of the profits of all clothing it drove consumers to purchase from the chain, with the store being Style.com's preferred retailer (over, say, Saks Fifth Avenue). Feeney made a fancy presentation to Neiman Marcus about why they should do it, but later learned they only said yes because Anna told them to.

"She deserves a lot of credit, which I don't believe she gets, for taking a wild risk to use her name and reputation to push a very unwilling fashion industry into the digital age," said Feeney. "In hindsight, fashion online seems obvious. It was anything but at the time."

A year after launching Vogue.com, Condé Nast made a decision that would have far-reaching impact on *Vogue*'s digital business. Anna would eventually find herself in the middle of it all, fighting for her magazine's supremacy, but at the time she was one among many who couldn't foresee how messy the company's digital business would become.

The root of the battle to come was the launch of Style.com. Condé Nast wanted to use it to extend a digital presence to *WWD* and its sister publication *W*, which was focused on a wider audience. (Newhouse owned both publications after acquiring Fairchild Publishing in 1999 for $650 million.) It was the same approach the company had taken with Epicurious.com, which hosted *Gourmet* and *Bon Appétit*: Uniting them in one site enabled the two publications to share resources while also preventing them from competing against one another. Newhouse's idea was that all of Condé Nast's fashion brands would exist under this "uber fashion site," Feeney said, which he decided to call Style.com. Vogue.com would retain its core specialty, hosting runway slide shows, but now appear as a channel on Style.com.

At the time, the Style.com URL was owned by the Express Company, the parent company of Express clothing stores. Feeney said she negotiated the cost of the URL down to $500,000, and proudly presented the offer to Newhouse.

"No," Newhouse told her. "Pay him a million. I don't want to be in his debt. I don't want him to think I owe him any favors." Newhouse couldn't foresee that, in twenty years, with postrecession coffers dried up, it was especially remarkable that his company had that much money to waste.

Chapter 18

THE DIVORCE

Anna must have known it was going to be a bad story.

It was 1999, and not long after she did the interview with the writer from *New York* magazine, she got a call from her former colleague Jordan Schaps, who still worked there editing covers.

An assistant answered the phone with the usual greeting: "Anna Wintour's office."

"Anna Wintour, please," said Schaps.

"She's not in right now," the assistant said. Sometimes Anna did tell her assistants, "I'm not here," if the phone rang and she was in the middle of something or didn't want to be bothered. But she wasn't the kind of person who avoided people—even if it was for an unpleasant conversation.

"Please tell her that her friend Jordan called," Schaps said, and left a phone number.

New York was doing a cover story on Anna, pegged to her breakups from two people: her husband, David Shaffer, and her deputy editor, Kate Betts. She was eleven years into the job. And when she was interviewed for the story, *Vogue*'s revenues were up 9 percent from 1998's $149 million. It was the perfect moment, at the apparent apex of her success, her icon status well established, for the press to tear her down. And in one respect, she'd made it easier for them.

Twenty minutes later, Schaps's assistant told him, "There's an Anna Wintour on the phone."

Schaps's goal was to convince her to pose for an original cover photo. She had sent over photographs for him to choose from, but he didn't like any of them. The best one was a shot of her in a fur coat with her sunglasses on and hair in her face.

"We all know it's going to be a piece-of-shit article, but we all know that a fabulous cover, that's all people take away with them. They don't read it, or they don't absorb it—they see it. I want you looking triumphant on the cover," he told her.

Anna was a visual person. If this argument would resonate with anyone, it was her. "Perhaps you're right. Let me think about it. I have to go. I'm taking my children to their tennis matches this afternoon," she said.

It was the end of the week, and Schaps had a photographer on hold to shoot Anna on Monday. On Monday, Anna called him back and said she would do the shoot if she could pick the photographer. Schaps said he couldn't agree to that, but she could draw up a list of five names and let him choose. They decided on Herb Ritts.

More than a year before Anna received Schaps's phone call, Shelby Bryan attended socialite Anne Bass's fund-raising ball for the New York City Ballet with his wife, Katherine. They sat next to Anna, who attended with Shaffer. Bryan had been to so many of these parties that little struck him about the evening except for Anna, whom he found both attractive and brilliant. He had only a vague sense of who she was, at that point, and was intrigued enough to call her and invite her to lunch. "I think that we both were fond of each other over a relatively short period of time," Bryan said.

Neither hid that they were married—their spouses naturally came up in conversation—and an affair unfolded.

Bryan was born in the town of Freeport, Texas, outside of Houston, and had attended the University of Texas at Austin, where he'd briefly been on the football team until it became clear he lacked sufficient talent. *Texas Monthly* described him as an "urbane cowboy" with "undeniable Texas bona fides," including being the great-great-great-great-nephew of the Father of Texas, Stephen F. Austin.

He studied art and history, the latter being one of the few subjects Anna actually enjoyed at North London Collegiate, and went to the Université Grenoble Alpes in France for his final year of college. Smart and driven, he then earned a law degree from UT. He worked briefly for Ralph Nader before enrolling at Harvard Business School, then cofounded Millicom, one of the first cellular telephone companies in the US, which brought him to New York. After retiring in 1995, he decided to take a job as CEO of ICG, a fiber optic networking business. By 1999, the company had annual revenues of $500 million, with a projected $1 billion in 2000. He was the first boyfriend Anna had with that kind of wealth.

Bryan was also known for his work for the Democratic Party. Between 1995 and 2000, he gave $350,000 to the party and its candidates. In 1997 and 1998, he served as the national finance chair for the Democratic Senatorial Campaign Committee, which pulled in more than $54 million. His friends included Al Gore and the Clintons.

Months after they first met, Bryan and Anna boarded a commercial flight to Houston. Bryan was splitting his time between there and New York, and Anna had something to do in Houston, so they traveled together. On the plane, Bryan noticed she was reading the same book he was. It was long, and he was already about a third of the way through, while Anna had just started reading from page one. Bryan considered himself a fast reader, but Anna was turning the pages more rapidly, and it actually annoyed him a little.

"I felt like she wasn't really—couldn't have been concentrating on reading it that fast," he said. By the time they landed three and a half hours later, she had been finished with the book for about fifteen minutes.

"You didn't really read that book, you sped-read," he told her.

"Well, I think I did," she replied. Bryan quizzed her by asking what she thought of a certain character. She said she thought another one was more interesting, but it was such an obscure character that Bryan now had to have Anna explain to him who it was. "I was really impressed with her intelligence," he said.

Once in Houston, Bryan could tell it wasn't her favorite place. "I think she prefers to be in Paris or London, frankly," he said, "but she wasn't a bad sport."

Bryan's job required him to travel internationally constantly. And he planned his business trips to Europe so he and Anna would overlap when she was traveling there to see fashion shows.

Bryan and Anna, despite their different backgrounds and contrasting accents (he spoke with an unmistakable Texas drawl), had a lot in common. They were both punctual. They both enjoyed theater, ballet, and the visual arts. Bryan also enjoyed fashion, though Anna never gave him advice on what to wear, the way she did her friend the tennis player Roger Federer. Like her, Bryan had "strong opinions." (He loved the opera as well, but, while Anna went with him, it wasn't her favorite activity.)

By the summer of 1999, their affair had been splashed across the tabloids. "I didn't like it. I was married," said Bryan. "The press, as it turned out, I guess was correct, but they were getting ahead of our relationship." With their romance out in the open, Bryan was able to attend the couture shows with Anna in Paris.

Delicious gossip column fodder, the affair played out on the sidelines of runways, and incited speculation over which spouse would get each couple's Manhattan townhouse (Bryan vacated his by mid-July, and Shaffer was said to want his and Anna's Sullivan Street house, but she kept it and he moved into a townhouse on Downing Street in Greenwich Village that he bought for $1.7 million).

Shaffer, on the other hand, was a man most comfortable behind the scenes. He still read all of Anna's editor's letters and gave feedback on the magazine that her staff often guessed she was repeating at the office, but even at parties he had attended with Anna, he'd maintained an aloof detachment from her world.

It wasn't as if Anna had seemed miserable with him. Toward the end of the nineties, they seemed to have a smooth domestic life despite the complexities inherent in a blended family that included two sons from his previous marriage. But Anna was reportedly bored by her relationship with Shaffer—which also began when she was with another man—and dazzled by Bryan, who had money, impeccable connections, and good looks. However, looks didn't seem to be what Anna primarily admired in men; after a lunch with Bill Gates, when Microsoft was on the rise, she came back to the office and told Laurie Jones how attractive she thought he was. Jones just thought, *God, she's attracted to people who are powerful.*

Unlike Shaffer, whom friends called "complicated," Bryan was straightforward. Though Anna agonized over how the divorce would affect her children, she initiated proceedings in September 1999. Anna knew, from her own father, how painful having a cheating parent was, yet here she was inflicting that same pain on her kids.

Vogue event planner Stephanie Winston Wolkoff, who developed a friendship with Anna, discussed personal matters with her and found herself in situations with Anna that other staff didn't. When they were in Los Angeles for work, she went bowling with Bee and Anna (Anna wore jeans and did put on the bowling shoes). Once in London for an event, she found herself in a hotel room with Anna, talking about Shaffer, in a scene that disturbingly foreshadowed the one in *The Devil Wears Prada* where Miranda Priestly reveals she's in the midst of a divorce and cries in her Paris hotel room with Andy.

One reason the divorce was hard was that Anna was the bread-winner. "Was she sad? Of course she was sad," said Winston Wolkoff. "Did she show it in the office a lot? No. She just kept going." Anna was remarkably good at compartmentalizing, which bothered some staff, but not Winston Wolkoff. She said, "As much as I had a personal relationship with her, as soon as I was in the office, it was like there was no personal relationship."

As Anna's relationship with Bryan intensified, she started, in a highly unusual move, shutting her office door to take what were presumably his calls. She was spotted leaving the Parc Vendôme apartment building with him early in the morning, wrapped in chinchilla that was obviously evening wear.

Bryan's appeal, the press reported, was partly his deep political connections. (When his separation from his wife became official, President Clinton called Katherine from Air Force One with his condolences.) But Anna had her own connection to Hillary (in addition to helping with her clothing choices as first lady and featuring her on the cover of *Vogue*, she had hosted a breast cancer fund-raiser with her at the White House). It might have been true that Bryan made her more interested in politics and political fund-raising, but it was routine sexism to pin the desires of a remarkably powerful woman on the accomplishments of her new boyfriend. "She had strong political opinions already," Bryan said. "I didn't have to do anything."

Yet people who were close to Anna were surprised she ended up with Bryan. He was smart and cultured—he would steal away from boring lunch conversations about Condé Nast to listen to Wagner CDs—but, Condé Nast staff who interacted with him at parties said, he could be crass and seemed to lack her self-control. Having grown up in a world that demanded a high degree of decorum, Anna expected that from everyone she worked with, but most of all from herself. No matter how short her emails are, she often takes time to begin with "Dear So and So." Bryan was the kind of guy with a sense of humor straight off the trading floor of the stock exchange in the eighties. Three people with knowledge of his behavior said he joked freely about things like how good he was in the sack and grabbed women's butts. "I've never done that," Bryan said, denying any inappropriate behavior. People wondered how Anna got through a day without slapping his hand five times. To managing editor Laurie Jones, some of his behavior toward Anna "was just not kind."

Tom Ford met Bryan on a pheasant shooting trip at the home of a mutual friend around five years into the relationship. (Ford has since become a vegan and stopped designing with fur, "but I was living in England, and people go shooting and you get invited to really amazing, great houses and it's fun," he said.) Ford, who was born in Austin and

had Texas roots in common with Bryan, said, "To me, he was very familiar because he was like very many Texas men that I grew up with. He
says what he thinks, he's not afraid of saying things that other people
might be shocked at, he can be very off-the-cuff, and kind of in that way,
the opposite of Anna. When I realized, *Wow, this is who she has chosen to
be with and he's kind of wild,* I thought, *Wow, okay. This is a totally different
side here I didn't know.*"

By that night in September 1999 when Anna walked into the studio
with Herb Ritts, she was in the process of divorcing Shaffer. At around
seven thirty, Schaps arrived, wheeling in the bike he rode everywhere.

"Oh my god, he's still on that bicycle," Anna said.

She had brought Talley along as her stylist. He'd liked her idea to
wear a simple white tank top under a light-colored Chanel suit. Ritts
shot some photos with the jacket on, some off. Talley, who felt his role
on set that day was to make her feel comfortable given the uncomfortable nature of the story, told her she looked great.

Anna had frequently sought Talley's opinion on her clothes since
becoming *Vogue* editor-in-chief, and he was happy to oblige. "It was
my moral duty. I thought it was a moral code that I considered a great
honor. As Grace Coddington once said, 'André Leon Talley's the only
person who's seen her in her underwear.' But that is not true. I mean,
she always went behind a screen or in a dressing room and would come
out in the dress or the toile and I would see her, not in her underwear,"
he said. (Coddington said she doesn't remember making such a quip).

Within half an hour, they had what they needed.

Anna appeared on the September 20, 1999, cover, a month and
a half before her fiftieth birthday, behind the words "WINTOUR'S
THAW" in chunky red capitals, the ends of her hair looking freshly
shorn, her crossed arms slender and muscular. She is unsmiling, with
a gaze that comes across as a challenge, as if to say, *You want to come
for ME?*

The story reported—likely erroneously—that she was losing interest in running *Vogue*. On top of the divorce, *Vogue* fashion news editor

Kate Betts had just left to become editor-in-chief of *Harper's Bazaar*—reportedly due to mounting frustrations working under Anna—after Liz Tilberis had died of ovarian cancer. It also reported something Bryan many years later called "made up": that when President Clinton appointed Bryan to his advisory board on foreign intelligence, aides asked Bryan to sit it out until the affair gossip blew over, but he refused.

"We were both unhappy with it," Bryan said of the story. But he never spoke to the reporters writing about his relationship with Anna. He didn't want to aid their credibility.

In the midst of all of this, Anna was working on the biggest endeavor of her philanthropic career. The Met had asked her to chair the Costume Institute's annual gala moving forward, because Tilberis was gone, and they had gotten used to working with Anna and she had proven successful. Planning that kind of event for an institution like the Met was a thankless job, with countless opinions about what should have been done differently and unfailing complaints about seating. But Anna signed on and gave it her all, bridging the fashion industry and the museum. Predictably, her association was all critics needed to denounce the exhibits as commercialism masquerading as art. Plus, brands coming in with checks meant society donors were on the way out, leaving wealthy New Yorkers seriously disgruntled. None of that concerned Anna, and after she planned it in 1999, the Met Gala would never be the same.

Myra Walker, a fashion history professor at the University of North Texas in Denton, had been a disciple of head curator Richard Martin since she saw his and Harold Koda's 1987 show on fashion and surrealism at FIT. While they were there, they came up with the idea to do a "Frock 'n' Roll" show. It never happened at FIT, but Martin finally got the chance to do it at the Met.

In 1998, Walker learned that Martin had an aggressive form of melanoma and had had lung surgery; knowing he was going to finally do the rock 'n' roll show, she offered her help. Martin said he might take her up on it because his interest in music stopped with Elvis. She moved to

New York and, given Martin's decline, basically took over the project—a challenging task, since Martin was both beloved and experienced. In the end, though, her hire would turn out to be essential in ways few could have imagined.*

Looking for a sponsor, Anna approached Tommy Hilfiger. The designer had dubbed 1999 his Year of Music, making Lenny Kravitz the face of his ad campaign and putting on two elaborate rock-themed fashion shows, one with Sugar Ray performing and the other with the band Bush. Hilfiger liked the idea of having his name on an exhibit at the Metropolitan Museum of Art. Plus, he respected Anna. He wrote a check for $1 million. Hilfiger was also launching a fragrance with Estée Lauder that year, so he invited Aerin Lauder, a young, stylish socialite and businesswoman who fit the *Vogue* image, to join as cochair.

The politics of collaborating with the Rock & Roll Hall of Fame in Cleveland and various rock stars whose clothes were in the exhibit were tricky. Prince wanted a cut of the Met's ticket sales. Madonna wanted her clothes to be in their own case, specifically not next to Britney Spears's. Securing Madonna's famous cone bra designed by Jean Paul Gaultier was, at one point, in question.

"I don't care," Anna told Jeff Daly, who designed *Rock Style* and many other exhibits at the Met, "figure it out. Make Madonna happy, make Michael Jackson's people happy, make the Beatles happy." Which was another way of saying: make Anna happy.

Everything Anna wanted to do, for this and subsequent galas, revolved around raising more money. How could she make the experience so desirable that she could eventually charge $275,000 for a single table?

Part of the appeal of having Hilfiger as the sponsor was the brand's connections to celebrities. The company booked, for their table, *Party*

---

* At her first meeting with Walker, Anna had told her, "If you need our help or need to do any research in the *Vogue* archives, let us know." However, as the exhibit came together, Anna had almost nothing to do with her, and, as with her new assistants who might not last, didn't bother learning her name, a Met staffer said, instead calling her "Myrna."

of Five star Jennifer Love Hewitt, who was allowed to bring her mom as her date. A Hilfiger partner, however, was encouraged not to bring family and friends, but to host glamorous people, like models from the Hilfiger ads. The same consideration went to people working the event, from *Vogue* staff to waiters. "It was a very photogenic group that had to be there," said Winston Wolkoff.

Vogue and Hilfiger decided to have Sean Combs, then known as Puff Daddy, perform, and he attended with his girlfriend, Jennifer Lopez. Also attending were Whitney Houston and Bobby Brown, Christina Ricci, Maxwell, Elizabeth Hurley, Gwyneth Paltrow and her dad Bruce, Steven Tyler, Tom Ford, Missy Elliott, and Mary J. Blige. (The *Washington Post* remarked, "The rapper Lil' Kim wore a studded pink bikini so unabashedly skimpy that it would have caused the windows in the room to fog up, if there had been any.") There were society types like C. Z. Guest, Jayne Wrightsman, and Nan Kempner, as well as fashion luminaries such as Carolina Herrera and Oscar de la Renta and his wife, Annette. Record executive Russell Simmons crashed without a ticket. When Combs performed, an attendee overheard Henry Kissinger remark, "Who is this fluff daddy?"

It was the flashiest and most shocking party the Met had ever thrown. The museum's traditional benefactors had probably never seen—and would perhaps never see again—a live rap performance. This was not a typical uptown New York charity event. As she had done with all the magazines she edited, Anna had cracked off the shellac and unleashed the future's much more hip possibilities. But Richard Martin didn't live to see it, having lost his battle against cancer one month earlier. His absence had been tangible.

The party raised $3 million for the museum. Anna, however, ended the night in tears. She had barely slept the past two nights. This was supposed to be, after a difficult year and a public divorce, her first public date night with Bryan, but he left early, and Talley saw her leaning against the wall, in her John Galliano gown with a thick caterpillar of red fox fur around her shoulders, mascara-laced tears running down her face. "It was not correct for him to make her cry like that in public," said Talley. "She was vulnerable." Anna's friend Oscar de la Renta escorted her out the back of the museum to her car. (Bryan said he didn't remember making her cry.)

It was the second and only other time after her mother's death that Talley can remember Anna losing her composure and breaking down.

Anna's new relationship was different from her marriage. She and Bryan never married and never moved in together. Once their relationship was public and they'd separated from their spouses, they settled into a rhythm of seeing each other on the weekends, often in Mastic, because they were so busy with work during the week. Anna would read drafts of *Vogue* articles on the weekend, but she almost never asked Bryan's opinion.

She returned with him to Houston on occasion, where she'd arrange to have her hair done, which struck Bryan as perfectly ordinary. "I haven't been around women who don't get their hair done. Where are they, those women?" said Bryan, pointing out that Anna is, after all, photographed frequently. "If she comes out with her hair all draggly and here's a leader of women's fashion, I think there'd be eyebrows raised."

With friends, Bryan liked to talk about how much he despised his hometown of Freeport. So one day, much as he disliked the hourlong drive to get there, he took Anna so she could see Freeport for herself. The site of Dow Chemical, the largest integrated chemical manufacturing plant in the Western Hemisphere, the town has a population of around twelve thousand, few trees, and tiny, flat houses. The only prettyish part, Bryan Beach, is named for Bryan's family. During their drive through the town, Anna was silent.

"Anna, what do you think? You're so quiet," Bryan said.

"It's worse than I'd thought," Anna replied.

They never got out of the car.

Anna's biggest influence as an editor and one of the most important people in her life, her father, Charles Wintour, died on November 4, 1999. In his will, he said, "I DO NOT leave a share in my residuary estate to my daughter ANNA WINTOUR SHAFFER as she is well provided for but I wish her to know that I am very proud of her great success and achievement and I am equally pleased that she has combined her career so happily with her family life."

At Charles's memorial service in London, on what was surely one of the most difficult days of her life, Anna was still a target. PETA left her a bouquet of flowers with a note that read, "Please also remember all the animals who lose their parents because of the insensitivity of people who still promote fur."

Anna's relationship with her father had been complicated. She adored, admired, and emulated him, but was scarred by his infidelity. He had opened the world of publishing to her and took her interest in fashion seriously. Her famous persona and editorial instincts were very much a product of being Charles Wintour's daughter, and now that staggeringly powerful influence was gone.

Anna would talk about his accomplishments and impact on her for the rest of her career, something she never did regarding her mother. In 2019, she told CNN's Christiane Amanpour, "He loved what he did, and it was so inspiring growing up in a house full of journalists and editors and always being aware of what was happening in the world. It made me love the news and it made me love culture. It was all around us and he brought what he did home and those kinds of people—politicians, editors—they were at the house at all times. And how lucky was I?"

Her defense of his character against those who emphasized his frosty demeanor was perhaps partly in defense of herself, maybe even her way of keeping her memory of him alive, and she would continue her methodical rise in his image.

After the *Rock Style* show, the Costume Institute was supposed to open a show about Chanel on December 6, 2000. But Karl Lagerfeld, at the urging of his friend Ingrid Sischy, withdrew support for it and had it canceled at the last minute.

It was a rare instance where Lagerfeld didn't seem concerned with pleasing Anna, who told *WWD* that, without Richard Martin, "there was nobody there to mastermind what the Met wants." Never mind that Myra Walker was filling in as interim curator and had already put together the entire show.

But after the show was canceled, Anna and Lagerfeld had a *froideur*, said Talley. Lagerfeld wouldn't talk to her on the phone, though she still wore his clothes and they exchanged faxes. In 2004, Anna asked Talley if he thought it was a good time to ask Lagerfeld to revisit the Chanel show. Talley thought for a minute and told her she should go ahead.

"It was almost like getting nails out of a coffin to get Karl on the phone," Talley recalled. But at last, he took Anna's call. She closed the door to her office and did what Talley said she does best: "She could get people to say yes when they said no," he said. "When Anna suggests it, the people are going to listen and are going to want to please her." The Chanel exhibit opened in May 2005, making Lagerfeld—one of the great icons of fashion—no exception.

Chapter 19

DOT.COM

Style.com was a problem for Anna. From its launch, it was set up so that she didn't have direct control over it. However, she didn't want Vogue.com—even if it was part of this non-*Vogue* thing—to fail. She also felt Style.com would be more successful if it had a more robust *Vogue* presence.

After Joan Feeney left CondéNet, Jamie Pallot was announced as Style .com's editor-in-chief on May 31, 2001. Anna signed off on his appointment, but she liked to have her own people in charge of things, and a little more than three months later her former accessories editor, Candy Pratts Price, then working on initiatives like *Vogue*'s VH1 Fashion Awards as head of programming, was announced as fashion director for Style.com.

Pratts Price said she ended up at Style.com after Anna asked her to "take it over," and she had strong ideas about where the site should go. Runway slide shows were no longer unique to Style.com, as publications like *New York* had started running them as well. "Everybody can run a bunch of slides," Pratts Price told Anna. "We should do a magazine for a Mac."

"It's a great idea," said Anna, who seemed to feel she didn't have to worry about the site so long as Pratts Price was there.

Pallot had the same idea. As it was, the site had become a fashion industry resource, but that was limiting because only a small number of people needed to reference look eighteen from Prada's spring 2000 show. But rather than work seamlessly together, some of the Style.com staff started to see Pratts Price as Anna's check on anything that might be too un-*Vogue*-y. "I think everybody felt that I was very just *Vogue* and not really Style.com because of my relationship with Anna," said Pratts Price. She was the only person from Style.com who traveled with the *Vogue* team to European fashion shows, staying with them at the Four Seasons. She knew how Anna felt about certain collections, and would inform reviewer Nicole Phelps. "I would say, Anna or *Vogue*, they love those chamois pants," she recalled. (Anna's primary interest in the site in the early years seemed to be its reviews.) Pratts Price often went to meet with Anna in her office to discuss her ideas. Anna put in phone calls and helped Pratts Price get access when she couldn't herself.

If Anna had ambitions to run Style.com at that point, she never shared them with Pratts Price. According to the latter, Anna's primary concern was maintaining consistency across the *Vogue* brand. "You're not going to say, 'There's nothing worse than chamois pants,' and then all of a sudden there's a whole issue on chamois pants. Wouldn't that be ridiculous?" she said.

If Anna objected to any content, the directive to remove or change it would often come through Pratts Price. One early video Style.com produced featured the Scissor Sisters, a performance art pop band named for a lesbian sex act. They were getting fitted for costumes by Zaldy, who designed tour looks for Michael Jackson and Britney Spears. According to two people, Pratts Price issued a directive from Anna to "get this gay porn off my site." (Pratts Price said she doesn't remember this.) Anna's word ruled, and the video came down.

Even if Anna didn't fully understand the medium, it became apparent around the time of the Jackie Kennedy show at the Met in 2001 that the internet was a useful tool for promoting parties. The morning after an event, people could click through images of the rich and famous wearing fancy dresses at the Met Gala or a movie premiere. After Anna transformed the gala from a charity party for sequined socialites to a celebrity event with mainstream appeal, interest in attending started to explode.

Stephanie Winston Wolkoff was officially *Vogue*'s events planner, and unofficially the "general." She planned all *Vogue* parties, including the gala. (Her team consisted of one assistant, whom Anna treated as her third assistant. If she knew her name, she didn't use it, instead calling her "Stephanie's girl." When her assistants weren't available, "Stephanie's girl" was summoned to answer Anna's phone or take the book to her house at night.)

Planning the gala began with creating the guest list. Winston Wolkoff would draw up a list of 775 people, including emerging designers, establishment designers, *Vogue* cover stars, and actors from big films. Then Anna went through it all, crossing off names and adding others. "Anna created the whole entertainment and fashion world that was on the red carpet of the gala," said Winston Wolkoff.

To sell the tables, Winston Wolkoff would send out personalized letters to designers, hand-signed by Anna, asking them to commit. "It wasn't as easy as you'd think," said Winston Wolkoff. Some people wanted a table for free, but her goal was to get people to spend as much as possible. People who didn't get invited called and asked to attend, promising a huge donation so long as they could just get a ticket. Some were designers who were just starting out but not big enough to be on the initial invite list. Hollywood agents also started calling, trying to get their stars in. "We're happy to take your donation," a representative from *Vogue* would tell them. "But we have no more tickets to sell." Said Winston Wolkoff, "You could have had a billion dollars, you were not going to get that ticket. . . . There had to be a reason for you to be in that room."

Representatives for the Kardashians called trying to get them in. "The Kardashians had zero style, and their whole reason for who they were was nothing that tied to *Vogue*," said Winston Wolkoff, a significant knock against them being, in Anna's eyes, that they weren't known for "making a difference." They were of the same ilk as other banned guests in the aughts—the Hilton sisters*, who never attended, and Nicole Richie (whom Anna eventually did allow in).

Once a table was purchased, Winston Wolkoff helped the purchaser fill it with Anna-approved guests. These guests, many of them celebrities, didn't have to pay, though many made a donation. Celebrities came with requests, and *Vogue* made every effort to accommodate them. If someone wanted a certain brand of tequila placed under their table, Winston Wolkoff would make sure to have a bottle of it on hand, but wouldn't put it under the table (she had a guest pass out in the bathroom once). They also wanted to smoke. "It was a huge thing, and everyone wanted to be able to do it," she said. Though the Met didn't allow it, that didn't stop guests from smoking anyway.

And there were some guests Anna would really go out of her way for—like Tom Ford, Karl Lagerfeld, and Harvey Weinstein—who she made sure were discreetly pulled out of the line queued up before the red carpet so they didn't have to wait.

Anna and Winston Wolkoff were terribly concerned over where guests sat, just as Anna had been with the very first parties she hosted at her house as *Vogue*'s editor. After Jennifer Lopez and Marc Anthony started dating but wanted it to be kept a secret, Winston Wolkoff and Anna decided to seat them back-to-back at separate tables, so they could be together but not appear like an item. Certain people had personal issues and couldn't sit next to each other. Others were competitive and had to feel like they had better seats than other people—which was one reason Anna never sat at the best table. "Every area had someone that was prominent enough for everyone to see around them, but they didn't feel that they were next to the bathroom," said Winston Wolkoff.

But Anna also wanted to mix everyone up so that business deals could happen. She might seat an emerging designer next to an inves-

---

* The Hilton sisters were successful, however, in getting into the VH1/*Vogue* Fashion Awards held in the fall of 2001. After *Vogue* denied them tickets, someone at VH1 let them in, without consulting the magazine. They attended wearing red satin dresses—Nicky's had a cowl neck and Paris's an asymmetrical hemline—and diamond necklaces. The amount of attention they got on the red carpet horrified Anna, according to a source close to the incident.

tor, or a model next to a cosmetics executive. She broke up couples on purpose to encourage what seemed like these serendipitous moments. "Anna wanted people to meet other people, and that's where a lot of business came out from," said Winston Wolkoff. "It's part of building the industry." They would seat a *"Vogue* socialite" like Aerin Lauder as an unofficial table host, to facilitate conversation amongst the groups of strangers.

A welcome guest at *Vogue* events, though he was somewhat a parody of a society person in New York at the time, was Donald Trump. Anna had known Trump since the early eighties when she was invited, as an editor at *New York*, to visit what was then a construction site—"not exactly my scene," she remarked—for Trump Tower: "I was amazed and flattered that Donald took it on himself to give me a personal tour— such was his pride in the building." Anna and Trump saw each other at New York events over the years, and he was welcome at hers for the simple reason that he paid, even if his Met Gala contribution was just $3,000 for two of the cheapest tickets.

But sometimes he coughed up more. On the night of April 17, 2001, Anna slipped into a silky orange evening gown, tied a scrap of fur around her neck to warm her shoulders, and went to host a screening of Baz Luhrmann's film *Moulin Rouge*, which she had previously honored by putting its star, Nicole Kidman, on the cover of *Vogue*. The night was meant to raise money for AIDS charities by auctioning off designer dresses inspired by the movie. The bidding took place after the screening at an event at the restaurant Brasserie 8 1/2. Among those enjoying the champagne, caviar, and steak frites were Kidman, designer John Galliano, Rupert Murdoch, and Anna disciples Harvey Weinstein and Donald Trump, who were reveling in her circle and attempting to burrow their way even deeper.

When a black Versace dress came up for auction, Trump and Weinstein bid against each other. The crowd started chanting, "Donald! Don-ald!" and he won with a $30,000 bid only to discover that the dress, which had severe boning in the waist, didn't fit his girlfriend, Melania Knauss. But the dress was beside the point. Trump was, by showing up and opening his checkbook, ingratiating himself with Anna in a way that would pay off with valuable publicity for his brand.

Trump and Knauss, who wore a white Dolce & Gabbana pantsuit, were pictured in a recap of the event in *Vogue*.

In the May 2003 issue of *Vogue*, Knauss was photographed and interviewed for a feature on cleaning out her closet. The story reported that Trump had "explored a presidential run three years ago, which would have made Melania a prospective first lady, a role she is surprisingly equipped for clotheswise."

In the spring of 2004, Anna tried to hire twenty-two-year-old Ivanka Trump for a role at *Vogue*. Donald encouraged his daughter to take it. "I think you should consider it, Ivanka," he told her. "Working at *Vogue* sounds very exciting. Anna's the best in the business. You could learn a lot from her." Ivanka declined, unwilling to "delay my dream of being a builder." Around the same time, in one publicity stunt feeding off another, Trump proposed to Knauss at the 2004 Met Gala for the *Dangerous Liaisons* exhibit, for which she wore the Versace dress that hadn't previously fit.

After the gala, Knauss went to meet with Anna in her office with former *Vogue* publicist Paul Wilmot. Trump had called Wilmot to ask him to represent Knauss as she worked with *Vogue* on an upcoming story. Trump, Knauss, and Anna had agreed that Knauss would pose for the cover of *Vogue*, and the story would follow her as she attended the couture shows in Paris that summer to shop for a wedding dress. Anna's decision to put Knauss on the cover perplexed members of her staff, who regarded her as one of Anna's tackier visitors.

The following year, Melania appeared on the February 2005 cover in a custom John Galliano couture wedding dress, approved by Anna and selected with Talley's help. The issue came out before Anna and Talley attended the actual wedding in late January, where the new Mrs. Trump wore a dress the general public had already seen on *Vogue*. "That actually was not a very remarkable cover," said Sally Singer, who wrote the cover story at the time. "It's not like when they did the Spice Girls or Madonna the first time." With around 417,000 copies sold at newsstand, sales were, compared to those featuring actresses like Sandra Bullock—and the Ivana Trump cover from many years earlier—paltry.

The only TV on the *Vogue* floor was in Anna's office. At 8:46 a.m. on the morning of September 11, 2001, American Airlines Flight 11 crashed into the North Tower of the World Trade Center, three and a half miles south of Condé Nast's Times Square headquarters.* Most people weren't at work yet, but the six or seven who were, including assistants and Condé Nast president and CEO Steve Florio, gathered in Anna's office to watch the news.

It was the middle of New York Fashion Week, and Lisa Love was in town to attend. When she got to the office at nine, Anna looked to her and said, "Lisa, what should we do?" Love thought Anna saw her as the resident survivalist, given that she lived in earthquake-prone Los Angeles.

"We go get the children," Love said.

She and Anna got in her car and drove as far uptown as they could, toward her kids' schools. As soon as they left the office, they were no longer just colleagues, Love felt. That was the day that bonded them as close friends. First, they picked up Charlie from his school in the Upper West Side. Bee was on the other side of Central Park, which was closed, so they got out of the car and ran some twenty blocks in their heels, Anna terrified for her children. Twenty years later, she would describe "vivid memories" of the park's "absolute quiet."

After the kids were picked up, they all went to Oscar de la Renta's apartment on Park Avenue. He wasn't there since he was supposed to have his fashion show that day, but Annette de la Renta let them in, and they all gathered in the bedroom, the news playing on TV in the background. Anna couldn't get home since access to her house was hindered by closures below Fourteenth Street, so she stayed in a hotel uptown until she could return.

---

* In 1999, Condé Nast had moved its offices four and a half blocks to 4 Times Square.

Meanwhile, at the office, the staff wondered if they would be allowed to go home. Eventually the building was evacuated. Anna started thinking immediately about what she, as editor-in-chief of *Vogue*, should do in the wake of the tragedy. With everyone scrambling and stunned, the fashion industry needed a leader, and she was who they'd be looking toward.

On September 12, 2001, Anna went to work. Anna always went to work. After she'd had a facelift at the end of 2000, she went back to work with yellow bruises still visible because she wasn't fully healed, prompting members of her staff to worry that, after major surgery, she was at work instead of at home resting. It was why in the early aughts her reaction to one senior editor being out of the office for Yom Kippur was to ask in a staff meeting, according to one person present, "Is she off being Jewish?" But this time it wasn't just about her work ethic. She seemed to believe that if *Vogue* stopped, if fashion stopped, if the world stopped, the terrorists would have won.

The message that trickled down to the staff from Anna was that 9/11 was a horrible, unthinkable tragedy, but the best thing to do was to keep going. *Vogue* wasn't a place where the staff felt comfortable saying they were uncomfortable, so Anna's team followed her back to the office, despite feeling completely traumatized and wary of being in the middle of Times Square. The one extraordinary step toward self-care that some of them took was wearing flats to the office, in case they had to run down the stairs.

Anna's assistant, Aimee Cho, spent most of September 12 pulling together donations from the *Vogue* fashion closet—T-shirts, jeans, pants, socks, sneakers—everything utilitarian that could be given to first responders. Meanwhile, Winston Wolkoff and her assistant were instructed to proceed with the planning for the New Yorkers for Children charity benefit, scheduled for September 19, that Anna was hosting along with New York's mayor Rudy Giuliani, who wanted the event to go forward. Some receiving calls informing them the benefit was still on were horribly offended, especially those who had lost loved ones in the attacks. The *Vogue* team just had to listen to their reactions, and try not to cry.

Anna immediately assigned a spring fashion preview story to Grace Coddington, meant to celebrate the fashion show season that 9/11 had effectively canceled. Within about a week, Coddington and her team were shooting the story with Czech model Karolína Kurková and photographer Steven Klein. In the opening photo, Kurková wore a white Calvin Klein tank and black corset and pants while holding a huge gold fringe–trimmed American flag, with an American flag scarf in her hair. When she wasn't holding flags in the photos, she stood in front of one, leaned against bunting, or had tiny flags painted on her nails.

In one photo, Kurková posed on the precipice of a New York City rooftop, a small flag in each hand, facing away from the camera and looking into an office building on the other side of the street. With Kurková teetering in her white stiletto pumps close to the edge of a ledge—even though it was about three feet wide—the crew became uncomfortable. On television and in the papers, images were circulating of people jumping to their deaths from the towers before they collapsed. "I remember looking, and there were people in the offices opposite us looking, thinking, *Oh god, is this another bomb?*" said Coddington. "It was very [much] in the front of our minds."

Anna never expressed concern about the photos or the tastefulness of this particular shot. "I think it had to be very fearless. That's what it was supposed to come across as," said Coddington. Like her shyness, Anna's ability to empathize is debated. Some felt that she was incapable of it. Her ex-husband, David Shaffer, around the time of the divorce, told friend Anthony Haden-Guest, "Anna has no empathy." But others thought that Anna did possess empathy—it just seemed like she left it at home, strictly reserved for certain aspects of her personal life. How on earth, her team wondered, could she look at that image and not make the connection, as her crew had done, with people jumping out of the towers?

Chapter 20

A NEW ALLIANCE

The year 2001 wasn't great for magazines, even before the September 11 attacks. After 9/11, marketers were worried about appearing insensitive and cut their spending across the board, resulting in lost ads at *Vogue*. The magazine finished 2001 with ad pages down 1.9 percent, and the January 2002 issue's ad pages were down 30 percent from the previous year. On top of that, Giorgio Armani pulled all ads from *Vogue* at the end of 2001, not because of 9/11 but because he was upset about the number of fashion credits he was getting.

Vogue needed help.

In early 2002, Anna walked into Si Newhouse's office and said, "I want Tom Florio as my publisher." Florio was the publisher of *GQ* at the time. He had been successful there and liked it, and had no interest in leaving when his brother, Steve, the CEO and president of Condé Nast, called and told him Newhouse would be calling to talk about him going to *Vogue*.

"Publisher of *Vogue* is the most important job at Condé Nast," Newhouse said, "even more important than being the CEO." He convinced Tom Florio to go meet with Anna.

"You're not going to like me as publisher," he told her. "It's not going to work. I'm outspoken, I'm going to get you angry. You're going to go to Si, you're going to get me fired—I don't want to do this."

Anna insisted he was wrong. "I'll be the best business partner you ever had," she said.

The only thing that Anna said would bother her was if Florio started running around with models. Otherwise, he could trust her not to go to Newhouse to complain.

Richard Beckman, the publisher Florio was asked to replace, was a former rock promoter known within the industry as Mad Dog. Following a sales meeting in June of 1999, he allegedly tried to force two women to kiss by pushing their heads together. One woman's nose slammed into the other's forehead, resulting in an injury so bad she had to have surgery, and a lawsuit that Condé Nast ended up settling for a sum between $1 million and $5 million. (Executives were said to be concerned not about the women but about *Vogue*'s health at the time, and didn't want to make a big leadership change, so Beckman kept his job, but publicly apologized to the staff.) Anna was appalled by the incident—she and Beckman had never been particularly compatible—but "she wouldn't have thrown down the gauntlet and said he has to go," said Laurie Jones.

Well before Beckman got to *Vogue*, Condé Nast had, like many companies, a shameful history when it came to its treatment of women. Lower-ranking women were outright harassed. In the early nineties, Steve Florio once called a young assistant into his office while he was with another executive to say, "We've been discussing it. And we both decided that you need to start wearing shorter skirts." They burst into laughter and the young woman tried to do the same, but felt humiliated.

Susan Bornstein, who worked on the business side of *Vogue*, said Norman Waterman, the associate publisher, harassed young women all the time. When he grabbed Bornstein's breasts in a meeting, she told him to get his hands off her. Newhouse may not have known about this behavior, but "he liked the bullies," Bornstein said, and rewarded machismo, though he didn't behave that way himself. "Si wouldn't do that. It was part of his alter ego."

Waterman's behavior was so well known in the company, someone who worked with him at *Vogue* said, that Anna was likely aware of it. But *Vogue*'s publishing team did not report to Anna. Human resources had a file on Waterman, the person said, and used to talk to him about his behavior. But they never fired him because of it, probably because he was making ad sales and bringing in money.

Tom Florio assured Anna he had no interest in working at *Vogue* for access to models. On February 4, 2002, he moved into the *Vogue* publisher's office. And Anna hadn't lied to him—as he would see, she was indeed the best business partner he ever had.

Early in his tenure, Tom Florio and Anna had breakfast. They agreed that if they were going to work together, they had to be honest with each other behind closed doors and present a united front when those doors opened.

Florio explained that he thought *Vogue* had an image problem in the industry. On one side were people like Domenico De Sole, the CEO of Gucci, working alongside designer Tom Ford, who would not start their fashion shows until Anna was in her seat. Other fashion executives would call and ask her opinion on what their designers were doing and which designers to hire. But on the other side were brands who felt *Vogue* was rude because if Anna didn't like what they were doing, she would ice them out of the magazine. Such was the dynamic: designers, celebrities, and models wanted to appear in the magazine because there was no such thing as a negative *Vogue* feature; under Anna, those chosen for the pages of the magazine were presented because there was something about them to celebrate with praise and happy photos. But if you weren't there at all—well, that was a big negative.

"We're like Harvey Weinstein," Florio said.

"What do you mean?" Anna asked.

"Everyone knows we have the juice, and everybody wants to work with us, but people feel we're aggressive, we're rude," he said. "What if we told people if you really didn't like something? Just the way you do it for Oscar de la Renta and you do it for Domenico and you do it for so many people who really rely on you for your input and honesty. What if that was just our approach? You would sit with people and tell them if you like something or didn't like something and why, but you did it like you were talking to your daughter. We don't do it in a dismissive way."

"Why would we do that?" she wanted to know.

"Because if you do that, then you'll be like the McKinsey of fashion," Florio said. "We'll have a value proposition that's so much bigger than losing business because of us not writing people up."

Anna agreed. But that didn't mean all of *Vogue*'s relationships with the fashion industry would be fixed overnight.

One of the earliest meetings Florio took with a brand as *Vogue*'s publisher was at Max Mara in Milan. He brought the magazine's lead market editor, Virginia Smith. As Florio remembered it, Giorgio Guidotti, who did public relations for the clothing brand, turned to Smith and said, "We give you all this advertising and we don't get any editorial."

Florio believed part of his job was to protect the editors. He never had Anna out selling ads and didn't want to outright promise that Anna would cover a brand in exchange for business. "You've got to be kidding me. You are the laziest motherfucker I have ever sat with," he remembered telling Guidotti. "You're sitting with my editor. You could pitch her on an idea and you're beating her up for editorial."

Late that night in his hotel room, his fax machine whirred. A note came in from Anna that said, "Tom, thank you very much for being so supportive and defending our editors. However, you don't need to be that tough on people."

Meanwhile, *Vogue*'s relationship with Giorgio Armani was being covered in the press as a delicious and dramatic feud. "With Anna," Florio noted, "when it came to the actual product, if you lost your mojo, she didn't cover you." That's what had happened with Armani. "It's unusual in the fashion industry because even at *GQ*, we would have covered him," Florio added. "We might not have covered him as much, but we liked him. We knew him. We had made money from him for fifteen years. Because the guy's not the coolest penny on the block, we're not going to drop them." (Editors at several Condé Nast publications said that they'd seen Armani try to hold out advertising in exchange for more editorial coverage, so the problem wasn't unique to *Vogue*.)

Then there was Azzedine Alaïa, whose clothes Anna loved wearing in the eighties and featured in *Vogue* early in her editorship. But in early 2003, when Alaïa staged his first haute couture show in ten years, no one from *Vogue* was there. Alaïa told the press he didn't invite them because they had been ignoring his clothes. He later said Anna "behaves like a dictator," and went on to tell an interviewer:

> When I see how she is dressed, I don't believe in her tastes one second. I can say it loudly! She hasn't photographed my work in years even if I am a best seller in the U.S. and I have 140 square meters at Barneys. American women love me; I don't need her support at all. Anna Wintour doesn't deal with pictures; she is just doing PR and business, and she scares everybody. But when she sees me, she is the scared one. . . . Anyway, who will remember Anna Wintour in the history of fashion? No one.

Though she never explained it publicly, Anna had reasons for ignoring him. Alaïa had stopped showing during fashion week in the nineties, which meant editors had to make a special trip to Paris to see his shows. And, Coddington explained, his clothes weren't getting into stores on a schedule that would allow *Vogue* to photograph them for an issue knowing the items would be available for purchase when the issue came out. Anna "didn't like to disappoint people and put them in the magazine if you couldn't buy them," said Coddington. Alaïa then made it worse by deciding he wouldn't allow *Vogue* to have any of his clothes or "photograph anything unless we did a full story on him, and he wouldn't bend. And she didn't really say anything. She just ignored it and moved on, as is her way," said Coddington. "And then the rift became bigger and bigger. It's like a bad marriage. So ultimately, no, he wasn't in the magazine, sadly because I love his things, but he was difficult. He was brilliant, but he was very difficult."

Fortunately, Alaïa wasn't a business concern, like Armani. Steve Florio, Condé Nast's CEO, and Si Newhouse had gone to see Armani before Tom Florio started. As Steve later told his brother, Armani had said, "You should fire Anna Wintour. She's over, she's not cool, she doesn't get it. Glenda Bailey"—the new editor-in-chief at *Harper's Bazaar*—"she gets it." That Condé Nast's owner and CEO would make the pilgrimage to Armani was a sign of how serious they considered the rift. Tom Florio believed his brother and Newhouse may well have seriously considered Armani's demand, but they didn't do anything right away.

There was one other thing working against Anna at this time. And that was a memoir by one of her former assistants thinly veiled as a novel.

One of Anna's two assistants around Christmas of 1999 was the kind managing editor Laurie Jones called a "girl of privilege." This particular assistant's father was a diplomat, and this particular assistant wanted to take a full month off for the holidays—which doesn't work for most bosses, especially not Anna Wintour.

Along came Lauren Weisberger, who had just graduated from Cornell. Jones and Anna decided to hire her. However, quickly there were worrying signs that Weisberger wasn't going to work out, the biggest being that she clearly wanted to be a writer.

Assisting Anna wasn't about being a journalist, it was about delivering hot lattes quickly in high heels. Very few young women who succeeded in the job successfully moved to editorial roles. Sometimes they successfully joined the fashion department, but the reality was that people who were fabulous assistants for Anna probably weren't going to be the next Joan Didion. They also probably weren't going to be the next Anna.

Predictably, Weisberger "couldn't get any assignments from us," said Jones. Weisberger was "a lovely girl," she added, but "not a great writer, poor thing." After being on the job for months, Weisberger asked Richard David Story, an editor who was leaving *Vogue* for *Departures* magazine, if she could go be his assistant there. He was amenable and she went with him, but when she tried to get published in *Departures*, she again struggled. Reading her material, Story told her to get writing lessons.

Following his advice, Weisberger enrolled in a creative writing course and, as could have been predicted, started writing a novel about what she knew, as writing teachers often suggest, and what she thought would be most interesting to others, which was assisting Anna Wintour. Her instructor asked to show her material to a book agent, Deborah Schneider, and she said yes even though she was far from a complete draft. Schneider called and said, "If she wants to sell this book, I can sell it this afternoon."

On May 21, 2002, *WWD* reported that *The Devil Wears Prada* had sold to Doubleday for a reported $250,000. When Anna learned about the book, she said to Jones, "I cannot remember who that girl is."

For the November 2002 issue, *Vogue* dispatched Annie Leibovitz, one of Anna's favorite photographers, to photograph the stars of the film *Chicago*. Catherine Zeta-Jones and Renée Zellweger posed together in twenties vaudeville clothing. The film was one of Harvey Weinstein's productions for Miramax, and he wanted the actresses to appear on the cover in costume. But Anna—despite the twenties being her favorite fashion era—almost never put costume on the cover; women were supposed to be able to buy the clothes *Vogue* featured.

Still, it was strange that this cover didn't work. How do you take a bad photo of Zeta-Jones and Zellweger? But even the team at Miramax could see that it wasn't working.

Working at *Vogue* for Anna, there was no plan B, only plan A (which is why, once after a box of Met Gala invites was mistakenly thrown out, chatter in the office was about finding the landfill they would have been taken to). So Anna asked for a reshoot, requesting Weinstein provide Miramax funds. "There definitely was a reshoot and it definitely was a fortune, and he was definitely asked to pay for all of it or part of it and he did," remembered Amanda Lundberg, Miramax's then-publicist. Certainly Weinstein was eager to stay in Anna's good graces—but in fact, for big stories like this where the inside photos were meant to mirror the film, studios often covered some of the costs, which could include erecting a set for *Vogue*'s photographer and providing the film's hair and makeup and lighting teams for the day.

Weinstein and Anna were developing a relationship that went deeper than Anna covering his films in the magazine. In 2011, he said, "When I wasn't doing so well, Anna would throw a party and put me next to Bernard Arnault [chairman and chief executive of Louis Vuitton]," crediting those encounters with producing business deals.

Still, "having someone on the cover [of *Vogue*] was a huge, humongous deal," said Lundberg. There wasn't another magazine that would do a beautiful shoot and celebratory eight-page story on a film and its stars the way *Vogue* did. Sure, you could go with *Vanity Fair*, but its philosophy wasn't that everyone featured should be celebrated, and the story could be snarky. Plus, Weinstein was increasingly obsessed with Anna's approval and having some sort of foothold in her world.

For Weinstein, it was an enormous advantage to be able to dangle Anna's name to woo actresses into his films and into his sphere. "To be able to say . . . 'I can get you on the cover of *Vogue*. I can get you a meeting with Anna Wintour.' That was very important to him," said Lundberg.

For Anna, who would attend the Oscars and sit next to Weinstein many years later, the relationship made sense as well. The kinds of movies she liked to cover in *Vogue* were the kinds of movies he liked to make—visually tasteful and starring of-the-moment actresses. In that way, despite being a reptilian creature known even then as capable of vile behavior, Weinstein approached his films the way Anna approached her magazine. Editors like Anna generally didn't enjoy dealing with Weinstein—but they each got something from the other. And Anna always seemed good at maintaining relationships with people she didn't like if she thought they could be useful to her.

"The sky was the limit. And if Anna wanted something, Harvey would pay for whatever she wanted," Lundberg added. "He perceived fashion as the ultimate acceptance. If you're friends with Anna Wintour that's just like, you've arrived."

The cover that ran for the November 2002 issue is simple. Zeta-Jones and Zellweger wear red lipstick, sheer black tights, and custom-made Ralph Lauren gowns, one in black and one in white, with fluttering off-the-shoulder sleeves. It was not what Weinstein had envisioned, but he got what he had wanted.

The first week of February 2003, *The Devil Wears Prada* was published. All signs pointed to it being big—Weisberger promoted it on the *Today* show, the first print run was 100,000 copies, and Wendy Finerman, the producer who optioned it for film, was known for the Oscar-winning *Forrest Gump*.

Yet Weisberger, while talking up her *Vogue* work experience in the press, insisted that—despite the character of Miranda Priestly, who tortured protagonist Andrea Sachs with endless, sometimes impossible, and seemingly trivial demands—"nothing was based on Anna."

In a profile by the *New York Times* media columnist David Carr that ran shortly after the book came out, Anna said, "I always enjoy a great piece of fiction," and, "I haven't decided whether I'm going to read it or not."

But along with many of her colleagues, Anna did read it. "No one was too excited about the book or got very upset about it because it was difficult to read. I know Anna read it and she was sort of bemused. She wasn't offended. She wasn't bothered by it at all," said Jones.

Friend William Norwich agreed that Anna "really didn't care" about the book even after it spent six months on the *New York Times* best-seller list. "I don't think Anna is as interested in the cultural phenomenon that she is as the rest of us are," he said. Anna has said to friends, "I'm so bored by me." This is one reason she doesn't plan to ever write a memoir. Norwich explained, "She doesn't want to stop working to reflect."

At *Vogue*, however, if Anna was brushing off Weisberger's book, her staff weren't. "It was an incredibly hurtful book," said Lisa Love. Weisberger's version of Anna wasn't the predominant one held by her staff, who were deeply loyal to her. Weisberger's obvious betrayal only reinforced their allegiance. And despite Anna's seeming indifference, some in the office had the perception that she *was* in fact really upset about it, which only served to heighten the chronic anxiety among those who worked with her.

Aimee Cho was Anna's assistant when the book came out. She had managed to read an early galley going out to media in addition to the finished book, allowing her to appreciate how the text changed "quite a bit"—she recalled the earlier version was even more negative about its Anna character.

"Everything felt very true to life, but through a negative lens," said Cho, who liked her job. "I always understood that [Anna] would deal with it, and she would deal with it well. I think at the time, the stress to me was more that these choices that I felt like I'd made in my life and felt good about could be looked at so negatively."

Cho had started assisting Anna in 2000 after graduating from Brown, where she studied religion. She had been trying to break into journalism with no success when she met Cindi Leive, editor-in-chief of *Glamour*, who passed her résumé to Condé Nast human resources. Within a day of meeting with HR, Cho was asked to go see Anna.

When Cho arrived at the office for the interview, Anna was standing up watching tennis on her television. Cho said hello and introduced herself so Anna would know she was there. She turned the TV off and walked behind her desk, and the interview formally began. Anna asked Cho about college and what magazines she read. Cho had been reading *Vogue* for as long as she could remember—she had read all of Anna's editor's letters and had her very first issue, with the famous bejeweled Lacroix on the cover.

Like many of Anna's assistants, Cho recognized that if you kept up with her needs—to book her daily hair and makeup, file receipts from the chef who cooked dinners for events at her house, get tickets for her friends to specific US Open matches, make sure she had that morning latte—she was not totally unaware of you. Cho never forgot that her job was to look out for Anna, but she also felt like Anna was looking out for her.

One Wednesday, Cho had to drop something off at Anna's house. On her way back to the office, while she was on the phone with Anna's nanny, two men came up and grabbed her bag. She and bystanders took off after them, but they hopped a subway and got away. A police officer saw the chase and took Cho to a precinct. As she was making her statement to an officer, there was a knock on the door and Cho was told that someone was trying to reach her.

It was Anna's other assistant. Anna's nanny had called the office to alert them she'd heard something bad going on while she and Cho were on the phone. What happened next was a process of calling police precincts until they had tracked Cho down and made sure she was okay. That they found her in such a short amount of time was undoubtedly the product of Anna's nearly military way of running *Vogue*.

When Cho got back to the office, Anna asked her how much money she'd had in the stolen bag. Cho answered, then Anna opened her purse, took out cash, and gave it to her. Then they both went back to work.

From where Tom Florio sat, *The Devil Wears Prada* was a blow to Anna—a huge betrayal. The magazine *InStyle* was becoming increasingly competitive, and *Vogue* had lost a lot of business—profits were half what they were under Ron Galotti—including Armani's. Any one of those things was reason for alarm; all three happening at the same time meant borderline panic.

Florio told Newhouse he was going to go see Armani.

"It's really bad, don't go," Newhouse told him.

Florio went anyway. He wasn't successful in getting Armani back at first. The press was still playing up his feud with Anna. (On October 1, 2002, in an item about Armani's show, *WWD* reported, "Anna Wintour and her team were present but seated in Siberia of sorts, off to the side of the theater-style stage.") Eventually, though, Florio convinced Robert Triefus, who ran Armani's communications, that the story had gotten away from them. "Why don't you give me just enough business to make it go away?" Florio said. "I'm not saying make me your number-one book. But I will make sure you're positioned like a big advertiser, even though you're only running, like, six pages a year. But I'm also going to go back now and talk to the editorial staff and say, 'Armani is a client. So everybody just sort of think about what they say.'"

Florio's pitch worked. Armani came back in the February 2003 issue, and the press quieted down.

In a way, what Florio was doing wasn't that alien to what *Vogue* had done in the past. Coddington said Anna never forced her editors to include certain labels. Anna sometimes told them, "We haven't put in Armani in a million years. Can you try?" But, Coddington said, "There wasn't a gun to your head or anything. You were encouraged and you were thanked if you did—not financially. I think that everybody has to be considered and, yes, if there's a problem, when someone says they're about to pull their advertising, then you don't turn around and say, 'Fuck you,' you actually try to help and to retain that advertising because it would be stupid otherwise. That's what pays my wage."

With the Armani problem solved and *The Devil Wears Prada* on its way to becoming a film, Anna turned her focus to her next big endeavor: cherry-picking the next generation of top American designers.

Chapter 21

MUTUAL BENEFIT

Some of the most important opportunities Anna found for *Vogue*, like Seventh on Sale, sprang from crisis. The CFDA/*Vogue* Fashion Fund, which minted the next generation of design talent under her watch, was no different.

The community witnessed this after September 11, when every remaining New York Fashion Week show was canceled. "Every single one of us at *Vogue* were obviously devastated, paralyzed, unable to fathom what was happening, and as I saw all this unfold, I thought, *What can I do to mobilize my team? What can I do on a tiny, tiny scale? What can all of us do that can be in any way helpful?*" Anna said. "What we talked amongst ourselves about is that we will not be defeated, we will go back to work, we will lead."

In the wake of the attacks, it was easy to see a focus on fashion as vain and oblivious to the tragedy that had just occurred. Yet for Anna, and many others, fashion at its best represents optimism about the future. In a show of influence, she used some of *Vogue*'s money and connections to put together a fashion show for ten up-and-coming New York designers. *Vogue* took care of booking models, hair and makeup, and other aspects of production, and got representatives from Barneys,

Bloomingdale's, Henri Bendel, Neiman Marcus, Bergdorf Goodman, and Saks Fifth Avenue to attend. Aimee Cho remembered Anna, as usual, seeing the collections in advance.

*V*ogue was inundated with calls from designers vying to be included, and, inspired by their enthusiasm, Anna wanted to do the event again. "I really started to understand more fully how hand-to-mouth these businesses are for young designers. It's always been tough; there isn't anything new about that. But when they have to compete in a marketplace with so many big companies, these smaller designers often don't have the same resources and are probably the last ones in line when it comes to factories and fabrics," she told *WWD* around that time. She approached the Council of Fashion Designers of America (CFDA) to suggest they work with her and *Vogue* to create an annual fund to help young designers. She got Si Newhouse to write a check for $1 million and placed her editors on the selection committee.

The CFDA/*Vogue* Fashion Fund is now one of the primary ways young designers are launched to lasting prominence in the American fashion industry, and—perhaps one and the same—how they gain access to Anna. By throwing money and *Vogue* behind it, Anna was now essentially funding the brands she liked (though it's true the winners are selected by committee, the committee consists of Anna and her people). Each year, the ten finalists become part of the *Vogue* "family," building their relationship with the magazine. Over ten years, that's a hundred designers who have become loyal to *Vogue*.

The first winners of the fund's top prize became Anna's darlings for the next two decades: Jack McCollough and Lazaro Hernandez, who created the label Proenza Schouler.

Hernandez famously first encountered Anna in 2000. He was in Miami flying back to New York, where he was studying at Parsons, and his mom was with him at the gate. When the flight attendant called to board first class, Hernandez saw Anna get on the plane. "Mom, that's Anna Wintour," he said.

"Who?" she said.

"The editor-in-chief of *Vogue*. She's a really important woman," he told her.

"Well, go talk to her!" his mom said.

Hernandez took his seat in the back of the plane and worked up the nerve to give Anna a note. He had no paper on him, so he scribbled on an air sickness bag.

"I promised my mom I would talk to you," he wrote. "I'm a student at Parsons. I'm not looking for anything, but I want to work for free, I want to be an intern, I want to learn about the industry, and I know that you can probably open a door for me."

He approached her in first class. "Ms. Wintour," he said. Anna didn't respond. He dug deeper and gathered the courage to tap her on the arm. She still didn't respond. "Now I know she was sleeping, but I was like, *What the hell? She's just straight-up ignoring me as I'm making physical contact*," Hernandez said.

There was a drink on the table next to her seat, so he picked it up and placed his note underneath. By the time he got off the plane, she was gone.

A week or two later, Hernandez got a call from Michael Kors's assistant; Anna had told Kors that Hernandez was bold and he should meet him. That landed Hernandez an internship, which was a huge deal because those internships were nearly impossible to get.

Later that year, Hernandez was backstage helping the Kors team get ready for a show when Michael grabbed him and said, "Come, you should meet Anna."

Anna, who always got to shows early, was sitting in the front row by herself. They walked out to the runway and over to her. "I want you to meet Lazaro. This is the kid who passed you the note on the plane," Kors said.

"Congratulations," she said. "How's it going? Are you learning? I'm so glad it was able to work out."

*   *   *

Their senior year at Parsons, Hernandez and McCollough got permission from the dean at the time, Tim Gunn (who would go on to become a celebrity thanks to mentoring designers on *Project Runway*), to design their senior thesis collection together. Kors gave them fabrics, and Marc Jacobs, for whom McCollough was interning, helped them find factories to make the clothes.

After the pair won the designer of the year prize at Parsons' annual fashion show, one of the judges, Barneys buyer Julie Gilhart, bought their entire collection. When Anna heard about this, she had one of her fashion assistants, Lauren Davis (who later cofounded online shopping platform Moda Operandi under her married name, Lauren Santo Domingo), call them in for a meeting.

The two designers packed the collection into garment bags and lugged it up to Anna's office at 4 Times Square, where they hung it on rolling racks for the meeting. When they walked into her office, Hernandez said, "Hey, remember me?"

"Oh my god. I cannot believe that you're the one from the plane," she said.

"I think from that moment on, she's like, 'Wow. The kid that I gave that opportunity actually now is in my office, completely unrelated.' It's like she made our careers happen," said Hernandez.

The next day, Grace Coddington called the collection in to feature it in a story shot by Helmut Newton.

In early 2003, Harvey Weinstein brought a television idea to Anna and Tom Florio. Miramax, as it tended to do when Weinstein spotted a better deal, had just screwed over Condé Nast by pulling out of a film event they had planned to partner on around the holidays. Weinstein decided to bring a reality show to Anna and Tom Florio as a make-good.

The series, called *Project Runway*, would pit fashion designers against each other in a competition, and Weinstein and his team at

Miramax felt they needed a magazine to give the winner a cover or other coverage as a partner to legitimize the show. His years of courting Anna enabled him to get show creator Eli Holzman meetings with her and Florio.*

Both *Vogue* and *Elle* were singled out as potential media partners, and *Elle* had responded favorably to the pitch. Miramax expected *Vogue* to be chilly, given Miramax pulling out of the film event, which was probably why Weinstein sent Holzman over without him to the Condé Nast building.

Once there, Holzman was taken to a meeting room with very high ceilings and a "stunning, I don't know, thousand-dollar floral arrangement," he said. In the middle of the cavernous room was a table for two. Holzman sat down and then Anna came in. An assistant followed with fruit plates for each, bearing a few perfect slices of star fruit, a few strawberries, and four or five blueberries.

Anna tended to take meetings in her office, but she may have been trying to make Holzman feel special because she had an agenda. She likely knew Weinstein wanted *Vogue* to partner with Miramax on this reality show, but she wanted Miramax instead to make a show about her nascent CFDA/*Vogue* Fashion Fund.

Anna and Holzman had a long conversation. Anna, who thought *Project Runway* was just a stunt, spent most of the meeting telling Holzman about the Fashion Fund. Holzman's goal was to convince her to do a documentary on it instead of a show, so they talked about how that might work.

Holzman did in fact think Anna's idea would make a great film, but that's not really why he was there. Miramax was more concerned that if she was able to proceed with her idea to do a show on the fund, it would compete with *Project Runway*. *Elle* was already interested in

---

* Weinstein originally wanted to do a show about models, but Holzman, who had seen success with *Project Greenlight* about first-time filmmakers, thought fashion designers would make a better show; he threw the bit about designers choosing their models into the pitch so Weinstein still thought it was a show about models, according to a source with knowledge of the show's origins.

Project Runway anyway, and Weinstein was just as happy to end up with them as with *Vogue*. Holzman was there not to save Anna's concept, but to try to kill it.

In the end, Anna and Florio passed on *Project Runway*. The concept was hard to envision and there was no guarantee the taste level would match that of a magazine that served esteemed guests perfect slices of star fruit beneath floral arrangements that could have graced a royal wedding.

That said, Florio was a little annoyed with the decision. He wanted to get *Vogue* on television as a potential revenue stream. The CFDA/*Vogue* Fashion Fund hadn't been set up as something for him to monetize; he respected that Anna wanted to use it to enhance the magazine's position as the leader of the industry, but it wasn't paying the bills.

Even two years into *Project Runway*'s existence, after it had become a massive success, Anna stood firm on her decision. Speaking at a conference, she said, "Resist any cheapening of the brand, however popular and lucrative it might be in the short term"—referring to *Vogue* passing on the show. "*Vogue* is not in the business of making entertainment out of the struggles of new designers. We're in the business of nurturing the next generation of American talent."

After Proenza Schouler won the fund's top prize of $200,000 and mentorship in 2004, McCollough and Hernandez were such darlings of New York fashion that they became the template for success. Other young designers believed that if they could just get in front of the right person—really, Anna Wintour—they too could launch their own businesses and succeed. Yet even with that $200,000, "we were so in debt at that point that, like, the money kind of came and went," said McCollough. "But what stayed was we got a mentorship with Rose Marie Bravo"—then the CEO of Burberry—"which Anna made happen, and that was a relationship that lasted for years and years. She even sat on our board and invested in the company years later. That for us was so beneficial on so many levels. Lasted much more than the money lasted, that's for sure."

Over time, McCollough and Hernandez went from meeting with Anna once a season to being her friends. Anna asked them to bring out the photo cake with Jake Gyllenhaal at her daughter Bee's fifteenth birthday party. They took Anna to party with them at Bungalow 8 after the Met Gala in 2004 (she left within minutes, declaring the cigarette smoke "gross"). "She's been painted as this slightly icy figure, so I think to the outside, it can be a little scary. It's only once you get to know her that you realize she's not that person whatsoever," said McCollough.

"She's full-throttle career and full-throttle family and I think she has no time for bullshit," said Hernandez. "I think maybe that's a little bit of the bad rap she gets, or whatever. She doesn't have time to chit-chat about what's going on and just hang out with people. She's dealing with her family and she's dealing with work and she's busy."

However busy, Anna has remained there for Hernandez and McCollough. In the beginning of their careers, they received tempting offers at European fashion conglomerates. Anna was the first person they called for advice because she knew about all the suitors and would be honest with them about how to handle each.

Investors regularly call Anna asking which labels to invest in, and she makes introductions, which was what she did in this case. "We were just so young," said Hernandez. "So she became in a lot of ways like our fairy godmother—we'd just call her up and be like, 'This is happening,' or 'We're running out of money,' or 'We need a new investor.'" Andrew Rosen, who started Theory, invested in Proenza Schouler in 2011 after Anna made the introduction.

"Where a lot of her power stems from is that she's so generous to so many people," Hernandez said. "She does so much for so many people that when she asks something of you, you do it. Not because she's this powerful figure, just because she's hooked you up and she's done so much for you that of course you're going to."

Some in fashion would argue that McCollough and Hernandez are lucky to have benefited from Anna and *Vogue*'s wholehearted sup-port from the very beginning of their careers. Designer Isaac Mizrahi enjoyed Anna's support for three decades, even though it seemed to wax and wane as the years went on. Mizrahi was forced to close his label in 1998 after he lost financial backing; though he eventually relaunched, he was left "jealous of others [Anna] paid attention to," he wrote in his memoir, *I.M.* Finally, at one of his shows in the early 2010s after the relaunch, he was waiting for Anna to take her front-row seat. After twenty minutes, it became clear she wasn't coming, and they let someone else have it. "It was a blow," he wrote. "I took it as a sign that my years as a couturier were waning." Mizrahi added, "For such a glamorous business, it's such a hard and arduous task. There are a lot of easier ways to get laid or get famous."

Anna's interest in designers can also be painfully fleeting.

Zang Toi received Anna's support beginning in 1989, shortly after she started at *Vogue.* "She fell in love with what I do. I was the first Asian designer that was championed by Anna Wintour," said Toi, who is Malaysian.

One of Anna's market editors came to see his very first collection, which included just thirteen pieces. She took Polaroid pictures to take back and show Anna, and the magazine ended up borrowing three looks. They sent two back and asked to keep the third, a bright-orange and pink baby-doll dress, which they photographed in Morocco for a story about young designers in the February 1990 issue.

Toi's clothes started appearing in the magazine regularly. The next month he was profiled in a story about "designers to watch in the 1990s," describing him as "small, dark, with an animated face and full lips [resembling] an exotic sprite." Shortly thereafter, Anna came by herself to Toi's 200-square-foot studio to see his second collection, taking notes the whole time. On the rack, she noticed a red denim trench coat with gold stitching and heart-shaped buttons.

"Can I look at the trench coat?" she asked.

"It's not finished yet," said Toi.

"It's okay. Can I see it?" she pressed.

She asked Toi to put it on one of the women in his office, wrote some more notes, and then left. Two hours later, the market editor called from *Vogue.* "Anna wants that trench coat as soon as it's done. Let us know—a messenger will pick it up," she said. Toi sent the coat over, and it appeared in the February 1991 issue of *Vogue*.

Toi was grateful for Anna's support. In fact, he found her warm. "She gave us great press in the first year. That cemented my reputation," said Toi, who started attracting a clientele of very wealthy, private jet–owning women. Anna even personally sponsored Toi for a competition for young designers in 1990, which he won, further bolstering his name.

Leading up to the spring 1991 show season, she went to see him and view the collection. "You should have a fashion show," Toi remembered her saying. "You are such a great designer. You are my favorite young designer. They'll worship what you do."

"I don't have that much money," Toi told her. Runway shows are expensive—designers have to pay for the venue, models, hair and makeup—and there's no guarantee it will lead to more clothing sales. Anna encouraged him to do one anyway, so at the last minute he rented a ballroom in a hotel and successfully staged his first show.

Toi's friendly relationship with Anna and *Vogue* continued through the mid-nineties. He recalled her always coming to see his collection a few days before his fashion show, and she never told him to do anything to his clothes. One day, however, she couldn't make it. Two members of her team went to see Toi's collection, but he missed their visit, which had been rescheduled for a time he was supposed to be at lunch with an editor from *Harper's Bazaar*.

When he got back from lunch, his assistant told him, "They loved the collection, they thought it was beautiful, but they told me two dresses were not very *Vogue*. Don't show them." Toi didn't think anything of it. He had around forty-five looks in the show; so what if *Vogue* didn't like two of them? Anna always photographed his clothes—and besides, this directive was coming from a market editor, not from Anna directly.

Toi said Anna didn't attend his show that season, but *Vogue* had requested seven or eight front-row seats. Toi left the offending dresses in the show. From then on, he couldn't get Anna or her team to come to his shows or to see his collections in his studio. For Toi's business, it didn't matter; the ladies with the private jets stuck with him, and "they couldn't care less what Anna Wintour has to say," he said.

The last time the two saw each other was at a Bill Blass fashion show around ten years after Toi had fallen out of favor. Toi had been stopped by reporters when Anna appeared. She looked at him for two minutes, saying nothing, and then walked off with her bodyguard.

Chapter 22

BIG VOGUE

Under Anna, *Vogue* had become the biggest, most valuable magazine in its category, and she had leveraged that position to function as the GM for the entire fashion industry. She helped John Galliano find financial backing in the mid-nineties when he needed it, setting him up to helm LVMH-owned Givenchy before Christian Dior, and recommended Marc Jacobs to design Louis Vuitton. And she was mobilizing the fashion world for the philanthropic work she hoped would outshine in her legacy what she did as an editor, the way her mother's lasting impact on the world was not her movie reviews but her social work. But there was always another way to be bigger, to work harder.

To do more.

In the aughts, the *Vogue* brand expanded into *Men's Vogue, Teen Vogue*, and *Vogue Living*. Anna started calling her empire "Big Vogue." Editing them all was "like planning a dinner party. You need to have the pretty girl, the controversy, and something reassuring," she was reported to have said. But not every dinner party ends well.

Teen Vogue arrived in 2003. Anna had asked Amy Astley, *Vogue's* longtime beauty director, to create prototypes; she made four over the course of two years. When she was working on the test issues, Anna went home at night with two books, one for *Vogue* and one for *Teen Vogue*. (Her staff had to finish all their *Vogue* work each day and then get their *Teen Vogue* work done, and sometimes Aimee Cho waited around until ten o'clock at night for that *Teen Vogue* book.)

Astley described her vision as a magazine for young women that was about beauty and style as self-expression, career development, health, and mental wellness—not about finding a boyfriend. Anna's best advice, she reflected, was to make the magazine very "you."

Teen Vogue was tested a handful of times before Newhouse committed to making it a permanent publication, though its two 2001 issues had only 123 ad pages combined, and it reached a fraction of the audience of the competing *Cosmo Girl*. Critiques of the issues were that it was too upscale for teenagers and looked and felt too much like *Vogue*. Bee Shaffer, who thought she wanted to go into journalism but didn't have a strong interest in fashion, was placed on the masthead because, Astley told the *New York Observer*, "She's obviously the ideal *Teen Vogue* reader. She and her friends are a ready-made focus group. They're smart and really sophisticated and clearly know a lot about fashion, but they're still normal girls." (Bee first attended the Met Gala in 2004 at age sixteen wearing a Rochas gown.)

But when Newhouse faced competition, he threw money at the problem, so *Teen Vogue* was treated as extravagantly as *Vogue* itself. Herb Ritts was hired to shoot the first 2003 cover with singer Gwen Stefani on a beach in Malibu.

Charles Churchward, *Vogue's* design director, went to the shoot. He knew that a beach shoot always included a setup with the person running along the edge of the water. Stefani liked to have music playing, but it was hard to do that outside on a beach when she was running, so Ritts got a flatbed truck to drive speakers blaring loud music alongside her as she ran down the beach, "like you were inside a disco," said Churchward. "And it was like, 'Oh my god. Wow. How have we gotten this far?'"

They got that far because Condé Nast was at peak excess in the early 2000s. Churchward said, "It just all grew, because, like, we wanted more, we wanted it to be better, and we were successful, but sooner or later, that takes a toll."

In what would prove a miscalculation, Anna poured more energy into her *Vogue* spinoffs than she did into *Vogue*'s digital presence on Style.com. But Astley noted that she saw the digital future coming. *Teen Vogue* was the first title at Condé Nast to have a social media manager.

When Anna was planning the 2003 Met Gala, which celebrated the Costume Institute exhibition *Goddess: The Classical Mode*, concerning the influence of classical dress on contemporary fashion, she probably didn't expect her cochair Tom Ford to have such strong opinions.

Ford was the lead designer at Gucci, and agreed to cochair and sponsor for a few million dollars. In those days, "money was unlimited," Ford said. "You did it for promotion of the brand, you did it because it was Anna."

Ford would have liked to take over all the planning, and Anna did let him get deeply involved, which was an experience that bonded them as personal friends. Ford wanted to approve the food and the table settings, so Stephanie Winston Wolkoff arranged to fly the chef to him in London for a demo. Ford said, "What we served had to look right on the plate together. I not only had to see it plated, but if the colors didn't work together of the vegetables and the whatever, they had to go. I remember she commented on that. It was like, 'But those are carrots.' And I was like, 'I know, but they're orange, they can't go next to that color, that doesn't look good. It's just not going to happen.'"

Anna was also particular about the food, though at tastings, she barely tasted. "She would make sure it looked beautiful," said Winston Wolkoff. She banned chives, garlic, onions, and parsley, which get stuck in your teeth and make your breath smell. Also for odor-related reasons, fish was never served (once, there was a cold lobster salad). Anna's favorite foods were lamb chops, steak, and French-style green beans. But the dish she seemed to love serving at *Vogue* events over any other was chicken pot pie, ideal to Anna because it's a one-course meal that has everything (protein, vegetables, etc.). For dessert, she loved crème brûlée.

Ford was particular about other aspects, including waiters' hair being perfectly slicked back (hiring waiters was "like a casting call," Winston Wolkoff said, but Anna trusted her to select the right fifty people). Winston Wolkoff had to take gum from their mouths the night of the party. Anna was also always concerned about the behavior of everyone who might be there, from guests to waitstaff to performers, Winston Wolkoff said. (If a guest, in Anna's eyes, was badly behaved, that could affect their prospects for *Vogue* coverage down the line, said another *Vogue* editor.)

Anna attended that year's gala wearing a slim, silky white gown by John Galliano, with a dramatic feathered jacket for her walk into the museum, up bare granite steps, because the entry hadn't yet become a proper red carpet. Anna, who was "militant" at the party, said Winston Wolkoff, moved people along if they spent more than twenty seconds talking to her as she greeted each guest at the top of the stairs. About 80 percent of the guests who followed would be wearing something she had approved (most stars welcomed the help getting dressed because it's free styling). Her and Ford's other cochair was Nicole Kidman, who attended wearing a dress by Ford himself and arrived on the arm of Adrien Brody. Both had won top Oscars (she for best actress, he for best actor), and "everybody went crazy," said Andrew Bolton, a Costume Institute curator who was attending the gala for the first time. Bolton would later become the chief curator in charge of the whole depart-ment, but that night, "I must have looked so out of place, such a newbie, because an actress asked me to get her a glass of wine and she thought I was a waiter," he said. "I must have looked really uncomfortable."

*M*en's *Vogue* was the kind of magazine that could only have been born in the fertile advertising climate that would soon feel prehistoric.

Publishers like Florio could sell so much advertising in the early and mid-aughts that it made perfect sense for *Vogue* to publish a supplement about men's fashion that could be sold to a men's brand. Jay Fielden, *Vogue*'s arts editor under Anna, edited a few of these supplements, which attached to *Vogue* and featured covers of celebrities like actor Colin Farrell and soccer star David Beckham.

Their success got Newhouse thinking, Florio recalled, that there could be a men's magazine targeting the highest end of the market, which the category's dominant titles, Hearst's *Esquire* and Condé Nast's *GQ*, weren't quite doing. *Men's Vogue*, Newhouse and Fielden thought, could reach men with disposable income who liked fancy watches, nice cars, and bespoke suits, who might own a skiing cabin with a dead animal's head on the wall.

Fielden made a forty-page mock-up of the idea to show to Newhouse, with Anna's full support. In early 2005, Newhouse greenlit the fall launch of *Men's Vogue*, with Anna serving as editorial director and Fielden as editor-in-chief—but even with Fielden ostensibly in charge, there was no question whose magazine it was.

Anna discussed *Men's Vogue* with Shelby Bryan on a trip to New Zealand, where they stayed just three days, for her stepson's wedding. "I told her it was a foolish thing to do," Bryan said.

Anna ran *Men's Vogue* the same way she ran *Vogue* and *Teen Vogue*, and was especially involved in the beginning. She took home the book every night and interviewed potential staffers herself to assess their pedigree for the *Vogue* brand. She approved every caption, photo, and piece of clothing that appeared. As time went by, she became less and less hands-on (not that she was ever hands-*off*).

The staff never observed a power struggle between her and Fielden. Then again, there was also something huge working in Fielden's favor: he was a straight man. There weren't many straight men in Anna's world, and from her early career days she seemed to turn on her signature flirtatious charm in their presence.

"She adored Jay. She likes the boys," said Jones, who also worked on *Men's Vogue*. Fielden also showed up to work well-dressed, had taste, and fully respected Anna as an editor.

For Anna, *Men's Vogue* wasn't just a business opportunity or power grab; it was *fun*, even if she didn't care deeply about men's suiting. It was a departure from the thing she had been chained to for almost two decades. And Fielden, who came to *Vogue* from the *New Yorker*, ensured it carried the appropriate amount of prestige and intellectual heft. Whereas Anna never ran critical stories in *Vogue*, she decided that in *Men's Vogue* she and Fielden could, which enabled them to take a weightier journalistic approach to topics like politics.

Anna and Fielden knew from the beginning that people were going to laugh at *Men's Vogue* for the same reasons they laughed at the movie *Zoolander*. Though gender fluid dressing would later become mainstream, at the time, what even *was* high-end men's fashion, for the target reader? Lace tank tops? Judging by a lot of what came down the runways at Men's Fashion Week shows in Paris and London, cutting-edge men's fashion didn't have broad appeal.

But that's not what Anna wanted to feature, not because it was uninteresting to her, but because there wasn't a big enough audience. The *Men's Vogue* reader was "somebody who's really comfortable with strong women, loves being a father—like, a whole new male sensibility," said Tom Florio. "Their wives worked. So we wanted to create this very high-end magazine for [men who] were involved in the decoration of the house. . . . And I just don't think anybody got it other than me and Anna."

Nonetheless, the New York media world was ruthless in its coverage of *Men's Vogue*. "With George Clooney on the cover and Gucci sprinkling the pages," *Gawker* wrote shortly before the magazine's official debut, "the new title aims to speak at a male demographic not yet realized: The man who has it all, but still aspires to be a knicker-wearing fop toting a big rifle and a dead quail or pheasant or whatever."

At the end of the day on September 8, 2005, Anna called Fielden into her office to discuss the next morning's *Today* show segment about *Men's Vogue*. As part of the magazine's launch, they had nabbed a prime slot with host Matt Lauer. Anna wanted to make sure Fielden felt comfortable before they faced a live morning show interview together.

"I think you just make the point that we're trying to do something different for this kind of guy," she said.

The next morning, they met at NBC's studios around 6 a.m. In the greenroom, Anna seemed anxious. Public speaking and television appearances often made her nervous, but she always stood her ground and did them anyway. Nevertheless, her voice shook when she spoke, she clasped her hands, and she tucked her chin toward her collarbones.

Finally they went on the air. Lauer opened by posing the question, "Will men care?"

Anna and Fielden talked about their desired audience ("someone with grown-up taste") and the topics *Men's Vogue* would cover ("there's hunting, there's food, there's wine, there's golf, there's sports"). Then Lauer turned to her and said, "Anna, this is a weird topic to come up in conjunction with this, but sexuality sometimes is brought up when they talk about magazines like this. There is a perception, I think, in some cases, that some of the men's magazines have begun to cater to a gay readership."

"Right," she said.

"And so, what are your thoughts on that, and how do you then look at that in terms of this magazine?"

Anna said, "Well, I agree with that, I think that a lot of the men's magazines are targeted towards gay men. And obviously that's more of what we call an industry of fashion customer. But I think a lot of straight men are quite disconnected from some of the fashion that they see on the runway. And again, that's something that Jay, I think, has very successfully addressed in *Men's Vogue*, that this is reality-based fashion, this is fashion for men like yourself, Matt."

It was the kind of thing she would probably never say fifteen years later; the *Men's Vogue* staff were surprised that she said it even then. Lauer had clearly baited her. Even if his question made sense given the conversation around *Men's Vogue*, it was strange to pose on a morning show. But given Condé Nast's fear that men would look at it and think it was gay and not pick it up, the *Men's Vogue* team figured she probably felt like she had no choice.

Anna did occasionally express concern about *Men's Vogue*'s stories looking "too gay," and tended to prefer women appearing in shoots alongside men. But while some were quick to see her as homophobic, others thought she was using politically incorrect language to zero in on a certain point of view. Some staff thought her concern was unnecessary, given that the magazine was staffed—like *Vogue* and Condé more broadly—mostly by white straight people who could be trusted to uphold that perspective. It made for splashy headlines but was unsurprising when *Men's Vogue* rejected a Marc Jacobs Men's ad shot by Juergen Teller featuring two men, Dick Page and James Gibbs, kissing.

Despite the endless mirth over *Men's Vogue* in the New York media world, the magazine did well. In her oversight of editorial, she dealt with some of the same problems *Vogue* did when it came to celebrities.

In 2007, Fielden had booked actor Owen Wilson and director Wes Anderson for a shoot that was supposed to be for the cover. However, on location at Coney Island, Wilson showed up hours late, then spent his first hour swimming in the ocean, which limited the time they had to get the pictures. When the story of Wilson's behavior got back to Anna, she and Fielden argued about whether any of the photos were good enough for a cover. Fielden believed they were. Anna wasn't sure.

By that time, reverting on a celebrity cover wasn't done. Hollywood and its publicists were powerful; it was up to them to dole out access to stars, and editors didn't want to piss them off. But Anna bought herself some leeway by never explicitly guaranteeing a cover. If she was going to lend the prestige of *Vogue* to someone, she wanted them to play by her rules.

Plus, *Men's Vogue* didn't have a problem with access. Celebrities, other than *Daily Show* host Jon Stewart, generally wanted to appear in the magazine or on its cover. (Stewart had turned down a cover offer repeatedly because he felt *Men's Vogue* was, as a concept, ridiculous.)

And *Men's Vogue*'s covers were, compared to *Vogue*, diverse. Denzel Washington and Will Smith appeared on back-to-back covers in 2007. Anna knew it was important to feature Black cover subjects, according to one person familiar with her thinking, but she also thought twice about doing it, as she had previously indicated to readers in that July 1997 cover letter. "Black people don't sell," this person remembered her saying, regarding *Men's Vogue* covers. It was a statement that editors like herself sometimes heard in high-level meetings; the company had provided her and other editors-in-chief with research and newsstand sales data for many years, and expected them to make editorial choices accordingly.

Harvey Weinstein himself kept tabs on *Men's Vogue*, maybe because he knew it was important to Anna. One Sunday night in 2007, he wrote her a suck-up email that said, "After reading *Men's Vogue*, I became interested in Peter Blake's work as an artist and Sebastian Koch as an actor in one of my movies. You're definitely influencing my work and my life."

But as much as Anna wanted stars on her covers, she needed the partnership to be respectful, for those being photographed to take it as seriously as her staff did. She reduced the Wilson/Anderson shoot to an inside story.* Some saw it as a power move, but for those interested in getting their clients into one of her magazines, the message was clear: they'd need to behave.

Anna continued to do what she could to help *Men's Vogue*'s publishing team succeed. She kept track of which labels they were chasing, and the strategies for reeling in their ad dollars. She never went on meetings with the sales team, and she never asked clients to confirm their buys, but she would encourage advertising with conversations along the lines of "We're so proud of what *Men's Vogue* is doing. We'd really appreciate your support." And her overtures worked.

As *Vogue* grew, so did Anna's celebrity. In May of 2005, news broke that Meryl Streep would play Miranda Priestly, the Anna character from *The Devil Wears Prada*, in the feature film.

Director David Frankel was adamant that he wouldn't participate in an Anna Wintour takedown. "Anna Wintour does extraordinary work and this is going to be a love letter to working women who do excellent work," he told the studio. He wanted the film to portray "the sacrifices you have to make to do that, and one of the sacrifices is not being so

---

*   Ralph Lauren ended up on the cover of that issue.

nice. If that's what it takes, that's what it takes." That, of course, was not how the book framed things.

The studio insisted they weren't doing "the Anna Wintour story," and Streep insisted she wasn't playing Anna Wintour. Frankel said Streep actually based her character on her experiences with actor/director Clint Eastwood and director Mike Nichols, saying, "The fact that Clint Eastwood didn't raise his voice and Anna Wintour never raises her voice, you can find parallels." But no matter what Frankel said, Anna was—as she was for the book—undeniably the inspiration. The film's production designer even sneaked into the Condé Nast building to take pictures of Anna's office in order to replicate it.

Right after Streep signed on, she bumped into designer Isaac Mizrahi and said, "I agreed to play Anna Wintour. Am I crazy?" She asked Mizrahi to look at the script, but before he agreed, he went to lunch with Anna to make sure she wouldn't feel betrayed if he helped with the movie. "[S]he had the opposite reaction to what I expected. She seemed delighted and told me not to hesitate," he recalled in his memoir.

Frankel found other designers to read the script and offer feedback, but they only agreed to do so under absolute secrecy because they were so scared of Anna. He knew Naomi Campbell from a previous project, and got her to commit to a role, but she then mysteriously bailed. Gisele Bündchen ended up as the beauty editor after clearing the appearance with *Vogue*.

Many people in the fashion industry and New York City, as far as Frankel could tell, possessed a deep fear of somehow crossing Anna. Designers were terrified to loan clothes to the costume designer, Patricia Field of *Sex and the City* fame. Frankel couldn't film at the Metropolitan Museum of Art or Bryant Park (where fashion week was held) because people were afraid of pissing off Anna. He couldn't even film at the Museum of Modern Art because people on the board were affiliated with Anna and afraid of her. The ball scene had to be filmed in the American Museum of Natural History, which was, Frankel said, "the one place she had no influence."

*   *   *

The Devil Wears Prada premiered on June 30, 2006. But before plebeians could see it, Anna got to attend a special screening on the night of May 23 at the Paris Theater in New York. The public relations team for the film invited her, and she accepted and attended with Shelby Bryan, her daughter, Bee, and *Vogue* contributing editor William Norwich. Maybe she was curious, maybe she wanted to support the charity auction that followed the screening, or maybe she saw it as a brilliant PR opportunity for herself: Anna, ingeniously, wore Prada. (This wasn't unusual, as she often wore Prada dresses, customized just for her.)

Frankel sat behind Anna and Bee. Anna had a seat at the end of the row and, though she had a habit of dashing out of plays that bored her, watched the whole movie. At one point, Bee turned to her and said, "Mom, they really got you." After the credits, Anna slipped out before the schmoozing started.

The impact the movie had on her image was incalculable. She was running Big Vogue, her magic touch all the more reason for Condé Nast to put out yet another spinoff, *Vogue Living*, which would launch before the end of the year. She finished the year 2006 as one of Barbara Walters's Most Fascinating People, and became a mainstream celebrity, like Cher or Madonna, recognizable by her first name alone. This was never her goal, said close friend Anne McNally: "She sees it as part of her job. She's very conscious that this is a persona that is existing at the moment because she has that job, and the minute she doesn't have that job, she knows it's going to be different."

But for now, she had become Big Anna, and with her star power now transcending fashion and media, it would be terribly hard for Condé Nast ever to let her go.

Chapter 23

THE CRASH

Originally, R. J. Cutler, fascinated by an article in *New York* magazine about the planning of the 2005 *Dangerous Liaisons*–themed party, had wanted to make a documentary about the Met Gala. Cutler, who had previously coproduced *The War Room* about Bill Clinton's 1992 presidential campaign, managed to get a meeting with Anna's public relations director, Patrick O'Connell, and pitch the idea. But while *Vogue* and Anna were receptive, the Met wasn't. Even so, Cutler didn't want to give up on doing a *Vogue* film. "Listen, we'd love to work with you guys. Maybe there's another idea. Maybe there's another way. Don't be shy," he told O'Connell.

Weeks later, O'Connell called him and said they had an idea. Cutler flew from LA to New York, got a manicure, and went to meet Anna for the first time in a conference room at her Times Square office. Anna, sitting in her seat at the head of the conference table, suggested Cutler make a film about *Vogue*'s September issue. Such a film by such a filmmaker served *Vogue*'s commercial interest but also Anna's interest in being taken seriously by a political documentarian.

"How long do you work on it?" he asked.

"We start in January after couture, and in August or the end of July, we put it to bed."

Cutler liked that the process was many months and culminated in an event, which was closing the magazine's all-important issue. But there was something he needed to get out of the way, one-on-one with Anna now, and not with lawyers later: he needed the final edit of the film.

"If we're going to do this, I need that final cut," Cutler told her. "You deserve that any film that's made about you be taken seriously, and a film that Anna Wintour has final cut on, I don't believe would be taken seriously."

Anna said immediately, "My father was a journalist, I'm a journalist, and that won't be an issue."

When Cutler's crew started filming in the beginning of 2007, most of the *Vogue* staff had no idea who they were or what they were doing there. Anna hadn't told them that a documentary crew was coming. In fact, the first person who was truly welcoming to Cutler and his crew wasn't anyone from *Vogue*—but Anna's daughter, Bee. But Anna assigned various staffers to take them around and show them things. André Leon Talley was assigned to babysit Cutler during the couture shows in Paris one day and took him to Charvet to get custom-made shirts. "The days when I wore my Charvet made-to-order clothes, it was a different Anna," said Cutler.

Cutler's crew was able to capture some candid moments, like when contributing editor Edward Enninful presented photos of a location for his color-blocking shoot with Steven Klein to Anna. "It's so gloomy, Edward. Where's the glamour?" she said. "It's *Vogue*, okay? Let's lift it." Later, after a run-through for the same shoot in which Anna had rejected some of the looks he'd presented, he found Grace Coddington, who seemed to understand his pain. "I want to kill myself!" he said, stressed.

"Why?" Coddington asked.

"I don't know what I'm doing anymore," he said.

Coddington tried to make him feel better. "Don't be too nice, even to me," she advised. "No, honestly—because you'll lose."*

Coddington's ability and willingness to push back against her boss made her an indispensable character for Cutler's film. The only problem was she found his crew particularly annoying. "They were driving me mad. They were in our offices for a year. I hated it," she said. During filming at the couture shows in January, she accused Cutler's sound person of clobbering her in the head with a boom microphone. "I love Grace so much, but nobody had clubbed her," Cutler said. "But she used that to propel herself through her frequent refusals of access."

Anna had her access limits too. At one point, cameras focused, a worried Tom Florio came into her office.

Vogue, like its sister magazines, had been funding a corporate initiative called Fashion Rocks, which included a television special and an annual *Fashion Rocks* print supplement. This involved putting a portion of ad pages—say, twelve of twenty-four bought by a brand like Calvin Klein—into *Fashion Rocks*, which meant they weren't running in *Vogue*. But pages and revenue were all that mattered, especially in the September issue.

"Anna, this is becoming a problem," he said.

She asked the camera crew to leave.

"The September 2007 issue is going to be a pamphlet if we don't do something."

Florio's idea to make up for the revenue lost to this initiative was to sell digital content along with the print pages. Only he didn't sell Style.com—he was, purposefully, never empowered to sell Style.com. Instead, he decided to entice print advertisers with the promise that their ads would also be shoppable on a new online video site called ShopVogue.TV. Here, readers could buy products that they saw on the site's four channels of original programming (one was called "60 Sec-

---

* Enninful's color-blocking shoot was ultimately killed and reshot by Coddington. But Enninful ended up working on a portrait of makeup artist Pat McGrath, which was published.

onds to Chic"). It was branded content before the industry ran on branded content.

"I'll show you all the content to make sure you're cool with it," Florio told Anna. She agreed and told him to move forward.

Vogue's advertisers responded well: they all wanted to be a part of ShopVogue.TV, which exploded ad sales in the 2007 September issue. Florio would later credit the program with driving a hundred additional pages of advertising into the magazine. As Florio was raking in September ad bookings, he got a call. It was from Newhouse, Condé Nast CEO Chuck Townsend, and Sarah Chubb, the head of CondéNet. They were not happy. "What are you doing?" they asked. "You just went off and created a digital channel on your own. We need to have a meeting."

What Florio and Anna were doing was undermining the company's existing websites. Unfortunately, the existing digital setup made such a clash inevitable: Florio was only incentivized to sell print pages. And Anna, by not having official oversight of Style.com, was similarly motivated to care only about her magazines.

Florio spoke with Townsend before the official meeting. "You're going to have to shut this down," Townsend told him.

Florio told him how much business he had booked. Townsend was incredulous, but said, "Well, you're about to go into this meeting, and it's going to be rough for you."

Florio reported back to Anna: "I'm getting called into this meeting with Si and all these other people are there."

"I'm coming with you," she said.

In the meeting, Anna watched Florio hold his ground. People were angry that he'd charged ahead and created digital properties for *Vogue* when *Vogue* was already supposed to have a digital property. But Florio stood behind their decision. After he did so, Anna stood up.

"You know," she told the room, "we just put out the biggest issue in history." Indeed, the September 2007 issue was, with 727 ad pages and 849 total pages, the magazine's biggest ever—and the biggest in the history of monthly consumer magazines. "You should all be congratulating him, this is a waste of all of our time. I think this meeting should be over." And she walked out.

Florio's programs stood.

But the episode about ShopVogue.TV had revealed a bigger problem: how unclear Condé Nast's digital strategy was. For Anna to strengthen the *Vogue* brand and expand her own power, she needed to run *Vogue*'s website. But, despite architecting Big Vogue, that was still years off.

There was no question that being a "*Vogue* brand" had value in the industry. As Scott Sternberg, who launched the clothing line Band of Outsiders (for men in 2004 and women in 2007), said, "*Vogue* was the pinnacle. *Vogue* was, depending on how you look at structure, either at the top of the pyramid or the entire foundation of the whole thing. Like, everything pointed to *Vogue*."

Sternberg had applied for the CFDA/*Vogue* Fashion Fund because of the $200,000 prize. But he also realized that, with a nascent women's-wear business and its high price points necessitated by the cost of pro-ducing his clothes, he needed the validation of magazines like *Vogue* and people like Anna. His business model was wholesale, meaning that selling clothes to stores like Saks Fifth Avenue was crucial; and to build a big wholesale business, buzz was what mattered. Anna was the indus-try's chief allocator of buzz.

After Sternberg became a finalist for the fund in 2007, he entered Anna's orbit. *Vogue* started calling in his clothes for photo shoots, and he noticed that things just got easier for him. "It was like a one-stop shop for relevancy," he said. Anna never pushed Sternberg to design certain things. But he felt she gave him smart advice, like when she told him not to spend time and money building out a Band of Outsiders store in New York, but to just roll racks into the unfinished space and start selling clothes. "That always stuck with me because she was one hundred percent right. We lost eight months of sales and momentum building out this perfect store," said Sternberg, "which was one of the death knells of my brand."

Indeed, in 2015, he announced that Band of Outsiders was going out of business. He should have listened to Anna.

As editor-in-chief of *Vogue*, Anna occupied the dual role of editor and fashion industry advisor.

After William McComb was named CEO of Liz Claiborne in 2006, Anna invited him to lunch. She was concerned about a deal that had been under discussion between his predecessor at Claiborne and Narciso Rodriguez, a designer she had long supported. Rodriguez needed capital to extricate himself from the arrangement he had with the Italian manufacturer Ferretti and regain control of his brand, so he had called Anna. Anna suggested he talk to Liz Claiborne. Then, McComb started.

Anna took McComb to db Bistro Moderne near her Times Square office. She didn't seem particularly interested in establishing a friendship; what she really cared about was that Rodriguez didn't end up with another bad partner. She wanted McComb to follow through with the deal that had previously been discussed. "It was all business. It was all very, very straightforward. She didn't broker the deal. She wasn't involved in negotiating or working it behind the scenes. She was just sort of the idea champion. And she obviously spoke to the genius that he is, and the genius that he could be," said McComb.

McComb was still new, and continued the initiatives of his predecessors, including the deal with Rodriguez, meeting with Anna about it several times. But not long into the partnership, it became clear to him that it wasn't going to fit in with his planned transformation of the company, and they'd need to get out of it. So Anna stepped in again, this time to steer the disentanglement. "In the end, it was good for Narciso," said McComb. "We just no longer were going to be able to do the kinds of things in spending that he would've needed from a good partner, so we freed him again." Rodriguez was able to keep his name and the control of his brand, as Anna hoped.

It was this kind of behind-the-scenes power brokering that had designers deeply afraid of crossing Anna. In an incredibly difficult business, designers want her as a champion and advisor because it can make all the difference.

McComb rang her up again when Isaac Mizrahi's five-year deal with Target was nearing its end in 2007. The Target line sold as much as $300 million each year, but it wasn't the best deal for its designer, who wanted a partner that would help fund and revive his runway shows. McComb knew that Mizrahi and Anna were friends, so he called to get her advice. Would Mizrahi be good for Liz Claiborne? Would Liz Claiborne be good for Mizrahi? Anna said yes to both, and McComb went out and made the deal.*

While Liz Claiborne was a big advertiser across Condé Nast's publications, McComb never got the impression that ads had anything to do with how accessible Anna was to him. She appreciated his conviction that designers mattered—this included all the brands he oversaw, from Lucky Brand to Kate Spade to Juicy Couture. For Anna, as fashion's chief mentor, designers' success was her success.

That said, McComb was under no delusion that his company's ad buys earned him the invitation to purchase seats at a few Met Galas. "I'm sure Anna has no regard for me, but she had met me and she knew me, so as a business weenie, I think she trusted that I would know my place," which was, he added, "kind of the point of it."

And sometimes no ads at all were required for notice. When her assistant Aimee Cho left *Vogue* to start a line of trench coats, Anna covered it in the magazine. One day when Anna had to go to fashion week around the corner from her office and it was raining, she asked her assistants to assemble a mini-rack of trench options for her to wear. Anna's assistant called Cho, who was then working close by, to tell her to rush a coat over for Anna to consider. Cho did, and Anna picked the coat—which was a coup for her line. Just like that, and once again, Anna had given a designer a boost.

---

* Only, through no fault of Anna's or McComb's, the Mizrahi line never got off the ground. It was supposed to go to wholesale market in September 2008, the same month that Lehman Brothers collapsed and, McComb said, "The world ended."

*   *   *

Because *Vogue* was so plugged into fashion companies, Anna and Florio had noticed something during an early 2008 trip to Europe: the discrepancy between the euro and the dollar was so large—rising to $1.60 in April 2008—that brands like Gucci struggled to make a profit on goods sold in the US and were having to mark them down to make sales. Less profit at Gucci meant less money to advertise in *Vogue*; and if Gucci was hurting, it meant nearly everyone in Europe must be in pain.

Florio was worried that pain would seriously hurt *Vogue*'s business.

Realizing that the effects of the exchange differential could have a disastrous impact on their fiefdom, Anna and Florio came up with a plan A, plan B, and plan C to save money. Plan C, the most dramatic, involved not replacing staff who quit and not going abroad for photo shoots.

And then it got worse. When Bear Stearns collapsed in early 2008, Florio called a meeting of Condé Nast publishers. As someone in corporate sales was gloating about being up 10 percent here and 10 percent there, Florio stood up in frustration. "Let me tell you something, I'm seeing something completely different," he said. He explained that he was worried about Bear Stearns and what it would mean for other banks and Condé Nast's business.

A senior person on the corporate business team dismissed him and said, "Well, if that happens, we're all screwed anyway."

Florio, stunned, went to Anna's office. "We're in trouble. The arrogance that I just witnessed is going to put us in a situation where we're going to lose money—we're going to lose a lot of money—unless we do something," he told her. They agreed to go to plan C. Florio, doing his part to cut back, started staying in a room at the Ritz in Paris that was cheaper than the one he'd been reserving for 2,100 euros a night. "In 2008, controlling your costs at that company was revolutionary," said Florio. Doing her part, Anna sent fewer editors to Europe for the shows. Talley said his salary was cut by $50,000 to $300,000, which bothered him because fashion editors were making upwards of $700,000 (as Laurie Jones remembered it, the cut was due to his performance more than the recession). As a result, *Vogue* was one of two magazines in the company that made a profit in 2008.

But while their foresight had been *Vogue*'s financial salvation, 2008 was also the year of one of Anna's biggest career missteps. April's *Vogue* was the "Shape Issue," which Anna said in her editor's letter was "dedicated to fashion and fitness for all."

Vogue seldom photographed men for the cover, and only ever alongside women. George Clooney had previously appeared with Gisele Bündchen wrapped around him on the cover of the June 2000 issue. Bündchen was young at the time and had no idea who Clooney was, which might have eased the rapport; nonetheless, it aided Bündchen's reputation of being good with men who might have no experience on high-fashion shoots. This made her, in *Vogue*'s mind, a logical pairing for April's male cover subject, LeBron James, who would be the first Black man to appear on the cover of *Vogue*.

The shoot took place in Cleveland on a day when the temperature was below zero. Every heater they had was on James and Bündchen and not the crew. Despite the tough conditions, James was a total pro.

The shot Anna approved for the cover, taken in a studio, depicted James dribbling a basketball, teeth bared and mouth agape, with his arm around the waist of Bündchen, in a silky green slip of a dress.

Vogue's senior editors warned Anna that that cover was problematic, that for some it brought instantly to mind images of King Kong with Fay Wray. "There was a lot of, 'Anna, this is not going to go over well,' but she was dismissive," said Laurie Jones, the managing editor. "Anna does not see stereotypes. She sees the passion and she sees the personalities and she sees the celebrity. And I don't think that that image—she just didn't see it."

Anna's decisiveness was what her staff greatly appreciated about her. But this was a time when it got the better of her. Jones said, "She had always such confidence in things. If we'd had someone who was twiddling her thumbs saying, 'Well, should I, or shouldn't I?' we'd have all gone crazy."

As soon as the cover hit, any fanfare over James's landmark appearance was replaced with offense. ESPN columnist Jemele Hill wrote, "Now, maybe the point was to show the contrast between brawn and beauty, masculinity versus femininity, strength versus grace. But *Vogue*'s quest to highlight the differences between superstar athletes and supermodels only successfully reinforces the animalistic stereotypes frequently associated with black athletes," adding that, "as always, it's important to question who was in the room when the cover decisions were made." In this case, it wasn't just who said what in that room, but the person who ultimately made the decision. And that was Anna.

Still, Jones thought, Anna didn't seem bothered by the backlash. It wasn't the sort of thing that would deeply trouble Si Newhouse either— maybe for a minute, but then he'd move on. And around the office, *Vogue* staffers mostly didn't understand why people were so upset about the image. The controversy was treated as a nuisance that would blow over.

That summer in Paris, the crew for one of Grace Coddington's couture shoots was out to dinner when the cover came up. Sonya Mooney, Coddington's assistant, said the group couldn't understand why people were so upset about it. She told them it was a racial trope, part of a troubling history of depictions of Black men.

"The conversation just screeched to a halt," said Mooney. "It wasn't willful ignorance, but just the level of ignorance of just—nobody stopped to think about how that could be offensive. Because it didn't even register on the radar of anyone."

The *Men's Vogue* team had a bad feeling about 2008. No matter how much Anna loved its existence, its staff, and working on its pages, there was nothing she could do to change the reality that the nearly three-year-old magazine—and the very idea of its archetypal reader—was living on borrowed time.

Things had certainly started well, but then the novelty seemed to wear off with advertisers, who were no longer prioritizing *Men's Vogue*. In the annual budget meeting for 2008, Si Newhouse was really unhappy. Not with Anna specifically, but that *Men's Vogue* was losing money. Of course, Newhouse had set it up that way, and expected a loss. A fashion feature shoot, independent of exorbitant photographer fees, could easily cost $50,000, the beauty of the final product always put before the budget. But it was now clear that there wasn't a big enough audience to suggest the magazine had a profitable future.

The only way to compensate for high expenses was by maintaining higher revenue, but, like a storm cloud, Fielden had returned from the men's fashion shows in Europe and said, "Advertising is going dark." Meanwhile, the magazine was meant to be putting together a benefit for the film program at the Museum of Modern Art that would be like its own Met Gala. Bonnie Morrison, *Men's Vogue*'s special projects editor, said she was supposed to sell around forty tables for $100,000 each. Morrison called all her contacts—at Chanel, Tommy Hilfiger, other fashion labels—but she couldn't get commitments. Brands had already budgeted for the year and didn't have $100,000 lying around for a film benefit, even if it was for *Men's Vogue*. The sponsor, Louis Vuitton, had only pledged $100,000, but due to the economy planned to pay half in 2008 and half in 2009.

On the morning of October 30, 2008, Morrison went straight to a meeting at MoMA instead of the office. There, someone from the museum told her, "We just got a message saying that your magazine has been shut down."

Once the *Men's Vogue* staff of around thirty-five people had arrived at the office that morning, Condé Nast CEO Chuck Townsend came down with Anna.

"With market conditions being what they are, we have to fold the magazine," Townsend said. "It's my personal favorite magazine, and I'm sorry to see it go."

Fielden said a few words, and Anna nodded vigorously at his side with visible tears in her eyes. Even though the magazine's numbers were indisputably down and the financial crisis was underway—Lehman Brothers had gone under the previous month, and the economy's dominoes had continued to fall—senior staff who worked at the magazine were shocked. *Men's Vogue* hadn't lost nearly as much money as the short-lived luxury business publication *Portfolio*, which was closed a few months later and cost the company $100 million. Condé Nast lost

30 percent of its revenue in 2009 as a result of the crash, and chose to stop funding startup titles. But even much older magazines, such as *Gourmet*, couldn't survive.

Newhouse, perhaps upset by the closure, and certainly in keeping with his reticent communication style, didn't go down to speak to the staff. He had other people to do that for him. The next day, he met with Fielden in his office and said, in his halting style, "Mr. Fielden, I did not want to do it. I wasn't going to do it, but they made me do it. And that is all I have to say to you." There was no point noting that Newhouse *was* "they." Fielden would stick around to finish the forthcoming supplemental issues of *Men's Vogue*, but then, with no place for him after that, left the company.

The day after *Men's Vogue* folded, Anna told a sympathetic friend, "I've moved on."

The financial crash of 2008 marked a turning point for Condé Nast, but also for the entire media industry. Companies slashed their advertising budgets. Subscriptions fell. And, perhaps most important, the way people read changed dramatically. After 2008, there would never again be as much money as there had been for Condé magazines. In the first half of the year, *Vogue*'s total circulation fell 6 percent and newsstand sales fell 15 percent from the same period in 2007. And while *Vogue* would hang on to its glory days longer than most titles—and Anna herself would hang on to her unbelievable Condé Nast–expensed lifestyle longer than any other editor-in-chief—the industry was rapidly shifting to digital media, a reality for which no one in or outside the company had a good business model.

For Anna, it was proof that her fame and grit weren't enough to keep magazines going. *Teen Vogue* had found an unexpectedly great promotional vehicle in MTV's reality show *The Hills*, on which cast members Whitney Port and Lauren Conrad were filmed interning for the magazine (Anna approved the deal but never watched the show), and managed to hang on. But by the end of 2008, *Vogue Living* (overseen by Hamish Bowles) had also folded after publishing just one stand-alone issue. And soon rumors started circulating that Anna was going to retire and be replaced by Carine Roitfeld, the editor-in-chief of *Vogue Paris*.

Anna had now been running *Vogue* for twenty years, and even though Newhouse dismissed the reports as "the silliest rumor I've ever heard," it revealed that a segment of the fashion and media industries were agitating for a power change. The truth was there was never a possibility, as far as executives knew, of Anna leaving at this time. Her annoyance was evidenced that fall at the National Book Awards, when *New York* reporter Charlotte Cowles asked her about retiring.

"I'm so sorry," Anna replied. "I think that's an extremely rude question. Leave me alone."

"May we ask what you would do if you did retire?" Cowles asked.

Anna said, "No. Just go away."

Even though for Anna, going away was the last thing on her agenda.

Chapter 24

POLITICS AND PAIN

I n the fall of 2009, after a disastrous year for media, Anna had
something that no other editor had: a movie.

Of course, she'd "had" a movie before, but that was fiction,
her actual existence obliquely acknowledged, the workings of her magazine airbrushed. Anna arranged to premiere *The September Issue* at the
Museum of Modern Art on August 19, 2009, in advance of its September release date. The day of the premiere, R. J. Cutler's publicist,
Amanda Lundberg, formerly of Miramax and now a partner at the public relations firm 42West, went to walk through the space. Anna's team,
used to getting what they wanted at the Met for the gala, asked if they
could move art from the walls for aesthetic purposes. A representative
from the museum explained, "That's an exhibit."

Months earlier, at the end of the editing process, Cutler had
arranged for a screening at the Soho House in New York for the *Vogue*
staff. Anna missed the screening with her team, instead receiving a
much more intimate screening days later. For that viewing, she'd
invited several *Vogue* writers, including her drama critic, Adam Green,
and her only bridesmaid, *Vogue* television critic Joan Juliet Buck. Afterward, Anna had notes for Cutler, the main one being, "It feels like a

home movie about two old ladies [Anna and Coddington] squabbling in a hallway." Cutler said, "She wondered where the glamour was." To him, this was a different movie, about two women who were at the top of their game, about their dynamic and their work together.

Anna said, according to another source with knowledge of the incident, that maybe it was time for Cutler to bring on another director.

Fortunately for Cutler, per their original agreement, she had no say over the final cut, but he thanked her for her feedback and invited her to send any more notes as they came to her. Rather than write her own notes, Anna forwarded the critiques written by her *Vogue* team. One was titled "How He Fucked Up."

Anna tried to dangle her "support" for the film as a reason for Cutler to acquiesce. She was supposed to appear at the Sundance screening, but she didn't have to go. It didn't matter to Cutler—if she didn't support it, he could pitch it as "the movie Anna Wintour doesn't want you to see."

Tom Florio had no misgivings. *The September Issue* was arguably the hottest documentary of the season, with tickets sold out in theaters around the country. Anna ultimately decided to support it, not only by going to Sundance but also by doing a segment on David Letterman's show. Still, underneath seemed to be a distinguishable tartness. Anna laughed when Coddington said to her, "It's crazy. Why is there so much of me in it?" Anna told her, "Go do all the publicity for it. It's your film anyway."

As *The September Issue* rolled toward its general release, Anna was probably thinking more about the ongoing impact of the 2008 recession. The economy's collapse had made shopping almost taboo—something the haves of the downturn were only doing covertly, if at all, as the have-nots lost their houses in foreclosures—which hurt fashion brands, which hurt *Vogue*. What she and Florio needed to do was get people to shop again. Jump-starting shopping—the physical kind, inside a store—became *Vogue's* new altruistic mission.

Anna arranged for all the international editors of *Vogue* to meet in Paris to brainstorm. She believed the solution to many problems began with a party, and they came up with Fashion's Night Out, an evening during which stores would organize festivities to get people to come into them.

By now it had been established that when Anna asked the fashion industry to jump, they asked how high, and Fashion's Night Out was no different. Anna approved the ideas from the brands participating, her feedback often being, "That's not big enough."

"It's like, do you expect us to get U2 to play?" said Bonnie Morrison, then working in fashion publicity. Events took place in more than eight hundred stores across New York City on one evening in September 2009, many of them involving free booze. Anna began her night at Macy's in Queens, where, wearing a perfectly tailored Fashion's Night Out shirt, she posed for photos with Gwen Stefani. Other events included having actresses-turned-fashion designers Mary-Kate and Ashley Olsen bartend (Bergdorf Goodman), *Vogue* editor-at-large Hamish Bowles doing karaoke (Juicy Couture), and the designers for the brand Vena Cava getting soaked in a dunk tank (Bird, a store in Brooklyn). There was something deeply bizarre about Anna and her team mixing with the masses, as if this was something *Vogue* had stood for all along—but these were extraordinary times.

As it turned out, the problem wasn't getting people into stores—it was getting people to actually buy things in the stores. The night became so chaotic that people ended up nearly rioting in the streets. The chaos, instead of inspiring purchases, just made shoplifting easy. Still, it kept going and kept growing, and by 2012, the annual event had expanded to five hundred US cities and thirty countries around the world. But after 2012, it was canceled, Condé Nast declining to provide a reason.

The demise of Fashion's Night Out was a relief for many in the industry. But it also made clear that shopping parties weren't going to alter the effects of an economic downturn and that, as had been the case after September 11, high fashion wasn't a panacea to the world's problems—nor was it viewed very widely beyond the halls of *Vogue* as something that deserved special efforts to save.

*   *   *

In September 2009, a few months after Bee's graduation from Columbia University, R. J. Cutler's *The September Issue* was released, to mostly
positive reception. In the *New York Times*, however, critic Manohla Dargis slammed Cutler for "a take so flattering he might as well work there,"
noting that Anna probably only supported the film because fashion's
darker issues—"the models starving themselves, the exploited Chinese
workers cranking out couture fakes and the animals inhumanely slaugh-
tered for their fur"—were left out. The film also put Tonne Goodman
in an awkward spot with actress Sienna Miller, whose cover shoot was
a story line in the film. Goodman was taped describing Miller's hair as
"lackluster." "I have apologized to Sienna about one trillion times for
saying that on camera," Goodman said. "We just pulled all her hair off
of her face. And her face is beautiful, but it was the right thing to do."

But the biggest impact the film had wasn't on Anna or *Vogue*—but
on Grace Coddington, who, after decades contentedly working in the
industry's trenches, became, at sixty-eight years old, a celebrity—the
very thing that had always repelled her.

And Anna, who wasn't the type of boss to be threatened by the success of her staff, let the moment belong to Coddington.

Though those closest to Anna often describe her as loyal, she has cut
off long-standing friendships.

In late 2010, Anna decided she wanted an interview with Asma
al-Assad, the wife of Syria's president, Bashar al-Assad, who had a look
that Anna felt suited *Vogue*. It was assigned to her friend Joan Juliet
Buck.

Buck was concerned about taking on a story that touched Middle
Eastern politics, on which she was not an expert. "I'm not a political
reporter," she told her editor.

"That's not what we want," the editor replied. "It's museums. The
first lady's getting the Louvre to help excavate the ruins in Syria. You
like ruins."

Buck went to Damascus for a nine-day trip, during which she didn't visit the ruins of Palmyra, as she had been expecting, but she did go with the first lady to a youth center where teens discussed democracy. Her last day there, a Tunisian fruit seller set himself on fire and the Arab Spring began.

When she got home, she told her editor they should hold the story. But the editor disagreed, adding, "No one's going to notice your piece anyway."

In line with *Vogue*'s tradition of only featuring subjects who deserve to be celebrated, Buck filed the requisite puff piece. It described Asma al-Assad as "glamorous, young, and very chic—the freshest and most magnetic of first ladies." It called Syria "the safest country in the Middle East." Buck had also gotten time with Bashar al-Assad, reporting that he said he studied eye surgery "because it's very precise, it's almost never an emergency, and there is very little blood." The story failed to mention that Assad was a dictator (one who killed thousands of civilians and hundreds of children the year the article came out). Instead, it noted that Assad won his election with "a startling 97 percent of the vote."

Laurie Jones said she told Anna they shouldn't run the story. It wasn't the kind of thing features editors would raise in a group meeting, but they could express concern about such issues to Jones, who relayed it to Anna. But Anna liked the opening photo of Asma, clutching a magenta wrap around her shoulders, on a vista high above the city of Damascus—and the photos were still what decided what ran or didn't. "We tried and tried and tried to talk her out of that," said Jones. "The human rights, all the indignities and how awful her husband was. And Anna just wanted that picture. She wanted the piece."

She also figured that the story could simply be taken down from the website if it caused a problem, but didn't realize the site was, in Jones's words, "primitive," and didn't operate quickly.

Almost as soon as the story went online, the backlash began. "The attacks were immediate, blistering, and universal. Every day I was shamed online, called a shill for the Syrians; I read the comments in disbelief," Buck wrote in her memoir. She got no more assignments from *Vogue* that year, then her contract was canceled.

After the story ran, Anna never called Buck. Their friendship, which began in London more than fifty years ago, was over. Laurie Jones, who had worked for Anna for twenty years, said, "That was, to me, the most contentious of any editorial problems that happened at *Vogue*. . . . You know, she didn't get upset about anything. But that story—that was one that we just begged her not to run."

Jones admired and respected Anna a lot, despite their occasional disagreements over many years working together, but nothing made her seriously reconsider her role until Hurricane Sandy struck New York City in late October 2012. The storm wreaked unprecedented destruction on the city and surrounding region, leaving all of downtown Manhattan without power for days. The flooded subway system was also closed down, crippling transit around the city at the same time.

After the storm, Anna called her. "Laurie, I want everyone back in the office tomorrow," she said. It was the same attitude she'd always had: you get back up, you keep going.

But for someone with Anna's lifestyle, it was easier to keep going. Though she lived in downtown Manhattan, she had been able to move uptown to the cushy confines of the Mark Hotel, where she had electricity and hot water and luxury. While she had a chauffeured car to get her to work, members of her staff were leaving apartments without power to walk across the Brooklyn Bridge to get to the office.

Jones was in Connecticut and couldn't get to work because downed trees were blocking her road, and she wasn't going to do something like trudge through the wreckage until she could find a passing car and try to hitch a ride. A few months later, she retired. "It was just too much after all that," she said.

On July 5, 2011, Anna attended her friend Karl Lagerfeld's couture show for Chanel in Paris. She often wore Chanel couture, so the show was always an opportunity for her to shop as well as come up with ideas for the magazine. However, this time she was shopping on an unusually tight timeline. The next day, French president Nicolas Sarkozy would award her the Légion d'Honneur—one of the highest honors in France—and she needed something to wear.

Right after the show she went with Talley to Chanel's Paris headquarters, across the street from where she was staying at the Ritz. This was one of the most elite shopping experiences in the world, and Anna took it seriously. A handful of Chanel staff would greet her at the top of the couture house's famous staircase, then she would proceed to a room to find the dresses hanging on racks. She would select things to try on, and Talley would offer his comments. That evening, he suggested she try a navy suit with white trim. Anna went into the dressing room and tried it on, then came out and looked in the mirror and asked Talley what he thought. Normally Anna does three or four fittings for her couture, but the ceremony was the next day, so the clothes were adjusted to her quickly and sent over that night. (She wore her usual Manolo Blahnik sandals with crossed straps—for special occasions with more lead time, such as the Met Gala, a fabric swatch was sent over so the shoes could be custom-made in Italy.)

The next morning, Talley went with Anna to the ceremony. He found spending time with Anna socially to be "extremely intense."

Talley sat in the corner during the ceremony at the Élysée Palace, holding Anna's purse. Other guests included Lagerfeld, Donatella Versace, and Tommy Hilfiger. Afterward, Talley and Anna got back in the car to go to a reception at the American embassy.

Anna noticed her phone was missing. "What have you done with my phone?" she asked Talley.

"I don't have your cell phone," he said. "You never took it out of your purse. I would never go in a woman's purse."

When they got to the reception, Talley called the Ritz and asked the concierge to check Anna's room for her phone. He found it on Anna's desk and sent it to the embassy. Talley handed Anna the phone, which she accepted with a grunt and a hair flip.

The next morning, Anna sent Talley a note on a ripped envelope from the Ritz, thanking him for all his help.

* * *

There was little question that the fashion industry itself leaned heavily Democratic. But having Anna aligned with the party created a connection to the whole industry.

Barack Obama had been the lucky face of not one but two *Men's Vogue* covers. His first was the September/October 2006 issue, when he was a senator; the second was October 2008, toward the end of his first presidential run. Leading up to the 2008 nomination, his campaign appreciated that Anna Wintour supported him when it seemed everyone in New York was still a Hillary Clinton loyalist. "I don't want to give myself credit that's undeserved, but I think that it was my suggestion that we support Barack Obama," said Shelby Bryan, who had heard him speak. "I said, 'I think it'd be really important for the American people, especially for Black people, to have a president who is Black, and he's quite capable.' And she was all on board immediately."

Anna had hoped to feature Clinton in an issue of *Vogue* as well. "Imagine my amazement," she wrote in her editor's letter, "when I learned that Hillary Clinton, our only female presidential hopeful, had decided to steer clear of our pages at this point in her campaign for fear of looking too feminine. The notion that a contemporary woman must look mannish in order to be taken seriously as a seeker of power is frankly dismaying. How has our culture come to this? How is it that *The Washington Post* recoils from the slightest hint of cleavage on a senator? This is America, not Saudi Arabia." It seemed possible that Anna was shrewdly dodging the prospect that Clinton's rejection had nothing to do with greater issues of femininity, but with Anna switching her allegiance to Obama.

Doubling down, before his second *Men's Vogue* cover came out, Anna was working to raise money for Obama. Anna, who wanted political stories in every issue whether or not her audience read them, had spent decades featuring politics in *Vogue*—Julia Reed profiled presidential opponents George W. Bush and Vice President Al Gore, and Bush's national security advisor, Condoleezza Rice, among others. Now Anna threw her philanthropic might behind influencing the election. In June 2008, after Obama secured the Democratic nomination, she chaired a fund-raiser with André Leon Talley, Calvin Klein, and Shelby Bryan. The guest of honor was Michelle Obama, who was already flirting with fashion iconography; for $10,000, a donor could attend dinner with her at Klein's house.

In September 2008, Anna and actress Sarah Jessica Parker hosted a cocktail party as part of the Obama campaign's Runway to Change initiative, for which designers like Narciso Rodriguez and Vera Wang made items like tank tops and tote bags to sell on Obama's site, with proceeds going toward the campaign. The collections were Anna's brain-child. Each time new merchandise went up for sale, it sold out within a day. Anna made the collections a staple of her fund-raising efforts each presidential election year, helping to develop her reputation for being one of Obama's hardest-working, lowest-maintenance fund-raisers. The campaign saw her as someone who put on high-dollar events with-out asking for anything in return. A lot of bundlers raising much less than Anna asked for things, like fifteen minutes with Obama for them-selves and their family members. But Anna ran her events with the same military precision she runs everything, from house parties to the Met Gala, and made it easy for the campaign. And while it would have been impossible for Anna never to have thought about the possibility of a Michelle Obama *Vogue* cover (she would eventually be featured on three, giving *Vogue* a full day with her for each one, an extraordinary amount of time for someone in her position), her focus was indisputably on the much bigger picture.

In 2012, Anna continued hosting fancy fund-raising dinners with her fancy friends. She called Tom Ford and asked him to host one with her at his house in London. "I will always say yes. Because I agree with it," said Ford. "I feel like a complete slouch," he added. "Mostly, I give money. Anna actually gets involved."

When Obama's campaign needed money that year after the con-vention, she was a natural go-to. The campaign called Anna to ask if she could do more for them, adding as an enticement—and one Anna probably did not need—that she would make a great ambassador.

After Obama won and ambassadors started stepping down so oth-ers could have a turn, the campaign realized that the offer to Anna would have to be addressed. Anna's name was brought to Obama as a potential ambassador to the Court of St. James's, one of the fanciest, most prestigious appointments. Obama thought she was worthy of consideration. The campaign already knew her pretty well from all the fund-raising she had done and found no disqualifying red flags.

But then Matthew Barzun, the campaign finance chair, expressed interest in the UK ambassadorship. Barzun outranked Anna in the pecking order. Still, the campaign owed Anna, after all she had done for them, at least a conversation about the appointment.

Alyssa Mastromonaco, an Obama advisor, went to meet with her to tell her that Barzun was interested in the Court of St. James's. Anna understood what that meant—that he would get priority for the role— but was impressed that Mastromonaco had the courage to tell her face-to-face when none of the men working on the campaign even bothered to say anything to her after election day. Anna also showed no sign that she was upset about the news; she got it.

Part of Mastromonaco's mission was to ask Anna if there was anything else she'd be interested in. "What about France?" she said.

"I don't know," Anna said. "This wasn't my dream to begin with. They told me to think about it. I'll think about it."

But when Mastromonaco reported back to the Obama team that she'd asked Anna to think about France, they revealed that the only thing Secretary of State Hillary Clinton wanted on her way out was for hedge fund manager and Obama bundler Marc Lasry to get France. Obama hated to go back on what Mastromonaco had told Anna, but felt he had no choice because it was Clinton's only ask. (Lasry never became ambassador to France, withdrawing from consideration following reports of his ties to a gambling ring.)

Anna seemed to have no problem with the news that France was off the table. Despite reports in the media that she was angling for an ambassadorship as a way out of Condé Nast, it was never clear to Obama's team that she actually wanted to move forward. Nor was it obvious to her bosses, Si Newhouse and Chuck Townsend. She never raised the prospect of leaving for an ambassadorship with them. And Newhouse didn't worry about it either, figuring she would never give up her spectacular job and power base for the thankless position and comparatively meager low six-figure salary of an ambassador, which, for the wealthy people who get the appointments, is more formality than enticement. Ambassadors have to pay for all the entertaining they do, and it was never clear that Anna would have been able or willing to take on such a burden.

But she had another way of moving forward. Anna had hinted during these postelection conversations that she would be more than fine. Shortly after her ambassadorial prospects shifted, Condé Nast announced that she was, finally, getting a promotion to the role people had thought she would get twenty years before: artistic director of the company, giving her purview over *Vogue* plus nearly every other magazine at Condé Nast.

Anna hadn't said anything about the promotion to her old friend Anne McNally, who found out about it in the media. She texted Anna congratulations; Anna replied, "Thank you, Anne. I'm probably going to get a lot of flak for it."

Chapter 25

ANNA WINTOUR,
ARTISTIC DIRECTOR

I n late 2012, Si Newhouse, now eighty-five, relinquished day-to-day duties in the magazine division. "Anna, without even having to think twice about it, is the most qualified person to pick up that torch and carry it into the future," Condé Nast CEO Chuck Townsend said at the time. Her artistic director position immediately established Anna "as one of the most powerful women in magazine publishing," reported the *New York Times*.

Si Newhouse's kingdom was now Anna Wintour's.

C ertainly, there was logic to her promotion, announced on March 12, 2013: Anna, now sixty-three, had clearly been successful with *Vogue*, which remained the crown jewel of the company. Anna said she saw the role as "almost like being a one-person consulting firm," similar in nature to the advising she did on the side of her editor-in-chief job already, helping pair designers with investors or designers with fashion houses. She had been acting, in essence, as the artistic director of the fashion industry.

But the appointment seemed illogical to some editors at the company. What success had Anna had with magazines outside of *Vogue*?

Men's Vogue, *Vogue Living*, and *HG* hadn't succeeded. How would she now be able to successfully manage nearly all of Condé Nast's portfolio, magazines as varied as *Wired*, *Golf Digest*, and *Brides*?

The job of artistic director required a different skill set from running one magazine brand. It wasn't about pushing a singular vision forward, as Anna had expertly done at *Vogue* since she started, but rather about nurturing the necessarily disparate visions of different editors. Whatever his faults, Newhouse, as Anna knew from experience, had nurtured a variety of editorial visions. Certainly he loved fostering competition between his magazines and his editors-in-chief. (*Vanity Fair* editor-in-chief Graydon Carter didn't let his editors discuss their stories on the elevator, for fear of being scooped by another Condé Nast title; *Men's Vogue* and *GQ*'s rivalry was so fierce that editors from the latter were offended when Anna showed up alongside Fielden at Men's Fashion Week and appeared to ice them out.) But Newhouse, though he clearly treasured some of his magazines more than others, mostly left his editors alone. Anna, however, had never run *Vogue* according to the will of her staff. The vision was hers and hers alone, and she hired people who were happy to execute it. People who couldn't or didn't like executing that vision didn't last.

Anna, Graydon Carter, and *New Yorker* editor-in-chief David Remnick had always reported directly to Newhouse (after he became ill, they started reporting to Townsend), circumventing the company's editorial directors, like Tom Wallace and, before him, James Truman. That reporting structure held, with Anna managing all other editors-in-chief, and Carter and Remnick still reporting to Townsend. Yet executives knew Anna's promotion had the potential to be awkward because she remained editor-in-chief of *Vogue*, meaning other editors-in-chief were now reporting to a competitor. But executives' desire to elevate Anna as the face of the company outweighed concern over potential pitfalls.

Complicating the dynamic, Anna was stepping into the role at a time when letting each magazine operate as its own independent province had become financially impossible, meaning operational changes would have to be implemented. Adding to the company's increasingly precarious financial future, print magazines—Anna's expertise—were a dying medium. How long would print really last as Condé Nast's most profitable revenue stream? Under Anna's oversight, the magazines would have to maintain their famously high standards while continuing to cut costs.

In 2010, Condé had cut budgets at some magazines by about 25 percent, having arrived at the figure after consultants from McKinsey & Company came in to advise on how to manage the fallout from the recession. But things never turned around. By the end of 2012, news leaked that Condé Nast titles had to cut 5 percent from their budgets in 2013 on top of the 10 percent cut they were asked to make in the summer of 2012 (there were some exceptions for Newhouse's favorite titles, including the *New Yorker*).

All of this was obviously bad news: Anna's success as artistic director of Condé Nast was up against tremendous obstacles. Yet this was the good news too: no matter what she did, the dire state of the magazine business meant that any mistakes she might make could be masked or excused by the industry's decline.

While Anna's professional responsibilities grew, so did her Mastic estate. In the summer of 2013, Anna bought the neighboring six-acre lot and house for $350,000, less than half off the $799,000 asking price. Her compound now comprised a lower house and an upper house, two swimming pools, and many converted barns, most for guests to sleep in but also a "bistro barn" for dining.

The Anna in Mastic is strikingly unlike the one at the office. "We probably walk ten miles a day, just back and forth between her houses, doing chores, lifting things, and setting the table," said Lisa Love. "She asks you if you want a towel. That seems so small in detail but she's like anyone else. It'd be like if you go to visit any friend you have. 'Can I get you a glass of water? Would you like something to drink?' All of the catering to that doesn't seem apparent at the office, but definitely is in her home life."

Anna liked to start her weekend days at Mastic by putting on a dark-blue or maroon Prada tracksuit for her 8 a.m. tennis game. "She just never misses shots," said Miranda Brooks. Then she and Brooks would do the garden walk-through to find plants that needed fixing. For meals, Anna's chef prepared tons of food—lamb, fish, chicken, cold soups, roasted potatoes—all served family-style. Brooks has tried to convince Anna to plant a vegetable garden, but she won't because "she doesn't like vegetables," she said. (In fact, her go-to lunch, after Condé Nast moved offices to 1 World Trade Center, was a steak and Caprese salad without the tomatoes from the nearby Palm restaurant.)

Lunches and dinners at Mastic might include around thirty people, and those who don't manage to slip away will have to play games, like the one where everyone around the table has to name, say, artists from the sixties—and if you can't think of someone when it's your turn, you have to dump a glass of water on your head, as Anna has done. After dinner, the guests might move to one of the barns on her property where a little disco ball spins. Everyone drinks and dances, including Anna, who loves to dance, until she slips away before everyone else.

Each summer, she held Camp Mastic for thirty of her closest friends and family members. They could take art classes, swim, or sing—and, of course, play tennis with her instructor (or Roger Federer, who came one year for her birthday). "She has a whole tennis camp and there are trophies and everything like that. It's usually a family member [who] wins. But it's very highly competitive. That's in her family," said Lisa Love. She also held "movie nights and casino nights and theme events constantly. She likes to party." She seemed to remain bemused by the location of her luxurious forty-acre compound, squarely in the middle of working-class Long Island, once creating "Mastic Sur Mer" T-shirts as a joke for all her guests.

And finally, eighteen years after she bought the house, she must have thought the hedges were lush enough to have the gardens photographed for publication for the first time. However, when Brooks and Anna saw the story in the *New York Times*'s *T* magazine, they were upset. "I think they were so excited to see that she had such a wild and loose garden that they sort of deliberately chose pictures where it really looked close to disheveled," said Brooks. "It's just so lush and delicious, and so many flowers in the summer and so many beautiful places to go, and it's not really there." She added, "It's *highly* looked after to get that appearance."

In early 2014, a cultural phenomenon was reaching its apex in the zeitgeist, so of course Anna was thinking about it. Kim Kardashian and rapper-slash-fashion designer Kanye West, who had been friends with Anna for years by that point, were getting married. Anna said to Grace Coddington, "Kim and Kanye are getting married. Why don't you do a take on them with actors from *Saturday Night Live?*"

Coddington replied, "Well, if we can get them, why don't we do the people themselves?"

"Oh my goodness," Anna said, giving Coddington a funny look, realizing that was the right idea. "That would be fantastic."

Before the shoot was officially booked, Anna and West discussed face-to-face what would be a turning point for the *Vogue* brand. Kardashian was a woman who had been barred from attending the Met Gala for all those years. When she finally went for the first time in May 2013, Winston Wolkoff, who was no longer planning the gala but stayed friends with Anna, thought, *Anna really sold her soul to the devil.* But she also understood Anna's change of heart. "At the end of the day, *Vogue*'s a business," she said. "I think that at a certain point you're going to have to give in to what culture, what people want."

Anna later said of the cover choice, "Kim and Kanye were part of the conversation of the day and for *Vogue* not to recognize that would have been a big misstep. But at the same time I knew that it would be deeply, deeply controversial and that many of our readers and our audiences would be horrified."

She knew she had to keep the entire thing secret. Coddington, who almost never styled celebrities, requested custom wedding dresses from designers for Kardashian to wear. Coddington sometimes commissioned custom looks for a shoot, as she did with her famous *Alice in Wonderland* spread where she had designers like John Galliano and Karl Lagerfeld all make dresses in blue. For Kardashian's dresses, Coddington provided only her measurements. Designers might have had a feeling of who they were designing for based on those, but didn't get confirmation until Kardashian showed up for her fittings. "All the designers were super-excited about it," said Hamish Bowles, who wrote the accompanying story.

Vogue staff knew something was up when Coddington left Paris Fashion Week early for a secretive shoot. Mark Holgate, *Vogue's* fashion news director, speculated that she was actually off to shoot Catherine Middleton, the Duchess of Cambridge.

Anna told Coddington and Bowles to wear disguises when they went to Los Angeles to shoot with Annie Leibovitz (even though a shot of the couple walking along the Seine in Paris appeared in the spread, it was fake—the pair were actually shot running along a private airport runway in LA and then photoshopped into Paris). If anyone saw *Vogue* staff with Leibovitz and Kardashian, they would know where the pictures were running. So Coddington tied a scarf around her instantly recognizable voluminous red hair, tucked it under a hat, and put on dark glasses. In the art department, a cover Holgate remembered featuring model Kate Upton was put up on the board so that Kimye's wouldn't leak to the press.

One day back at the office, Anna called in Holgate to discuss her editor's letter, which he was writing each month, for the May issue. When he stepped into the office, two highly unusual things happened. First, her assistants closed the door behind him. Then Anna came around her desk, holding a manila envelope. It was all so strange and dramatic that Holgate thought for a moment he was about to be fired.

"Mark, there's something I want to show you," she said, and took the real cover out of the envelope. "This is top secret. This is going to be the cover. I want you to write another letter."

Of course, the backlash was immediate when the cover finally dropped, Kardashian wearing an ivory A-line duchess satin dress by Alber Elbaz for Lanvin, and West in a dark Saint Laurent blazer by Hedi Slimane. The hashtag #boycottvogue trended on Twitter, and people threatened to cancel subscriptions, the broader public embracing the classism *Vogue* had long projected, for which they would later scorn Anna.

It wasn't Coddington's favorite set of pictures. She liked the one of Kanye photographing Kim taking a selfie with her baby, North. But the rest of the published images—of Kimye on a private plane, by the Seine, draped over a matte-black Lamborghini—she found "too expected and normal."

Holgate had been to many fashion shows with Anna, which in itself is an extraordinary experience. Usually Anna arrived early, saw the collection backstage, then went to her seat, where she might say to Holgate, "Lotta tweed," or, in the case of designer Demna Gvasalia's first collection for Balenciaga, "It looks great. Have we put the request in?" Which prompted Holgate to email the house from his seat to request access for a *Vogue* feature on Gvasalia's debut before the collection had walked before him down the runway. (Front-row conversations, Holgate said, usually revolved around business. "I'm not going to be saying to my boss," he said, "I don't know, 'Oh, I just saw a really great Balenciaga jacket at Dover Street Market.'")

But Anna didn't just gain advance access to major fashion collections. Her position in media culture itself sometimes seemed special, even to the people who worked with her every day. Holgate experienced this firsthand when attending an unusual meeting at a tiny screening room at the Soho House in the Meatpacking District. Anna had also assembled Hamish Bowles, market director Virginia Smith, creative digital director Sally Singer, and entertainment editor Jill Demling at the behest of actor Hugh Jackman for a meeting that felt, to Holgate, "surreal." Jackman had put together a pitch on the movie *The Greatest Showman*, which hadn't started filming. As Jackman asked the team for their input—on things like costumes and casting—Holgate got the impression he and Anna were friends. Jackman wanted ideas for an actress who would look great in period clothing, but also had a great singing voice, so Holgate suggested Adele (who ultimately wasn't cast).

Vogue published a feature on the film pegged to its release in the September 2017 issue with a photo portfolio shot by Annie Leibovitz. Bowles, who wrote the story, described Jackman as "absurdly charismatic," something he knew from that rather remarkable meeting. But readers of *Vogue* would never know that because it was never mentioned in the story, Anna's influence remaining, as it usually does, behind the scenes.

If editors-in-chief were wary of Anna when she became artistic director of Condé Nast, they had reason to be. In all her magazine editorships the first thing she did was fire most of the existing staff and bring in her own people. But Brandon Holley, who edited the shopping magazine *Lucky*, decided to try to work with Anna proactively. The magazine was ailing at that point. Ad pages were down 2.7 percent through April 2013, after a 20 percent decline in 2012.

Holley, who had the support of the executive team before Anna's promotion, hoped Anna could help *Lucky* book better photographers and models. She thought *Lucky*'s future was digital and, though she cared about print, saw it as a dying medium; Anna, with immense power in the fashion world, was better poised to improve the print product. Anna was primarily concerned with magazines' visuals, and left articles alone. But she soon became involved in granular aspects of *Lucky*, including attending run-throughs. Not long after that, Anna was on the floor several times a week, expressing strong views on what Holley and other editors should be doing, pushing them in a more high-fashion direction that looked, frankly, like *Vogue*.

In April 2013, about a month after she started her artistic director job, Anna brought in Eva Chen, who had worked at *Teen Vogue*, to "consult" on *Lucky*. By June, Holley was fired, and Chen was appointed *Lucky*'s new editor-in-chief. It seemed to Condé Nast staff that Anna wanted her own people in these editor-in-chief jobs, but Bob Sauerberg, Condé Nast's president at the time, said the turnover didn't stem merely from Anna's decisions: "Anna and I collaborated on every big decision made, with a lot of input on finance, consumer metrics, business strategy. We were advised by all of the groups, and we made the decisions together."

Lucky wasn't the only publication where people became concerned about looking like a *Vogue* knockoff. *Self*—whose editor-in-chief, Lucy

Danziger, was replaced with Joyce Chang from *Cosmopolitan*—received its own high-fashion photography makeover. Before long it was featuring cover models like Joan Smalls and Candice Swanepoel in sleek cutout swimsuits instead of celebrities like Fergie in shorts, and was referred to sneeringly in the building as "*Vogue* with a ponytail." One executive admitted that, with this approach, Anna had erred.

Over the course of her first few years as artistic director, Anna also replaced longtime *Allure* editor Linda Wells with Michelle Lee and *Condé Nast Traveler* editor Klara Glowczewska with Pilar Guzman, with the *Vogue*-like makeovers soon following. In the midst of this, Condé Nast moved out of its offices in 4 Times Square, surrounded by a vibrant theater and restaurant scene, and into 1 World Trade Center in the city's comparatively bland Financial District. Employees felt a similar drain on the originality of Condé Nast's titles under Anna. With the industry in decline, she might not have been able to do much in her role to boost the performance of various magazines. But the misses seemed to stack up: *Lucky* merged with online retailer BeachMint in 2014, which closed it in 2015; *Self* eliminated its print edition in 2017, only to be followed by *Glamour* and *Teen Vogue* in 2018. As all this unfolded, staff across titles wondered if Anna's promotion had been for the best.

Throughout all of this, Anna's team was expecting her to be less involved with the *Vogue* brand now that she had so many other responsibilities. But, as far as they could tell, she gave up none of her *Vogue* and *Teen Vogue* duties. Instead, she found more hours in her day by waking up as early as four some mornings (though sometimes she sleeps in until five thirty) and asking her *Vogue* staff to schedule meetings on her calendar instead of drifting in and out of her office when they wanted to talk to her. "There was really no change at all" in her *Vogue* involvement, said Hamish Bowles.

Anna's hours always amazed Bowles. When they attended Paris Fashion Week together in the early 2000s, he had stayed out late at an after party, returning to the Ritz between 4 and 5 a.m. As he swung through the doors, Anna was on her way out to play tennis an hour outside the city. "Good morning," she said, laughing, as they passed. By 9 a.m., having played, come back, and had her hair and makeup done,

Nonie Wintour with Anna (left), James, Nora, and Patrick, photographed in their St. John's Wood home in London for a January 5, 1964 *Observer* newspaper article.

Anna walking down the runway to take her seat at a fashion show while working as fashion assistant at *Harpers & Queen* in the early seventies. Monty Coles

Anna on set in Jamaica while working at *Harper's Bazaar* in 1976.
Francois Ilnseher

Anna, with photographer Rico Puhlmann on set in Jamaica
for *Harper's Bazaar* in 1976. Francois Ilnseher

Anna on set in Toronto shooting for *Viva* in 1977. STAN MALINOWSKI

Anna and her father, Charles, in 1986, when Anna got her first editor-in-chief job at British *Vogue*. JON TIMBERS/ ArenaPAL

Anna in 1986, as editor-in-chief of British *Vogue*.

Anna and her young son Charlie appearing in a 1987 newspaper article, when she was the outgoing editor of British *Vogue*.

Anna's first American *Vogue* cover, November 1988, starred model Michaela Bercu wearing a $10,000 Christian Lacroix couture jacket and $50 Guess jeans. The image was so unexpected that the printers, Anna later said, wondered if it was a mistake.

For the cover of *Vogue*'s May 1989 issue featuring Madonna, editor André Leon Talley said Anna didn't want anything too "bombastic." She chose this simply styled portrait of the then-scandalous pop star in the pool.

Anna, about a year into her *Vogue* editorship, with her husband, David Shaffer, at a Tiffany for Men launch in September 1989. Roxanne Lowit

Anna with Alexander Liberman at Seventh on Sale, the AIDS charity fundraiser *Vogue* cosponsored and helped organize, November 1990. Roxanne Lowit

Anna seated next to husband David Shaffer at the CFDA Awards in New York in 1991, where she won editor of the year and her ex-boss Tony Mazzola was humiliated. RON GALELLA/GETTY IMAGES

Anna and David Shaffer with their children, Bee and Charlie, at *Vogue*'s 1991 Christmas party. ROXANNE LOWIT

A Polaroid of Anna and
close friend Anne McNally,
taken in the nineties by Karl
Lagerfeld. KARL LAGERFELD

Anna dancing at a
Vogue party, November
1993. ROXANNE LOWIT

Anna with Karl Lagerfeld (and Helena Christensen behind him) at Italian *Vogue*'s thirtieth anniversary party in Milan, October 1994. ROXANNE LOWIT

Anna with David Shaffer hosting her very first Met Gala opening the *Haute Couture* exhibit, December 1995. ROXANNE LOWIT

Anna seated front row with André Leon Talley, 1996.
EVAN AGOSTINI/GETTY IMAGES

For the October 1998 issue, Oprah appeared on the cover of *Vogue* with what Anna described in her editor's letter as a "*Vogue* makeover." For the shoot, she wore custom designer clothes and allowed her hair to be done by Garren, *Vogue*'s chosen stylist, instead of her own.

Hillary Clinton appeared on the cover of *Vogue*'s December 1998 issue as first lady in the wake of the Monica Lewinsky scandal. She wore a custom Oscar de la Renta gown, created with Anna's input.

Anna with Si Newhouse at *Vogue*'s 1998 Christmas party. ROXANNE LOWIT

Anna posing for a 1999 *New York* magazine cover story pegged to her divorce from David Shaffer and the departure of her deputy editor, Kate Betts.

GEORGE W. BUSH'S SECRET PLAN TO CONQUER N.Y. ● WOLFF ON CBS-VIACOM

NEW YORK

Amid a blizzard of gossip about an affair and the defection of a key protégée, *Vogue*'s ice queen suddenly seems vulnerable. But for Anna Wintour, maybe that's not all bad—she's just as powerful without the sunglasses.

WINTOUR'S THAW

By Kevin Gray

Anna and boyfriend
Shelby Bryan at the
CFDA Awards in New
York, June 2000.
Roxanne Lowit

Anna and Karl Lagerfeld at
the Met Gala opening the
Chanel exhibition in 2005.
Patrick McMullan / Getty
Images

Anna and boyfriend Shelby Bryan at a tennis match in 2009.
Michel Dufour / Getty Images

Kim Kardashian and Kanye West appeared on the April 2014 cover of *Vogue* pegged to their wedding, styled by Grace Coddington. Coddington almost never worked on celebrity shoots, and in the end found most of the images "too expected and normal."

Anna and Queen
Elizabeth II at a
fashion show in
London, February
2018. Yui Mok/
Getty Images

Anna and daughter
Bee at the Met Gala
opening the exhibit
for *Fashion and the
Catholic Imagination*,
May 2018. Jamie
McCarthy/Getty
Images

Anna and cohosts of the 2019 Met Gala opening the *Camp* exhibition, from left: Serena Williams, Harry Styles, Alessandro Michele, and Lady Gaga.

she was in her front-row seat at the first show of the day, flawless alongside a drained Bowles.

*V*anity Fair editor-in-chief Graydon Carter wanted as little to do with Anna as possible, and she seemed to sense it. When she was promoted, she didn't try to oversee him. But she did try to include his magazine in her cost-cutting plans. One day in the summer of 2016, Anna called him and said, "We're going to pull all your art department, photo department, fact-checking, and copy department onto another floor, combined with other magazines."

Carter, about to go to *Vanity Fair*'s New Establishment Summit in San Francisco, was furious. *Vanity Fair* ran complex stories that he felt were best served by a team of fact-checkers who didn't also have to work on other titles like *Teen Vogue*. "You've got to be fucking kidding me. I'm getting on a plane, I'm not going to talk about this right now," he said.

When he got back, he brought it up with her. "You didn't talk to anybody about this, you're just doing it. This makes no sense," he said.

She replied, "No, I talked to lots of people."

Carter said, "Like who did you talk to?"

Anna said, "People in Silicon Valley."

"What the fuck do they know about anything?" Carter said. He wasn't the only editor who was angry about this—no one wanted to lose control of their team.

Carter was in the process of renewing his contract. He moved forward with it, with two stipulations: he wouldn't be required to attend meetings on the executive floor—meaning Anna's Editorial Task Force meetings, for which she invited luminaries to speak with Condé Nast editors-in-chief—and that his staff would be left alone.

Carter had previously felt *supported* by Anna. She had given him writing assignments at *Vogue* and *HG*. In his first two years editing *Vanity Fair*, when the job felt especially difficult, she was reassuring. "If Si has any doubts about you, he certainly hasn't mentioned them to me," she told him.

But now, more than twenty years later, that feeling was gone.

*　　*　　*

While Anna's power was steadily growing inside Condé Nast, it was growing outside the company too. On Monday, May 5, 2014, about two months before her son, Charlie, married his college sweetheart, Elizabeth Cordry, Michelle Obama paid a visit to the Metropolitan Museum of Art to cut the ribbon opening the Anna Wintour Costume Center.

"I'm here because I'm so impressed by Anna's contributions, not just to the fashion industry but also to this great museum," said the first lady. The remodeled center, now emblazoned with Anna's name, contained the Costume Institute's galleries, a library, the conservation laboratory, and offices. It was made possible with a donation from the billionaire Tisch family, who were major arts philanthropists, as well as the money Anna had raised through nearly twenty years of hosting the gala.

"The truth is, I'm here today because of Anna. I'm here because I have such respect and admiration for this woman who I am proud to call my friend," Obama told a crowd that included a stunning lineup of major fashion designers—Proenza Schouler's Jack McCollough and Lazaro Hernandez, Marc Jacobs, Oscar de la Renta, Donatella Versace, Calvin Klein, Ralph Lauren. She added that "fashion isn't an exclusive club for the few who can attend a runway show or shop at certain stores. This center is for anyone who cares about fashion and how it impacts our culture and our history."

This sort of recognition for her philanthropy was what Anna had told friends she really wanted as her legacy—more than fame in publishing or additional magazines to run back at the office. Which may have been why a different side of Anna came out that morning, one that her staff rarely saw, one that was emotional, overwhelmed with pride, the elation clearly visible on her face.

Anna hadn't really had eyes and ears at Style.com since Candy Pratts Price, the *Vogue* accessories editor turned executive Style.com fashion editor, had been cut following the recession. When it became clear that Style.com couldn't afford to keep paying Pratts Price, Anna had signed off on letting her go and became even less involved with the site.

In 2010, Anna was further disengaged from Style.com when Condé Nast folded the site into Fairchild Publishing (*Women's Wear Daily*'s parent company) and moved its staff into that office. The website was meant to operate with more independence than ever from Condé Nast and Anna, and it started thriving editorially. But this digital strategy didn't make sense to Anna. *Vogue* was the world's best fashion media brand, and, rather than having its own robust presence online, its content was going toward helping Style.com. In 2010, Condé Nast executives came to the same conclusion when they let Anna spin Vogue.com off from Style.com in order to better leverage the *Vogue* brand digitally.

To create *Vogue*'s site, she decided to use an outside company called Code and Theory instead of Condé Nast's existing technology. Code and Theory maintained the website, and Tom Florio was easily able to sell ads on Vogue.com.

But by the summer of 2013, Condé Nast's digital business was starting to look better. The websites were no longer functioning as dumping grounds for favors to advertisers or cheap ploys for print subscriptions. With the exceptions of Style.com and Epicurious, Condé Nast's magazine editors were running their own sites and their publishers were selling ads for them. The sites were pulling in around a couple of hundred million dollars a year, inspiring the company to make bigger investments in the websites. Meanwhile, Vogue.com was stuck at around a million unique visitors a month, and no one in the company really knew what Anna was doing with it since it was being managed outside the company.

Understanding how to run digital media required work on Anna's part. "It wasn't a natural thing for her to work with less fact-checking and thirty-minute turnarounds," said Bob Sauerberg, Condé Nast's president. Sauerberg told her that Vogue.com had to post stories more quickly and hire editors with expertise in the online news cycle. "I was telling her all this every day, but I don't know if she trusted what I was saying." Her mind seemed to change after she went to Silicon Valley to hear the same advice from people running tech companies. "Being Anna's boss is an interesting process. You don't really want to tell her.

She has great pride in figuring things out, so you just sort of want to lead her to an outcome and let her figure her own way," explained Sauerberg. After the trip, she seemed to have a shift in thinking, which Sauerberg described as: "I've got to move quicker, I've got to find people that look different, I've got to be more expansive in my thinking and the talent that I surround myself with. I can't just have a print person that I ask to do digital, if they don't know how to do it; that just doesn't get me what I need to do."

Anna, aware that her site wasn't competitive, looked to Ben Berentson for assistance. Berentson, who had worked for *Glamour* from 2009 to 2012, helped build up that magazine's website to five million unique visitors and had become something of a digital guru at Condé Nast, going from magazine to magazine to help editors establish plans and operations for their websites. Meanwhile, executives at the company were thrilled—they had been waiting for Anna to come to them and say she wanted *Vogue* to "go big" digitally. Guided by Berentson, Anna was able to successfully pitch her bosses to fund an expanded Vogue .com, which she would bring back to Condé Nast's platform.

With new corporate investment and staff, Vogue.com relaunched and started publishing original fashion photo shoots, cleverly reimagined in a video or GIF format. The site grew from around one million unique visitors to five million in under two years.

Then Anna got hold of Style.com's financials. She finally saw that the site had never made money, and, based on that, according to someone involved with digital at the time, pitched Conde Nast's corporate executives to let her absorb and integrate the site into her increasingly strong Vogue.com. With Style.com in existence, the company would never fund runway shows on Vogue.com; with Vogue.com in existence, the company would never fund more daily content on Style.com. This meant neither site would ever reach its full potential. Weeks later, the executives came back to Anna and said, "We won't roll Style.com into Vogue.com, but you can run it"—which was exactly what she didn't want at this point.

Some saw this takeover as a Machiavellian power grab. Others saw it as an untenable situation given the competitive relationship Style

.com had to Vogue: of course Style.com rolling up under *Vogue* management would be awkward, and there would be nothing Anna could do to change that.

Anna must have realized Style.com had stars on its roster, like street style photographer Tommy Ton and critic and fashion industry personality Tim Blanks. She set about trying to keep them happy. When she flew to London at the end of 2014, she met with Blanks, summoning him to a room off the lobby of the Ritz, where she was staying.

Blanks had known Anna since he hosted a fashion television show for which he had interviewed her in the late eighties and early nineties. They'd had a warm rapport back then, but their relationship had chilled over the years.

He was late to the meeting, and Anna got right to the point.

"I want to assure you that Style.com and Vogue.com will continue," she said. "They will have their own separate tracks, but complement each other. But you're not doing enough. I want you to do social media." She suggested Blanks look at the Twitter feed of Stuart Emmrich, the *New York Times* Styles section editor she would hire years later to run Vogue.com.

"What do you think of Throwback Thursday?" Blanks asked. Style .com had been running a video series with footage it had licensed from *Fashion File*, his old TV show, of old runway shows by designers like Helmut Lang and Claude Montana.

"Irrelevant," Anna said.

"Why? It's the most popular thing we have on the platform," Blanks said.

"Nobody wants to go back into the past. You have to go into the future," Anna said.

He fundamentally disagreed with her; fashion informed the future by also reflecting the past. "Kids love it, Anna. Kids love looking at that stuff. Kids love looking at the things they missed," Blanks said.

The disconnect was one of many the Style.com staff would encounter. Anna wasn't terribly digitally savvy and didn't have a great understanding at that point of why certain stories were popular or where traffic came from. It felt to the Style.com team like a print editor stepping in where they had previously enjoyed being managed by digital people—those who knew that people on the internet, unlike Anna Wintour herself, loved nostalgia. The Style.com staff didn't want to hear who *Vogue* staff thought they should hire and fire, nor did they want feedback from Anna's people on what they were doing.

As this dragged on, Jonathan Newhouse, Si's cousin, who was running Condé Nast International, was cooking up an idea for an e-commerce website that was supposed to make up for the company not buying Net-a-Porter years before, valued in March of 2015 at $775 million. The site would focus on shoppable editorial content, but not actually fulfill any orders or manage customer service. In one meeting presenting the new site to top Condé Nast editors, a senior *Vogue* staff member couldn't hide their dismay at the idea.

One day in early 2015, Anna called Berentson into her office and shut the door, which she almost never did. She explained that Bob Sauerberg, now Condé Nast's CEO, was going to give Condé Nast International the Style.com brand and URL for its store.* Embracing the new endeavor, Anna joined Sauerberg on its board. "Obviously, it allowed her to prevent any shackles to evolve *Vogue*," Sauerberg said. "She always wanted to do that." If there was no Style.com brand, there was no need to preserve it as a media entity—which meant its staff's futures were now in jeopardy.

As always, Anna kept moving. With Style.com being turned over to international, Anna was now free to execute her plan for Vogue.com as the future of digital fashion at Condé Nast, and in media more broadly.

---

* The e-commerce initiative that took Style.com away from Anna cost the company $100 million, London's *Telegraph* reported, and would ultimately fail.

Chapter 26

CHANGES

Teen Vogue was on a winning streak leading up to 2015. Ad sales in digital and print were up, and the magazine had cut a lot of costs, so the business was looking strong. When not accounting for administrative costs that all titles paid out of their budget, for things like their office space and the shared mail room, the magazine had record earnings (although when factoring in that $3 to $5 million in administrative costs, the magazine wasn't profitable). This gave *Teen Vogue* leadership the confidence to make a pitch to the higher-ups—one that had, in the past, always failed.

Amy Astley, the title's editor-in-chief, had realized that a teen magazine wasn't going to sustain itself on paper. She had already been transitioning her resources to digital media; when a print position opened up, she shifted the head count to her web staff whenever she could.

But her magazine had a big problem from a business standpoint—it had from the beginning. And that was the word *teen* in its title. Most advertisers didn't want to market to teens, who were viewed as not having significant disposable income. And besides, *teens* don't even want to identify as teens. This was why *Teen Vogue*'s audience was always pitched as 16- to 24-year-old women who were in college or getting their first

job. So Astley and her publisher, Jason Wagenheim, pitched what publishers before had: dropping *Teen* from *Teen Vogue*, maybe renaming it
Miss Vogue, or casting it as a relaunched *Mademoiselle*, which had closed
in 2001 because of declining ad sales. But they felt their strongest concept was *Story by Vogue*, which would feature underrepresented voices,
much as the brand had been doing during that period with a push
for diverse and inclusive storytelling. The August 2015 cover featuring three Black models—Imaan Hammam, Lineisy Montero, and Aya
Jones—was widely celebrated. In the accompanying cover story, beauty
editor Elaine Welteroth wrote that their careers "play[ed] a major role
in a progressive sea change that positions diverse faces at the forefront
of fashion." Astley later described it as her "favorite *Teen Vogue* cover
ever, of all time."

Anna had always been involved in *Teen Vogue*. No matter how
much her responsibilities expanded, she always went to the monthly
run-throughs of the print issues. She sometimes went to the floor of
its offices just to check out what was going on. She looked at the book
about once a month and dressed it up with her beloved Post-its, but
mostly seemed concerned with the cover and fashion shoots, not other
sections like beauty.

She also always knew who was advertising in the magazine. When
brands tried to pull ads, all the publisher had to say was, "Anna's really
disappointed that you're not supporting us," and the ads stayed. It was
a way of reminding clients that Anna knew who was in—and who was
out. With that kind of power, it wasn't surprising that Condé Nast
wanted to leverage her influence across all its magazines.

And Anna had always been adamantly against dropping *Teen*. Her
thinking made sense: If *Teen Vogue* becomes "young women's *Vogue*,"
does that make *Vogue* "old ladies' *Vogue*"? That wouldn't have been an
appealing position to advertisers. And it didn't make sense to undermine *Vogue* when it was one of the company's biggest and most reliable
revenue drivers.

Phillip Picardi was twenty-two years old and had only been in his
job nine months as the editor of *Teen Vogue*'s website when he suddenly
found himself amidst anguished executives decades older than him try-

ing to figure out how to save the brand. "I don't think I'd ever seen such important people in a boardroom at that point in my career so impassioned and so upset," he recalled. "I didn't realize they knew something I didn't, which was, it doesn't matter what you get them—this game is over."

Over the course of a year, Astley and Wagenheim had pitched Anna and other executives on their ideas—to drop *Teen* and phase out print. But they never took it seriously. So in November 2015, the pair made one final presentation to the higher-ups, including Anna, with an edited pitch that was no longer about the primacy of *Teen Vogue*, but merely about its survival.

Anna and the other executives accepted their proposal: to combine *Vogue* and *Teen Vogue*'s operations to save on costs. That same afternoon, Wagenheim was let go.

Astley told her team the news through tears.

With Wagenheim out and *Vogue* and *Teen Vogue* somehow combining, Astley was in a vulnerable position. Everyone was in a vulnerable position.

Picardi was too. He was on the treadmill at Equinox before work one morning when he got a call from a Condé Nast number at seven forty-five. "This is, like, the famous Anna Wintour move—you get called on her time and you better be there early, baby, okay? You better be there early, you better be there *dressed*," he said.

It was Anna's assistant on the phone telling him Anna would like to meet with him. Picardi thought he was getting fired. He ran to his locker to change, but all he had to wear was a mesh Helmut Lang T-shirt, ripped light-wash American Eagle jeans, and his New Balance running sneakers, having forgotten his work shoes at home. He rushed to the office and went to Anna's forty-second-floor executive suite. It was so bizarrely well-decorated that, as soon as he entered, he felt like he was in an English country house.

Anna was sitting at a round table. "Take a seat," she said. "I've heard great things."

He sat.

"You're going to be reporting in to Ben Berentson now along with Amy [Astley]," she said. "Let me know how it goes, and keep me abreast of the progress that you guys are making on the website. We're very happy with the growth and we need you to keep the growth going."

Anna wasn't one for explaining. And Picardi still didn't know what was going on.

The next six months at *Teen Vogue* felt bizarre, probably most especially for Astley, who was starting to talk about how she had done *Teen Vogue* and was ready to move on. One day not long after Wagenheim's departure, an email went out saying that Anna would like the *Vogue* Group—including leaders from *Vogue* and *Teen Vogue*—to meet. No one knew what it was about, and since most of the *Teen Vogue* staff didn't interface much with Anna, the mood was not cheerful.

Anna always sat at the head of the table, but when she entered the conference room, Astley—who thought she was meant to run the meeting—was in her chair. Anna, in front of everyone, told her to get out of the seat. From another chair, Astley started going down the lineup for the next issue. But Anna kept interrupting. Every time Astley opened her mouth to say something, Anna just cut her off by saying, "Okay." Astley had started working at *Vogue* as a beauty associate more than twenty years ago, and now Anna seemed to be testing her all over again. If Astley managed to get more than a few words out, Anna would turn to one of her staffers and say, "What do you think?"

This was something Anna did often in meetings. Back when she was overseeing *Men's Vogue*, she asked special projects editor Bonnie Morrison what she thought of a rack of dresses that another editor had selected. *This is a test*, Morrison remembered thinking in that moment. *How do I make sure that I answer correctly so that she asks my opinion in the future? Because I've also now, in front of the other people at this run-through, been seen as someone whose opinion she solicits. If we go into another meeting and she doesn't solicit my opinion, my evaluation is that I will be seen to have failed the previous test by all of my colleagues and they will not only not fear me, they won't respect me.*

What was Astley's team supposed to say in front of their boss, whom they liked? That they disagreed with her decisions? That they thought she was doing her job wrong? There was a sense that they were auditioning for Astley's job in front of both Anna and Astley. But at the same time, they knew they all had to leave that room and keep reporting to Astley.

Astley set her sights on a new editor-in-chief job.

Maybe it was Anna's management style, descended from the proudly Machiavellian Alexander Liberman. Maybe it was the postrecession decline of Condé Nast. But now her name and Condé Nast's were not enough to keep people.

The Vogue.com team, including Anna, had tried to handle the takeover of Style.com sensitively and preserve what people loved about the site. But staff like Tim Blanks felt like they had been bulldozed. Many of Blanks's colleagues still perceived it as a hostile takeover, even though to Anna and her team this was a logical, business-minded way to preserve both sites. Despite personal appeals to stay, Blanks was among those who went elsewhere.

But Vogue.com, with or without Style.com's best talent, was successful. The team increased the audience to ten million monthly unique visitors while retaining all the advertisers and cutting costs And Anna enjoyed working on it. It was something new that, unlike the print magazine, could still grow. She started making cameos as herself in Vogue .com videos, including one in which she appeared with Ben Stiller and Owen Wilson, filmed backstage at the Valentino show to promote *Zoolander 2*.

Part of the reason *Vogue*'s access to celebrities was so great was that Anna personally called and pestered stars if her team couldn't get them to do what they wanted. Her attitude was, "Give me a break—we're doing all this stuff for them, they can tweet." The only person Anna couldn't bend to her will was Beyoncé, who appeared on the September 2015 cover of *Vogue*, and insisted on directing her own cover shoot video. Her team simply sent over the tape and left Vogue.com to publish it. (The video wasn't what they would have done, but it got a lot of views because it was Beyoncé.)

As the site grew, Anna became addicted to traffic numbers. The year 2015 was the first that Vogue.com did massive coverage of the Met Gala. The site set a single-day traffic record that year and in each subsequent year the day after the party, which was significant because they were now selling tons of advertising against the content. Whereas *Vogue*'s sales team hadn't been allowed to monetize the party in earlier years, now the company wasn't in a position where it could leave that money on the table.

The values of the younger generation now embodied by *Teen Vogue*, that every platform and brand should be imbued with a deeper social and political message, was likely becoming apparent to Anna outside of the Condé Nast offices.

Aurora James applied to the CFDA/*Vogue* Fashion Fund in 2015, two years after she had started Brother Vellies, her line of luxury shoes and accessories sustainably made by artisans in Africa. She didn't think she had any shot at winning a prize—to her, winning was just getting into the program. Her first event was at a hotel in the West Village, and Anna came in to address the group of finalists. James had worn Rachel Comey jeans, a vintage blouse, and springbok sandals, and "I was terrified," she said.

James met with Anna many times over the course of the next several months, including once at her Brooklyn store. Despite being incredibly intimidated, James decided the best way to interact with her was by answering all her questions as honestly as she could. "I was talking about sustainability back then. I was talking about artisan work. I was talking about the fashion calendar being too fast. I was talking about all these things that truly this woman did not really want to hear. No one really wants to hear a younger generation critiquing the way that they've gone about things," said James, one of a small number of Black designers ever to become a Fashion Fund finalist.

But it went beyond that. In exchanges with the fund judges and separately with Anna, James added nuance and perspective to elements of the business that had been ignored or taken for granted by the majority of those running labels, stores, and magazines, such as "using fur, which is a controversial thing amongst white people who don't understand Black African culture and farming. So that's about people wanting to put their own moral compasses onto other cultures, which is a type of colonialization being disguised as being progressive."

At that time, high fashion and activism didn't go hand in hand. Yes, Anna had organized fund-raisers and events intended to boost awareness of issues like the AIDS epidemic and breast cancer, in addition to her political bundling for Democrats. In 2013, she partnered with Vera Wang to raise money for New York-Presbyterian Hospital's Youth Anxiety Center. "Vera and I both have children the same age, and once they become teenagers and go off to college, it can be such a difficult age—they look grown up and are meant to act grown up, but they're not," Anna said in 2015. But these efforts had been sporadic, isolated, and without acknowledgment that solving the problems the charities raised money for might involve self-examination and consideration of a different sort of guest list.

"You might have to decide," Anna told James, "whether you want to be a full-time designer or an activist."

James replied, "I might not have to decide." Anna looked at her and gave a slight smile.

"I think it was actually a moment that we both sort of realized, *Oh, you can, actually*. We don't have to be just one-dimensional humans or women or creative people anymore," said James.

James won the Fashion Fund's top prize. The $200,000 cash award was huge for her, and she made it last as long as she could. But she also won access to Anna. She knew she could email her if she needed something and that she would get a quick response. "I wish I bothered her more often, because I feel like I know that she would have been on board to help with things that I probably needed more help with at different times," said James, citing a "not great contractual deal" that she felt Anna could have steered her away from. Designers ask Anna for

advice constantly; Tory Burch recalled emailing her at 5:30 a.m. needing advice, only to get an immediate reply to say Anna would call her
at 6:30 after playing tennis. Burch has since asked for advice on any
number of things, including whom she should hire for senior design
positions, for which Anna sends a list of names.

But Anna also lobbied for James. After the creative director of the
LVMH-owned label Edun stepped down in 2016—the same year that
Anna hired her first Black assistant—Anna recommended James for the
job. Edun had been founded by Bono and his wife, Ali Hewson, with
the mission, much like that of James's label, of bolstering African communities by making clothing there ethically and sustainably. If James
had gotten the job, that would have been a huge win for women in fashion, particularly Black women; very few women, and even fewer Black
women, have ever served as creative directors at big labels.

"Do I know why LVMH decided not to hire me for that job and
instead hire no one?" said James. "I have no idea. You would have to ask
them that. But I do know that she really fought for it."

Things were changing not only at the CFDA/*Vogue* Fashion Fund.
In late January 2016 came an announcement that stunned the fashion
world: Grace Coddington, Anna's creative director for twenty-five years,
would step down and become a freelancer, paid by the story, instead of
a salaried staffer. The stories she used to tell in *Vogue*'s glory days were
no longer possible in an age of budget cuts, when the website had fifty-
four employees and the emphasis was increasingly on getting things
online and doing everything more cheaply. Anna wanted to change the
way Coddington worked. Coddington, then seventy-four, didn't want
to change.

"Well, maybe you should just freelance and do a few shoots now
and then," Anna told her. Coddington agreed.

"I like everything done absolutely immaculately. And that is not the
way of the world now. And I could never just let things go the way they
are," said Coddington. "I questioned, I think, too much. She wants to
have a young team about her that could jump on a plane and go and do

what she wanted them to do. And to bring that fresh new blood in. So I said, 'Fine.'"

Coddington had never seriously considered leaving *Vogue* over the course of her two-plus decades working for Anna. "Sometimes it was so hard, and she's a tough person to work for. She has very high standards and it's difficult. But apart from that, she was always really fair and honest and straightforward with me. So I respected that. And I thought, *I'm not going to get it better anywhere else, so certainly I should stay here.* Sometimes I had to do boring things, but sometimes I got the opportunity to do something very rewarding."

Coddington spoke about the change in role without bitterness, because she felt like Anna had always looked out for her. In addition to helping Coddington negotiate her retirement package twenty years earlier, she'd also introduced her to a financial advisor. "She didn't just work with me day to day. She took care of me afterwards," said Coddington.

She's remained loyal to Anna since leaving *Vogue*, "not that she demands it. You do give it freely, because I really, really respect her as an editor. And I don't know anybody else that could do what she does."

The change in Coddington's role wasn't the only new development within the company. The generational shift in attitudes about identity and social responsibility was brought into stark focus during the next phase of *Teen Vogue*.

In May 2016, Anna called Phillip Picardi into her office again. She told him that he would henceforth run *Teen Vogue* along with Elaine Welteroth, the beauty director, and Marie Suter, the creative director, each of whom was called in for a short, unceremonious meeting with Anna, passing each other in the elevator banks as their turns came. Picardi would continue overseeing the website but now report to Anna. His old boss, Amy Astley, was becoming editor-in-chief of *Architectural Digest*. While staff had the impression Anna had saved her out of loyalty after Astley had worked faithfully for her since joining the beauty department at *Vogue* in 1993, the appointment was more the result of Astley being proactive. Anna was quickly convinced that Astley, whose first job out of college had been working for Nancy Novogrod—Anna's successor at *HG*—would be right for the title. "Amy was looking for a new thing, and I think she was capable of doing multiple brands, but she was interested in that," said Bob Sauerberg.

Welteroth, the beauty director, was told the same thing in her meeting with Anna—that she would oversee print and lead the brand with two other people. She would receive a $10,000 raise, said Anna, whose company expenses around this time included repairs to the HVAC system at her home, for upwards of $5,000. "You're the editor of *Teen Vogue*," Anna told her. "Sign this paper."

Like Picardi, Welteroth felt confused. She was being made the second Black editor-in-chief of a Condé Nast magazine (the first was Keija Minor, who became editor-in-chief of *Brides* in 2012). Yet she wasn't getting the title of editor-in-chief, she wasn't getting a better office, and she wasn't getting a raise that felt commensurate with the job she was being asked to do. And she felt she couldn't say anything to Anna about it because an HR person had previously told her that Anna "does not discuss money."

Anna may have thought of giving three people the reins to *Teen Vogue* as a brilliant, hip new way to run their brilliant, hip young brand. But to *Teen Vogue*'s new leaders, the whole thing felt confusing. And to at least one colleague, it seemed like all Anna had done was set up a fight club. Was this Anna's way of innovating or a move learned from her mentor Alexander Liberman, who admitted to "hiring two people for the same job and letting them compete for it"?

But the fight appeared, from the outside, to be directed elsewhere. The magazine was now becoming known for coverage that was diverse, inclusive, and politically progressive—things consumer magazines like *Vogue* and *Teen Vogue* historically had not been. As formulated (unofficially) by Picardi, Welteroth, and their colleagues, *Teen Vogue*'s thesis was that the boomer generation's status quo was no longer acceptable. Donald Trump was running for office, fomenting racism across the country, and *Teen Vogue*'s target audience—the most diverse generation in history—was fired up and fed up. The way Anna had run her magazines for so long directly clashed with the way millennials and Gen Z thought about work and opportunity. Anna's way or the highway, in an era when the media business was ailing and opportunity within the industry was more limited than it had ever been, wasn't something they were likely to accept.

Welteroth wrote in her memoir *More Than Enough* about the day she became editor of *Teen Vogue*: "I have thought back to that moment many times and grappled with a sense of shame and even blame over how powerless I felt in what from the outside looked like the most empowered moment in my career. Even years later, it's hard to untangle one feeling from the other."

As soon as Welteroth got back to the *Teen Vogue* floor after being offered the position, Anna and Astley had gathered the staff into Astley's office to make the announcement. Welteroth hadn't even had time to think about how to negotiate—yet there was Anna saying, "Elaine, come on over," with Picardi and Suter standing next to her, ready to make the announcement about *Teen Vogue*'s new triumvirate.

Welteroth felt she had been forced into accepting a situation that Anna may have thought was empowering her, but actually undermined her. She wondered, she wrote in her memoir, "*Would* any of it have gone down this way if I were a White man?" There were other things that made Welteroth's new job uncomfortable, like being called into Anna's office because of her "tone."

Anna came through the art department once a month to review the covers and fashion layouts, which were her primary concern, with Welteroth and Suter. She didn't micromanage the content but she did want to see all the photos and the accompanying clothing credits. She reminded them that while activism was part of the content thesis, this was still a fashion magazine. To the degree that they could, Welteroth and Suter wanted to create a new image identity for *Teen Vogue*, but Anna's specific preferences (the same she'd had for years: gardens, natural makeup, floral dresses, a big European fashion credit) made that hard. When Anna left sticky notes on the *Teen Vogue* book, they sometimes said "dark" or "depressing," which disturbed one editor when they appeared on pages where none of the people were white, but seemed to another like her reaction to a new, less cheerful aesthetic that was more modern than the English garden party look Anna had pushed for decades.

Still, Anna, a major Democratic fund-raiser, fully supported the thing that might have been more repellent to advertisers than the word *teen*: *Teen Vogue*'s left-leaning political coverage. On December 10, 2016, after Donald Trump had been elected president and after Anna had cried before her team about it, TeenVogue.com published the story that would go viral, headlined "Donald Trump Is Gaslighting America" by Lauren Duca. The media were stunned to see that kind of political essay coming out of *Teen Vogue*. "It was a scathing piece that, for some, came as a surprise, feeding off the stereotype that the magazine's pages are too full of makeup tips and celebrity gossip to have room for serious and thoughtful political commentary," wrote Katie Mettler in the *Washington Post*. Picardi and Welteroth went on *The Daily Show* to talk about it. Dan Rather became a fan of theirs.

Political coverage was exactly the kind of thing Anna had always wanted *Vogue* to be recognized for—but, with her ethos that the magazine should feature the subjects it felt deserved celebration instead of those it would criticize, had been unable to do. She sat back while Picardi and Welteroth doubled down on anti-Trump coverage. She thought Picardi, then twenty-five, was a prodigy. She was excited to see *Teen Vogue* exalted at a time when print was dying. Web traffic went from two million to twelve million and—bonus—print subscriptions tripled.

Though it didn't get the same recognition, Vogue.com was doing progressive coverage of its own. In the fall of 2016, the website published a feature by Rebecca Bengal on the fight to stop the Dakota Access Pipeline at the Standing Rock reservation in the Dakotas. A few months later came a feature by Chioma Nnadi on Alpha Kappa Alpha, the first sorority for African American women, to which then-senator Kamala Harris belonged. In 2018, when Alexandria Ocasio-Cortez won her House seat, Vogue.com was one of the first outlets to interview her.

But to many people at Condé Nast, Anna's management style didn't align with these progressive stances. The company established a diversity and inclusion council around this time, and Bob Sauerberg put Anna in charge of it. The council brought employees together to talk about diversity and inclusion, and reported its findings back to Anna on a set schedule. "I think when she started this communication outreach, and everybody really started talking openly, she saw it. I think it's just like the Silicon Valley trip, when she sees something and hears it, she can immediately shift gears and go, 'Whoa,'" he said. "'We've got to deal.' So you can see through her actions, in both content and in her hiring, some real action steps to move the company forward in that regard."

Yet it was unclear to some employees how seriously Anna was taking her role as council leader. When one staff member came to her with a concern about the council, Anna seemed uncharacteristically uneasy during the conversation, and dismissed the urgency of the group's work. She said that fixing diversity and inclusion was "easy." Her message, the person recalled, was that the problem had been solved and she was—as she generally was with her problems—ready to move on and not dwell on it.

A year into her job, Welteroth was enjoying the work but tired of the environment in which she had to do it. "As a brand, we had risen to prominence for activating and empowering young women and people of color—but it became clear that we were editorializing values that were not reflected in the company culture," she later wrote in her memoir.

So she met with Anna. She laid out how she had been doing the job without getting the office, the salary, and the respect that typically came with being an editor-in-chief at Condé Nast. She told Anna she could no longer work under those circumstances, and was fully prepared to walk away.

Anna immediately said, "Will you give me twenty-four hours to make it right?" She had no questions for Welteroth. It was as if she knew, either instantly or all along, that Welteroth was completely right.

Less than twenty-four hours later, Anna gave her everything she asked for.

While Anna became more invested in youth activism through the headline-making progressive work of her editorial staff, she did something that, to the outside, seemed completely at odds with her political beliefs. As much as she had come to despise Trump, she felt the need to invite him to the building to meet with her colleagues. Graydon Carter, whose needling of Trump had become a story during the campaign, didn't want to attend, but Anna kept asking him to go, saying, "Graydon, he's going to be the president of the United States. We're just all going to have to work with him." Carter would just reply, "You might have to. I don't have to work with him."

Besides, many important Democrats—including Hillary Clinton, who would sit through the inauguration—were trying to send a uniting message to the country that Trump deserved a chance to lead. (Anna's desire to have that meeting may have been why, in December 2016, she bothered issuing a statement through her PR team apologizing for comments she was reported to have been overheard making that "Trump's foundation has done nothing," and "Its board is packed with relatives, and he's going to use his presidency to sell himself and his brand and profit personally for himself and his family.")

Anna had agreed for the meeting to be off the record, meaning none of its contents could be reported; in fact, all Editorial Task Force meetings, including an earlier one with Hillary Clinton, were conducted off the record. But this was Trump, and the editors were angry that he had been welcomed into the building, especially without being required to go on the record. Graydon Carter sat in the meeting with a scowl while Anna tucked clasped hands under her chin, grinning at her guest of honor. But the other editors-in-chief in the room seemed horrified by Trump's rhetoric, not yet normalized. Trump advisor Kellyanne Conway was in the meeting, and seen typing a message on her phone that read, "Your hair looks great, Mr. President" (probably because the entrance to 1 World Trade Center tended to be so windy). Carter then wrote in his editor's letter, "The get-together was off the record. (Not my wish. Nor was the meeting itself.)"

Later that year, with the meeting behind her and the nature of Trump's presidency by then abundantly clear, Anna was free to go on James Corden's *Late Late Show* and say Trump was the one person she'd never have back to the Met Gala.

*   *   *

While *Teen Vogue* became the shiny example of what diversity and inclusion should and could look like in consumer youth media, *Vogue* itself seemed to lag behind.

On some level, Anna knew that her magazine needed to change, which was why she started hiring editors who would push for a more diverse vision. But, a creature of habit, she often simply fell back on working with her favorite people, like photographer Mario Testino. *Vogue* seemed to run like a country club, where if you didn't know someone who was already a member, you might as well not even apply. (One former *Vogue* staff member recalled hearing in the office, when an assistant position opened up, "Anna wants to fill that assistant spot with either a socialite or a princess.") So getting new talent into the magazine sometimes required a fight. One editor, determined to expand the scope of *Vogue*'s female gaze, pushed for Harley Weir, a young woman photographer from Britain, to shoot for the magazine after she had shot major campaigns and seemed to be on her way to becoming the next big thing. After the editor pitched her repeatedly over the course of a year, she only got into the magazine—first appearing in the September 2016 issue—after signing with prestigious talent agency Art Partner and getting face time with *Vogue* editors at exclusive events, proving she fit into the *Vogue* world.

However, other talent seemed destined for *Vogue* success. Descended from the Swansons who founded the frozen dinner brand, Claiborne Swanson started as Anna's assistant in 2008 after previously appearing in the September 2007 issue in a story called "American Beauties" about "daughters of the social establishment" who had not "gone the way of reality shows and public scandals." She left the role in early 2009, pivoted to a photography career, and got her first credit in the magazine in the October 2010 issue. Staff at *Vogue* observed that those who didn't come from a prominent family or have Ivy League degrees weren't afforded similar preferential treatment.

When new photographers wanted to work with diverse models, Anna made comments like "Don't we have enough gays"—or "enough

men" or "enough lesbians" or "enough Black people"—"in this issue?"
The message seemed to be—not that Anna ever explained these
comments—that diversity was fine up to a point. Another person who
worked closely on fashion spreads with her and recalled her expressing
this concern said this wasn't proof that she didn't champion diversity in
editorial—if she didn't, *Teen Vogue* wouldn't have been what it became—
but revealed a desire to represent every reader.

Anna's commentary on photos she saw in The Book remained
unsparing. (Her staff had previously encouraged her to look at PDFs
instead of making an assistant wait for a book to take to her house every
night, but Anna refused.) Often her Post-its contained single words,
like "yes" if she liked a picture or "no" if she didn't. But she could be
harsher; one editor described getting feedback on a Post-it that read
"awful" with three underlines. This is one reason images in *Vogue* were
so heavily retouched (and every image in *Vogue* is retouched). Photographers like Testino would send in retouched selects from a shoot, and
then *Vogue* editors would retouch them again so that Anna wouldn't see
something that would cause her to kill an image. They knew she didn't
like certain things, like too many wrinkles in a face or a dress, so they
softened lines in people and clothing before she saw the pictures. She
once asked her photo department to retouch the fat around a baby's
neck. By the time the retouching was complete, layers of individuality
and idiosyncrasy had been massaged away. Even the most convention-
ally beautiful dealt with this erasure. In one meeting about beauty ideas,
an editor pitched a piece about Gwyneth Paltrow's Goop skin-care line,
and Anna—who was personally self-conscious about the appearance of
her neck in photos and videos—said, "If you do it, just make sure we're
retouching her because she's looking quite rough these days." In the
resulting photo, Paltrow had not one visible wrinkle.

One of Anna's biggest strengths as a leader would prove, in the
age of woke media, to be one of her biggest weaknesses: being decisive but often incapable of both changing her mind and inviting different perspectives into her sphere. Anna was treated like a monarch in a
royal court. Only a small number of people had a rapport where they
could freely converse with her, while the rest of her staff believed that

an unspoken rule was that you could not look at her or talk to her unless she first talked to you.

For the March 2017 "diversity"-themed issue, the problems with this management style became quite clear. Anna had the idea to dress supermodel Karlie Kloss as a geisha for a fashion editorial, two people with knowledge of the planning process said. She was, like Testino, a *Vogue* favorite, and *Vogue* had done this sort of thing before, dressing white models in culturally appropriative clothing; there was no backlash, for instance, to an editorial featuring Kloss dressed as the Mexican painter Frida Kahlo in the July 2012 issue. In the June 2007 "Escapes" issue, Keira Knightley was photographed in Africa wearing high fashion and herding cows with the Maasai (someone who spoke up about the shoot being colonial in nature and offensive was told by a senior member of Anna's staff that the photos cost money and would run).

But staff at *Vogue* knew that the geisha story would be a problem. They decided not to post it on Vogue.com, hoping that no one would notice. However, when you cast Karlie Kloss, whose fans scan magazines and post all her photos, you can't avoid it ending up online.

After Kloss tweeted an apology, Anna was angry. The Asian American Journalists Association reached out next, and a representative from *Vogue* spoke with them, but it felt perfunctory and their recommendations went ignored.

Anna had many opportunities to reconsider this shoot. She would have seen those images scores of times before they went to print, between time spent every day in the art department and taking the book home every night. She must have been unable to imagine the qualitative damage it would inflict. While her instincts about acceptable controversy had been spot-on previously, like the cover of Madonna in the pool, now they were faltering.

Even after that issue, it wasn't clear that Anna fully grasped what was problematic when it came to race. In the November 2017 issue, model Gigi Hadid appeared in a fashion spread of clothes that *Vogue* was calling "glamleisure" in a park alongside a group of Black basketball players, who appear as props—a longtime offense by fashion magazines, but still—surprisingly tone-deaf by 2017.

* * *

In 2017, despite the professional challenges brought on by the media's decline, Anna enjoyed a bustling and happy family life. That year marked a personal milestone for Anna: her daughter-in-law, Elizabeth Shaffer, gave birth to her first grandchild, a girl named Caroline. Bee Instagrammed a photo of herself smiling, holding the baby, who was wearing a tiny knit cap from the hospital. Her caption congratulated her brother and sister-in-law, adding, "Looking forward to many more chic hats!!!"

Months later when Caroline was crawling, Anna took a vacation to the Dominican Republic with Anne McNally, where they babysat together. "She *loves* the grandchildren," said McNally, who saw Anna play with Caroline and change her diapers. Anna was delighted when a second granddaughter, Ella, followed on February 3, 2019. It's not like the kids know their grandmother is *the* Anna Wintour. But of course, even while babysitting, McNally said, "She is still Anna."

Around this time, Phillip Picardi became frustrated with Anna's decision to fortify the print side of the *Teen Vogue* brand. The print budget was still bigger than his online budget. (This was because, as Picardi remembered it, Anna thought the print edition could be saved; it could not, and would eventually go online only, leading to Welteroth's departure in early 2018.)

Still, Picardi said he enjoyed having Anna as a boss. In the weekly editorial meetings she held with her *Teen Vogue* triumvirs, she laughed, asked questions, and genuinely seemed interested in what they were doing. When Picardi blushed telling her about a sex story that was a top traffic driver, she said, "Phillip, trust me, there's nothing you're telling me I've not heard before. I know that you think it's all revolutionary." Early in their tenure, he realized Anna wasn't the same as her persona. After they had asked an assistant to hold a door for Anna, she told them, "You know, I don't need someone to hold the door for me."

"If you let her micromanage you, she will micromanage you. But I never got the impression that Anna wanted more people to manage. I got the impression that Anna wanted to be leveraged. And I think those are two different things," said Picardi. "We would often run into the editors who were having trouble. And they were like, 'Well, don't you have to send her a million things for approval?' We would never set up a process like that. How are you going to undermine yourself by creating some sort of process that empowers someone to say no to you every step of the way?"

"There are certain editors who look after themselves, and I only have to see them once a year," Anna has said. "And all I can do is congratulate them. And say what a wonderful job you're doing. There are others that need rather more of my attention."

Anna eventually heard that Picardi, who was interviewing at competing companies, was unhappy. She invited him to a salmon lunch in a Condé Nast conference room. "I'm your boss. If you have a problem, I would like to hear about it from you and not from other people, because that's the kind of respect that I give you," she said. "So, what do you want?"

Picardi then pitched her an idea for a new digital media brand for LGBTQ youth, called *Them*. Anna embraced it and Picardi began meeting with her and other executives over the next three months to develop a business plan. When it was done, Picardi had to present it to the entire executive committee. Anna attended, and sat in her chair at the conference table wearing her sunglasses.

There was almost no way for Picardi to know, as he was being grilled by Condé Nast CEO Bob Sauerberg—although Sauerberg himself certainly did—that 2017 was going to be an especially difficult year, with losses that would eventually total more than $120 million, according to the *New York Times*, and that cuts were coming. (Some loss was expected that year, given the company's decision to make one-off investments in certain things, but about $30 to $40 million of the total caught executives off guard.)

Finally, Anna took off her sunglasses and said, "How much do we need to raise to convince you?"

The whole room turned to look at Anna, who had said nothing up until that point.

Sauerberg just said, "What?"

"If you think that you don't want to fund it because we don't have the resources to do so, let's go get the resources and build a proof of concept. How much?" she said.

"I need at least $1.5 million," Picardi remembered him saying.

Anna plucked her Condé Nast ID badge off the table, turned to Picardi, and said, "Congratulations on the greenlight, Phill. I'm very excited to work with you on this." And walked out of the room.

Then she made calls—to the CEO of Calvin Klein, the CEO of Burberry, executives at Apple and Google. "Hi, this is Anna," she greeted people. "Thank you so much for being on the call with us. We really appreciate you supporting the new Condé Nast venture for the LGBTQ community." Then she hung up the phone and let the salespeople finish the call.

Sauerberg said he didn't demand the usual financial review, which would have taken weeks, before greenlighting *Them*. He knew that Condé Nast employees, who regularly asked him about things like gender-neutral bathrooms, were concerned about the issues *Them* would cover, and he saw Picardi as a unique talent. "They were very convincing that the marketplace was just ready for a new voice, something that was very contemporary, very forward-thinking," said Sauerberg, "It's not like launching a *Portfolio*."

Them launched in October 2017.

While Anna was working to launch the new venture, Condé Nast was making headlines for two stunning resignations. In September, Graydon Carter announced he was leaving after running *Vanity Fair* for twenty-five years. A week later, *Glamour*'s editor-in-chief of sixteen years, Cindi Leive, announced she was also departing. Circumventing his boss, Carter told only a handful of his direct reports he was quitting before the story came out in the *New York Times*. He wanted to control the narrative on his way out, but the truth was, he was leaving because of Anna—he didn't want to work with the centralized teams she was creating, which served multiple titles. In 2018, following Welteroth's departure, Phillip Picardi left to become editor-in-chief of *Out*. Along with the *New Yorker*'s David Remnick, Anna was one of the last celebrity editors left standing.

Remnick helped Sauerberg, in need of a new editor-in-chief for *Vanity Fair*, find Radhika Jones, editorial director of the *New York Times* books department. Sauerberg wanted Jones to be able to work independently from Anna, and not be required to get her approval on content or cover choices, which Anna had been doing with other magazines in the same market as *Vogue*, like *Glamour*. "Her artistic director role, which was really set up to be an oversight role, not a day-to-day thing—it's hard for her to not do day-to-day things," Sauerberg said. But Anna still ended up "coaching Radhika and integrating her into the company, and into the industry."

Her power had, once again, expanded.

While Anne McNally said Anna hasn't changed since they met in the seventies, other friends find her much more regal. The woman who used to giggle and hug her friends at dinner and occasionally even get drunk has been replaced by a queenlike figure who doesn't want a kiss hello on the cheek, though she still has a twinkle in her eye. André Leon Talley wrote in his memoir that Anna "has mercilessly made her best friends people who are the highest in their chosen fields."

One friend of more than twenty years, the playwright David Hare, described Sienna Miller as being especially close to Anna. Photos of Anna and the actor Bradley Cooper going to dinner and boarding a plane together have been splashed across the internet. Anna viewed tennis star Serena Williams as one of her closest friends. It's a distinction Williams affords to Anna too, even though they mostly see each other at events like the Met Gala and Oscars parties. When Williams met her husband, Reddit founder Alexis Ohanian, she wanted him—like all her past boyfriends—to meet Anna. Ohanian even reached out to Anna to get her advice on an engagement ring. "From the second I got engaged, I barely said yes before I was calling Anna," Williams said, "'because I'm not doing this without you.'"

In fact, Williams wanted Anna's advice on everything. When she was struggling with tennis before she won her twenty-third Grand Slam, she called Anna after losing a few finals.

"It helped catapult me to winning Wimbledon," said Williams (who, for the record, has never played tennis with Anna).

Celebrities are probably comfortable company for someone like Anna. Like her, they understand the burdens and advantages of having power, money, a busy travel schedule, and therefore little time for friendly socializing.

On Tuesday, February 20, 2018, Anna was in her usual front-row seat along the runway at London Fashion Week to see the latest from young designer Richard Quinn (known for his brilliant use of prints) when the whole room gasped. In strode actual royalty, Queen Elizabeth II herself, in a pale-blue skirt suit with black gloves and a black handbag, which she placed at her feet after taking her seat on a velvet cushion set upon an armchair—right next to Anna.

The Queen was there to honor Quinn with the very first Queen Elizabeth II Award for British Design. Anna had previously interacted with the Queen in May 2017, when she became a dame in a ceremony at Buckingham Palace and, she later said, the Queen couldn't figure out where to pin the brooch signifying her new status on her pink Chanel suit.

But mostly what people remembered about the Queen's appearance at Quinn's show were the photos of her and Anna—Anna with sunglasses on—chatting and smiling. Anna later recounted discussing with the Queen "how long we've both been in our jobs." The photos went viral (*Vogue* posted one of the images on Instagram, a rare Anna-approved cameo in the feed) as fans delighted in the two mysterious, world-famous icons coming together and apparently enjoying each other's company.

Anna was also amused by it. "It was hilarious, and the photos were just absolutely hilarious," said David Hare. "You would be amazed at how much time we spent laughing. Because it's just, there is a ridiculous side to her life." With Hare and his wife, the fashion designer and artist Nicole Farhi, Anna can let her guard down. "Anna has a survival technique in public. Of course she does, but that doesn't mean that's who she is," he said. "I think people who think that Anna is about power have her completely wrong. I think she's about curiosity and doing. And it's completely different. She is in the position she wants to be, because it's a position from which she can see anything or get to meet anyone. . . . And she's not remotely blasé."

The viral popularity of the images of Anna and the Queen confirmed what she was, seemingly, finally recognizing: the future was digital, and she was walking clickbait.

In 2018, *Vogue*'s creative digital director, Sally Singer, had the idea to put Anna on YouTube. She came up with the series *Go Ask Anna*. People on the street were filmed asking banal questions for Anna to answer; then Anna was filmed sitting at her desk delivering replies. Singer specifically didn't want the series to be *about* Anna, enhancing her already deep mystique. Yet the series is only interesting because it stars Anna.

But the purpose of the videos wasn't just to satisfy Anna's evergreen ambition to be current and modern. It was also to connect "non-*Vogue*" people—the question askers on the street—to the brand and to Anna. Other Condé Nast brands were making videos with ordinary-looking and average-dressing people, who would in no way have fit into Alexander Liberman's ideal of Condé Nast. This was Anna's and *Vogue*'s way of satisfying that demand. Besides, YouTube drove revenue. And Anna always had her eye on the bottom line.

The sales team wanted to sell the series to a sponsor, and bandied about the idea of Anna appearing on camera with the advertiser's product. It wasn't a scheme she loved, despite the sales team's enthusiasm. Having a Starbucks cup on her desk would have been a natural fit—she drank Starbucks all the time—but the ask was trickier when sales people wanted her to appear with, say, a chocolate brand. In that instance, Anna was loyal to Swiss milk chocolate, Suchard in particular, but agreed to appear on camera only with Ferrero Rocher or Lindt, according to someone who attended a meeting where a potential chocolate sponsor was discussed. There were limits, however: She was said to have insisted she not be filmed with dark chocolate. You could only ask so much.

Chapter 27

THE MET GALA

The first Monday in May is, at the Metropolitan Museum of Art, the Anna Wintour Holiday. It has historically been* one of three days each year the museum is closed, along with Christmas and Thanksgiving, so the museum can set up for what has evolved from the Party of the Year to the far glitzier Oscars of the East Coast, its current moniker.

On Monday, May 7, 2018, Anna arrived first, at six o'clock exactly, as she always did. She floated up the steps, which were covered with hand-stenciled, cream-colored sisal carpet, wearing a silver Chanel couture gown and (always dressed for the event's theme) a diamond cross dangling from a long chain around her neck, heralding the 2018 exhibit, *Heavenly Bodies: Fashion and the Catholic Imagination*. Her usual resplendence was, this time, more symbolic of her resilience than usual. For about a month, she had been fending off rumors that she would leave Condé Nast after the July 7 wedding of her daughter to Francesco Carrozzini, the son of beloved Italian *Vogue* editor Franca Sozzani,

---

* Before the coronavirus pandemic that began in 2020 forced more frequent closures.

who had died recently.* (Bee's wedding, like her brother's, took place at Mastic; it was officiated by actor Colin Firth, and had a strict no-social-media policy.)

Anna took her place on the receiving line in the museum's Great Hall, with a mighty thirty-foot-high floral replica of a three-tiered papal tiara looming above her—it had been made with 80,000 roses and weighed 4,000 pounds. Anna was *happy*, as she always is on this night, a year in the making, an evening that every preceding year's Met Gala has paved the way for. But she never relaxed—this was still work. "Where is everybody? It's time," she said to her team. "Where are they? Can you tell me where they are? Where are they?"

The *Vogue* staff knew. Everyone had an arrival time, and *Vogue* people knew where their cars were, what cars they'd arrive in, if they'd left the house, if along the way their zipper had broken and had to be fixed.

Beneath Anna in the basement, her digital staff sat at laptops and furiously published content. (*Vogue* had even hired a movement coach to direct guests in eight-second videos showing off their outfits for Instagram.) Though working, those in the basement wore gowns and formal wear since they were usually allowed upstairs for a few minutes to watch the performance—this year, Madonna. The *Vogue* fashion team borrowed designer outfits for those who needed them, which was useful if you were a sample size 0 or 2; staffers who were bigger were often embarrassed to ask for larger sizes. The staff were then photographed in the dresses for Anna's most senior fashion editors to approve.

At dinner, where everything had been thought of down to the back-less chairs for guests who wore gowns that wouldn't fit into a regular seat, Anna would fuss about details. When Kim Kardashian wore a custom latex Thierry Mugler dress that redefined *tight* to the camp-themed party in 2019, Anna kept saying to Lisa Love, "Can you please tell her to sit down?" Love had to explain that, actually, Kardashian physically couldn't sit.

---

* Franca died of cancer on December 22, 2016; when Anna learned the news, it was one of the few times she was seen crying at the office.

*   *   *

As the publishing industry crashed in the aftershocks of the 2008 recession, Anna's Met Gala did the opposite. It grew in prominence and starriness until it became unrecognizable compared to the first party Anna had hosted in 1995. Some would argue it also grew in sheer profligacy, as the museum attempted to realize every one of Anna's desires to improve the quality of the party. Yet in her mind, every decision she made was about driving up that cost to raise more and more money for the museum.* In 2008, tables could be purchased for $75,000 and tickets for $7,500. By 2018, tables cost a minimum of $200,000 and tickets $30,000.

As soon as the gala finished, work would begin on the next one; in the early fall, 7 a.m. meetings at the Met began taking place every four to six weeks. The planning process was a tug-of-war between *Vogue*/Anna and the Met. The museum's team wanted to keep the costs and footprint down, while *Vogue* wanted the party to be the sort of thing that demanded a 4,000-pound floral arrangement. The planning was really an attempt to whittle the cost from between $5 and $7 million to between $3 and $4 million, but each year, to make everything more impressive and more exclusive, the budget went up.

As with her assistants, Anna had a habit of not learning the names of some people at the Met that she worked with—year after year—to plan the party, a former staff member recalled. Sometimes she addressed them as "you" and pointed; other times she called them variations on

---

* Each year, Anna could afford to exclude people willing to pay. A good example of this was when Liz Claiborne's William McComb wanted to bring Tim Gunn, his company's creative director and *Project Runway* star. Gunn had been on Anna's bad side ever since writing in his book *Gunn's Golden Rules* and stating publicly that the most ridiculous thing he'd seen in fashion was Anna getting carried down the stairs by her two bodyguards in a fireman's lock to swiftly exit a fashion show venue. Despite Anna's public relations person and lawyers demanding a retraction, Gunn said he stood by his comment and never made one. Suffice it to say, McComb said it was made clear to him that there was no way Gunn would be allowed in.

their names. Her directives were often so absurd the Met team just laughed them off. Once, when walking through the Egyptian galleries, where the display cases were empty because they were being replaced, she turned to the Met team and said, "Where is she? Yes, *you*—can you go into the basement and just bring up a bunch of art and put it in these cases?" At another point she gave a staff member the impression that she found the Temple of Dendur ugly and said she wanted to board it up, but had to compromise and simply erect Katy Perry's stage in front of it.

While the Met fretted over creating the space, the *Vogue* team sold the tables and drew up the guest list. *Vogue* invited two hundred guests to sit at brands' tables. "Every celebrity wants to be dressed, and makeup, and hair, and somebody has to pay for that," said Lisa Love. "And it can't come out of the *Vogue* budget."

Though celebrities never paid to attend and instead were paid for by their table host (some did, however, make a donation to the Costume Institute), the museum itself assumed some responsibility for the various needs of this demanding crowd. There was the year Karl Lagerfeld attended and the Met had to work with his team to procure his desired beverage, Coca Cola Light, which was locked away in an office in the museum for protection. George and Amal Clooney requested and were given a private bar so they could have a drink away from the other (lesser?) A-list celebrities; the museum also had its bookstore outfitted with upscale rental furniture for Amal, so she had a private place to change clothes. During the gala, the museum is dotted with such greenrooms for various stars, like Sarah Jessica Parker and Anna and her daughter, Bee, to touch up hair and makeup. For the biggest stars, the Met has spent more than $100,000 on a private jet to bring them to the party, as it did one year for Beyoncé and Jay-Z. Performers, on the other hand, are compensated, sometimes incredibly well. After a long negotiation, Rihanna charged more than a million dollars to perform at the gala for *China: Through the Looking Glass*. (When the Chinese government didn't want to send items to the Met for the exhibit, fearing they'd be damaged, Anna made a day trip there to meet with government officials, successfully convincing them to make the loans.)

While the costs and extravagance have gone up, so have the funds raised. In 2011, the total income was $12.5 million, and the party and exhibit expenses $5 million, for a net sum raised of $7.5 million. In 2018, the total income was $20.5 million and the expenses $8.5 million, for a haul of $12 million. Kimberly Chrisman-Campbell, a fashion historian and curator, said, "For the costume industry [that fund-raising]'s very important, because it is a very high-maintenance collection, and you do need conservators, you do need the staff, you do need a lot of storage space. And the Met has very successfully leveraged the Costume Institute gala to support its collection. And it is, I think it's fair to say, the best collection in the world."

"The only thing about the Met that I wish hadn't happened is that it's turned into a costume party," Tom Ford said. "That used to just be very chic people wearing very beautiful clothes going to an exhibition about the eighteenth century. You didn't have to look like the eighteenth century, you didn't have to dress like a hamburger, you didn't have to arrive in a van where you were standing up because you couldn't sit down because you wore a chandelier. I miss the days when people just wore beautiful clothes. I don't design costumes. Whenever anyone asks me to dress them, the first thing I say is, 'I'll make you a beautiful dress, I'll make you look great, we can talk about it, tell me your favorite color, but I'm not going to make a costume.'"

But Anna loved the over-the-top looks. She especially loved the yellow fur-trimmed cape gown Rihanna wore for the *China: Through the Looking Glass* gala, which the internet later compared to an omelet. "It's that English part of her. She's loves a dress-up party," said Love.

A different kind of spectacle occurred when Scarlett Johansson walked the *Heavenly Bodies* carpet in 2018, though she was wearing one of the more demure evening gowns of the night, by Marchesa. It was the first major red-carpet appearance for the label since its designer Georgina Chapman's husband, Harvey Weinstein, had been brought down in a defining story of the decade.

On October 5, 2017, the *New York Times* published Jodi Kantor and Megan Twohey's article about his long history of paying off sexual harassment and assault accusers. It was followed five days later by an explosive story in Condé Nast's the *New Yorker* by Ronan Farrow, which contained additional damaging accounts of sexual assault and harassment by Weinstein.

Weinstein had long been a known bully. Someone working closely with Anna at the time said there was no indication that she knew about the allegations detailed in the *Times* and the *New Yorker*. Nonetheless, her loyalty to certain people ran deep, and she and Weinstein seemed to have a relationship that went beyond a typical industry friendship. This was why Anna repeatedly made the allowance—afforded to no one else—for him to split the cost of a table at the Met Gala with Tamara Mellon, the Jimmy Choo cofounder. And it seemed to explain why Anna had to be talked out of having lunch with Weinstein at his invitation after the *Times* story broke (to avoid the possibility of being photographed together). It was also presumably why it took a full eight days after the *Times* story came out for her statement denouncing his behavior to appear in the paper.

Before she issued that statement, Anna cut off contact with Weinstein and set up a call with his wife, whose fashion career she had been supporting for more than a decade. On *The Late Show with Stephen Colbert* the day after the gala, Anna said, "Georgina is a brilliant designer and I don't think she should be blamed for her husband's behavior. I think it was a great gesture of support on Scarlett's part to wear a dress like that, a beautiful dress like that, on such a public occasion." A dress that Anna, as she did for most of her guests, had likely approved.

The very same week of that gala, Chapman's profile in the June 2018 issue of *Vogue*, her first interview about Weinstein since the *Times* story broke, was published on Vogue.com. "When I went to see Georgina not long after the news broke, she was near mute with shock, trying to process the emotions—anger, guilt, revulsion, fear—as well as grappling with the terrible wider human cost in all of this," Anna wrote in that issue's editor's letter, also posted online. "I am firmly convinced that Georgina had no idea about her husband's behavior; blaming her for any of it, as too many have in our gladiatorial digital age, is wrong."

But Anna also seemed to view it as her job to rehabilitate her favorite designers felled by scandal, and this was why intervention was controversial. Anna got to decide who deserved to be saved. When John Galliano, one of her all-time favorite designers, was fired from Christian Dior after being filmed spewing an anti-Semitic tirade at a bar in 2011, saying "I love Hitler," Anna sprang into action. Before she managed to place him in a job at Maison Martin Margiela, she was the one who called Parsons to ask if Galliano could have a faculty appointment. The school was prepared to give him a three-day class to teach, but was forced to cancel it after a wave of backlash.

Anna's move to rescue Marchesa was also controversial. In one essay, *New York* magazine's *The Cut* editor-in-chief Stella Bugbee wrote, "This is not a designer with Galliano-level talent. Chapman's career was funded and made possible by affiliation with her powerful husband and his equally powerful fashion-editor friend. Now that editor has ensured her return to the very red carpet where so many actresses were pushed to wear her dresses, despite her affiliation with a known bully and abuser. This is how Anna Wintour chooses to use her power."

Anna's alliances with powerful men came under further scrutiny when, following Weinstein's downfall, *Vogue*'s favored photographers Mario Testino and Bruce Weber were also accused of sexual misconduct as part of the #MeToo movement. Anna announced that month that, despite them being her personal friends, *Vogue* would stop working with them right away. Patrick Demarchelier was the next long-standing *Vogue* photographer to face accusations of misconduct.

Tonne Goodman, still one of Anna's top editors, was close with Weber and Testino, who was the godfather to her son. "I'm not making excuses for any of this behavior," she said, admitting it was a complicated topic for her to discuss. "They were proven guilty without due process." She never discussed the accusations or her feelings about them with Anna. "I do not know this, but I'm assuming that she was as heartbroken as we were," she said.

None of the reported allegations against the photographers specifically involved incidents that happened at *Vogue* shoots. High-profile shoots like that tended to be tightly controlled, unlike private casting sessions involving agents sending models to meet with photographers in hotel rooms. But as celebrities entered fashion, the outgoing supermodels were replaced by a generation of anonymous mannequins, who were often very thin, very young, and from very poor families.

Helena Suric, who worked as *Vogue*'s bookings editor at the time, said Anna was always concerned about the well-being of models, who were among the youngest and most vulnerable people in the high-fashion industry. She wanted modeling to once again become an industry that created one-name stars (Gisele, Naomi, Christy, Linda) and used to insist on meeting every model prior to her being cast for a *Vogue* shoot. It was like a typical go-see—Anna would ask where they were from or what they were studying in school. She liked models who could hold their own in conversation with her, like Kendall Jenner and Ashley Graham.

As with designers, certain models were able to develop relationships with Anna and had her ear. When Graham got pregnant, she reached out to Suric, who was no longer working at *Vogue*, to ask her advice about how to get a *Vogue* cover. Suric told her to email Anna and share her news and say she'd love to do something with *Vogue*—and she appeared gloriously pregnant on the January 2020 issue.

Before #MeToo, Anna's worries about models had centered around thinness and health, not sexual harassment. "Anna was very concerned about body size of models. Like, if I had a dollar for every time she and I spoke about whether a model was too thin—it was a huge thing," said Suric. Many of the Post-it notes Anna left on the *Teen Vogue* book were comments about how models looked too slender. Suric said, "I have literally argued with her over whether someone was too skinny or not. Like, 'that's just how her arms are.' It was a constant conversation."

Vogue had previously worked with the Council of Fashion Designers of America on its Health Initiative, which was supposed to combat eating disorders and had begun a decade before #MeToo, but Anna thought it was important to only cast models age eighteen or older, partly because that's when a woman's body changes, hoping it would help address the issue of extreme thinness.

"We really started to step up our efforts as advocates, beyond just, like, let's host forums about how models shouldn't be too thin," said Suric. *Vogue* held focus groups with leaders in the fashion industry, and came up with the Code of Conduct, which also forbade alcohol and drugs on shoots, required models to agree in advance to being photographed nude or in revealing clothing, and decreed that photographers could complete no work on set that hadn't been approved by Condé Nast.

Casting director James Scully, who participated in the focus groups, said Condé's pledge not to work with models under eighteen "basically went industry-wide, and what it really did was it stopped the flow of underage girls flooding the markets, because it was really, really becoming dangerous." He added, "It was a way for both *Vogue* and Condé Nast to protect themselves, because anything that could have or would have happened on any of those shoots? It could have come back to haunt them."

Showing long-contracted photographers like Testino the door not only made a statement about behavior, it had another huge impact on *Vogue*: it made room for new talent. While Anna liked to position herself as a champion of new designers, she hadn't done nearly as much for people working in other facets of fashion and media, like photographers. When Beyoncé insisted on having a Black photographer shoot her September 2018 cover, *Vogue* suggested twenty-three-year-old Tyler Mitchell, who had been shooting for Vogue.com. The cover went on to be widely celebrated. But a lot of people were left wondering why it took so long for Anna to hire a Black cover photographer in the first place.

The 2019 gala, opening the *Camp* exhibit, was the last one the Met was able to hold before the coronavirus pandemic swept the globe and made throwing parties dangerous. Anna attended wearing a cape of feathers by Chanel over a beaded gown, inspired by the essay "Notes on 'Camp,'" in which Susan Sontag writes, "Camp is a woman walking around in a dress made of three million feathers." Yet the feathers were a curious choice. The previous fall, Burberry had announced it would no longer use real fur and it was around that time that Anna had decided she no longer wanted to wear real fur herself. (Gucci went fur-free earlier, in October 2017, under designer Alessandro Michele.) Some of Anna's furs were sent back to the designers, including Celine and Fendi, some were donated to the Costume Institute, and others were sold, the profits going to charity.

It was the first time in all her years hosting that Anna left her perch greeting guests just inside the museum entrance, next to her friend Serena Williams, to watch a red-carpet arrival. Lady Gaga spent sixteen minutes on the steps—after Anna approved the extra time—stripping from one dress to another, then another, and then just glittery underwear. Anna, a devoted theatergoer, loved it. (Plus, unlike a play, this performance was blessedly short. Anna's impatience can be evident when she starts crossing and recrossing her legs in her seat; she is known to get bored and leave Broadway shows less than an hour after they start.)

That year, Anna also held the special distinction of being immortalized on a tote bag and as a patch being sold in the museum gift shop. Known for being a commercial editor and art world influencer, now she was in one of the world's most famous museums, as commerce itself. "We were trying to think of people who had a very specific look and a very specific identity. I think to be a 'camp' icon, you need to almost be a caricature of yourself and have a very specific look that is instantly recognizable, a play on yourself in a way," said curator Andrew Bolton. Other icons chosen for the collection were Karl Lagerfeld and Susan Sontag.

It was fitting. Anna has told friends she wants to be remembered not as an editor, but as a great philanthropist, though what she will be remembered as, most certainly, is an icon.

Epilogue

THE PANDEMIC

The end had come.

At Paris Fashion Week in 2020, which Anna attended in late February, people were going home early. At the time, media columnist Ben Smith wrote in the *New York Times*, Anna reportedly sent the message to her team that the pandemic "was not a big deal." But *Vogue* fashion director Virginia Smith said Anna was concerned. They saw that American designers who had gone to Paris to show their collections, expecting to sell their clothes, simply couldn't because so many retailers had gone home early without placing orders.

In March, when the US was going into lockdown with the scope of the pandemic potentially enormous but unclear, Anna called Tom Ford, then serving as president of the Council of Fashion Designers of America.

"We have to do something. What are we going to do?" she asked.

"Well, I don't know how much there is to do, sadly. A lot of people are going to go out of business," said Ford.

"No. We have to do something. What can we do? Will you help me?" she said. Her team had been calling designers and knew how bad things were getting. Anna wanted to help fashion companies pay their rents, their staff's salaries, just survive.

Ford and Anna decided to set up a fund through the CFDA and called it A Common Thread. Ralph Lauren donated $1 million. The public was invited to contribute. The fund raised more than $5 million and was disbursed to 128 recipients. Aurora James, the Brother Vellies designer and 2015 CFDA/Fashion Fund award winner, had lost 90 percent of her sales in March and was unable to secure a government loan for her business—but was able to make payroll thanks to the grant she got from A Common Thread.

Anna was adjusting to her new reality, which included a 20 percent pay cut, working from home, wearing track pants during the day, taking up jogging, and eating Bee's homemade blueberry muffins. Instead of having racks of clothes wheeled in and out of her office, she was conducting run-throughs on Zoom calls, using images from *Vogue*'s runway slide shows instead of actual clothes. Her old colleagues could only surmise how frustrating working that way must have been for her.

Meanwhile, the pandemic, which disproportionately affected BIPOC Americans, made abundantly clear the distinction between the haves and the have-nots. Following the police killings of Breonna Taylor on March 13, 2020, and George Floyd on May 25, 2020, protests swept the globe as millions demonstrated to demand justice for Black people. In an op-ed on Vogue.com published almost a week later, arguing that presidential candidate Joe Biden should choose a woman of color as his running mate, Anna wrote, "The need for change should fall especially on those of us who enjoy incredible privileges; *we* need to listen and learn and take action to ensure social justice and basic human rights for people of color in this country. . . . I respect and honor the anger and rage behind these protests, and I stand with those calling out that Black Lives Matter—even as I do not advocate violence and feel true pain at the damage to our cities and communities."

Months later, against the backdrop of the pandemic and social justice protests, with Donald Trump still in office and the 2020 election just months off, the media industry's systemic lack of diversity and inclusion was thrust into the spotlight. This was what *Teen Vogue* editors Phillip

Picardi and Elaine Welteroth had been shouting about from their plat-form all along: young people were exhausted by the status quo, includ-ing the systemic racism that Anna's generation had seemed largely blind to. And that oppression was felt acutely in the workplace.

First came upheaval at the young women's site Refinery29, where senior leaders resigned after allegations of a toxic work environment. Then came a staff uprising at *Bon Appétit*, where editor-in-chief Adam Rapoport—one of Anna's direct reports—stepped down after staff accused him of marginalizing people of color, including, in one instance, asking his Black, Stanford-educated assistant to clean his golf clubs.

Anna's management style had never seemed more mismatched for a particular moment. By endorsing Black Lives Matter and attempting to position *Vogue* as a progressive publication, she had taken a stance, but many *Vogue* followers felt it wasn't legitimate or authentic. Though her imperiousness had been lionized in *The Devil Wears Prada* when the film came out in 2006, it seemed now like a liability, perhaps as it should have been perceived all along.

Anna's strategy to get ahead of PR crises was to apologize quickly, hope that would make the problem go away, and move on. On June 4, she sent her staff an email—quickly leaked to the *New York Post*'s Page Six—in which she confessed, "I know *Vogue* has not found enough ways to elevate and give space to Black editors, writers, photographers, designers and other creators. We have made mistakes too, publishing images or stories that have been hurtful or intolerant. I take full respon-sibility for those mistakes." Less than a week later, the *New York Times* published an article headlined "Can Anna Wintour Survive the Social Justice Movement?"

The media industry seemed certain that in fact even Anna Wintour, the icon, could not.

Around the same time that the *New York Times* asked if Anna would "survive the social justice movement," Anna emailed Aurora James wanting to learn more about the 15 Percent Pledge. James had launched the initiative in early June 2020, asking companies like

Target to commit to stocking 15 percent of their shelves with products made by Black-owned businesses. "Let's put time on the calendar and talk about the Pledge," wrote Anna. "I want to really understand what it is."

James explained it to her on a Zoom video call, but at that point James had been focused on signing up retailers—she hadn't thought about *Vogue* or any other magazine signing it.

Soon James was so busy with the 15 Percent Pledge that she barely had time to talk to anyone on the phone. But her friend the painter Jordan Casteel had been trying to reach her, so finally at 10 p.m. one night, James called her back.

"I have to tell *Vogue* in the morning whether you're on board to work on this project with me," Casteel said.

"What's the project?" James asked.

"I'm doing a painting for the cover for September and we want it to be a portrait of you," Casteel said.

James was confused. Who calls asking to paint your portrait for the September cover of *Vogue*?

"Why?" she asked.

"I started thinking about women of color in fashion, and I've been admiring your 15 Percent Pledge," Casteel said. "So I told them that I wanted to paint you and everyone was really excited and I told them that I would ask you, so they've been waiting all week to find out if you're on board."

James said yes, and two days later she was posing in a blue Pyer Moss gown on the roof deck of her building in Brooklyn for a photo that would ultimately become Casteel's painting, one of two artworks that appeared on the September 2020 cover of *Vogue*.

Shortly after Casteel took the photo, Anna asked James if she wanted to get on another Zoom call. James had never seen her as excited as she was on that call: she was excited about the September issue, she was excited about getting through the pandemic, she was excited about the upcoming election. And she had a question for James: "Could the pledge translate to the publishing industry?"

*   *   *

Anna's excitement about supporting a cause for people of color in publishing had been preceded by appointing André Leon Talley creative director of *Vogue* in 1988—as he later put it, "the highest-ranking Black man in the history of fashion journalism." But thirty-two years later, he published his memoir, *The Chiffon Trenches*. In the book, he discussed his relationship with Anna, including the times he felt she'd slighted him, their falling-out in the nineties and subsequent rapprochement, and being replaced on the Met Gala red carpet by a YouTube star.

On the press tour for his book, which became a *New York Times* best seller, he called Anna "a colonial broad," saying on Sandra Bernhard's podcast, "She's part of an environment of colonialism. She is entitled and I do not think she will ever let anything get in the way of her white privilege."

Anna was hurt by his book and his comments, and those in her inner circle were flummoxed by the scathing remarks: "Simple human kindness. No, she is not capable," he wrote. Yet Anna, as far as they could tell, had been exceedingly kind to him—employing him when he needed work, expensing his fabulous life to the company, getting him an interest-free company loan when he needed to pay his taxes and buy a house for his grandmother. When she became concerned about his weight, Anna also staged an intervention in a conference room at Condé Nast's Times Square offices, and arranged for the company to pay for a three-month program at the Duke Lifestyle and Weight Management Center in Durham, North Carolina.

But the weight loss was never permanent, and Talley fell out of her social circle. Invitations to dinner parties stopped. His relationship with Anna was reduced to perfunctory happy birthday exchanges and him attending her fittings when summoned. "I think she thought I was too fat and too old," Talley said, acknowledging that her job also keeps her exceedingly busy, along with her family. "She just became bigger than life. She has no time for me."

Talley's book further fueled the narrative about Condé Nast and its leadership being racist and phony in their commitment to, as Anna later put it to the *New York Times*, "doing the work." But Laurie Jones said that Anna's actions toward Talley were never vindictive. "Anna never wanted to cross André, that's the irony of all this. She never wanted to upset André. She felt so sorry for him. He was this guy who had been mistreated and he was Black and he was gay and all these awful things had happened to him his whole life. And she was so sensitive to that," she said.

Yet Anna never sought to get her side of the story into the press, and she was quickly recast as a woman whose methods were toxic and flippant instead of admirably unapologetic and routinely misunderstood. She didn't invent Condé Nast and the fashion industry's long-held values, but she was rewarded by upholding that belief system to an unprecedented degree. *Vogue*'s whiteness and elitism have historically resulted in praise and magazine sales. Anna's treatment of assistants was questioned, but then quickly lionized by *The Devil Wears Prada*. During Anna's years at Condé Nast, the company placed many women and gay men in powerful positions, making it more progressive than much of the rest of white collar America. Yet, with all her power and her knack for sensing cultural shifts, she failed to trumpet diversity and inclusivity and to rethink Condé Nast on behalf of its progressive young workforce until it seemed like she was forced to. It is this very oversight that those who have worked closely with her find shocking.

Shortly after news of Anna's breakup with Shelby Bryan appeared in the press—though they had broken up much earlier for reasons Bryan couldn't remember—the *New York Times* published another story about Anna on October 24, 2020, with the headline "The White Issue: Has Anna Wintour's Diversity Push Come Too Late?" "Under Ms. Wintour, 18 people said, *Vogue* welcomed a certain type of employee—someone who is thin and white, typically from a wealthy family and educated at elite schools," Edmund Lee wrote. "Of the 18, 11 people said that, in their view, Ms. Wintour should no longer be in charge of *Vogue* and should give up her post as Condé Nast's editorial leader." The story also touched on her relationship with Edward Enninful, who became editor-in-chief of British *Vogue* in 2017, quickly earning acclaim for modernizing and diversifying the magazine: "The two are said to have a difficult working relationship, according to people in New York and London who have directly observed their dynamic."

Unfortunately, what seemed to be missing from this conversation was acknowledgment that while Anna had made mistakes and operated in a largely exclusive way over the course of decades while she was in power, she was also a product of the company. She worked for men like Alexander Liberman who expected staff to be attractive. She worked under the auspices of research that purported to tell editors exactly which magazine covers would sell, which historically didn't include people of color. For Anna, having been so rewarded for aligning with these values, any incentive to question them probably only would have come from within.

Weathering the negative press in the social justice era of media hasn't been easy for Anna.

"I think her concern is, how is this going to affect our numbers?" said friend William Norwich of how she feels about criticism in general. "She is an employee and she's an honorable employee. When she was able to make her numbers, then she can be relieved. No wonder they keep her around."

But Anna is not solely at the mercy of executives or the general public. She has chosen to stay in her job, retaining her icon status, with all of its pitfalls and perks.

People who have worked closely with Anna over the years suspect that running Condé Nast in the digital age with its gutted budgets must be drudgery for her. They marvel that she's still doing it, under such intense scrutiny and pressure, when she could be spending her seventies enjoying caviar and champagne by one of her Mastic estate's two pools. But they also marvel that she has, unlike her two predecessors at *Vogue*, made repeated efforts—however stumbling—to adapt to her time.

After *Them* founder Phillip Picardi left Condé Nast in August 2018, Anna approached Whembley Sewell, then twenty-five years old and working on branded content and social media for *Teen Vogue*.

"I'm not a traditional editor. I said this to her face, I'm like, 'I don't carry a red pen, I'm not underlining sentences,'" recalled Sewell, who had worked in social media and video but didn't have the standard portfolio of clips. "I'm not David Remnick. She was very receptive to that."

Sewell—a queer Black woman—became the executive editor of *Them* in 2019. The next year, Katie Grand, the famous stylist and editor-in-chief of the edgy and niche UK-based fashion magazine *Love*, announced her departure twelve years after she founded the title. Condé Nast had to decide whether or not to keep the magazine going. Anna chose to hand over the title to Sewell to run along with *Them*. She was among a group of editors-in-chief of color, including Radhika Jones at *Vanity Fair* and Dawn Davis at *Bon Appétit*, working under Anna. (Sewell wasn't an editor-in-chief for long; in the summer of 2021, she announced she was leaving Condé Nast for a role at Netflix.)

For decades, those who worked with Anna knew that making her wait for anything was the cardinal sin. As it turned out, a lot of people had been kept waiting for her to modernize Condé Nast and *Vogue* as both workplaces and cultural barometers, and for too long. Perhaps one of Anna's great challenges going forward is to keep realizing that.

The fashion industry is predicated on the understanding that there is an "in" and an "out." In Anna's world, people occupy those distinct buckets. Some are always "out"—low-performing assistants, the Penthouse Pets she was forced to cast as models at *Viva*, the Met's event planners who tell her she can't hang a dropped ceiling over a priceless statue. Some, whose success, power, creativity, and beauty are undeniable, are therefore always "in," like Serena Williams, Roger Federer, Michelle Obama, and Tom Ford. Some begin as "in" and get moved to "out," like Talley. Others begin as "out" and switch to "in," like Kim Kardashian. But being "in" is often polarizing, as New York congresswoman Alexandria Ocasio-Cortez saw when she attended the 2021 Met gala in a white gown by Aurora James that read "TAX THE RICH" in red on back. Entering Anna's world, even just for a night, stirred up a swarm of critics, among them *New York Times* columnist Maureen Dowd, who wrote, "A.O.C. wanted to get glammed up and pal around with the ruling class at an event that's the antithesis of all she believes in, a gala that makes every thoughtful American feel like Robespierre . . ."

The ability to make decisions about who matters is the great source of Anna's power—along with her ability to put people in the "out" bucket in an instant. "If you get frozen by her, that's it. She's a Scorpio, you're done," said Lisa Love. "It's that cold." It's why, with her in power, fashion designers, writers, editors, photographers are never safe. What if they get frozen out?

James said, "If you're trying to climb a social ladder in New York and you're trying to get invited to the Met Gala, that's something different. You're never going to be able to feel success. You're always going to feel unsuccessful. If you're just looking for powerful people's validation, then that's a whole different ball game that you're playing. But if you're talking about a love of clothing, a love of expression, a love of color, a love of culture, a love of how putting things on can make women feel about themselves and their place in the world, those are measures of success that no one woman is ever going to be able to stop someone from feeling."

While there are those who think she should be fired or forced to resign, Anna's influence remains profound and unmatchable. She ended the disastrous year of 2020 with a promotion, announced in mid-December, to Condé Nast's chief content officer, giving her oversight of all magazine brands, including the *New Yorker* and every international title. It seemed that no amount of bad press could shake her ascendancy. (The same was painfully not true of Alexi McCammond, whom Anna hired to run *Teen Vogue* in the spring of 2021 before backlash over decade-old tweets led her and Condé Nast to, as she tweeted, "part ways.") The mere mention of Anna's name remains enough to prevent advertisers from pulling money from Condé Nast magazines. Her phone call is all it takes to get a brand to sponsor a museum exhibit for millions of dollars. She is, in a capitalist society, exactly the kind of person a company like Condé Nast wants to keep at all costs, no matter how many lower-level workers think she should resign, and no matter how exclusionary her management style has been.

Anna has built her own kingdom. And the world's most beautiful, most powerful people are living in it. The rest are just looking on. Anna surely has a plan for her exit from Condé Nast and for her future—but, aside from telling friends maybe she'll do something where she's being paid for her advice instead of giving it away for free, she hasn't told them what it is. It's not in her nature to talk about herself.

Author's Note

When I started working on this book in late 2018, the first sources I approached for interviews had one of two takes on how this was going to go for me. The first group thought Anna Wintour's fearsome reputation was more gossip column fodder than reality, and that she would surely help. The other group thought she would do everything in her power to shut it down, perhaps by issuing warnings to sources not to talk to me—as she had done to an author of a previous unauthorized biography—or by using the clout of Condé Nast to try to intimidate my publisher.

Though I do not know Anna, I am not entirely a stranger to her, having interviewed with her twice for jobs. The first time, I was called on a weekend to interview the following week for a *Vogue* writing job for which I was ultimately rejected. The second time, about six years later, I was pregnant with my son in early 2018. I wrote up some ideas for her, but was uninterested in a full-time role, and we never ended up working together. She thanked me for my edit memo and invited me to reach out again after I had my baby. The day before I went into labor with my son, who is now three, I got a call from my literary agent about possibly writing this book.

After I undertook this assignment, frustrating stretches of weeks passed during which no one would talk to me. Finally I started making progress by reporting on her early life and career, which people were less skittish about discussing, and working my way forward to the present day. A year and a half after starting, having interviewed more than a hundred sources, I heard from a Condé Nast public relations person who works with Anna, and who'd discovered that I was working on this book. We spoke on the phone and I explained that this aimed to be a biography of Anna as a woman in a unique position of power. I later heard back that Anna "respectfully declined" to speak with me, but I was provided with contact information for some of her colleagues and friends. (Prior to publication, Anna declined two additional formal interview requests.)

Access then came easier, both to Anna's friends and colleagues and to others who, previously convinced by many years of sexist coverage and false rumors that I couldn't possibly be constructing a fair portrait, agreed to speak. I quickly learned that part of Anna's power is that people who have known her at different periods throughout her life tend to feel protective of her. Their stories were nonetheless illuminating, and helped paint a remarkably intimate picture of an incredibly secretive figure.

Not everyone was able to talk about Anna on the record, and anonymity was granted so that these people would feel comfortable speaking freely. Both anonymous and on-the-record accounts were corroborated when possible. Dialogue is re-created from sources' memories and may not be exact. Readers should not assume accounts of specific meetings and conversations came from people who participated in them.

I am unbelievably indebted to all of this book's more than 250 sources, many of whom spent hours talking to me. I am particularly grateful to those who went on the record: Verrinia Amatulli, Jim Anderson, Meredith Asplundh, Andy Bellamy, Susan Bidel, Peter Bloch, Andrew Bolton, Eric Boman, Michael Boodro, Ingrid Boulting, Hamish Bowles, Patricia Bradbury, Kathleen Brady, Celia Brayfield, Joe Brooks, Miranda Brooks, Stephanie Brush, Gay Bryant, Maggie Buckley, Tory Burch, Carol Devine Carson, Paul Cavaco, Alex Chatelain, Aimee Cho, Kimberly Chrisman-Campbell, Nancy Chilton, Charles Churchward,

Grace Coddington, Monty Coles, Richard Cork, R. J. Cutler, Catherine Daily, Jeff Daly, Gary Delemeester, Jill Demling, Wanda DiBenedetto, Debborah Dichter, Joe Dolce, Gabé Doppelt, Jean Druesedow, Suzanne Eagle, Susan Edmiston, Liz Eggleston, Michel Esteban, Joan Feeney, Wendy Finerman, Jill C. Fischman, Tom Florio, Tom Ford, David Frankel, Freddy Gamble, Rick Gillette, Tonne Goodman, Wendy Goodman, Beth Greer, Barbara Griggs, Valerie Grove, Claire Gruppo, Bob Guccione Jr., Anthony Haden-Guest, David Hare, Deborah Harkins, Rose Hartman, Clare Hastings, Gay Haubner, Lazaro Hernandez, Mary Hilliard, Sarajane Hoare, Jade Hobson, Michael Hodgson, Annabel Hodin, Mark Holgate, Eli Holzman, Barbara Hulanicki, Francois Ilnseher, Helen Irwin, Aurora James, Leslie Jay-Gould, David Johnson, Laurie Jones, Anne Kampmann, Mary Kenny, Harry King, Marilyn Kirschner, Willie Landels, Vivienne Lasky, Guy Le Baube, Jim Lee, Stacey Lee, Freddie Leiba, Sue Llywellyn, Evelyn Lorentzen Bell, Lisa Love, Zazel Lovén, Amanda Lundberg, Patricia Lynden, Mairi Mackenzie, Julie Macklowe, Sarah MacPherson, Jacques Malignon, Stan Malinowski, Terence Mansfield, Bill Marlieb, Michele Morgan Mazzola, Jack McCollough, Bill McComb, Aline Brosh McKenna, Nancy McKeon, Kelly McMasters, Anne McNally, Earl Miller, Sonya Mooney, Alma Moore, Alida Morgan, Michele Morris, Bonnie Morrison, Kathy Mucciolo, Peggy Northrop, William Norwich, Nancy Novogrod, Patricia O'Toole, Adrienne Parker, Phillip Picardi, Gail Pincus, Rachel Pine, Corky Pollan, Phyllis Posnick, Candy Pratts Price, Beverly Purcell, Mike Reinhart, Linda Rice, Cheryl Rixon, Michael Roberts, Jessica Rogers, Bob Sauerberg, Jordan Schaps, Laurie Schechter, James Scully, Dennita Sewell, Whembley Sewell, Lesley Jane Seymour, Sadia Shepard, Alexandra Shulman, Sally Singer, Tae Smith, Virginia Smith, Emma Soames, Scott Sternberg, Helena Suric, Cynthia Swartz, André Leon Talley, Zang Toi, Oliviero Toscani, Keith Trumbo, Rochelle Udell, Sara Van Sicklen, Claire Victor, Carol Vogel, Myra Walker, James Wedge, Carol Wheeler, Serena Williams, Kim Willott, Paul Wilmot, Stephanie Winston Wolkoff, Bruce Wolf, Rosie Young, and Chuck Zuretti.

Many others were instrumental in helping me track down sources and clarifying facts, and I thank them as well.

This book would not be the same without the help of Raquel Laneri, who brilliantly conducted interviews with forty-one people. Raquel is a fearless collaborator whose research of the Metropolitan Museum of Art's Costume Institute, in particular, was vital to this project. Laura Silver conducted interviews in London and went through archives only accessible there. Additional research support was provided by Ko Im, Sue Carswell, and Lexi Hill. I am also thankful to Marc Goldberg, who helped me track down, sift through, and decipher hundreds of pages of court records.

Ben Kalin fact-checked this book with remarkable attention to detail, sensitivity, and thoughtfulness, and I thank him for his many hours of hard work.

While the back issues of the magazines Anna worked at were mostly accessible through the library, those of *Viva* magazine were not; thanks are owed to Rachel David and Jeremy Frommer for generously allowing me into your Creatd offices in Fort Lee, New Jersey—and for sending me home with Anna's entire archive.

I am also thankful to everyone who helped me at the New York Public Library, the source of a wealth of research material, including Arthur M. Schlesinger Jr.'s papers, which contained hundreds of pages of Charles Wintour's letters, many handwritten. I spent many riveting hours reading and deciphering his often barely legible scrawl. Additionally, I looked at every magazine spread I could access that Anna had styled over the course of her career, along with many more she oversaw as editor-in-chief at *Vogue*.

A number of books were instrumental in my research, including *Alex: The Life of Alexander Liberman* by Dodie Kazanjian and Calvin Tomkins, *Newhouse* by Thomas Maier, and *Citizen Newhouse: Portrait of a Media Merchant* by Carol Felsenthal. The memoirs of Liz Tilberis (*No Time to Die: Living with Ovarian Cancer*), Grace Mirabella (*In and Out of Vogue*), Grace Coddington (*Grace: A Memoir*), André Leon Talley (*The Chiffon Trenches: A Memoir*), and Elaine Welteroth (*More Than Enough: Claiming Space for Who You Are (No Matter What They Say)*) provided vivid recollections of Anna at different junctures of her career, and are also frequently cited.

I am not the first person to write a biography about Anna. Jerry Oppenheimer's *Front Row: Anna Wintour: What Lies Beneath the Chic Exterior of Vogue's Editor in Chief* provided an enormously useful blueprint for these pages.

Finally, for allowing me access into her world, I am grateful to Anna.

Acknowledgments

Karyn Marcus plucked me out of the blogosphere when I was writing obsessively about Prince William and Kate Middleton's wedding circa 2010. I never thought that nearly a decade later the blogosphere would have gone the way of shoulder pads and that I would have the opportunity to work with her on such an ambitious book. Karyn, thank you for believing in me all these years and giving me a chance with this difficult, fascinating assignment.

Aimée Bell, thank you also for entrusting me with this book. It would not be what it is without your support throughout a long and challenging reporting process and your deep knowledge of the world illustrated in its pages, which your feedback helped bring to life.

Rebecca Strobel also has my sincerest gratitude for her thoughtful edits and help throughout this process. Rebecca, thank you for your patience and always being available to me.

I am indebted to the entire team at Gallery for championing this project: Jennifer Bergstrom, Jennifer Long, Sally Marvin, Jill Siegel, Mackenzie Hickey, and Julia McGarry. Jon Karp, thank you also for your enthusiasm and kind words about this book.

My agent, Gillian MacKenzie, has been a wonderful partner. Thank you for always having my back and being there to advise me, on this book and beyond.

Geoff Shandler, thank you for your brilliant edits. You were the very best killer of my darlings and I thank you for your hard work and thoughtfulness.

A number of friends kindly read drafts of this book along the way and gave me feedback. Others told me I could do it at my most frustrated moments. Thank you Samer Abousalbi, Omar Alvi, Ashwini Anburajan, Doris Johnson, Dara Kapoor, James Lim, Meredith Goldberg, Patti Greco, Justin Ravitz, Kyra Richards, and Maria Velisssaris.

My family are a constant source of love, support, and encouragement. Thank you, Pamela, Marc, Lorri, Alyssa, Ray, Joan, and Marilyn.

Holly, Mark, Jack, and Kai: I miss you constantly and love you all so much. Thank you for providing much-needed moments of pure joy throughout the years I was working on this.

Mom, you have always given me the best advice. I'm not sure I would have been able to do this had I not inherited your fortitude and had you to encourage me every step of the way. I love you and thank you for being the greatest mom.

My dad is not here to see this book, but his advice, sense of humor, and love will forever impact my work.

Words cannot express how grateful I am for my children, Colby and Lila, the absolute joys of my life. Marcela, thank you for taking the very best care of them while I was working on this book.

And to my husband, Rick, who lived through this difficult and scary assignment at my side: thank you for telling me to keep going when no one would talk to me, for understanding when I had to disappear all those nights and weekends to meet deadlines and conduct interviews, and for reading more drafts of these words than anyone else. I could not have done it without you.

Notes

Introduction

1 Of course, she was wearing the sunglasses. . . . scared, in shock: Interview with Phillip Picardi, August 10, 2020, and numerous people present at the meeting.

1 Anna started the day as usual. . . . were waiting for her: Interviews with two background sources.

1 wearing tall python boots: Interview with Phillip Picardi.

1 Anna told the first assistant . . . you were late: Interviews with two background sources.

2 Phillip Picardi, the editorial director: Interview with Phillip Picardi.

2 Seats at the white conference room table: Background interviews with numerous people present in the meeting.

2 "There's an article that came out": Interviews with Phillip Picardi, and background source who was present.

2 "With the bitter election": Alexandra Steigrad, "Did Anna Wintour and *Vogue*'s Hillary Clinton Advocacy Go Too Far?" *WWD*, November 9, 2016.

3 While Clinton thought Anna: Hillary Clinton spokesperson to author, June 24, 2021; interview with Bob Sauerberg, July 13, 2021.

3 Her then-boyfriend: Interview with Shelby Bryan, July 21, 2021.

3 Surveying her staff: Interviews with Phillip Picardi and background source who was present.

3 As she spoke, her voice caught: Interviews with numerous sources present in the meeting.

3 It was something that happened rarely: Interview with Stephanie Winston Wolkoff, May 1, 2021.

3   She once described [her sunglasses]: Fiona Sinclair Scott and Christiane Amanpour, "CNN Exclusive: Anna Wintour Says It's Time to 'Stand Up for What You Believe In,'" CNN.com, April 19, 2019, https://www.cnn .com/style/article/anna-wintour-interview/index.html.

3   she hadn't the night before: Interview with Shelby Bryan, July 21, 2021.

3   She was crying: Interviews with numerous sources present in the meeting.

3   "But he's the president": Interviews with Phillip Picardi and background source who was present.

3   Her statement made, she departed: Interview with Phillip Picardi.

3   [The staff] then texted: Background interview.

4   Before Trump was inaugurated: Background interview.

4   Ivanka, a long-time acquaintance . . . the February 2005 cover of *Vogue*: Interview with Stephanie Winston Wolkoff, May 1, 2021.

4   *Who wouldn't want an audience*: Background interview.

4   Her team tried twice: Stephanie Winston Wolkoff, *Melania and Me* (New York: Gallery, 2020), 335.

4   But she *did* give a fuck: Interview with Stephanie Winston Wolkoff.

4   "I don't know what it is": Interview with Laurie Schechter, February 14, 2020.

5   "She makes it very clear": Interview with Grace Coddington, December 19, 2020.

5   "I haven't ever heard her say": Interview with Tonne Goodman, June 10, 2021.

5   Sally Singer, who worked for Anna: Interview with Sally Singer, January 14, 2021.

5   "If I were on her good side": Interview with André Leon Talley, March 20, 2021.

6   has amassed more than $250 million: Email from Metropolitan Museum of Art spokesperson to author, June 14, 2021.

6   First-time director Bradley Cooper . . . went to Lady Gaga: Interviews with two background sources.

6   "The amazing thing": Interview with Tom Ford, October 22, 2020.

6   When she walks the halls . . . and check what's on their computer screens: Interviews with two background sources.

6   Staff responsibilities go beyond: Interview with Mark Holgate, July 15, 2021.

7   As one of her old friends: Interview with Annabel Hodin, May 20, 2019.

7   yes, she's changed their diapers: Interview with Anne McNally, May 6, 2021.

7   "She's very family-minded": Interview with Emma Soames, May 17, 2021.

7   "There is a person there": Text message from Stephanie Winston Wolkoff, May 2, 2021.

7   "Anna played an important role": Email from Jill Demling, June 21, 2021.

8   Her closest friends said: Interviews with Anne McNally, Miranda Brooks, Emma Soames, and others.

8   They wondered if fashion: Background interview; André Leon Talley, *The Chiffon Trenches* (New York: Ballantine, 2020), iBook, 307.

Chapter 1: Origins

9   Born Eleanor Baker: Radcliffe deceased student file for Eleanor Trego Baker.

9   Her father, Ralph Baker . . . specialized in trusts: "Professor Baker of Law School Dies at Age 78," *Harvard Crimson*, November 8, 1966.

9   before his death, established: Ralph Baker will and trust documents probated in Middlesex County, MA.

9   Nonie had enrolled . . . their mutual friend: Arthur M. Schlesinger, Jr., *A Life in the Twentieth Century: Innocent Beginnings, 1917–1950* (New York: Houghton Mifflin, 2000), 201.

9   The son of a major general: Michael Leapman, "Obituary: Charles Wintour," *Independent*, November 5, 1999.

9   Petite and slim, Nonie: "Miss Eleanor Baker," *Harrisburg (PA) Telegraph*, January 6, 1949.

9   Charles wore glasses: Schlesinger, *A Life in the Twentieth Century*, 192.

9   At Cambridge, Charles coedited *Granta*: Charles Wintour, *The Rise and Fall of Fleet Street* (London: Hutchinson, 1989), xi.

9   Nonie had spent the summer: Radcliffe deceased student file for Eleanor Trego Baker.

10 her direct and spare use of language: Charles Wintour, letter to Arthur Schlesinger, undated, Arthur M. Schlesinger Jr. papers, Manuscripts and Archives Division, New York Public Library (hereafter cited as Schlesinger papers, NYPL).

10 After graduating: Charles Wintour, letter to Arthur Schlesinger, July 2, 1939, Schlesinger papers, NYPL.

10 Germany's invasion: "Sept. 1, 1939 | Nazi Germany Invades Poland, Starting World War II," *New York Times*, September 1, 2011, https://learning.blogs.nytimes.com/2011/09/01/sept-1-1939-nazi-germany-invades-poland-startingworld-war-ii/.

10 Charles being out of a job: Charles Wintour, *The Rise and Fall of Fleet Street*, xii.

10 barely two months: Charles Wintour letter to Arthur Schlesinger, undated, Schlesinger papers, NYPL.

10 Before he knew what his assignment would be: Charles Wintour letter to Arthur Schlesinger, September 12, 1939, Schlesinger papers, NYPL.

10 the same day the first enemy aircraft: C. Peter Chen, "Battle of Britain," World War II Database, July 2010, https://ww2db.com/battle_spec.php?battle_id=95.

10 Charles was so ecstatic: Charles Wintour letter to Arthur Schlesinger, February 14, 1940, Schlesinger papers, NYPL.

10   While a bit less euphoric: Nonie Wintour letter to Arthur Schlesinger, February 7, 1940, Schlesinger papers, NYPL.

10   They married: Marriage announcement from the Bakers, Schlesinger papers, NYPL.

10   and then celebrated: Charles Wintour letter to Arthur Schlesinger, July 30, 1940, Schlesinger papers, NYPL.

10   Charles slid into depression . . . the faithful type: Charles Wintour letter to Arthur Schlesinger, June 7, 1939, and undated letter to Arthur Schlesinger, Schlesinger papers, NYPL.

10   Feeling that a ground rule had been established: Charles Wintour letter to Arthur Schlesinger, August 22, 1940, Schlesinger papers, NYPL.

10   Charles's affairs would go on: Background interview.

11   Nonie—then about six months pregnant . . . conveniently in Rhodesia: Charles Wintour letter to Arthur Schlesinger, August 22, 1940, Schlesinger papers, NYPL.

11   In late November: Charles Wintour letter to Arthur Schlesinger, December 23, 1940, Schlesinger papers, NYPL.

11   Half a decade would pass: Charles Wintour letter to Arthur Schlesinger, November 24, 1945, Schlesinger papers, NYPL.

11   Just months after having Gerald: Charles Wintour letter to Arthur Schlesinger, March 1, 1941, Schlesinger papers, NYPL.

11   Still, Charles was aware: Charles Wintour letter to Arthur Schlesinger, October 11, 1944, Schlesinger papers, NYPL.

11   Nonie stayed with Charles . . . the Staff College: Charles Wintour letter to Arthur Schlesinger, February 2, 1942, Schlesinger papers, NYPL.

11   She finally sailed home: Charles Wintour letters to Arthur Schlesinger, March 29, 1944, and October 11, 1944, Schlesinger Papers, NYPL.

11   Charles began another affair: Charles Wintour letter to Arthur Schlesinger, July 6, 1945, Schlesinger papers, NYPL.

12   Trianon Palace Hotel: "History of Waldorf Astoria Versailles—Trianon Palace," https://www.trianonpalace.fr/en/discover/about-trianon-palace/hotel-history/.

12   Sitting in a garret: Charles Wintour, *The Rise and Fall of Fleet Street*, xi.

12   Lord Beaverbrook was a wealthy Canadian: "In the Beaver's News Kingdom Empire Propaganda Comes First," *Newsweek*, April 28, 1952.

12   before moving to London . . . advised Winston Churchill during the war: Woodrow Wyatt, "Beaverbrook: The Last of the Press Lords," *Harper's*, July 1956, 48.

12   published a portfolio of newspapers . . . of any publisher in the world: "In the Beaver's News Kingdom Empire Propaganda Comes First," *Newsweek*, April 28, 1952.

12   Having failed to become prime minister: Woodrow Wyatt, "Beaverbrook: The Last of the Press Lords," *Harper's*, July 1956.

12   Once the war ended . . . on London's upscale Park Lane: Charles Wintour, *The Rise and Fall of Fleet Street*, xii.

12 Charles found him disarmingly warm: Charles Wintour, *The Rise and Fall of Fleet Street*, xii.

12 Monday, October 1, 1945: Charles Wintour telegram to Arthur Schlesinger, September 28, 1945, Schlesinger papers, NYPL.

12 He asked Charles to write: Charles Wintour, *The Rise and Fall of Fleet Street*, xii.

12 He had one final night out: Charles Wintour letter to Arthur Schlesinger, November 24, 1945, Schlesinger papers, NYPL.

12 Gerald was five: Charles Wintour letter to Arthur Schlesinger, February 2, 1946, Schlesinger papers, NYPL.

13 Nonie and Charles had their second son: Charles Wintour letter to Arthur Schlesinger, October 11, 1947, Schlesinger papers, NYPL.

13 (known as Jimmie): Charles Wintour letter to Arthur Schlesinger, February 16, 1948, Schlesinger papers, NYPL.

13 the little girl . . . named Anna: Charles Wintour letter to Arthur Schlesinger, November 17, 1949, Schlesinger papers, NYPL.

13 Aside from the baby's bout: Charles Wintour letter to Arthur Schlesinger, June 18, 1950, Schlesinger papers, NYPL.

13 That was until Tuesday, July 3, 1951: Jerry Oppenheimer, *Front Row: Anna Wintour: What Lies Beneath the Chic Exterior of* Vogue's *Editor in Chief* (New York: St. Martin's Griffin, 2006), 6.

13 Now ten years old . . . was pronounced dead: Report of the Death of an American Citizen, Gerald Jackson Wintour, August 28, 1951; Gerald Jackson Wintour death record in the Sub-District of Hampstead North in the Metropolitan Borough of Hampstead.

13 The story that would endure: Interview with Mary Kenny, July 25, 2019.

13 He had been bored: Charles Wintour letter to Arthur Schlesinger, August 11, 1949, Schlesinger papers, NYPL.

13 Still, when notified: Interview with Mary Kenny.

13 Charles shared Nonie's profound grief: Charles Wintour letter to Arthur Schlesinger, July 11, 1951, Schlesinger papers, NYPL.

13 Though he faced a maximum jail sentence: Charles Wintour letter to Arthur Schlesinger, November 18, 1951, Schlesinger papers, NYPL.

13 Later that month: *Queen Elizabeth* inbound passenger list, arriving from Southampton July 21, 1951; Charles Wintour letter to Arthur Schlesinger, July 11, 1951, Schlesinger papers, NYPL.

13 Charles . . . departed the States early: Charles Wintour letter to Arthur Schlesinger, November 18, 1951, Schlesinger papers, NYPL; 1951 passenger manifest.

14 No pictures of her brother . . . might fall out: Interview with Vivienne Lasky, July 19, 2019.

14 A profile of Beaverbrook: "In Beaverbrook's News Kingdom, Empire Propaganda Comes First," *Newsweek*, April 28, 1952.

14 Though Nonie was proud: Nonie Wintour letter to Arthur Schlesinger,

March 18, 1958 or 1959; Nonie Wintour letter to Miriam Schlesinger, undated, Schlesinger papers, NYPL.

14 She especially loathed: Oppenheimer, *Front Row*, 8–9.

14 Bored at home: Charles Wintour letter to Arthur Schlesinger, January 16, 1957, Schlesinger papers, NYPL.

14 writing as a film critic . . . "inspiring to all of us": Anna Wintour, interview by Tina Brown, Women in the World Conference, New York, April 12, 2019.

14 she almost never . . . even privately with friends: Interviews with Emma Soames, May 17, 2021; André Leon Talley, March 20, 2021; and others.

14 Anna's professional ambition: Background interview.

15 from political editor . . . the more upmarket *Evening Standard*: Charles Wintour, *The Rise and Fall of Fleet Street*, xiii; "Editorship Change," *Daily Telegraph*, April 24, 1959.

15 Wintours bought a large two-story house: Interview with Vivienne Lasky, July 19, 2019.

15 marveled at Anna's voracious reading: Interviews with Anne McNally, May 6, 2021; Laurie Jones, May 20, 2021; and others.

15 The Wintours' vacations: Interview with Vivienne Lasky, July 24, 2019; Charles Wintour letter to Arthur Schlesinger, April 14, 1957, Schlesinger papers, NYPL; Kevin Gray, "The Summer of Her Discontent," *New York*, September 20, 1999, https://nymag.com/nymetro/news/people/features/1460/.

15 Charles kept a strict professional schedule: Charles Wintour, *Pressures on the Press* (London: André Deutsch, 1972), 5–20.

15 "The family all knew": Luke Leitch, "Anna Wintour: Beneath the Bob," *Telegraph*, November 21, 2012, http://fashion.telegraph.co.uk/news-features/TMG9691700/Anna-Anna-beneath-the-bob.html.

15 "There was always this sense of deadlines": Gray, "The Summer of Her Discontent."

15 Sunday lunches were often dominated: Interview with Vivienne Lasky.

15 "The gospel in our house": Kevin Haynes, "Anna's Big Year," *WWD*, November 10, 1989.

15 Though Nonie had grown up: Nonie Wintour letter to Arthur Schlesinger, undated, Schlesinger papers, NYPL.

15 Anna later said: *The September Issue*, directed by R. J. Cutler (2009; New York; A&E Indie Films and Actual Reality Pictures).

15 But Nonie and Charles wanted to raise their kids . . . around the dining table: Interview with Vivienne Lasky, August 11, 2019.

16 Under Charles . . . "cannot afford to miss": Magnus Linklater, "Chilly Charlie: The Editor with a Real Touch of Genius: A Tribute to One of the Giants of Modern British Journalism," *Daily Mail*, November 5, 1999.

16 He hired foreign correspondents . . . "I recruited young": "Charles Wintour: Editor as Vital Talent Spotter and Mentor," 47 Shoe Lane, November 1, 2015, https://47shoelane.wordpress.com/editors/theme3/.

16   He valued his inexperienced staff's input: Interview with Mary Kenny.

16   For a Fleet Street editor . . . was set in the morning: Interview with Celia Brayfield, July 17, 2019.

16   In daily interactions: Interviews with Mary Kenny, Celia Brayfield, and others who worked for him.

17   When he took members of his staff: Interview with Mary Kenny.

17   His speech, indicative of: Interview with Valerie Grove, August 1, 2019.

17   The exception was his signature phrase . . . "from sheer authority": Interview with Celia Brayfield.

17   Staff were thrilled . . . who wrote for him: Interview with Valerie Grove, August 1, 2019.

17   Despite how he came off: Gray, "The Summer of Her Discontent."

17   Outside of work: Interview with Valerie Grove.

17   Many nights, he and Nonie: Georgina Howell, "Two of a Type" *Sunday Times*, July 13, 1986.

17   went out to parties . . . "more people than he likes": Charles Wintour, *Pressures on the Press*, 5–20.

17   Eventually, Nonie's attendance ebbed: Interview with Vivienne Lasky, July 16, 2019.

17   While Charles's staff thought: Interview with Mary Kenny, July 25, 2019.

18   Arthur Schlesinger described Nonie: Oppenheimer, *Front Row*, 3.

Chapter 2: Beyond School Uniforms

19   "It was impossible not to be aware": Anna Wintour, "Introduction," *Anna Wintour Teaches Creativity and Leadership*, MasterClass, https://www.masterclass.com/classes/anna-wintour-teaches-creativity-and-leadership/chapters/introduction.

19   Clothes for women: Interview with Liz Eggleston, June 28, 2019.

19   Nothing more dramatically signified this shift: Liz Atkinson, "Knees Up Dolly Brown!" *Daily Mail*, December 24, 1964.

19   Barbara Hulanicki, a fashion illustrator: Barbara Hulanicki, *From A to Biba*, (London: V&A Publishing, 2012), iTunes eBook, 209–18; interview with Barbara Hulanicki, May 15, 2019; Barbara Hulanicki and Martin Pel, *The Biba Years* (London: V&A Publishing, 2014), 31–33.

20   Hulanicki opened a pioneering boutique: Interview with Liz Eggleston.

20   She never made more than 500: Interview with Barbara Hulanicki, July 7, 2019.

20   Anna had little patience: Interviews with Vivienne Lasky, July 24, 2019, and August 11, 2019.

20   "could probably become a sprinter": Georgina Howell, "Two of a Type," *Sunday Times*, July 13, 1986.

20   In 1960: Jerry Oppenheimer, *Front Row: Anna Wintour: What Lies Beneath*

the Chic Exterior of Vogue's *Editor in Chief* (New York: St. Martin's Griffin, 2006), 10.

20   she had tested into: Interview with Stacey Lee, February 25, 2020.

20   running was not it: Interview with Anne McNally, May 6, 2021.

20   In 1960: Jerry Oppenheimer, *Front Row: Anna Wintour: What Lies Beneath the Chic Exterior of Vogue's Editor in Chief* (New York: St. Martin's Griffin, 2006), 10.

20   she had tested into: Interview with Stacey Lee, February 25, 2020.

20   "Queens College was": Interview with Emma Soames, May 17, 2021.

20   The school had rigorous academics . . . "or attach to people": Interview with Stacey Lee.

20   In 1963, Anna started: Email from NLCS archivist Sue Stanbury, May 13, 2019.

20   She wasn't warmly welcomed . . . when it came to Anna's family: Numerous interviews with Vivienne Lasky, 2019.

21   Her dad went to work: Interview with Barbara Griggs, September 20, 2019.

21   Her sister, Nora . . . literary journals: Numerous interviews with Vivienne Lasky.

21   Anna especially loved *Seventeen*: Alice Steinbach, "Always in Vogue," *Baltimore Sun*, May 22, 1990.

21   For Anna, it wasn't enough . . . to maintain Anna's approval: Numerous interviews with Vivienne Lasky.

22   After it came out in 1964: Background source; Gardner Jameson and Elliott Williams, *The Drinking Man's Diet* (San Francisco: Cameron & Co., 1964), iBook, 9.

23   Anna loved going over . . . a social circle there beyond Lasky: Numerous interviews with Vivienne Lasky.

23   In interviews, Anna has described: Linda Blandford, "Guardian Style: To *Vogue* with Red Herrings / Interview with Anna Wintour, Incoming Editor of *Vogue* Magazine," *Guardian*, March 20, 1986; Jan Moir, "The Very Cool Queen of Fashion," *Telegraph*, May 14, 1997.

23   They agreed . . . that she was silent: Interviews with Emma Soames and Anthony Haden-Guest, May 19, 2021; and others.

23   Lasky didn't see her as shy: Interview with Vivienne Lasky.

23   The dinner gatherings became increasingly tense: Interview with Mary Kenny, July 25, 2019.

24   Lasky and Anna adored their dads: Interview with Vivienne Lasky.

24   women who were prominent: Interview with Valerie Grove, August 1, 2019.

24   When Anna was around fifteen: Interview with Vivienne Lasky.

24   She got to study under Peggy Angus: Email from Sue Stanbury.

24   a famous artist: Rachel Cooke, "Peggy Angus Was a Warrior. Women Weren't Supposed to Be Like That," *Guardian*, July 5, 2014, https://www.theguardian.com/artanddesign/2014/jul/06/peggy-angus-warrior-painter-designer-tiles-wallpaper.

24   the curriculum bored her: Interview with Vivienne Lasky, July 19, 2019.

24 Occasionally, without any consequence: Interview with Vivienne Lasky, July 17, 2019.

24 At the end of the school week . . . one of their favorite clubs: Interview Vivienne Lasky, July 19, 2019;

24 Its slogan was: "Tonight's TV," *Daily Mail*, November 15, 1963.

24 As Anna described . . . "what more could anyone ask?": Anna Wintour, "London's Discotheques," *NLCS Magazine*, 1966.

25 Bouncers didn't check IDs . . . never about going wild: Numerous interviews with Vivienne Lasky.

Chapter 3: Fired and Hired

26 Anna's formal education ended: Email from NCLS archivist Sue Stanbury, May 13, 2019.

26 University had been an important part: Interview with Vivienne Lasky, August 11, 2019.

26 Years later, Anna told: Interview with David Hare, October 27, 2020.

26 She wanted to work: Interview with Emma Soames, May 17, 2021.

26 At the time, it was not unusual: *Education: Historical Statistics*, SN/SG/4252, House of Commons Library, November 27, 2012, https://researchbriefings.files.parliament.uk/documents/SN04252/SN04252.pdf.

26 Unsurprisingly, Nonie and Charles . . . "never threw it in her face": Interview with Vivienne Lasky, July 16, 2019.

27 On the other hand, her siblings: Linda Blandford, "Guardian Style: To *Vogue* with Red Herrings / Interview with Anna Wintour, Incoming Editor of *Vogue* Magazine," *Guardian*, March 20, 1986.

27 Charles seemed to appreciate it: Interview with Barbara Griggs, September 20, 2019.

27 But he also cared that fashion: Interview with Mary Kenny, July 25, 2019.

27 Charles denied that he ever pushed Anna: Michael Leapman, "Media Families, 23: The Wintour," *Independent*, July 21, 1997.

27 but in fact, she knew: Nigel Farndale, "'Nuclear' Anna Sets a Frosty Tone at *Vogue*," *Telegraph*, April 4, 1998.

27 He would sometimes ask her: Interview with Vivienne Lasky, July 19, 2019.

27 "I certainly grew up knowing": George Wayne, *Anyone Who's Anyone* (New York: HarperCollins, 2017), 175.

27 Still, some twenty years into: *The September Issue*, directed by R. J. Cutler (2009; New York; A&E Indie Films and Actual Reality Pictures).

27 He left behind an estate . . . would be nearly $119,000: Ralph Baker will and trust documents probated in Middlesex County, MA.

28 passed away in September of 1970: Anna Baker obituary, *Boston Globe*, September 8, 1970.

28 like the Mini she drove: Background source.

28   At work one day Charles . . . "she would do": Interview with Barbara
      Griggs.

28   Griggs then called: Interview with Barbara Hulanicki, May 15, 2019.

29   As Charles Wintour's daughter . . . "we would have hired, realistically":
      Interview with Kim Willott, September 3, 2019.

29   "I'm sure she was terrified": Interview with Barbara Hulanicki.

29   Staff said they were told: Interview with Kim Willott.

29   Celebrities like Brigitte Bardot . . . she seemed too reserved: Interview
      with Barbara Hulanicki.

29   Part of the craziness: Barbara Hulanicki, *From A to Biba*, (London: V&A
      Publishing, 2012), iTunes eBook, 271–72.

29   In a 2002 *Independent* profile: Deborah Ross, "The Deborah Ross Inter-
      view: Alexandra Shulman," *Independent*, July 22, 2002.

29   Anna had been working there: Interviews with Rosie Young and back-
      ground source.

30   Young certainly didn't get the impression: Interview with Rosie Young.

30   In the summer of 1967 . . . all wore white minidresses: "'The Way In' at
      Harrods," *Times (UK)*, April 5, 1967.

30   blue-and-black-striped floor: Gloria Emerson, "In London's Staid Har-
      rods, the 'Way In' Goes Far Out," *New York Times*, August 31, 1967.

30   The vibe resonated with Anna: Interview with Vivienne Lasky, August 11,
      2019; Anna's employment confirmed by Harrods archivist.

30   her colleagues included: "A History of Way In," provided by Harrods
      archivist.

30   working a retail job . . . "straight to the top": Interview with Vivienne Lasky.

30   Around the time Anna was working at Harrods . . . in a grown woman's
      closet: Interviews with Vivienne Lasky.

31   For someone who would . . . settled on something leather: Mary Kenny,
      "Why Anna Wintour Should Have No Regrets About Giving Uni a
      Miss," *Belfast Telegraph*, February 22, 2016, https://www.belfasttelegraph
      .co.uk/opinion/columnists/mary-kenny/why-Anna-anna-should-have
      -no-regrets-about-giving-uni-a-miss-34469152.html.

31   In a joint interview: Georgina Howell, "Two of a Type" *Sunday Times*,
      July 13, 1986.

31   she insisted on running political stories: Interview with Laurie Jones,
      December 5, 2020.

31   "Just because you like": *The September Issue*, directed by R. J. Cutler (2009;
      New York; A&E Indie Films and Actual Reality Pictures).

31   Her father had put: the headless corpse Magnus Linklater, "Chilly Charlie:
      The Editor with a Real Touch of Genius," *Daily Mail*, November 5, 1999.

31   Anna made one final attempt: Interview with Vivienne Lasky, August 12,
      2019.

32   But the classes weren't a complete waste . . . show her New York nightlife:
      Charles Wintour letter to Arthur Schlesinger, February 2, 1968, Arthur M.

Schlesinger Jr. papers, Manuscripts and Archives Division, New York Public Library.

32 Schlesinger, a prominent New Yorker: Charles Wintour letter to Arthur Schlesinger, April 5, 1968, Schlesinger papers, NYPL.

32 Anna started a relationship . . . inviting her parents over for dinner: Interviews with Vivienne Lasky.

32 his photos were appearing in major magazines: "Stephen Bobroff," Liz Eggleston (website), https://lizeggleston.com/category/photographers/stephen-bobroff/.

33 The two of them collaborated: "Student 1969 + I-D 1991: How Anna Wintour and Edward Enninful Started Their Journeys to the Top," Paul Gorman (website), https://www.paulgormanis.com/?p=21948.

Chapter 4: Anna Wintour, Fashion Assistant

34 When Anna showed up for an interview: Georgina Howell, "Two of a Type," *Sunday Times*, July 13, 1986.

34 Sitting down with editor Jennifer Hocking: Jerry Oppenheimer, *Front Row: Anna Wintour: What Lies Beneath the Chic Exterior of* Vogue's *Editor in Chief,* (New York: St. Martin's Griffin, 2006), 63.

34 Anna made a point of exaggerating: Nigel Farndale, "'Nuclear' Anna Sets a Frosty Tone at *Vogue*," *Telegraph*, April 4, 1998.

34 her boss, Willie Landels: Interview with Willie Landels, May 17, 2019.

34 Landels, an artist: "Willie Landels," Zanotta (website), https://www.zanotta.it/en-us/heritage/designers/willie-landels.

34 knew Anna's father: Interview with Willie Landels.

35 One of the first things Landels noticed: Ibid.

35 The glasses, which seemed like an eccentricity: Interviews with Clare Hastings, June 13, 2019, and Vivienne Lasky, July 16, 2019.

35 Her father suffered from macular degeneration: Charles Wintour letter to Arthur Schlesinger, June 23, 1997, Arthur M. Schlesinger Jr. papers, Manuscripts and Archives Division, New York Public Library.

35 causing vision problems: "Age-Related Macular Degeneration," NIH, https://www.nei.nih.gov/learn-about-eye-health/eye-conditions-and-diseases/age-related-macular-degeneration.

35 Anna claimed that her nearsightedness: Interview with Lisa Love, October 20, 2021.

35 Lasky remembered Anna unhappily having to wear glasses . . . Both Anna and her dad were thrilled: Interviews with Vivienne Lasky, 2019.

35 Both Anna and her dad were thrilled: Interviews with Vivienne Lasky, July 17 and 19, 2019.

35 in the March 1970 issue, debuted: Masthead, *Harper's Bazaar (UK)*, March 1970.

35 her last name hardly made her stand out: Interview with Terence (Terry) Mansfield, November 27, 2019.

35 Since the fashion pages were run . . . "told me to go on a shoot": Anna Wintour, "Introduction," *Anna Wintour Teaches Creativity and Leadership*, MasterClass, https://www.masterclass.com/classes/anna-wintour -teaches-creativity-and-leadership/chapters/introduction.

36 Anna was a perfectionist: Interview with Clare Hastings, June 12, 2019.

36 Landels didn't like how she dressed: Interview with Willie Landels.

36 Anna seemed to agree with him: Geraldine Ranson, "A New Realism in *Vogue*," *Sunday Telegraph*, April 6, 1986.

36 Eric Boman, who was trying to break into photography: Email from Eric Boman, May 28, 2021.

36 "She was good at finding people": Interview with Willie Landels.

36 In a late November 1971 spread: "Christmas Presents," *Harpers & Queen*, Late November 1971.

37 That's not to say that Charles failed to notice: Howell, "Two of a Type."

37 she had a type: Charles Wintour letter to Arthur Schlesinger, July 31, 1978, Schlesinger papers, NYPL.

37 Many of the men she dated: Background source.

37 Anna moved back into: Interview with Emma Soames, May 17, 2021.

37 Neville, a hippie . . . decided to move: Richard Neville, *Hippie Hippie Shake* (London: Duckworth Overlook, 1995), 24–68.

37 Writer Anthony Haden-Guest: Interview with Anthony Haden-Guest, May 19, 2021.

37 at a party in 1969 . . . they had dinner with her parents: Oppenheimer, *Front Row*, 58–60.

38 Neville continued using *Oz* . . . life in prison: Interview with Jim Anderson, December 12, 2019.

38 In the end, the *Oz* team was acquitted: Marsha Rowe and Geoffrey Robertson, "Richard Neville Obituary," *Guardian*, September 4, 2016, https://www.theguardian.com/media/2016/sep/04/richard-neville-obituary.

38 After almost a week in prison: Natasha Frost, "The Underground Magazine That Sparked the Longest Obscenity Trial in British History," Atlas Obscura, February 16, 2018, https://www.atlasobscura.com/articles/oz -magazine-obscenity-trial.

38 she would allude to the encounter . . . "my dad was quite cunning": "Anna Wintour's Valentine's Day Gift Ideas, Oscar Picks, and Worst Date Ever (ft. Kendall Jenner)," *Vogue*, YouTube video, February 6, 2020, https://www .youtube.com/watch?v=KtSocOBSbYg.

38 Clare Hastings landed as Anna's assistant . . . to what she ate: Interviews with Clare Hastings, June 12 and 13, 2019.

39 Sometimes she would send her steak back: Interview with James Wedge, May 24, 2019.

39 For a while, she paid Hastings . . . lie that she was out of the office: Interviews with Clare Hastings.

39   When not at work: Interviews with Emma Soames, Anthony Haden-Guest, and background source.

39   "Are you one of the beautiful people?": "Club Dell Aretusa—Kings Road, Chelsea," *Bowie Blog*, August 13, 2020, https://davidbowieautograph.com/blog/f/club-dell-aretusa---kings-road-chelsea.

40   At dinner, Anna sat silently: Interview with Emma Soames.

40   Her crew included: Interview with Anthony Haden-Guest.

40   "I know there was a lot of drinking": Tim Willis, *Nigel Dempster and the Death of Discretion*, (London: Short Books, 2010), 60.

40   She was always home: Interview with Emma Soames.

40   Part of Anna's job . . . and say, "Thank you": Interviews with Clare Hastings.

40   One photographer who did appeal: Interview with James Wedge, May 24, 2019.

41   As Anna developed a reputation . . . and they were published: Interview with Jim Lee, June 14, 2019.

41   Anna, always dressed immaculately . . . on the way to her seat: Interview with Monty Coles, May 24, 2019.

42   although she couldn't really draw: Interview with Clare Hastings.

42   In 1972, Anna started a five-year relationship: Background interview.

42   always simply Bradshaw . . . "He caused a stir": Jon Bradshaw, *The Ocean Is Closed*, (Houston: ZE Books, 2021), eBook, 15.

42   They moved in together: Interview with Vivienne Lasky.

42   While covering the lingerie market: Liz Tilberis, *No Time to Die*, (New York: Avon, 1998), 88–89.

43   In fact, Anna had quickly tired: Anna Wintour, "Introduction," *Anna Wintour Teaches Creativity and Leadership*.

43   In 1974, a more senior role . . . a promotion was well deserved: Interviews with Clare Hastings.

43   To help her case: Interview with Willie Landels.

43   "Over five years, I rose": Georgina Howell, "Two of a Type."

43   Hogg was dramatically different . . . "not being as good as she was": Interview with Clare Hastings.

44   As Michael Hodgson [recalled]: Interview with Michael Hodgson, June 13, 2019.

44   Anna "could be vile": Interview with Clare Hastings.

44   Once, things got so bad: Interview with Willie Landels.

44   After several months under Hogg: Interview with Clare Hastings.

44   Anna had no master plan: Louise Chunn, "A Wintour's Tale," *Guardian*, April 29, 1991.

44   She set her sights: Interview with Emma Soames.

45   After considering San Francisco: Charles Wintour letter to Arthur Schlesinger, February 20, 1975, Schlesinger papers, NYPL.

45   "She regarded New York": Interview with Emma Soames.

45   On Thursday, March 13, 1975: Charles Wintour letter to Arthur Schlesinger, March 14, 1975, Schlesinger papers, NYPL.

Chapter 5: A New Start in New York City

46 Anna was hired to oversee . . . was never even published: Interview with Harry King, November 26, 2019.

46 "a rather depressing start": Charles Wintour letter to Arthur Schlesinger, February 20, 1975, Arthur M. Schlesinger Jr. papers, Manuscripts and Archives Division, New York Public Library.

46 She and Bradshaw moved: Jon Bradshaw, *The Ocean Is Closed*, (Houston: ZE Books, 2021), iBook, 8.

47 Here, no one knew her as Charles Wintour's daughter: Alastair Campbell, *Winners*, (United Kingdom: Pegasus Books, 2015), iBook, 387–88.

47 Yet Anna would, many years later: Interviews with Laurie Jones, December 5, 2020, and background sources.

47 After interviewing: Interviews with several of Anna's *Harper's Bazaar* colleagues.

47 *Have we hired the wrong person?* . . . what she later described as business: Interview with Michele Mazzola, October 31, 2019.

47 what the crew figured . . . didn't meddle in what they were doing: Interview with Francois Ilnseher, March 9, 2020.

47 Michele was a bit disconcerted: Interview with Michele Mazzola.

47 This was unusual in American fashion: Interview with Francois Ilnseher.

48 *Bazaar*'s Gloria Moncur. . . to stamp her vision on *Bazaar*'s pages: Interview with Michele Mazzola.

48 Mazzola's primary concern was finances: Interview with Catherine A. Daily, October 29, 2019.

48 "All he did was capitulate": Interview with Alida Morgan, December 8, 2020.

48 Mazzola micromanaged budgets: Interviews with Keith Trumbo, October 25, 2019 and background source.

48 There wasn't always money: Interview with Alida Morgan.

48 Though Tony had approved Anna's hiring: Interview with Evelyn Bell, October 29, 2019.

48 those at the magazine thought: Background interview.

48 They, however, did: Interviews with Marilyn Kirschner, September 17, 2019; Zazel Lovén, September 17, 2019; and others who worked with her at the time.

48 Wendy Goodman . . . was struck by Anna's [dress and heels]: Interview with Wendy Goodman, June 29, 2021.

48 Anna liked clothes that showed off her legs: Interview with Marilyn Kirschner.

49 Goodman once snatched up: Interview with Wendy Goodman.

49 And then there was Anna's British accent: Interviews with numerous colleagues from the time.

49 a long-standing friendship with . . . Carrie Donovan: Interview with Carol Vogel, February 28, 2020.

49 Donovan, a highly respected editor: Profile of Carrie Donovan, *Avenue*, March 1986.

49 Anna "is a fashion person": "Spice Girls," *W*, August 1997.

49 "She was very clear-minded": Interview with Zazel Lovén.

49 That was made harder . . . what to do with them: Interview with Alida Morgan.

49 Michele . . . dressed casually: Interviews with Marilyn Kirschner, Wendy Goodman, and others who worked with her at the time.

49 her colleagues never forgot their mortification: Background interview.

49 Goodman thought her attire: Interview with Wendy Goodman.

50 Mazzola noted that she often: Email from Michele Mazzola, September 4, 2021.

50 Anna's taste was edgier: Interviews with numerous colleagues from the time.

50 Mazzola and his art department . . . Anna got what she wanted: Interview with Alida Morgan.

50 Goodman was in awe: Interview with Wendy Goodman.

50 "Tony was the boss": Interview with Marilyn Kirschner.

50 Yet when Anna and Tony clashed: Interviews with Evelyn Bell and background source.

50 part of it was Anna's shyness . . . He had a glow around her: Interview with Alida Morgan.

51 Bradshaw occasionally went to the office: Interview with Wendy Goodman.

51 In the spring of 1976: Interview with Alida Morgan.

51 she later called the rumors "fake news": "Spill Your Guts or Fill Your Guts w/ Anna Wintour," *The Late Late Show with James Corden*, YouTube, October 26, 2017, https://www.youtube.com/watch?v=gWQ3mhN_6iE.

51 Despite how well they got on . . . an off period with Bradshaw: Interview with Alida Morgan.

52 Another person Anna dated: Martin Amis, *Inside Story* (New York: Knopf, 2020), 312; and background source.

52 "She just was very suave": Interview with Wendy Goodman.

52 Mazzola liked themed issues . . . not a shill for *Bazaar*: Interview with Jill Fischman, October 8, 2019.

52 In mid-1976, not even a year into her tenure: Interview with Alida Morgan.

52 It didn't appear that . . . editing "fashion" out of his magazines: Marian Christy, "The Fine Definition of Style," *Boston Globe*, March 12, 1976.

53 Then Donovan—Anna's champion—left . . . Tony had fired her: Interview with Alida Morgan.

53 "She was very upset": Interview with Wendy Goodman.

53 "I was fired by the editor-in-chief": Anna Wintour, "Anna Wintour on Leaving London for New York," *Guardian*, May 19, 1997.

54 Tony denied firing Anna: Jerry Oppenheimer, *Front Row: Anna Wintour: What Lies Beneath the Chic Exterior of* Vogue's *Editor in Chief* (New York: St. Martin's Griffin, 2006), 109–10.

Chapter 6: Viva la Vida

55 Anna felt like . . . by her own admission, "a disaster": Linda Blandford, "Guardian Style: To *Vogue* with Red Herrings / Interview with Anna Wintour, Incoming Editor of *Vogue* Magazine," *Guardian*, March 20, 1986.

55 her parents' tumultuous marriage was finally ending: Charles Wintour letter to Arthur Schlesinger, February 14, 1977, Arthur M. Schlesinger Jr. papers, Manuscripts and Archives Division, New York Public Library.

55 Their divorce seemed difficult for Anna . . . they were better off apart: Interview with Vivienne Lasky, July 16, 2019, and email from Michel Esteban, May 6, 2021.

56 Charles, now fifty-nine: Charles Wintour letter to Arthur Schlesinger, February 14, 1977, Schlesinger papers, NYPL.

56 Anna never liked her: Background interview.

56 Nonie moved into a modest house: Interview with Vivienne Lasky, July 17, 2019.

56 She refused to take any money: Charles Wintour letter to Arthur Schlesinger, September 25, year unspecified, Schlesinger papers, NYPL.

56 *Viva*, the sister publication: Anthony Haden-Guest, "Anthony Haden-Guest Remembers Bob Guccione and *Penthouse*," Daily Beast, July 14, 2017, https://www.thedailybeast.com/anthony-haden-guest-remembers-bob-guccione-and-penthouse.

56 22,000-square-foot mansion: Bess Levin, "Falcone Buys *Penthouse* Penthouse," Dealbreaker, March 5, 2008, https://dealbreaker.com/2008/03/falcone-buys-penthouse-penthouse.

56 was bothered that *Viva*'s photos: Interview with Bob Guccione Jr., November 22, 2019; also Joe Cappo, "Associate Publisher Said Male Nudity Hurt *Viva*," *Atlanta Constitution*, June 25, 1976.

56 Jon Bradshaw's timing was perfect . . . Bloch asked Alma Moore: Interview with Peter Bloch, August 20, 2019.

56 Their relationship had ended: Jon Bradshaw, *The Ocean Is Closed*, (Houston: ZE Books, 2021), iBook, 17.

56 Moore had just let go of . . . When Anna accepted, she was amazed: Interview with Alma Moore, September 13, 2019.

57 "I needed a job": Blandford, "Guardian Style."

57 including the inadequacies of the American legal system: Judi Kesselman and Franklynn Peterson, "Rape . . . And Now a Friendly Word from the Enemy," *Viva*, June, 1977.

57 For Anna, the other odd aspect: Interview with Vivienne Lasky, July 24, 2019.

57 Keeton, whom he assigned to run the magazine: Interviews with Joe Brooks, August 22, 2019, and Alma Moore.

57 Keeton wanted *Viva* to compete: Background interview.

57 but it was still banned: Cappo, "Associate Publisher Said Male Nudity Hurt *Viva*."

57 A former dancer, Keeton: Interview with Joe Brooks.

58 The staff got the impression: Interview with Alma Moore.

58 Anna, who surely didn't want to lose: Interview with Bob Guccione Jr., November 22, 2019.

58 The first thing Anna did: Interview with Alma Moore.

58 Keeton brought two Rhodesian Ridgebacks . . . with the *Penthouse* logo: Interview with Stephanie Brush, May 10, 2019.

58 She rolled in a rack for clothes: Email from background source.

58 On days she came in: Interview with Bob Guccione Jr.

58 she propped up her clunky boots . . . "she was always the boss": Interview with Wanda DiBenedetto, June 19, 2019.

58 Guccione . . . edited everything: Interview with Bob Guccione Jr.

58 He liked to work through the night: Interview with Cheryl Rixon, November 7, 2019.

58 Meetings were held: Interview with Joe Brooks.

59 His son, Bob: Interview with Bob Guccione Jr.

59 the column in his house with his face: James Barron, "On the Block, a Peek into the Lifestyle of Bob Guccione," *New York Times*, August 17, 2009.

59 Anna became an expert at manipulating . . . Anna's ability to continue borrowing: Background interview.

59 Perhaps emboldened in her job . . . which is what Anna did: Background interview.

59 She also took advantage . . . and fly to one: Interview with Alma Moore.

60 Attempting a better version: Arthur Elgort, "Jamaican Jamboree," *Viva*, June 1977.

60 Moore . . . thought the photos were "ridiculous": Email from Alma Moore, October 9, 2019.

60 That may have been because Anna had gone: Background interview.

60 Anna blamed her assistant: Email from Alma Moore.

60 Stephanie Brush also started: Interview with Stephanie Brush, May 10, 2019.

61 Moore didn't love Anna's refusal: Interview with Alma Moore.

61 "There were all these little details" . . . Anna took a liking to Brush: Interview with Stephanie Brush.

61 which was unusual because: Interview with Alma Moore.

61 Anna would frequent the local bar: Background interview.

61 But she started inviting Brush to her office: Interview with Stephanie Brush.

61 While Anna didn't casually stroll: Interviews with Bob Guccione Jr. and Joe Brooks.

61 *Viva*'s art director, Johnson: Interview with Joe Brooks.

61 He was respected: Interview with Jacques Malignon, October 9, 2019.

62 Gunn worked hard and was friendly: Interview with Patricia Lynden, August 21, 2019.

62 Alma Moore liked Gunn a lot . . . didn't want to go herself: Interview with Alma Moore.

62 Their colleagues speculated that Gunn . . . Gunn never complained: Interview with Wanda DiBenedetto.

62 the cliché idea to make over members: Gay Haubner, "North Country Girl: Chapter 64—The Accidental Editor," *Saturday Evening Post*, August 8, 2018, https://www.saturdayeveningpost.com/2018/08/north-country-girl -chapter-64-accidental-editor/.

62 But of all their disputes . . . didn't even show up, sending her assistant instead: Interview with Cheryl Rixon, November 7, 2019.

64 There were the country scenes: Jacques Malignon, "Autumn Tweeds," *Viva*, September 1977; Stan Malinowski, "Sweaters Are Better," *Viva*, November 1977; and Guy Le Baube, "Country Classic, City Chic," *Viva*, September 1978.

64 "It's all very suggestive": Interview with Patricia Lynden, October 11, 2019.

64 While at *Viva*, Moore took a meeting: Interview with Alma Moore.

64 "The writing was on the wall": Interview with Debby Dichter, June 10, 2019.

64 "The magazine was losing so much money": Interview with Alma Moore.

64 At that point, Vivienne Lasky: Interview with Vivienne Lasky.

65 "Anna was not squeamish": Interview with Bob Guccione Jr.

65 In early 1978, Gunn went with Anna: Email interview with Michel Esteban, May 1, 2021.

65 the magazine never found a large enough audience: "Circulation Low, *Viva* Magazine to Stop in January," *New York Times*, November 18, 1978.

65 Anna immediately started sobbing: Interview with Patricia Lynden.

65 Just a week earlier, her father: Charles Wintour letter to Arthur Schlesinger, September 25, year unspecified, Schlesinger papers, NYPL.

Chapter 7: A Savvy Move

67 After *Viva* closed: Email interview with Michel Esteban, May 1, 2021.

67 There, Anna became closer: Interview with Anne McNally, May 6, 2021.

67 this period was her only true break: Email from Michel Esteban, May 4, 2021.

67 In the spring of 1980: Jerry Oppenheimer, *Front Row: Anna Wintour: What Lies Beneath the Chic Exterior of* Vogue's *Editor in Chief* (New York: St. Martin's Griffin, 2006), 152–55.

67 Anna and Esteban broke up: Email from Michel Esteban.

68 McNally moved to New York: Interview with Anne McNally.

68 In early 1980, *Savvy* magazine launched: Margalit Fox, "Judith Daniels, Editor of *Savvy* Magazine, Dies at 74," *New York Times*, September 4, 2013, https://www.nytimes.com/2013/09/05/business/media/judith-dan iels-74-editor-of-savvy-magazine-dies.html.

68 Without much leverage, she accepted: Interview with Claire Gruppo, December 3, 2019.

68 In early editorial meetings, *Savvy*'s staff: Background interview.

68 Daniels had spent years . . . good for them if they were: Background interview.

68 Still, she felt the kinds of fashion stories . . . and reasonable prices: Interview with Susan Edmiston, November 22, 2019.

69 stories like "What Your Business Card Says . . .": *Savvy*, March and June 1981.

69 "Anna was very strong-minded": Interview with Susan Edmiston.

69 When Anna got to *Savvy*: Interview with Claire Gruppo.

69 Anna was still receiving: Ralph Baker will and trust documents probated in Middlesex County, Massachusetts.

69 Gunn, as she had at *Viva*: Interviews with Susan Edmiston, Claire Gruppo, and Michele Morris, June 2, 2020.

69 Anna mostly spoke with her boss . . . wanted Anna's pages to be beautiful: Interview with Carol Devine Carson, September 25, 2020.

69 While at *Savvy*, Anna moved: Interviews with two background sources.

69 Michael Stone, who was well-off: Background source.

69 she set up a big white desk: Interview with Susan Edmiston.

70 When she was at the office . . . She pushed her own racks of clothing: Interview with Michele Morris.

70 "We just got the pictures": Interview with Carol Devine Carson.

70 Anna's expenses were . . . a point of contention: Interviews with Carol Devine Carson, Claire Gruppo, and Michele Morris.

70 For one cover shoot, Anna obscured: Email from Carol Devine Carson, October 13, 2020.

70 For another shoot, she photographed Tina Chow: Anna Wintour, "The High Style of Tina Chow," *Savvy*, March 1981.

70 Though the fee was a fraction . . . who could also "invent" them: Interview with Guy Le Baube, October 14, 2020.

70 they upset the magazine's readers: Interview with Claire Gruppo.

71 Daniels became so concerned: Interview with Susan Edmiston.

71 "It was a good gig for her": Interview with Claire Gruppo.

71 On Wednesday, March 18, 1981: Andy Warhol, *The Andy Warhol Diaries*, edited by Pat Hackett (New York: Warner, 1989), 365.

Chapter 8: In Vogue

73 The first time Laurie Jones saw her . . . Kosner laughed, then hired Anna: Interview with Laurie Jones, December 5, 2020.

74 Anna was again a bizarrely glamorous presence: Interview with Nancy McKeon, September 15, 2019.

74 Her bob obscured her face: Interview with Laurie Schechter, February 14, 2020.

74 She wore high heels: Background interview.

74   Anna brought in her own . . . a clothing rack: "Between the Lines," *New York*, July 6–13, 1981.

74   and a chic chair: Interview with Jordan Schaps, February 7, 2020.

74   She asked for whiteboards: Interview with Corky Pollan, May 6, 2020.

74   the newspaper-littered office: Interview with Patricia Bradbury, December 6, 2019.

74   she worked out of a cubicle: Interview with Laurie Jones.

75   capable of projecting the demeanor of an army general: Interviews with Patricia Bradbury and two background sources.

75   befriended the men's fashion editor . . . "She just moves on": Interview with Anthony Haden-Guest, May 19, 2021.

75   Anna felt like the outcast: Anna Wintour, "Case Studies: Lessons from Creative Leaders," *Anna Wintour Teaches Creativity and Leadership*, Master Class, https://www.masterclass.com/classes/anna-wintour-teaches-creati vity-and-leadership/chapters/case-studies-lessons-from-creative-leaders.

75   Occasionally she would put up her bob: Interview with Laurie Schechter.

75   The first time the staff noticed: Interview with Jordan Schaps.

75   Once Anna asked: Interview with Nancy McKeon.

75   Her closest friends were European ex-pats: Background source.

76   She stayed close with . . . "she was right about the man": Interview with Emma Soames, May 17, 2021.

76   But most of the fashion advertising: Interview with Tom Florio, August 12, 2020.

76   She convinced Kosner . . . he let her do it: Interview with Deborah Harkins, February 12, 2020.

76   he did once complain: Interview with Anthony Haden-Guest.

76   "He thought the world of her": Interview with Patricia Bradbury.

76   Anna specifically wanted to blend: Interview with Michael Boodro, April 28, 2021.

77   Le Baube wanted them to look . . . the buildings tilted behind them: Interview with Guy Le Baube, October 14, 2020.

77   Anna posed MacDowell: Anna Wintour, "In the Heat of the Night," *New York*, July 6–13, 1981.

77   Le Baube didn't feel they were particularly great collaborators . . . disdained when anyone wasted hers: Interviews with Guy Le Baube.

77   In the fourth issue: Anna Wintour, "Furs for All Seasons," *New York*, September 14, 1981.

78   In one 1982 issue: Anna Wintour, "Now, Voyager," *New York*, August 9, 1982.

78   Editor Nancy McKeon thought the trunk . . . "You don't eat that": Interview with Nancy McKeon.

78   One spring Friday night . . . "There was no reason to make her cry": Interview with Jordan Schaps.

78   Toscani said he didn't remember: Interview with Oliviero Toscani, June 16, 2021.

79 Anna worked with Toscani a number of times again: Interview with Jordan
    Schaps.

79 Anna's first assistant . . . notable as the model: Background interview.

79 Meisel, who was about as exacting: Background interview.

79 Kosner expanded her purview: "Table of Contents," *New York*, April 5, 1982.

80 Polly Mellen, began to feel: Jacob Bernstein, "More Mellenisms From
    Polly," *Women's Wear Daily*, March 8, 2002.

80 To save a shoot . . . "I was crying," Mellen said: Rosemary Feitelberg,
    "Polly Mellen Behind the Scenes," *WWD*, December 14, 2012, https://
    wwd.com/fashion-news/fashion-features/polly-mellen-behind-the
    -scenes-6541955/.

80 Mellen wondered if Anna: Jerry Oppenheimer, *Front Row: Anna Wintour:
    What Lies Beneath the Chic Exterior of* Vogue's *Editor in Chief* (New York:
    St. Martin's Griffin, 2006), 189–90.

80 she arranged a meeting with Mirabella: Jacob Bernstein, "More Melle-
    nisms from Polly," *WWD*, March 8, 2002; Anna Wintour, "Anna Wintour
    on Leaving London for New York," *Guardian*, May 19, 1997.

80 It was obvious that Anna and Stone: Interview with Chuck Zuretti, Janu-
    ary 6, 2020.

80 However, Anna professed disgust . . . his unprofessional behavior: Back-
    ground interview.

81 When it came time to shoot: Interview with Chuck Zuretti.

81 For the 1982 "Summer Pleasures" issue . . . "It's our cover": Interview with
    Jordan Schaps.

83 Schechter had gotten her start in fashion . . . Anna and the crew got their
    new van: Interview with Laurie Schechter.

83 *Vogue* employees later described being "hazed": Background interviews
    with four sources.

83 "clothes for a country weekend": Anna Wintour, "Days of Heaven," *New
    York*, November 8, 1982.

84 Alex Chatelain had been hired . . . "She destroyed my career": Interviews
    with Alex Chatelain, February 21, 2020, and May 26, 2021.

84 would later regiment her business lunches: Background interview.

85 The "Flower Wars": Interview with Laurie Schechter.

85 Shaffer, thirteen years older: "David Shaffer, MD, Professor of Psychiatry,
    Columbia University," Global Medical Education, https://www.gmeded
    .com/faculty/david-shaffer-md.

85 Anna met Shaffer—and his wife: Background interview.

85 In London, Shaffer and Bass had regularly held: Interview with Michael
    Roberts, November 21, 2020.

85 Though Anna was still with Stone . . . with her hair a mess: Interview with
    Laurie Schechter.

85 whose marriage with Bass fell apart: Background interview.

85 who had always resented feeling second fiddle: Background interview.

85 Schaps was glad to see Anna moving on: Interview with Jordan Schaps.

85 Laurie Jones also deemed him: Interview with Laurie Jones, May 20, 2021.

85 Shaffer was slightly hunchbacked: Background interview.

85 knew she wanted children: Interview with Laurie Jones.

86 Despite his occupation, Shaffer wasn't alien . . . long before he even met Anna: Background interview.

86 For Anna, the relationship provided: Interviews with Michael Roberts and background source.

86 But some friends saw something sinister: Background interviews with two sources.

86 Anna finally had nothing to prove: Interviews with Michael Roberts and background source.

86 Shaffer, though self-conscious: Interview with Anthony Haden-Guest.

86 seemed just as dedicated to her rise: Background interviews with two sources.

86 she styled a spread of models: Anna Wintour, "Metropolitan Life," *New York*, February 28, 1983.

86 Toscani loved a shot with Anna . . . "going to marry him": Interview with Oliviero Toscani.

87 The logical section for her to take on: Interviews with Nancy McKeon and Corky Pollan.

87 The most popular items . . . went through her trash can: Interview with Nancy McKeon.

87 Anna also had a habit: Interview with Laurie Schechter.

87 One rare exception to such treatment: Interview with Nancy McKeon.

87 Despite sitting on the other side of a cubicle wall . . . "She was very opinionated": Interview with Corky Pollan.

88 As Schechter put it: Interview with Laurie Schechter.

88 Liberman was a Condé Nast company man. . . sculpted steel into large-scale artworks: Jesse Kornbluth, "The Art of Being Alex," *New York*, October 12, 1981.

88 gray if it was fall, winter, or spring: Interview with Rochelle Udell, April 12, 2019.

89 He was so devoted to his art: Francine du Plessix Gray, *Them* (London: Penguin, 2004), 446.

89 Born in Russia . . . to excel in the arts: Dodie Kazanjian and Calvin Tomkins, *Alex* (New York: Knopf, 1993), 25, 54, 107.

89 While in theory he thus lived: Kornbluth, "The Art of Being Alex."

89 In 1962, a few years after newspaper magnate Samuel Newhouse: Thomas Maier, *Newhouse* (New York: St. Martin's Press, 1994), 45, 50.

89 And while friends thought working: Kornbluth, "The Art of Being Alex."

89 It was this story: Anna Wintour, "Introduction," *Anna Wintour Teaches Creativity and Leadership*, MasterClass, https://www.masterclass.com/classes/anna-wintour-teaches-creativity-and-leadership/chapters/introduction.

89 Anna has said she can't remember: Kazanjian and Tomkins, *Alex*, 310.

89 Though according to another account: Background interview.

89 Toscani also remembered Liberman asking him: Interview with Oliviero Toscani.

90 At age seventy, Liberman, a natural seducer, was taken: Interviews with numerous observers of their relationship.

90 Anna was honest: Interview with Rochelle Udell.

90 Liberman later said he felt: Michael Gross, "War of the Poses," *New York*, April 27, 1992.

90 Things moved quickly . . . instead of a plant: Kazanjian and Tomkins, *Alex*, 310.

90 Anna preferred cut flowers: Interviews with Laurie Schechter and André Leon Talley, April 10, 2021.

90 he had been a witness at Mirabella's wedding: Grace Mirabella, *In and Out of Vogue* (New York: Doubleday, 1995), 11.

91 Liberman, who claimed he couldn't bear to fire anyone: Kazanjian and Tomkins, *Alex*, 316.

91 In fact, his start at Condé Nast . . . ended up in Agha's job: Kornbluth, "The Art of Being Alex."

91 Mirabella couldn't override Liberman: Mirabella, *In and Out of Vogue*, 11.

91 He was responsible, one staffer said: Background interview.

91 When his father sent [Si Newhouse] to work . . . his new milieu: Maier, *Newhouse*, 55.

91 Unsurprisingly, when it came to: Deirdre Carmody, "Alexander Liberman, Condé Nast's Driving Creative Force, Is Dead at 87," *New York Times*, November 20, 1999, https://www.nytimes.com/1999/11/20/arts/alexander -liberman-conde-nast-s-driving-creative-force-is-dead-at-87.html.

92 Now Liberman and Newhouse felt *Vogue* needed a shake-up: Kazanjian and Tomkins, *Alex*, 310.

92 Though it wasn't clear how Anna and Mirabella: Gross, "War of the Poses."

92 Those who saw Anna and Newhouse together: Interviews with numerous sources who observed their relationship.

92 But to assume his attraction: Background interview.

92 There was something else about Anna: Interview with Gabé Doppelt, November 13, 2020.

92 Approval given, Liberman offered Anna the title of creative director: Kazanjian and Tomkins, *Alex*, 312.

93 she called Bruce Wolf . . . "there are a lot of sharks": Interview with Bruce Wolf, January 10, 2020.

93 Anna and Shaffer went to the Algonquin: Interview with Grace Codding-ton, December 12, 2020.

93 Anna also went to Kosner . . . remove himself from Anna's decision-making: Interview with Nancy McKeon.

93 Kosner was terribly upset to lose her: Interview with Deborah Harkins.

93 but to the rest of the staff: Interviews with Patricia Bradbury, Nancy McKeon, and others.

93   Anna called her dad: Interview with Corky Pollan, May 6, 2020.

93   Laurie Schechter was upset too: Interview with Laurie Schechter.

Chapter 9: Second Best

95   she and Shaffer took the next step: Public record of mortgage dated December 13, 1983.

95   It wasn't up to Anna's standards: Carol Vogel, "Home Design: The Splendor of Simplicity," *New York Times Magazine*, January 26, 1986.

95   Aside from an appreciation for twenties-inspired fashion: Background interview.

95   Anna's earliest *Vogue* colleagues [describe]: Interviews with Laurie Schechter, February 14, 2020; Anne Kampmann, May 21, 2020; and background source.

95   Though her stint as creative director has been characterized as: Interviews with numerous sources who worked at *Vogue* at the time.

96   she was a perplexing presence: Interviews with Anne Kampmann and background source.

96   Part of the confusion stemmed from the vague nature: Background interview.

96   She was clearly comfortable making decisions: Background interview.

96   something she had been longing for: Anna Wintour, "Introduction," *Anna Wintour Teaches Creativity and Leadership*, MasterClass, https://www.masterclass.com/classes/anna-wintour-teaches-creativity-and-leadership/chapters/introduction.

96   "As shy as she's sometimes described": Interview with Laurie Schechter, October 6, 2020.

96   First, there was the office vernacular: Interview with Laurie Schechter.

96   the organization oozed with theatrical showings of rank: Interview with Maggie Buckley, January 19, 2020.

97   "She was cool as a cucumber": Interview with Lesley Jane Seymour, January 13, 2020.

97   Anna was actually interested in the opinions: Interview with Maggie Buckley.

97   She never demanded that subordinates call her . . . called Mirabella by her first name alone: Interview with Laurie Schechter.

97   "She got the work done" . . . "they weren't physically assaulting us": Interview with Lesley Jane Seymour.

97   Editors brought extra chairs: Interview with Jade Hobson, February 4, 2020.

97   Run-throughs, the meetings where clothing was selected . . . "a belabored conversation, actually": Interview with Maggie Buckley.

97   Mirabella wanted to analyze: Background interview.

98   One of her favorite comments was: Interview with Beverly Purcell, February 27, 2020.

98 Mirabella's fashion editors didn't need to obsess . . . if a show had ended at 10 p.m.: Background interview.

98 sit there with her legs crossed: Interview with André Leon Talley, March 20, 2021.

98 couldn't hide how stunning she found this process: Interview with Maggie Buckley.

98 He liked quick decisions: Interview with Jade Hobson, February 4, 2020.

98 Mirabella had started: Grace Mirabella, *In and Out of Vogue* (New York: Doubleday, 1995), 22, 53, 56.

98 In 1962, Vreeland had arrived: Carol Felsenthal, *Citizen Newhouse* (New York: Seven Stories Press, 1998), 162–64.

98 After Vreeland became editor-in-chief . . . vitamin B_{12} shot: Mirabella, *In and Out of Vogue*, 103.

98 She remains known for the memos: Gigi Mahon, "S. I. Newhouse and Condé Nast; Taking Off the White Gloves," *New York Times Magazine,* September 10, 1989.

99 Vreeland asked Mirabella: Mirabella, *In and Out of Vogue*, 111, 134.

99 With the pages of Vreeland's *Vogue* . . . who conducted research for Newhouse: Thomas Maier, *Newhouse* (New York: St. Martin's Press, 1994). 58, 64–65.

99 an approach that treated magazines like toothpaste: Maier, *Newhouse,* 62–64.

99 Vreeland had no interest in Newhouse's new methodology . . . "the next editor in chief of *Vogue*": Mirabella, *In and Out of Vogue*, 139–40.

100 Mirabella's appointment drew an onslaught: Mirabella, *In and Out of Vogue*, 142.

100 She featured advertisers: Maier, *Newhouse*, 77.

100 But though the *Vogue* business was going strong . . . she wrote in her memoir: Mirabella, *In and Out of Vogue*, 193–96.

100 Liberman brought in Anna . . . "foisted upon me": Mirabella, *In and Out of Vogue*, 215.

100 staff observed [a] respectful professionalism: Interview with Maggie Buckley.

100 Mirabella saved the disparaging comments: Mirabella, *In and Out of Vogue*, 215.

101 the magazine had two distinct fiefdoms: Interviews with Lesley Jane Seymour and background source.

101 But the true sovereign at *Vogue* was Liberman: Interviews with Jade Hobson, February 4, 2020, and background source.

101 Liberman didn't involve himself: Interview with Anne Kampmann.

101 Anna's presence felt more curious than threatening . . . "something a little less moody": Background interview.

101 That [Mirabella] let it sail through: Interview with Laurie Schechter.

102 "In terms of fashion photography": Nora Frenkiel, "The Up-and-Comers; Wintour Displays Knack for the New," *Adweek*, March 1984.

102 created especially for *Vogue* by Dennis Ashbaugh: "The Strong Beat of Color," *Vogue*, February 1, 1984.

102 "Developing a creative eye": Anna Wintour, "Starting Out: Finding Your Voice and Succeeding," *Anna Wintour Teaches Creativity and Leadership*, MasterClass, https://www.masterclass.com/classes/anna-wintour-teaches -creativity-and-leadership/chapters/starting-out-finding-your-voice-and -succeeding.

102 "I'm working on every aspect": Frenkiel, "The Up-and-Comers; Wintour Displays Knack for the New."

102 Anna felt that Mirabella . . . didn't want her to succeed: Interview with Laurie Jones, December 5, 2020.

102 When photos came in: Interview with Maggie Buckley.

103 Anna sometimes recommended a reshoot: Background interview.

103 "She'd sit in on editorial": Mirabella, *In and Out of Vogue*, 215.

103 Jade Hobson, one of Mirabella's senior fashion editors: Interview with Jade Hobson.

103 The fashion team's vocal resistance: Interview with Laurie Shechter.

103 But it didn't really matter: Interview with Gabé Doppelt, November 13, 2020.

104 And he continued making his favoritism of Anna known . . . "can't survive without talent": Mirabella, *In and Out of Vogue*, 216.

104 All the while, Anna took mental notes: Dodie Kazanjian and Calvin Tomkins, *Alex* (New York: Knopf, 1993), 312.

104 At night, she took a dummy copy home: Interview with Michael Roberts, November 21, 2020.

104 But Anna would read articles: Background interview.

104 He called the office multiple times . . . would pick up Anna from work: Interviews with Laurie Schechter.

104 Volvo station wagon . . . "the shrinkmobile": Background interview.

104 They sometimes gave Schechter a ride: Interview with Laurie Schechter.

105 there was no meaningful change: Interviews with Anne Kampmann, Jade Hobson, and background source.

105 She had been following André Leon Talley . . . Talley didn't return her messages: Interview with Laurie Schechter, October 6, 2020.

105 when Mirabella called . . . Arthur Elgort showed it to her: André Leon Talley, *The Chiffon Trenches* (New York: Ballantine, 2020), iBook, 187–88.

105 As he left *Vogue* . . . too scary to speak to: Interview with André Leon Talley.

105 Now his job was to fill two pages: Talley, *The Chiffon Trenches*, 191.

106 For the December 1984 issue . . . to take Polaroids of his progress: Interview with André Leon Talley.

106 It wasn't terribly efficient . . . "after seventeen send-backs?": Talley, *The Chiffon Trenches*, 193.

106 Talley believed Anna had "intuition": Interview with André Leon Talley, April 10, 2021.

106 He wrote in his memoir, "We never really spoke": Talley, *The Chiffon Trenches*, 191.

160 perplexed by Mirabella's agonizing meetings: Talley, *The Chiffon Trenches*, 180–86.

106 Mirabella "didn't quite get me": Interview with André Leon Talley.

106 When Anna was in Paris . . . "when I'm ready to marry you": Georgina Howell, "Two of a Type," *Sunday Times*, July 13, 1986.

107 Before the wedding, she got a call: Email from Michel Esteban, May 6, 2021.

107 just two *Vogue* colleagues, Schechter and Talley: Interview with André Leon Talley, March 20, 2021.

107 Working with architect Alan Buchsbaum . . . "spare with an English flavor": Vogel, "Home Design: The Splendor of Simplicity."

107 "She's an edited person": Interview with Laurie Schechter.

107 Despite living her life in the spotlight: Interview with Anne McNally, May 6, 2021.

107 Anna wore a tea-length cream Chanel dress: Interview with Laurie Schechter.

107 She had gone to Bergdorf Goodman with Anna: Background interview.

108 Talley was stunned: Interview with André Leon Talley.

108 instead of throwing [the bouquet]: Talley, *The Chiffon Trenches*, 198.

108 on Tuesday, April 23, 1985, Beatrix Miller: "Sit. Vac," *Telegraph*, April 24, 1985.

108 Anna Wintour was expected to replace her: Peter Hillmore, "Mag Bag," *Observer*, July 14, 1985.

Chapter 10: A Tale of Two Vogues

109 "Oh my god, I'm back in England" . . . "It was the end of life as we knew it": Liz Tilberis, *No Time to Die* (New York: Avon, 1998), 137–38.

110 Anna had a hard time accepting the job . . . so far from Shaffer: Nigel Dempster, "She's a Princess in *Vogue*," *Daily Mail*, June 7, 1985; Georgina Howell, "Two of a Type," *Sunday Times*, July 13, 1986.

110 entrenched in his job at Columbia: James Fallon, "Anna Wintour Takes Charge," *WWD*, November 5, 1986.

110 On June 5, 1985 . . . "and prove executive chops": Tina Brown, *The Vanity Fair Diaries* (New York: Henry Holt, 2017), iBook, 379–81.

111 The next month, Anna was in the press: Peter Hillmore, "Guess Who's Coming to Dinner," *Observer*, July 14, 1985.

111 Brown told Newhouse: Brown, *The Vanity Fair Diaries*, 417.

111 claiming to think that she and Mirabella: Dodie Kazanjian and Calvin Tomkins, *Alex* (New York: Knopf, 1993), 312.

111 Mirabella, though still dismissing: Grace Mirabella, *In and Out of Vogue* (New York: Doubleday, 1995), 216.

111   Finally . . . Anna accepted . . . start the job in London in April: "Look: Start of the Wintour Season," *Sunday Times*, September 22, 1985.

111   Before Anna left for London . . . to start in six weeks: Interview with Gabé Doppelt, November 13, 2020.

112   Anna's appointment to British *Vogue* . . . a girls' boarding school: Rupert Christiansen, "Vogue's New Look," *Telegraph*, July 21, 1986.

112   [Miller] loved a beautiful duchess . . . never tried to dress fashionably: Adrian Hamilton, "Beatrix Miller: *Vogue* Editor Whose Own Talents and Her Nurturing of Others', Helped Set the Tone for the Swinging Sixties," *Independent*, February 26, 2014, https://www.independent.co.uk /news/obituaries/beatrix-miller-vogue-editor-whose-own-talents-and -her-nurturing-others-helped-set-tone-swinging-sixties-9152879.html; Joan Juliet Buck, "Beatrix Miller Obituary," *Guardian*, February 25, 2014, https://www.theguardian.com/media/2014/feb/25/beatrix-miller.

112   kept her long nails painted a glossy red: Patrick Kinmonth, "Recalling the Legacy of Beatrix Miller, Longtime Editor of British *Vogue*," Vogue.com, February 23, 2014, https://www.vogue.com/article/recalling-legacy-of-bea trix-miller-longtime-editor-of-british-vogue; Tilberis, *No Time to Die*, 137.

112   Anna, on the other hand . . . "a wide range of interests": Christiansen, "Vogue's New Look."

112   Tilberis didn't feel qualified: Tilberis, *No Time to Die*, 135–36.

112   Coddington, who liked being on shoots: Grace Coddington, *Grace* (New York: Random House, 2012), 162; interview with Grace Coddington, December 19, 2020.

113   she did convince Shaffer's friend: Interview with Michael Roberts, November 21, 2020.

113   She offered Laurie Schechter a job: Interview with Laurie Shechter, February 14, 2020.

113   Anna asked *Vogue* fashion editor Robert Turner: Background interview.

113   And she asked Talley: André Leon Talley, *The Chiffon Trenches* (New York: Ballantine, 2020), iBook, 200.

113   Anna [managed] to hire her old friend: Interview with Emma Soames, June 14, 2021.

113   Anna proceeded to fire almost everyone: Interview with Gabé Doppelt.

113   She also let go of [Shulman and Walker]: Interview with Emma Soames.

113   She did decide to keep Tilberis and Coddington: Interview with Gabé Doppelt.

113   "She was civilized and polite": Tilberis, *No Time to Die*, 136–37.

113   Vivienne Lasky reached out . . . Anna had moved on: Interview with Vivienne Lasky, July 17, 2019.

114   On a Friday night in April . . . The final touch was a large NO SMOKING sign: Tilberis, *No Time to Die*, 137.

114   In came Anna's desk: David Colman, "POSSESSED; A Desk to Depend on Through Thick and Thin," *New York Times*, August 17, 2003, https://

www.nytimes.com/2003/08/17/style/possessed-a-desk-to-depend-on
-through-thick-and-thin.html.

114 a stark departure from Miller . . . "a radical, radical change": Interview with Emma Soames, June 14, 2021.

114 leaving her house . . . her infant son, Charlie, named for her father: Howell, "Two of a Type."

114 After eighteen years under Miller: Nicolas Ghesquière, "Grace Coddington," *Interview*, November 28, 2012, https://www.interviewmagazine .com/fashion/grace-coddington.

115 Still, Coddington was habitually late: Tilberis, *No Time to Die*, 139–40.

115 But Anna also got her staff raises: Christiansen, "Vogue's New Look."

115 Overall the pay was low . . . . "You could say thank you": Tilberis, *No Time to Die*, 138.

115 Wanting to be especially involved: Interview with Gabé Doppelt.

115 Anna would sit there in her sunglasses: Tilberis, *No Time to Die*, 139.

115 Coddington noted she had a hard time: Coddington, *Grace*, 165.

115 Anna reviewed every photo . . . one by one: Interview with Gabé Doppelt.

115 she would put on her thick, round eyeglasses: Interview with Sarajane Hoare, October 23, 2020.

115 She also demanded "endless reshooting": Tilberis, *No Time to Die*, 139.

115 For her very first cover, Anna wanted: Coddington, *Grace*, 163.

116 Having said just a couple of years earlier: Tilberis, *No Time to Die*, 139.

116 It was an image of womanhood: Christiansen, "Vogue's New Look."

116 Anna later admitted that this approach . . . "I wanted to put my stamp on it": Michael Gross, "War of the Poses," *New York*, April 27, 1992.

116 Not everyone could handle Anna's new way: Interview with Gabé Doppelt.

116 Even though she hadn't managed to hire: Talley, *The Chiffon Trenches*, 193.

116 She also wanted to know what he thought: Interview with André Leon Talley, March 20, 2021.

116 He seemed the antithesis to her: Tilberis, *No Time to Die*, 137.

117 [Coddington] also found it strange: Coddington, *Grace*, 162.

117 As hard as it was for Anna to recruit . . . Hoare took the job: Interview with Sarajane Hoare.

117 such as the rumor (later called a "fabrication"): Andrew Billen, "Wintour Melts, a Little," *Times (UK)*, May 6, 2002.

117 Her father's old paper described: Tilberis, *No Time to Die*, 138–40.

117 *Private Eye* reported details of her contract . . . print an apology and pay her legal fees: Fallon, "Anna Wintour Takes Charge."

118 as she would over the course of decades: Interviews with Anne McNally, May 6, 2021; David Hare, October 27, 2020; and Lisa Love, October 20, 2020.

118 Emma Soames was stunned by these stories: Interviews with Emma Soames, May 17 and June 14, 2021.

118 But quickly Anna's British *Vogue* was successful: Fallon, "Anna Wintour Takes Charge."

118   she developed relationships with British designers . . . "probably did very well because of it": Interview with Grace Coddington.

118   During the first features meeting: Brown, *The* Vanity Fair *Diaries*, 667.

118   Still, while Tilberis claimed that Anna: Tilberis, *No Time to Die*, 141.

119   Photographer Bruce Weber: David Livingstone, "Seeing Broken Noses," *Globe and Mail*, September 15, 1987.

119   Jewelry designer Tom Binns made a pin: Gross, "War of the Poses."

119   Anna didn't seem to care: Michael Gross, "Notes on Fashion," *New York Times*, March 17, 1987.

119   Her departure was prompted not by discontent: Interview with Grace Coddington.

119   Coddington, whom Anna later called: Gross, "War of the Poses."

119   Tilberis, who was also struggling . . . felt that her boss started trusting her: Tilberis, *No Time to Die*, 142.

120   wearing the same Yves Saint Laurent suits and high heels: Interview with Sarajane Hoare.

120   She didn't have a big social circle: Interview with Michael Roberts.

120   This wasn't the only quality time she had with her son: Howell, "Two of a Type."

120   Anna was also the one flying to New York . . . "the magazine I wanted to edit": Linda Blandford, "Guardian Style: To *Vogue* with Red Herrings / Interview with Anna Wintour, Incoming Editor of *Vogue* Magazine," *Guardian*, March 20, 1986.

120   But Liberman also seemed to be making an effort: Interview with Grace Coddington, July 24, 2021.

120   When Anna struggled: Kazanjian and Tomkins, *Alex*, 313.

120   When Coddington was in New York for shoots: Coddington, *Grace*, 166.

120   Anna was vigorously denying speculation: "Eye Scoop," *WWD*, April 27, 1987.

120   In May, the *New York Times* reported: Michael Gross, "Notes on Fashion," *New York Times*, May 5, 1987.

121   She was also rumored to be in talks: Felsenthal, *Citizen Newhouse*, 281.

121   Though Anna later described receiving offers: Gross, "War of the Poses."

121   But she did fully intend to move back to New York: Charles Wintour letter to Arthur Schlesinger, July 9, 1987, Arthur M. Schlesinger Jr. papers, Manuscripts and Archives Division, New York Public Library.

121   it's possible she planted rumors: Brown, *The* Vanity Fair *Diaries*, 667.

121   Newhouse got on a plane to London . . . "no way to treat a lady": Gross, "War of the Poses."

Chapter 11: House & Garment

122   On the way to the hospital: Interview with Gabé Doppelt, November 13, 2020.

122 Anna had left work: Interview with Sarajane Hoare, October 23, 2020.

123 "I have an announcement to make": Interviews with Sarajane Hoare and Gabé Doppelt.

123 Before Anna departed . . . leaving Tilberis in charge on her own: Liz Tilberis, *No Time to Die* (New York, NY: Avon, 1998), 146–47, 54.

123 A week after she told the staff: Interview with Sarajane Hoare.

123 Louis Oliver Gropp, whom Anna was succeeding . . . "Yes," Newhouse said: Carol Felsenthal, *Citizen Newhouse* (New York: Seven Stories Press, 1998), 162–64.

124 Gropp stayed on until September 9: "Eye Scoop," *WWD*, August 26, 1987.

124 Though she hadn't officially started: Tina Brown, *The* Vanity Fair *Diaries* (New York: Henry Holt, 2017), iBook, 649.

124 making him her creative director . . . he admitted: André Leon Talley, *The Chiffon Trenches* (New York: Ballantine, 2020), iBook, 202.

124 The "problems" Newhouse was having: Felsenthal, *Citizen Newhouse*, 281.

124 Since the 1970s, the magazine: Dodie Kazanjian and Calvin Tomkins, *Alex* (New York: Knopf, 1993), 313.

125 considered the most upscale: Deirdre Donahue, "Decorating Magazines Move Up," *USA Today*, August 25, 1987.

125 Condé Nast had spent $8 million: "House & Garden's New Focus," *New York Times*, July 7, 1984, https://www.nytimes.com/1984/07/07/business /house-garden-s-new-focus.html.

125 Other competing home magazines: Donahue, "Decorating Magazines Move Up."

125 Yet in 1987, *House & Garden*: Cynthia Crossen, "Revamped *House & Garden* Is Aiming to Regain Ground in Crowded Field," *Wall Street Journal*, February 8, 1988.

125 Her company town car deposited her at the office: Talley, *The Chiffon Trenches*, 202–3; interview with Gabé Doppelt.

125 She, Doppelt, and Talley went through drawer after drawer: Interview with Gabé Doppelt.

125 In about three days, Anna reportedly threw out: Kazanjian and Tomkins, *Alex*, 313.

125 Anna also began sorting through the existing staff . . . "I hope you fall on your face": Elaine Greene Weisburg, "Early Wintour," *Voices*, http://irpvoicesonline.com/voices/early-wintour/.

125 Spending this time with Anna: Interview with Gabé Doppelt.

126 The new *House & Garden* tended to feature: Deirdre Donahue, "A Remodeled *HG*: Style Is In," *USA Today*, January 28, 1988.

126 and Steve Martin: *HG*, April 1988.

126 socialites like Baron Eric de Rothschild: Donahue, "A Remodeled *HG*: Style Is In."

126 To further telegraph to the world: Crossen, "Revamped *House & Garden*."

126 Liberman and Newhouse supported the change: Interview with Gabé Doppelt.

126 "I personally questioned the introduction of fashion": Kazanjian and Tomkins, *Alex*, 314.

126 One February night in 1988 . . . Calvin Klein: Brown, *The* Vanity Fair *Diaries*, 707.

127 most welcome, Anna's father: Interview with Carol Vogel, February 28, 2020.

127 Anna seemed overwhelmed by the event: Interview with Rochelle Udell, April 12, 2019.

127 Anna would go on "the diet of cream": Interview with Miranda Brooks, May 7, 2021.

127 Inspired by Parisian gardens, Anna had hired: Interview with Gabé Doppelt.

127 "You know you have a successful party": Interview with Michael Boodro, April 28, 2021.

127 So scattered throughout the space . . . he scolded her for it: Interview with Nancy Novogrod, June 3, 2020.

127 Newhouse gave a speech . . . from *New York*, Ed Kosner: Brown, *The* Vanity Fair *Diaries*, 708.

127 She featured so much fashion . . . subscription cancellations: Kazanjian and Tomkins, *Alex*, 314.

127 A Condé Nast executive told: Susan Heller Anderson, "*HG* Magazine Is Not What It Used to Be," *New York Times*, June 8, 1988.

128 But some people thought . . . "one of the most fun jobs I ever had": Interview with Michael Boodro.

Chapter 12: Anna Wintour, Editor-in-Chief

129 One June morning, Anna went . . . the loss of advertising under Anna: Interview with Nancy Novogrod, June 3, 2020.

129 Grace Mirabella was sitting in her office . . . "I'm afraid it's true": Grace Mirabella, *In and Out of Vogue* (New York: Doubleday, 1995), 9–11.

130 idle at his big black desk: Interview with Rochelle Udell, April 12, 2019.

130 By 1988, *Elle* had surpassed . . . reached 1.2 million people: Dodie Kazanjian and Calvin Tomkins, *Alex* (New York: Knopf, 1993), 316.

130 *Elle* had leaped to 850,000: Geraldine Fabrikant, "Murdoch Sets Deal to Sell Stake in *Elle*," *New York Times*, September 21, 1988, https://www.nytimes.com/1988/09/21/business/murdoch-sets-deal-to-sell-stake-in-elle.html.

130 Mirabella's weaknesses had become prominent: Interviews with Phyllis Posnick, January 18, 2021; Linda Rice, May 18, 2020; and background source.

130 Early in the spring of 1987 . . . he had acute pneumonia: Francine du Plessix Gray, *Them* (London: Penguin, 2004), 448.

130 However, without his usual involvement: Interviews with Phyllis Posnick, Linda Rice, and background source.

130 Staff filtered through: Background interview.

130 Phyllis Posnick, who became health and beauty editor: Interview with Phyllis Posnick.

131 When Liberman reviewed layouts . . . "not the woman for the job": Interview with Linda Rice.

131 Mirabella had another problem . . . this was a bad idea: Mirabella, *In and Out of Vogue*, 219–21.

131 So when Newhouse decided to go ahead . . . that, he claimed, was all Si: Kazanjian and Tomkins, *Alex*, 317.

131 when Mirabella did ask him about the rumors: Interview with Jade Hobson, February 4, 2020.

132 Noted Brown, "There didn't seem to be": du Plessix Gray, *Them*, 444.

132 After the news of Mirabella's firing . . . "It was like regicide": Interview with Lesley Jane Seymour, November 13, 2020.

132 Jade Hobson, a senior fashion editor: Interview with Jade Hobson.

132 Newhouse asked Mirabella to make an announcement: Mirabella, *In and Out of Vogue*, 223–24.

132 while Newhouse and Liberman had made their decision . . . "It was really, really awful": Kazanjian and Tomkins, *Alex*, 317.

133 Amy Gross, who ran the features: William Norwich, "The Dirt on Dirty Harry: Under Lock and Key?," *Daily News*, September 21, 1988; Woody Hochswender, "Patterns" *New York Times*, November 29, 1988.

133 Hobson, who hadn't wanted anything: Interview with Jade Hobson.

133 Liberman had previously brought over: Redazione, "Interview with Carlyne Cerf de Dudzeele," *Vogue Italia*, November 4, 2017, https://www.vogue.it/en/news/vogue-arts/2017/11/04/interview-carlyne-cerf-de-dudzeele-vogue-italia-november-2017/.

133 Grace Coddington, who had left (She and Calvin Klein remained friends): Interview with Grace Coddington, December 19, 2020.

133 André Leon Talley became creative director: André Leon Talley, *The Chiffon Trenches* (New York: Ballantine, 2020), iBook, 196.

133 While Mirabella finished out . . . all in a few minutes: Interviews with Laurie Schechter, February 14, 2020, and Maggie Buckley, January 19, 2020.

134 After these meetings: Interview with Linda Rice.

134 Phyllis Posnick was among: Interview with Phyllis Posnick.

134 Anna combined two copy: Interview with Lesley Jane Seymour.

134 She kept Maggie Buckley: Interview with Maggie Buckley.

134 And she kept Linda Rice . . . She said yes: Interview with Linda Rice.

Chapter 13: Calculated Risk

135 Anna's first day as editor-in-chief . . . "absolutely no truth to the whole thing": Liz Smith, "Wintour of Discontent at Condé Nast," *New York Daily News*, August 1, 1988.

136 But that morning, when she got to work: Thomas Maier, *Newhouse* (New York: St. Martin's Press, 1994), 78.

136 The affair rumors tarnished: Dodie Kazanjian and Calvin Tomkins, *Alex* (New York: Knopf, 1993), 318.

136 Anna later admitted that the Smith allegation: Ibid.

136 each time it seemed she might crack: Interview with Freddy Gamble, February 28, 2020.

136 Anna told her staff she wanted: Grace Coddington, *Grace* (New York: Random House, 2012), 204–6.

136 But she also made clear: Interview with Beverley Purcell Guerra, February 27, 2020.

136 Still, Doppelt remembered: Interview with Gabé Doppelt, November 13, 2020.

136 Richard Avedon had been shooting them: Kazanjian and Tomkins, *Alex*, 240–41.

136 Rather than fire Avedon . . . to reshoot anything: Philip Gefter, *What Becomes a Legend Most: A Biography of Richard Avedon* (New York: Harper, 2020), 506–7.

136 Insulted, he severed ties with *Vogue*: Maier, *Newhouse*, 78; Craig Bromberg, "The Glitzy Brits of Condé Nast," *Washington Journalism Review*, November 1989.

137 The eighties were the ideal era: Redazione, "Interview with Carlyne Cerf de Dudzeele," *Vogue Italia*, November 4, 2017, https://www.vogue.it/en /news/vogue-arts/2017/11/04/interview-carlyne-cerf-de-dudzeele-vogue -italia-november-2017/.

137 who loved mixing designer pieces: Ibid.

137 "The jacket was actually part of a suit": Anna Wintour, "Honoring the 120th Anniversary: Anna Wintour Shares Her *Vogue* Story," Vogue.com, https://web.archive.org/web/20120817004203/http://www.vogue.com :80/magazine/article/anna-wintour-on-her-first-vogue-cover-plus-a -slideshow-of-her-favorite-images-in-vogue/.

137 "The powers that be were a little surprised": Anna Wintour, "A Look Back at Iconic Vogue Covers," *Anna Wintour Teaches Creativity and Leadership*, MasterClass, https://www.masterclass.com/classes/anna-wintour-teaches -creativity-and-leadership/chapters/evolving-a-brand-a-look-back-at -iconic-vogue-covers.

137 Newhouse sent her a note: Interview with Michael Boodro, April 28, 2021.

137 *Vogue* staff hadn't been afraid . . . being shown the door: Interviews with Lesley Jane Seymour, January 13, 2020, and background source.

137 Mirabella had a bathroom in her office: Background interview.

138 But her manner didn't bother: Interview with Gail Pincus, April 21, 2021.

138 In one of her earliest features meetings: Background interview.

138 Another editor described: Ibid.

138 In run-throughs, where editors: Ibid.

138 Anna did ask questions . . . "'Yes. No. I want an answer'": Interview with Maggie Buckley, January 19, 2020.

139 If Anna didn't get what she wanted . . . "Why can't they just pick up the phone?": Interview with Lisa Love, October 20, 2020.

139 "She would want you to keep calling": Interview with Maggie Buckley.

139 While editing her first six issues: Interview with Lesley Jane Seymour.

139 "She really brought a breath of fresh air": Interview with Grace Codding-ton, December 19, 2020.

140 Unlike Mirabella, who liked being in her office . . . in other words, Ameri-can sportswear: Interview with Gail Pincus.

140 She didn't appreciate Ralph Lauren: Background interview.

140 Everything about Anna was fast . . . and then get out: Interview with Les-ley Jane Seymour.

140 With Anna, people say, "You get two minutes": Interview with Paul Cavaco, December 23, 2020.

140 Being late meant: Background interview.

141 the new glass walls were a huge adjustment: Interview with Lesley Jane Seymour.

141 "She's not a writer per se": Interview with Michael Boodro.

141 When staffers stood before Anna, they received The Look . . . even higher expectations: Interviews with Lesley Jane Seymour and Maggie Buckley.

141 During one search for a writer . . . the person was hired: Background inter-view.

141 In another instance . . . She would have to find someone else: Interview with Lesley Jane Seymour.

141 Once, spotting [*Hippocrates*] at the airport . . . Northrop and Posnick never had lunch again: Interview with Peggy Northrop, April 2, 2019; Peggy Northrop, "My September Issues," unpublished piece of personal writing shared with author, September 13, 2009.

143 Anna, too, ate [at 44]: Georgia Dullea, "The Royalton Round Table," *New York Times*, December 27, 1992.

143 In Anna's first year . . . Anna took it as a challenge: Anna Wintour, "Edi-torial Decision-Making," *Anna Wintour Teaches Creativity and Leadership*, MasterClass, https://www.masterclass.com/classes/Anna-anna-teaches -creativity-and-leadership.

144 A month after [the song's] release: "Pepsi Cancels Madonna Ad," *New York Times*, April 5, 1989.

144 Anna seemed to dislike LA: Interview with Lisa Love.

144 Any doubt she had about putting Madonna: Kevin Haynes, "Anna's Big Year," *WWD*, November 10, 1989.

144 Maggie Buckley booked Madonna: Interview with Maggie Buckley.

000 Talley went to Madonna's house . . . didn't want anything "bombastic": Interview with André Leon Talley, March 20, 2021.

144 "The fact that that very nice man": Anna Wintour, "Editorial Decision-Making," *Anna Wintour Teaches Creativity and Leadership*, MasterClass,

https://www.masterclass.com/classes/Anna-anna-teaches-creativity-and
-leadership.

145   Her instinct paid off: Nina Darnton, "What's in a Name?" *Newsweek*, June 5, 1989.

145   A year later, Anna doubted her instinct . . . easily justify the choice: Interview with Michael Boodro.

145   newsstand sales of nearly 750,000: Figure provided to author by Audit Bureau of Circulations.

145   Killing the cover with Cindy Crawford . . . would one day be working for Anna: Interviews with Laurie Jones, December 5, 2020, and May 20, 2021.

145   Grace Coddington had styled that shoot: Interview with Grace Coddington, May 17, 2021.

145   But now in 1993 . . . "We just can't run it": Interview with Laurie Jones.

145   Crawford, one of her favorite models: Interview with André Leon Talley, April 10, 2021.

146   The May 1993 cover instead ran: Cover credit, *Vogue*, May 1993.

146   Anna held occasional off-site meetings . . . and photographed beautifully: Interview with Laurie Jones.

146   Los Angeles–averse Anna: Interview with Lisa Love.

146   "She realized that she couldn't stay behind": Interview with Grace Coddington.

146   After her first year, *Vogue*'s revenue: Haynes, "Anna's Big Year."

Chapter 14: "In" versus "Out"

147   When she took over *Vogue*, she made hosting: Interview with Gabé Doppelt, November 13, 2020.

147   No matter what or who the party was for . . . "but we did it, and it worked": Interview with Gabé Doppelt.

148   "She likes conversation": Interview with Lisa Love, October 20, 2020.

148   Susanne Bartsch, a party promoter known as: "Bartschland," http://www .susannebartsch.com/about.

148   next to Henry Kissinger: Interview with Gabé Doppelt.

148   A few months into Peggy Northrop's new job . . . just wanted her to figure it out: Interview with Peggy Northrop, April 12, 2019.

148   Anna had been devastated by the loss: Interview with Laurie Jones, May 20, 2021.

149   Anna got Newhouse to underwrite . . . designer Carolyne Roehm: Melanie Kletter, "When Bigger Was Better," *WWD*, May 28, 2002.

149   As she did in the pages of *Vogue*: Interview with Gabé Doppelt.

149   Michael Kors donated . . . prior to the event: Jeannie Williams, "Touching Travis Tribute Makes Hayes' Birthday," *USA Today*, October 24, 1990.

149   Betsey Johnson contributed . . . and portraits by top photographers: Cathy Horyn, "Fashion Notes," *Washington Post*, November 18, 1990.

149   Robert Isabell . . . 12,000 yards of white voile: Cathy Horyn, "Snap, Sparkle, Shop: In New York, Designers' Benefit for AIDS Research," *Washington Post*, November 30, 1990.

149   Like Anna, Isabell's primary concern: Interview with Gabé Doppelt.

149   On opening night, Anna hosted: Horyn, "Fashion Notes."

149   Chanel designer Karl Lagerfeld . . . they also did it for Anna: Horyn, "Snap, Sparkle, Shop."

149   Anna attended the party looking glamorous: @oldmarcjacobs, "A Look from Perry Ellis by Marc Jacobs S/S 1991—modeled by Christy Turlington," Instagram, https://www.instagram.com/p/CGqJtHmAbnp/?utm_medium=share_sheet.

149   She had spent so much time: Horyn, "Snap, Sparkle, Shop."

150   But Anna was also terribly nervous . . . a disease then identified with gay men: Interview with William Norwich, December 16, 2020.

150   The event grew so much . . . raising $4.7 million: "Fashionably Late," *Advocate*, January 1, 1991.

150   No sponsorships were sold, no magazine coverage: Patrick Reilly, "Magazines Find Noble Causes Let Them Help Others, Themselves," *Wall Street Journal*, September 18, 1990.

150   Anna's staff thought that she viewed giving back: Interviews with numerous people who worked for Anna at *Vogue*.

150   But in an article about magazines: Reilly, "Magazines Find Noble Causes."

150   In February 1990, *Adweek* named her: Judith Newman, "Anna Wintour: Editor of the Year," *Adweek*, February 12, 1990.

150   over the first seven months of the year . . . *Elle*, rose slightly: Joanne Lipman, "*Vogue*'s Ads Sag in the Battle with *Elle*," *Wall Street Journal*, July 13, 1990.

151   *Elle*'s publisher, Anne Sutherland Fuchs: Lipman, "*Vogue*'s Ads Sag."

151   On December 4, 1990, Fuchs was named: James Barron, "Condé Nast Publications Get 3 New Publishers," *New York Times*, December 4, 1990.

151   started getting her hair professionally done: Interview with André Leon Talley, April 10, 2021.

151   But though she and *Vogue* cost a lot: Interviews with Linda Rice, May 18, 2020, and three background sources.

151   When she was told to keep her staff's salaries . . . as she expected from herself: Interviews with Freddy Gamble, February 28, 2020, and several background sources.

151   As the editor-in-chief . . . "natural, friendly, and warm": Anna Wintour, "Letter from the Editor: Traumas of a Cover Girl," *Vogue*, August 1996.

152   As a perfectionist, Anna had many checks . . . would be rushed to her via taxi: Interview with Maggie Buckley, January 19, 2020.

152   If it was somewhere else, a Polaroid: Interview with Lisa Love, October 20, 2020.

152   While editors came to know what she liked: Interviews with Lisa Love; André Leon Talley, March 20, 2021; and background sources.

152 After actress Uma Thurman divorced . . . no point even transcribing the tape: Background interview.

152 Anna decided to put Gwyneth Paltrow . . . "'in an old Ivory-soap commercial'": Wintour, "Letter from the Editor: Traumas of a Cover Girl."

153 Each time Anna killed one of Paltrow's shoots: Interview with Maggie Buckley.

153 Anna's judgments of women in the nineties . . . they respected her process: Background interview.

153 Staff printed out drafts for Anna to read: Interviews with Peggy Northrop, April 12, 2019, and Sarah Van Sicklen, September 16, 2020.

153 Sometimes she made more specific comments . . . "It didn't work. Let's move on": Interview with Michael Boodro, April 28, 2021.

153 At home, she would show articles to Shaffer: Interview with Laurie Jones, December 5, 2020.

154 "We all knew that Dr. Shaffer": Interview with André Leon Talley.

154 The final mark of approval . . . would parrot in frustration: Background interview.

154 In the eighties, billboards advertising *Forbes* . . . "was if you didn't give a crap": Interview with Michael Boodro.

154 In one features meeting in early 1994 . . . was stunned to hear this idea coming out of her mouth": Background interview with source present in the meeting.

155 a story in this vein ran: Georgina Howell, "Vogue Beauty: Eyeing the East," *Vogue*, May, 1994.

155 Writers, even those doing [just] short pieces: Interview with Laurie Jones.

155 Some editors, however were known for . . . spending extravagantly: Interviews with Linda Rice, Freddy Gamble, and background source.

155 In the beginning of Anna's editorship . . . bring back his receipts: Interview with André Leon Talley.

155 In 1990, he moved to Paris . . . "This was *Vogue*!": André Leon Talley, *The Chiffon Trenches* (New York: Ballantine, 2020), iBook, 239.

155 Talley said later . . . "Anna did not like to explain": Interview with André Leon Talley.

156 Freddy Gamble, who worked in [HR], said Talley: Interview with Freddy Gamble.

156 "She indulged him all the time": Interview with Laurie Jones.

156 Talley wrote in his memoir: Talley, *The Chiffon Trenches*, 241.

156 But Jones saw it as more than that: Interview with Laurie Jones.

156 enabling him to expense: Interview with André Leon Talley.

165 In 1995, fed up with what he saw as . . . and quit: Talley, *The Chiffon Trenches*, 289.

156 "Anna had her pets": Interview with Lesley Jane Seymour.

157 Anna chose Carrie Donovan . . . as Mazzola slumped in his seat: Michael Gross, "War of the Poses," *New York*, April 27, 1992.

157 When she got to the stage, she said: "Long Night's Journey," *WWD*, February 27, 1991.

157   In the audience, Anna's former *Bazaar* colleagues: Background interview.

157   Hearst announced Mazzola's retirement: Gross, "War of the Poses."

Chapter 15: First Assistant, Second Assistant

158   In the summer of 1991 . . . in close touch with the world of haute couture": Charles Wintour letter to Arthur Schlesinger, July 25, 1991, Arthur M. Schlesinger Jr. papers, Manuscripts and Archives Division, New York Public Library.

158   $1.64 million interest-free loan: Public record of mortgage dated February 28, 1993.

158   the new Greek revival-style house . . . attracted artists, musicians, and filmmakers: Steven Kurutz, "What Do Anna Wintour and Bob Dylan Have in Common? This Secret Garden," *New York Times*, September 28, 2016, https://www.nytimes.com/2016/09/29/fashion/new-york-secret-garden-anna-wintour-bob-dylan.html.

159   Just before they moved in . . . (Anna had dogs from then on): Interview with Miranda Brooks, May 7, 2021.

159   when she talked about her young children: Interview with Lesley Jane Seymour, January 13, 2020.

159   She took them to school . . . and avoided commitments on weekends: Nigel Farndale, "'Nuclear' Anna Sets a Frosty Tone at *Vogue*," *Telegraph*, April 4, 1998.

159   Anna herself sometimes went to the office on a Saturday: Interview with Meredith Asplundh, August 7, 2020.

159   instituting rules for her children . . . "behind my back already!": Farndale, "'Nuclear' Anna Sets a Frosty Tone at *Vogue*."

159   One, Lori Feldt, who lived in their home in 1997 . . . ended at 9 or 10 at night: Lori Feldt deposition, March 8, 2002, Lori Feldt against Conde Nast Publications, Inc., and Chemico Plus, Inc., d/b/a Riccardi Contracting, Supreme Court of the State of New York County of New York.

160   if her kids ever called, she answered the phone: Interview with Stephanie Winston Wolkoff, May 1, 2021, and others.

160   And she showed up physically . . . "as much as her job would allow": Interview with Susan Bidel, August 23, 2019.

160   Anna took them to work events . . . "an incredibly efficient woman": Interview with Laurie Jones, September 15, 2021.

161   poinsettias were banned: Sara James, "Memo Pad: Deck the Halls," *WWD*, November 30, 2005.

161   ("you never knew where that came from"): Interview with Maggie Buckley, January 19, 2020.

161   couldn't stand chewing gum (true, actually): Interview with Laurie Jones, December 5, 2020.

161   along with polka dots: Interview with Laurie Jones.

161 "I wouldn't have any staff": "Is Black Dead? Is It Finally Time to Go into Mourning for a Fashion Staple?," *Chicago Tribune*, July 18, 1990.

161 she actually *did* tell her staff: Interview with Sarah Van Sicklen, September 16, 2020.

161 Anna wanted Laurie Jones to help her build: Interview with Laurie Jones.

161 She has had at any one time . . . she had two to three [assistants]: *Vogue* mastheads 1988–2020, and interviews with Laurie Jones and several others.

161 The first assistant managed the other two . . . a view shared by many on her staff: All details in this section drawn from interviews with multiple background sources, except as noted in subsequent two endnotes.

162 "Usually someone in her office sends an email" . . . sends it over: Interview with Tom Ford, October 22, 2020.

163 means being her *personal* assistant: Interview with Laurie Jones.

164 Still, finding the right person . . . "who had experience and could really contribute": Interview with Laurie Jones.

164 Meredith Asplundh started as an intern . . . their office attire wasn't sufficient: Interview with Meredith Asplundh.

166 [Anna] never liked orchids: Interview with André Leon Talley, April 10, 2021.

167 Hamish Bowles first met Anna . . . were able to sidestep some oversight: Interview with Hamish Bowles, December 2, 2020.

168 Phyllis Posnick, who worked on photos . . . she laughed and said, "Okay": Interview with Phyllis Posnick, January 18, 2021.

168 Anna had editors make boards of Polaroids . . . "to do with what she was actually shooting": Grace Coddington, *Grace* (New York: Random House, 2012), 213–14.

168 Talley described an altercation with Cerf de Dudzeele: André Leon Talley, *The Chiffon Trenches* (New York: Ballantine, 2020), iBook, 286.

169 Anna seemed to dislike the chaos . . . competition for certain items was fierce: Interviews with several people who worked at Vogue at the time.

169 complaining to Anna was "pointless": Coddington, *Grace*, 214.

169 Anna liked over-the-top personalities: Interview with Laurie Schechter, February 14, 2020.

169 Anna "surrounded herself with strong independent thinkers": Talley, *The Chiffon Trenches*, 286.

169 Or as Lisa Love, *Vogue*'s West Coast editor, said: Interview with Lisa Love, October 20, 2020.

169 Just a few years into her job . . . her champion and mentor, Alexander Liberman: Edward Helmore, "New Brit on the Block; James Truman," *Times (UK)*, February 6, 1994; and Meg Cox, "James Truman Gets Star Status at Condé Nast," *Wall Street Journal*, January 26, 1994.

169 In February 1991, the seventy-eight-year-old Liberman . . . the work that was his identity: Francine du Plessix Gray, *Them* (London: Penguin, 2004), 455 and 486–91.

169   Unlike Grace Mirabella, Anna was never dependent on Liberman . . . for the remainder of his life only as a courtesy: Dodie Kazanjian and Calvin Tomkins, *Alex* (New York: Knopf, 1993), 322; and interview with Laurie Jones.

170   Anna said that her replacing Liberman was "never discussed": Rebecca Mead, "The Truman Administration," *New York*, May 23, 1994.

170   but people who worked with her believed she wanted more: Interviews with Lesley Jane Seymour, January 13, 2020, and background source.

170   In 1992, Graydon Carter received a job offer . . . "Act surprised when Si calls you": Background interview.

170   Gabé Doppelt, who had faithfully worked for Anna . . . Being shut out offended Liberman: Interview with Gabé Doppelt, November 13, 2020.

170   Some figured that Anna's coordinating: Background interview.

170   "The Doppelt appointment demonstrates . . .": Brian Leitch, "*Vogue*'s Gabé Doppelt Succeeds Amy Levin Cooper at *Mademoiselle*," *WWD*, October 2, 1992.

171   And the November 1993 issue . . . "'the ugliest girl in eighth grade' cover": Deirdre Carmody, "The Media Business: New Makeover for *Mademoiselle*," *New York Times*, March 21, 1994.

171   With readers and advertisers fleeing . . . taking a job at MTV: Deirdre Carmody, "Top Editor Resigns at *Mademoiselle*," *New York Times*, September 30, 1993; and interview with Gabé Doppelt, November 13, 2020.

171   By this point, Anna [said], Newhouse "distinctly felt" . . . to buy a house on Long Island: du Plessix Gray, *Them*, 488.

171   Anna was upset by the way Liberman was treated . . . despite the golden parachute: Background interview.

171   But Anna wouldn't become . . . the next editorial director of the company: Deirdre Carmody, "The Media Business: Conde Nast's Visionary to Bow Out," *New York Times*, January 26, 1994, https://www.nytimes.com/1994/01/26/business/the-media-business-conde-nast-s-visionary-to-bow-out.html.

172   But Doppelt thought it was a typical Newhouse move: Interview with Gabé Doppelt.

172   Liberman felt similarly, telling Truman: du Plessix Gray, *Them*, 488.

172   Udell hired Joan Feeney: Interview with Joan Feeney, February 6, 2019.

172   Udell believed the internet was the future . . . was, frankly, unthinkable: Interview with Rochelle Udell, April 12, 2019.

173   Udell and Feeney decided to start with food . . . to run the magazine's photo archive online: Interview with Joan Feeney.

173   Joe Dolce, a features editor, sent an email: Interview with Joe Dolce, June 26, 2020.

173   Still, from the beginning of the Epicurious.com project . . . she'd have to wait years for her website: Interviews with Joan Feeney, February 6, 2019, and December 21, 2020.

Chapter 16: A New Project, an Old Friend

174 an unseasonable forty-eight degrees: "Weather History for New York, NY," *The Old Farmer's Almanac*, https://www.almanac.com/weather/history/NY/New%20York/1995-12-04.

174 As the night's hostess . . . to just below her toned biceps: Aileen Mehle, "A Report on the Costume Institute Gala and the New Regime," *WWD*, December 6, 1995.

174 The event's sponsors were Chanel and Versace: Nadine Brozan, "Chronicle," *New York Times*, July 18, 1995.

174 After Anna, Naomi Campbell sparkled . . . Calvin Klein apron dress: "25 Years of Met Gala Themes: A Look Back at Many First Mondays in May," Vogue.com, April 27, 2020, https://www.vogue.com/article/met-gala -themes.

174 Along with fellow models . . . centerpieces filled with fruit: Mehle, "A Report on the Costume Institute Gala."

175 The Met's exhibit offered . . . a $1,000 ticket to the dinner: Nadine Brozan, "Chronicle," *New York Times*, October 9, 1995.

175 Anna would, in later years ensure: Text message from Stephanie Winston Wolkoff, July 17, 2021, and background interview.

175 "God forbid if they're fat": Interview with Sarah Van Sicklen, September 16, 2020.

175 Following the dinner was a dance party . . . admitted with $150 tickets: Brozan, "Chronicle," October 9, 1995.

175 They smoked and drank . . . [until] people were puking: Interviews with Sarah Van Sicklen, September 16, 2020 and background source.

175 at one gala . . . women peeing in the Great Hall: Background interview.

175 The Costume Institute, founded in 1937: "The Costume Institute," The Met, https://www.metmuseum.org/about-the-met/collection-areas/the -costume-institute#:~:text=The%20Costume%20Institute%20began%20 as,Neighborhood%20Playhouse%20founder%20Irene%20Lewisohn.

176 Beloved by his staff, Martin had been the editor . . . an invitation to write an article or speak: Interview with Dennita Sewell, July 29, 2020.

176 Martin had started at the Costume Institute . . . "no razzle-dazzle": Bernadine Morris, "Costume Change at the Met," *New York Times*, December 18, 1992.

176 Martin's charge was to reignite the department's buzz: Michael Gross, *Rogues' Gallery* (New York: Crown, 2010), 463.

176 "There was no one spearheading it": Anna Wintour, "Executing a Vision and Transforming the Met Gala," *Anna Wintour Teaches Creativity and Leadership*, MasterClass, https://www.masterclass.com/classes/anna-win tour-teaches-creativity-and-leadership/chapters/executing-a-vision-trans forming-the-met-gala.

176 However, part of the reason the Met needed her . . . if it were a designer: Background interview with source familiar with the planning.

177 she prevented boredom in her job [by] regularly finding new projects: Interview with Emma Soames, June 14, 2021.

177 "I think I was quite naïve": Wintour, "Executing a Vision and Transforming the Met Gala."

177 Martin, the chief curator . . . her rival Liz Tilberis, now editor-in-chief of *Harper's Bazaar*: Background interview.

177 Anna took Shulman to lunch: Email from Alexandra Shulman, September 22, 2021.

177 Her attitude was, "Great" . . . not ceding territory to anybody: Interview with Michael Boodro, April 28, 2021.

177 Tilberis had taken the *Bazaar* job . . . they couldn't also work for Anna at *Vogue*: Interview with Sarajane Hoare, October 23, 2020.

177 upwards of $1 million: "Eye Scoop," *Women's Wear Daily*, May 12, 1992.

177 Anna signed Steven Meisel: Ibid.

177 [Anna] started having her cover stars agree: Interview with Maggie Buckley, January 19, 2020.

177 She counter-offered to keep editors . . . [Newhouse] had her back: Michael Gross, "War of the Poses," *New York*, April 27, 1992.

177 In 1996, Tilberis hosted the party . . . which led to an easier rapport: Background interview.

178 Martin took great pride [in] the text he wrote . . . didn't mean it needed dumbing down: Interviews with several background sources.

178 One piece of text . . . The text stayed: Background interview.

178 On January 5, 1996: Eleanor Wintour's will, obtained by author as public record.

178 Nonie had been suffering from osteoporosis . . . undetected for months: Charles Wintour letter to Arthur Schlesinger, February 7, 1996, Arthur M. Schlesinger Jr. papers, Manuscripts and Archives Division, New York Public Library.

178 It was Nonie's osteoporosis that inspired Anna to take up tennis: Background interview.

178 after losing her mom, "she was very emotional about it": Interview with Laurie Jones, December 5, 2020.

178 She would credit her mom with instilling her social conscience: Kevin Gray, "The Summer of Her Discontent," *New York*, September 20, 1999.

178 When Anna was in London for the funeral . . . his dramatic resignation ten months earlier: André Leon Talley, *The Chiffon Trenches* (New York: Ballantine, 2020), iBook, 310.

178 "Probably at the time, his role was just not clearly defined . . . what you expect him to do": Interview with Laurie Jones.

179 Talley had spoken out publicly . . . "one of my oldest friends": Constance C. R. White, "Patterns," *New York Times*, March 7, 1995, https://www.nytimes.com/1995/03/07/style/patterns-637095.html.

179 When she called, Talley could tell . . . where he found Anna along with her dad and siblings: Talley, *The Chiffon Trenches*, 310–11.

179   At the funeral, Anna's brother Patrick . . . "so Anna had to do it": Charles
      Wintour letter to Arthur Schlesinger, February 7, 1996, Schlesinger papers,
      NYPL.

179   Talley sat in the back . . . and held her as she exited: Talley, *The Chiffon
      Trenches*, 311–12.

179   just before Nonie died, Charles . . . the right eye "was dodgy in the morn-
      ings": Charles Wintour letter to Arthur Schlesinger, February 7, 1996,
      Schlesinger papers, NYPL.

180   revealed a side invisible to most . . . no amount of power can shake that
      core: Interviews with several of Anna's close friends.

180   not that, Jones said: Interviews with Laurie Jones, September 15, 2021.

180   Despite their reconciliation, Talley did not go back . . . "my heart was still
      with the magazine: Talley, *The Chiffon Trenches*, 313 and 326.

180   a salary of $350,000: Interviews with André Leon Talley and Laurie Jones,
      May 20, 2021.

180   "Sometimes he would be very obliging" . . . "he had a great job": Interview
      with Laurie Jones.

181   A manager in human resources . . . "It is better to have André where you
      can see him": Background interview.

Chapter 17: Follow the Money

182   But at work, she was merely a subject . . . whether he was going to promote
      them or fire them: Background interview.

182   Ad pages were down in the first quarter of 1994 . . . *Bazaar* had nearly
      double its to $57.3 million: Garth Alexander, "The Gloss Comes Off at
      Condé Nast Magazines," *Times (UK)*, May 8, 1994.

183   Anne Sutherland Fuchs, whom he . . . at Hearst publishing *Esquire*: Lisa
      Lockwood, "Ron Galotti: *Vogue*'s Hired Gun," *WWD*, May 13, 1994.

183   at a seven-figure salary: Background interview.

183   Newhouse had fired him . . . move over to *Harper's Bazaar* and crush *Vogue*:
      Alexander, "The Gloss Comes Off."

183   The stories about Galotti's temper were legendary . . . A few months later,
      Galotti was fired: Jay McInerney, "Goodbye, Mr. Big," *New York*, April 30,
      2004.

183   Galotti was as ruthless . . . the most dominant fashion publication in the
      world: Background interview.

184   Before long rumors surfaced . . . that she would soon be out of a job: Alex-
      ander, "The Gloss Comes Off."

184   The September 1994 issue was an homage to glamour . . . "If you can't sell
      it, you can't advertise it": Amy Spindler, "How Fashion Killed the Unloved
      Waif," *New York Times*, September 27, 1994.

184   Anna mainly wanted to kill grunge . . . "she printed it, and people talked
      about it": Interview with Grace Coddington, December 19, 2020.

184 Galotti respected Anna as an editor . . . smart enough to view herself the very same way: Background interview.

185 By early 1997, business was looking up . . . "Everything looks pretty damn good": Lisa Lockwood, "March: The Record Breakers," *WWD*, February 27, 1997.

185 For 1997, the magazine's pages were up 10 percent overall: Lisa Lockwood, "Forecast '98: The Ad Page Challenge: How to Beat '97," *WWD*, October 23, 1997.

185 Packed with ads, its 734 total pages . . . the fifth-biggest of all time: Lisa Lockwood, "September Mags: Fat and Happy," *WWD*, August 21, 1997.

185 A 1997 ad for the shoe brand Candie's . . . "a decision was made": "Memo Pad: What a Relief," *WWD*, February 28, 1997.

186 But what Galotti really wanted was for Anna . . . She was more deliberate about shooting advertisers' clothing: Background interview with source with knowledge of the Da Silvano conversation.

186 Da Silvano, one of her and Newhouse's favorite restaurants: Kate Betts, "Ruth Reichl Dishes on the Last Days of *Gourmet* Magazine," *New York Times*, April 9, 2019, https://www.nytimes.com/2019/04/09/books/review/ruth-reichl-save-me-the-plums.html.

186 she seemed to like him: Interview with Laurie Jones, May 20, 2021.

186 But she also had an ally in company president and CEO Steve Florio: Interview with Tom Florio, April 19, 2021.

187 So, on September 30, 1993 . . . a protest against the magazine's coverage of fur: Nadine Brozan, "Chronicle," *New York Times*, October 1, 1993, https://www.nytimes.com/1993/10/01/style/chronicle-638293.html.

187 The PETA contingent marched . . . waited for security to come: Interview with William Norwich, December 16, 2020.

187 the police took the protesters: Brozan, "Chronicle," October 1, 1993.

187 the racks lining the *Vogue* office . . . a story about coats every August: Interview with Sarah Van Sicklen, September 16, 2020.

187 Although the magazine carried ads . . . brands who had licensed fur lines: Background interview.

187 Anna's assistants felt that part of their job: Interview with Meredith Asplundh, August 7, 2020.

188 In her September 1996 editor's letter: Anna Wintour, "Letter from the Editor: An American Moment," *Vogue*, September 1996.

188 It was these very words that, on December 19, 1996 . . . Christmas lunch with senior members of her team: "Memo Pad: Raccoon-ized," *WWD*, December 20, 1996.

188 The woman—who wore black . . . rather like roadkill: Grace Coddington, *Grace* (New York: Random House, 2012), 248–49.

188 Whacking it down: "Memo Pad: Raccoon-ized"; and Nadine Brozan, "Chronicle," *New York Times*, December 20, 1996.

188 Anna threw a napkin over the raccoon . . . "Well, that certainly broke the ice": Coddington, *Grace*, 248–49.

188   The Four Seasons later joked: Brozan, "Chronicle," December 20, 1996.

188   the only person who could tell Anna what to do: Interview with Anne McNally, May 6, 2021.

188   learned of a house for sale in Mastic, Long Island . . . a garden, which had been designed by Brooks: Interview with Miranda Brooks, May 7, 2021.

188   But the Hamptons . . . didn't want her life to be like the Met Gala: Interview with Anne McNally.

189   celebrities like film director Baz Luhrmann and *The Wire*'s Dominic West: Background interview.

189   Aside from trips to the Tortuga Bay: Interview with Anne McNally, May 6, 2021.

189   Anna, who actually dislikes cold weather: Interviews with several friends.

189   This eighteenth-century homestead . . . (though Anna never got one): Interview with Miranda Brooks.

189   Friends told Anna not to buy it: Background interview.

189   Anna would later describe the town . . . [leaking] into the drinking water: Kelly McMasters, *Welcome to Shirley: A Memoir from an Atomic Town* (New York: PublicAffairs, 2008), 248.

189   But McMasters wondered: Interview with Kelly McMasters, December 16, 2019.

189   she didn't care . . . she didn't often mix with the locals: Interviews with several friends.

190   she took on the work of transforming it . . . "not pretentious and long grass": Interview with Miranda Brooks.

190   That landscape went with the English country interiors . . . "a wonderful compound for my family": Mara Miller, *Carrier and Company: Positively Chic Interiors* (New York: Harry N. Abrams, 2015) via "Anna Wintour's House," Scene Therapy, December 16, 2020, https://scenetherapy.com /anna-wintours-house/.

190   Brooks convinced Anna and Shaffer . . . "and look at a full moon": Interview with Miranda Brooks.

191   The fur-related attacks against Anna . . . [settled] in 2004, for $2.1 million: Lori Feldt against Conde Nast Publications, Inc., and Chemico Plus, Inc., d/b/a Riccardi Contracting, Supreme Court of the State of New York County of New York; Dareh Gregorian, "Condé Clear$ Air—Pays Wintour Nanny $2M to Settle Toxic-Fume Suit," *New York Post*, October 20, 2004.

191   Anna was angry . . . because it resulted in Feldt's injury: Interview with Laurie Jones, May 20, 2021.

191   On Wednesday, December 17 . . . (fearing it would escalate the situation): Richard Johnson with Jeane MacIntosh and Sean Gannon, "*Vogue* Fights PETA Beef with Beef," *New York Post*, December 19, 1997.

191   But Anna simply carried on: Interview with Laurie Jones.

192   *WWD* called them . . . the cover acknowledged the "naysayers": Lisa Lockwood, "Anna's Ménage a Trois," *WWD*, January 9, 1998.

192   "that issue was taking a look back . . .": Orla Healy, "Girl Power," *New York Daily News*, January 15, 1998.

192   Shooting celebrities with *Vogue* standards: Interview with Laurie Jones.

192   "They're not really model size . . .": Interview with Grace Coddington.

192   "There was a lot more work": Interview with Charles Churchward, June 4, 2020.

192   have clothing custom-made for celebrities: Interviews with Tonne Goodman, June 10, 2021 and Paul Cavaco, December 22, 2020.

192   that an editor had a life-span of five years: Background interview.

192   "Every now and then we encounter . . . we have more than succeeded": Anna Wintour, "Letter from the Editor: No Ordinary Oprah," *Vogue*, October 1998.

193   In a November 1998 profile . . . "I would have a problem with that": Rick Marin, "She's Still in Vogue," *Newsweek*, November 23, 1998.

193   In 2009, when Morley Safer asked her . . . "take care of themselves in a healthier way": Amy Odell, "*60 Minutes* Outtakes: Anna Wintour on Fur, Photoshop, and Obese People," NYMag.com, May 18, 2009, https://www.thecut.com/2009/05/60_minutes_outtakes_anna_winto.html.

193   Anna personally spoke to designers . . . brought her hairdresser, Andre Walker, for the day: Interview with Paul Cavaco.

194   For the accompanying profile . . . "That's why it's so extraordinary": Jonathan Van Meter, "From the Archives: Oprah Winfrey in *Vogue*," Vogue.com, https://www.vogue.com/article/from-the-archives-oprah-winfrey-in-vogue.

194   The issue was the biggest in Anna's editorship: Lisa Lockwood, "Covers '98: Agony and Ecstasy," *WWD*, January 29, 1999.

194   Magazines that hadn't switched . . . "Nobody cares about models anymore": Alex Kuczynski, "Trading on Hollywood Magic: Celebrities Push Models Off Women's Magazine Covers," *New York Times*, January 30, 1999.

194   "And at the end of my presentation": Anna Wintour, "Evolving a Brand: A Look Back at Iconic Vogue Covers," *Anna Wintour Teaches Creativity and Leadership*, MasterClass, https://www.masterclass.com/classes/anna-wintour-teaches-creativity-and-leadership/chapters/evolving-a-brand-a-look-back-at-iconic-vogue-covers.

195   " . . . America is a country of people": Anna Wintour, "Letter from the Editor: Fashion's New Faces," *Vogue*, July, 1997.

195   André Leon Talley regularly sent . . . While she valued Talley's suggestions: Interviews with two background sources.

195   her off-handed response . . . "not every month is Black History Month": Interviews with two background sources.

196   After Tonne Goodman started in 1999 as fashion director . . . "who is not there to know what is going on": Interview with Tonne Goodman.

197   Anna sent [Hillary Clinton] a note . . . "sift through all of the fashion for her": "Notes," *New York Times*, February 7, 1993.

197   Clinton accepted the help: Hillary Clinton spokesperson to author.

197 The magazine offered help to Nathan: Interview with Laurie Jones, December 5, 2020.

198 "By sitting for the cover of *Vogue*": Alex Kuczynski, "Media: The First Lady Strikes a Pose for the Media Elite," *New York Times*, December 7, 1998, https://www.nytimes.com/1998/12/07/business/media-the-first-lady -strikes-a-pose-for-the-media-elite.html.

198 Like the Oprah shoot all the clothes were custom . . . "in satin instead of velvet": Interview with Paul Cavaco, December 22, 2020.

198 The week after the cover came out . . . being a political fund-raiser could be a very powerful thing: Kuczynski, "The First Lady Strikes a Pose."

199 When Miramax started producing costume dramas . . . "don't ask Anna Wintour to take off her sungasses": Interview with Rachel Pine, August 3, 2020.

199 In the summer of 1998 . . . a successful publisher at the Condé Nast title *GQ*: Robin Pogrebin, "Media: Publishing: Losing *Vogue*'s Publisher Could Hurt Condé Nast as Much as Tina Brown's Departure," *New York Times*, July 20, 1998.

200 Anna and Beckman didn't click: Interview with Laurie Jones.

200 Galotti had turned the *Vogue* business around: Kevin Gray, "The Summer of Her Discontent," *New York*, September 20, 1999.

200 The magazine charged the highest possible rates: Background interview.

200 For 1997, *Vogue* finished the year: Jane L. Levere, "The Media Business: Advertising: Harper's Bazaar Is Moving to Increase Ad Pages with a New Web Site and Television Campaign," *New York Times*, March 5, 1998.

200 In the spring of 1998, CondéNet editorial director . . . she'd showed him how it worked: Interviews with Joan Feeney on February 6, 2019, and December 22, 2020.

201 Given that she couldn't charge . . . sat on the back burner and never happened: Interviews with Joan Feeney and Rochelle Udell, April 12, 2019.

201 To start *Vogue*'s site: Interview with Joan Feeney.

201 "The big designers got in": Interview with André Leon Talley, April 10, 2021.

201 Publishing images of runway shows: Interview with Joan Feeney.

201 a letter on Vogue.com letterhead: Scan of letter provided to author by Joan Feeney.

201 The ask was extraordinary . . . Chanel customers could preorder what they wanted: Interview with Joan Feeney.

203 In 2013, Burberry would receive accolades: Teo van den Broeke and Zak Maoui, "How Burberry Became Britain's Most Important Brand," *GQ UK*, September 17, 2018, https://www.gq-magazine.co.uk/article/how -burberry-became-britains-most-important-brand.

203 In Vogue.com's infancy Anna also helped . . . "to think I owe him any favors": Interviews with Joan Feeney.

203 Newhouse owned both publications: Ravi Somaiya, "Condé Nast to Sell Fairchild Fashion Media for $100 Million," *New York Times*, August 19, 2017.

Chapter 18: The Divorce

205   not long after she did the interview . . . [Schaps] left a phone number: Interview with Jordan Schaps, February 7, 2020.

205   *New York* was doing a cover story: Kevin Gray, "The Summer of Her Discontent," *New York*, September 20, 1999, https://nymag.com/nymetro/news/people/features/1460/.

205   Twenty minutes later . . . They decided on Herb Ritts: Interview with Jordan Schaps.

206   Shelby Bryan attended socialite Anne Bass's fund-raising ball . . . an affair unfolded: Interviews with Shelby Bryan, July 20 and 21, 2021.

207   Bryan was born in the town of Freeport, Texas . . . His friends included Al Gore and the Clintons: Evan Smith, "In Vogue," *Texas Monthly*, October 1999.

207   He was the first boyfriend Anna had with that kind of wealth: Background interview.

207   Months after they first met . . . it wasn't her favorite activity: Interviews with Shelby Bryan.

208   By the summer of 1999, their affair: "Encore: People Watch," *Fort Worth Star-Telegram*, July 21, 1999.

208   "I didn't like it": Interview with Shelby Bryan.

208   the affair played out on the sidelines of runways: George Rush and Joanna Molloy, "Jerry Gets a Beauty Over-Hall," *New York Daily News*, July 14, 1999.

208   but she kept it and he moved into a townhouse: Deborah Schoeneman, "David Shaffer Guts Downing Street Home in a Real Big Hurry," Observer.com, February 14, 2000, https://observer.com/2000/02/david-shaffer-guts-downing-street-home-in-a-real-big-hurry/.

208   He still read all of Anna's editor's letters: Background interview.

208   and gave feedback on the magazine: Interview with Laurie Jones, December 5, 2020.

209   but even at parties he had attended . . . two sons from his previous marriage: Interviews with two background sources.

209   But Anna was reportedly bored: Gray, "The Summer of Her Discontent."

209   after a lunch with Bill Gates: Interview with Laurie Jones, May 20, 2021.

209   Unlike Shaffer . . . Bryan was straightforward: Interviews with two background sources.

209   Though Anna agonized . . . initiated proceedings in September 1999: Gray, "The Summer of Her Discontent."

209   *Vogue* event planner . . . "it was like there was no personal relationship": Interview with Stephanie Winston Wolkoff, May 1, 2021.

209   As Anna's relationship with Bryan intensified . . . obviously evening wear": Gray, "The Summer of Her Discontent."

210   she had hosted a breast cancer fund-raiser: Karen de Witt, "A 7th Ave. Campaign Goes to Washington," *New York Times*, September 22, 1996,

https://www.nytimes.com/1996/09/22/us/a-7th-ave-campaign-goes-to
-washington.html.

210   "She had strong political opinions already": Interview with Shelby Bryan.

210   were surprised she ended up with Bryan: Interviews with background
source; Tom Ford, October 22, 2020; and Laurie Jones.

210   He was smart and cultured: Background interview.

210   he joked freely about things like how good: Interviews with three background sources.

210   "I've never done that": Interview with Shelby Bryan.

210   People wondered how Anna got through: Interviews with two background
sources.

210   his behavior "was just not kind": Interview with Laurie Jones, December 5,
2020.

210   Tom Ford met Bryan on a pheasant shooting trip: Interview with Tom
Ford.

211   she was in the process of divorcing Shaffer: George Rush and Joanna
Molloy, "For Mogul, High Cost of Wintourizing," *New York Daily News*,
July 25, 1999.

211   Schaps arrived, wheeling in the bicycle: Interview with Jordan Schaps.

211   She had brought Talley along . . . "not in her underwear": Interviews with
André Leon Talley, March 20 and April 10, 2021.

211   Within half an hour, they had what they needed: Interview with Jordan
Schaps.

211   Anna appeared on the September 20, 1999, cover . . . until the affair gossip
blew over, but he refused: Gray, "The Summer of Her Discontent."

212   something Bryan many years later called "made-up": Interview with Shelby
Bryan.

212   "We were both unhappy with [the story]": Interview with Shelby Bryan.

212   The Met had asked Anna . . . she had proven successful: Background interview.

212   Planning that kind of event [was] a thankless job: Interview with William
Norwich, December 16, 2020.

212   leaving wealthy New Yorkers seriously disgruntled: Interview with Julie
Macklowe, August 5, 2019.

212   Myra Walker . . . essential in ways few could have imagined: Interview
with Myra Walker, May 4, 2020.

213   Looking for a sponsor, Anna approached Tommy Hilfiger . . . Plus, he
respected Anna: Background interview.

213   He wrote a check for $1 million . . . not next to Britney Spears's: Interview
with Myra Walker.

213   Securing Madonna's famous cone bra . . . make Anna happy: Interview
with Jeff Daly and Gary Delemeester, May 6, 2020.

213   Everything Anna wanted . . . could eventually charge: Interview with
Stephanie Winston Wolkoff.

213   $275,000 for a single table: Figure appeared on a Met Gala planning docu-
      ment provided by background source.

214   A Hilfiger partner, however was encouraged: Background interview.

214   "It was a very photogenic group": Interview with Stephanie Winston
      Wolkoff.

214   *Vogue* and Hilfiger decided to have Sean Combs . . . "if there had been
      any": Cathy Horyn, "A Rare Mix of Celebrity and Society," *Washington
      Post*, December 8, 1999.

214   Russell Simmons crashed: Interview with Stephanie Winston Wolkoff.

214   "Who is this fluff daddy?": Background interview with someone who
      heard the remark.

214   The party raised $3 million . . . She had barely slept the past two nights:
      George Rush and Joanna Molloy, "The Wintour of Her Discontent," *New
      York Daily News*, December 8, 1999.

214   but he left early and Talley saw her . . . losing her composure and breaking
      down: Interview with André Leon Talley.

215   Bryan said he didn't remember: Interview with Shelby Bryan.

215   She and Bryan never married . . . They never got out of the car: Interview
      with Shelby Bryan.

215   In his will, he said: Charles Wintour's will, obtained by author through
      public records request.

216   At Charles's memorial service . . . "people who still promote fur": "People,"
      Miami Herald, December 17, 1999.

216   "He loved what he did": "Anna Wintour on Her Father, Charles Win-
      tour," CNN.com, April 8, 2019, https://www.cnn.com/videos/fashion
      /2019/04/08/anna-wintour-interview-charlie-style-orig.cnn.

216   But Karl Lagerfeld . . . had it canceled at the last minute: Interview with
      Myra Walker; and André Leon Talley, *The Chiffon Trenches* (New York:
      Ballantine, 2020), iBook, 360.

216   Anna, who told *WWD*: Lisa Lockwood, "Karl's Blank Canvas: No Chanel
      Sensation for the Metropolitan," *WWD*, May 19, 2000.

217   [Walker] had already put together the entire show: Interview with Myra
      Walker.

217   Anna and Lagerfeld had a *froideur* . . . making Lagerfeld no exception:
      Interview with André Leon Talley, March 20, 2021.

Chapter 19: Dot.Com

218   She also felt Style.com would be more successful: Interview with Aimee
      Cho, October 16, 2020.

218   After Joan Feeney left CondéNet: "Style.com Names Online Media Vet-
      eran Jamie Pallot as Editor in Chief," *Business Wire*, May 31, 2001.

218   Anna signed off on his appointment: Background interview.

218 Candy Pratts Price . . . was announced as fashion director: James Fallon, "Price Named Style.com Fashion Head," *WWD*, September 5, 2001.

218 Pratts Price said she ended up . . . so long as Pratts Price was there: Interview with Candy Pratts Price, December 8, 2020.

219 Pallot had the same idea . . . that might be too un-*Vogue*-y: Background interview.

219 "I think everybody felt" . . . "Wouldn't that just be ridiculous?": Interview with Candy Pratts Price, December 16, 2020.

219 One early video . . . "get this gay porn off my site": Background interviews with two sources.

220 (Her team consisted of one assistant . . . take the book to her house at night): Background interview.

220 Planning the gala began . . . get people to spend as much as possible: Interview with Stephanie Winston Wolkoff, May 1, 2021.

220 People who didn't get invited called . . . "But we have no more tickets to sell": Background interview.

220 "You could have had a billion dollars" . . . (whom Anna did eventually allow in): Interviews with Stephanie Winston Wolkoff, and background source.

221 Once a table was purchased . . . to facilitate conversation among the groups of strangers: Interview with Stephanie Winston Wolkoff.

221 Tom Ford, Karl Lagerfeld, and Harvey Weinstein: Text message from Stephanie Winston Wolkoff, May 2, 2021.

222 A welcome guest . . . was Donald Trump: Background interviews.

222 Anna had known Trump . . . "such was his pride in the building": Anna Wintour, "Letter from the Editor: The Bold and the Beautiful," *Vogue*, February 2005.

222 Anna and Trump saw each other . . . two of the cheapest tickets: Stephanie Winston Wolkoff, *Melania and Me*, (New York: Gallery, 2020), 20.

222 On the night of April 17 . . . he won with a $30,000 bid: "Radical Lecture Cancels Class," *New York Post*, April 19, 2001.

222 only to discover that the dress . . . didn't fit his girlfriend, Melania Knauss: Background interview.

223 Trump and Knauss . . . were pictured: Alexandra Kotur, "Talking Fashion: Moulin Rouge Premiere: Kickoff Time," *Vogue*, June 2001.

223 In the May 2003 issue of *Vogue*, Knauss: Eve MacSweeney, "Vogue View: Out with the Old," *Vogue*, May 2003.

223 Anna tried to hire twenty-two-year-old Ivanka Trump: Ivanka Trump, *Women Who Work* (New York, NY: Portfolio/Penguin, 2017), 34.

223 After the gala, Knauss went to meet Anna . . . to shop for a wedding dress: Emails from Paul Wilmot, July 21, 2021.

223 Anna's decision to put Knauss . . . one of Anna's tackier visitors: Interviews with two background sources.

223 "That actually was not a very remarkable cover" . . . actresses like Sandra Bullock, paltry: Interview with Sally Singer, January 14, 2021.

223 With around 417,000 copies: Figure provided to author by Audit Bureau of Circulations.

224 The only TV on the *Vogue* floor: Interviews with Aimee Cho and background source.

224 At 8:46 a.m.: "September 11 Attack Timeline," 9/11 Memorial, https://timeline.911memorial.org/#Timeline/2.

224 Most people weren't at work yet . . . stayed in a hotel uptown until she could return: Interviews with Lisa Love, October 20, 2020, and May 25, 2021.

224 Twenty years later, she would describe: Anna Wintour, "What Does 20 Years Feel Like?" Vogue.com, September 10, 2021, https://www.vogue.com/article/anna-wintour-september-11-tribute-2021.

224 Meanwhile, at the office: Interview with background source.

224 Anna started thinking immediately about what [to] do: Anna Wintour, "The CFDA Vogue Fashion Fund," *Anna Wintour Teaches Creativity and Leadership*, MasterClass, https://www.masterclass.com/classes/anna-wintour-teaches-creativity-and-leadership/chapters/spotting-designer-talent-cfda-vogue-fashion-fund.

225 On September 12, 2001, Anna went to work: Interviews with numerous *Vogue* staff.

225 After she'd had a facelift: Interviews with Laurie Jones, May 20, 2021, and background source.

225 It was why in the early aughts: Background interview.

225 She seemed to believe that if *Vogue* stopped: Interview with background source.

225 The message that trickled down . . . was to keep going: Interview with Grace Coddington, May 17, 2021, and two background sources.

225 *Vogue* wasn't a place where the staff felt comfortable . . . in case they had to run down the stairs: Interviews with two background sources.

225 Anna's assistant, Aimee Cho, spent most of September 12: Interview with Aimee Cho, October 16, 2020.

225 Meanwhile, Winston Wolkoff and her assistant . . . listen to their reactions, and try not to cry: Background interview.

225 Anna immediately assigned a spring fashion preview . . . on the other side of the street: Interview with Grace Coddington, May 17, 2021; Sally Singer, "Amazing Grace," *Vogue*, November 2001.

226 With Kurková teetering . . . crew became uncomfortable: Background interview.

226 "I remember looking" . . . "That's what it was supposed to come across as": Interview with Grace Coddington, May 17, 2021.

226 Her ex-husband, David Shaffer . . . "Anna has no empathy": Interview with Anthony Haden-Guest, May 19, 2021.

226 But others thought that Anna did possess empathy: Interviews with Laurie Jones, December 5, 2020, and background source.

226 it just seemed like she left it at home . . . with people jumping out of the towers?: Interviews with two background sources.

Chapter 20: A New Alliance

227 The year 2001 wasn't great . . . down 30 percent from the previous year: Lisa Lockwood, "Mags Worry about Ads," *WWD*, September 21, 2001; and Lisa Lockwood, "Mag Meltdown Spills into 2002," *WWD*, December 14, 2001.

227 Giorgio Armani pulled all ads from *Vogue*: George Rush and Joanna Molloy, "Armani's in Fashion, but Not in *Vogue*," *New York Daily News*, October 31, 2001.

227 In early 2002, Anna walked into Si Newhouse's office . . . trust her not to go to Newhouse to complain: Interview with Tom Florio, August 12, 2020.

228 Richard Beckman, the publisher . . . had to have surgery: Keith Kelly, "Muzzle for Mad Dog—Condé Nast Will Pay Seven Figures to Settle Assault Suit," *New York Post*, September 22, 1999.

228 a lawsuit that Condé Nast ended up settling . . . publicly apologized to the staff: Alex Kuczynski, "Condé Nast Pays Woman Injured by Executive," *New York Times*, September 22, 1999.

228 Anna was appalled by the incident: Interview with Laurie Jones, May 20, 2021.

228 In the early nineties, Steve Florio . . . but felt humiliated: Background interview.

228 Susan Bornstein, who worked on the business side . . . "I don't think they really gave a shit": Interview with Susan Bornstein, August 7, 2019.

229 Waterman's behavior was so well known . . . bringing in money: Background interview.

229 Tom Florio assured Anna . . . we're not going to drop them: Interviews with Tom Florio, August 12, 2020, and April 19, 2021.

231 Editors at several Condé Nast publications: Interviews with three background sources.

231 Alaïa told the press . . . they had been ignoring his clothes: Cathy Horyn, "Fashion Review: Karl Lagerfeld's Understated Mastery," *New York Times*, January 26, 2003.

231 He later said Anna "behaves like a dictator": "Memo Pad: Alaia Aloud," *WWD*, May 8, 2009.

231 When I see how she is dressed . . . No one: Eric Waroll, "Azzedine Alaïa Interview," Virgine, May 25, 2011, http://www.virginemag.com/home /azzedine-alaia-interview/.

231 Alaïa had stopped showing . . . "He was brilliant, but he was very difficult": Interview with Grace Coddington, December 19, 2020.

231 Steve Florio, Condé Nast's CEO, and Si Newhouse . . . thinly veiled as a novel : Interview with Tom Florio.

232 a "girl of privilege" . . . clearly wanted to be a writer: Interview with Laurie Jones, December 5, 2020.

232 Very few young women . . . probably weren't going to be the next Anna: Interviews with Laurie Jones and background source.

232 Predictably, Weisberger "couldn't get any assignments" . . . "I can sell it this afternoon": Interview with Laurie Jones; "First Fiction: Publishers Spring into Action," *Publishers Weekly*, January 27, 2003.

233 On May 21, 2002, *WWD* reported: Lisa Lockwood, "Memo Pad: Wintour Tales," *WWD*, May 21, 2002.

233 When Anna learned about the book: Interview with Laurie Jones.

233 For the November 2002 issue . . . wanted the actresses to appear on the cover in costume: Email from background source.

233 despite the twenties being: "Anna Wintour on AOC and the Three Things She Never Leaves the House Without," *Go Ask Anna*, April 15, 2019, https://www.vogue.com/video/watch/go-ask-anna-video-aoc-the-hadids.

233 almost never put costume . . . to be able to buy the clothes *Vogue* featured: Background interview.

233 Still, it was strange . . . could see that it wasn't working: Interview with Amanda Lundberg, August 20, 2020.

233 once after a box of Met Gala invites was mistakenly thrown out: Background interview.

233 So Anna asked for a reshoot . . . "and he did": Interview with Amanda Lundberg.

233 for big stories like this . . . makeup and lighting teams for the day: Background interview.

234 "When I wasn't doing so well": Joshua Levine, "How to Get Ahead in Fashion: Rule No. 1: Make Friends with This Woman," *Times (UK)*, July 9, 2011.

234 Still, "having someone on the cover" . . . "That was very important to him": Interview with Amanda Lundberg.

234 Anna, who would attend the Oscars: Interview with Amanda Lundberg.

234 the relationship made sense . . . she thought they could be useful to her: Background interviews with two sources.

234 "The sky was the limit": Interview with Amanda Lundberg.

235 Weisberger promoted it . . . known for *Forrest Gump*: "First Fiction: Publishers Spring into Action."

235 "nothing was based on Anna": Sherryl Connelly, "Mags to Riches on a *Vogue* Idea," *New York Daily News*, April 14, 2003.

235 In a profile [that] ran shortly after the book came out: David Carr, "Anna Wintour Steps Toward Fashion's New Democracy," *New York Times*, February 17, 2003.

235 Anna did read it . . . "She wasn't bothered by it at all": Interview with Laurie Jones.

235 William Norwich agreed that Anna "didn't really care": Interview with William Norwich, December 16, 2020.

235 six months on the *New York Times* best-seller list: Sheelah Kolhatkar, "Devil Writes Nada: Why Is Weisberger Getting a Million?" *New York Observer*, October 10, 2005, https://observer.com/2005/10/devil-writes -nada-why-is-weisberger-getting-a-million/.

235 Anna has said to friends, "I'm so bored by me": Interviews with William Norwich and Gabé Doppelt, November 13, 2020.

235 "It was an incredibly hurtful book: Interview with Lisa Love, October 20, 2020.

235 some in the office had the perception that she *was*: Interviews with Aimee Cho, October 16, 2020; Lisa Love; and background source.

236 Aimee Cho was Anna's assistant . . . Then they both went back to work: Interview with Aimee Cho.

237 From where Tom Florio sat . . . Florio's pitch worked: Interview with Tom Florio.

238 Anna never forced her editors to include certain labels . . . "That's what pays my wage": Interview with Grace Coddington.

Chapter 21: Mutual Benefit

239 "Every single one of us at *Vogue* were obviously devastated . . . we will lead": Anna Wintour, "The CFDA Vogue Fashion Fund," *Anna Wintour Teaches Creativity and Leadership*, MasterClass, https://www.masterclass.com/classes/anna-wintour-teaches-creativity-and-leadership/chapters/spotting-designer-talent-cfda-vogue-fashion-fund.

239 she used some of *Vogue*'s money and connections . . . Saks Fifth Avenue to attend: Peter Braunstein, "Young Designers to Show Today," *WWD*, September 21, 2001.

240 Aimee Cho remembered Anna: Interview with Aimee Cho, October 16, 2020.

240 *Vogue* was inundated: Braunstein, "Young Designers to Show Today."

240 "I really started to understand": Eric Wilson, "CFDA, *Vogue* Form Designer Grant Fund," *WWD*, September 25, 2003.

240 Each year, the ten finalists become part of the *Vogue* "family": Interview with Sally Singer, January 14, 2021.

240 Hernandez famously first encountered Anna . . . a story shot by Helmut Newton: Interview with Jack McCollough and Lazaro Hernandez, November 18, 2020.

241 scribbled on an air sickness bag: Bob Morris, "The Age of Dissonance: Fashion Isn't for the Meek," *New York Times*, February 11, 2001.

242 In early 2003, Harvey Weinstein brought a television idea . . . floral arrangements that could have graced a royal wedding: Interview with Eli Holzman, September 23, 2020.

244 [Tom] Florio was a little annoyed: Interview with Tom Florio, August 12, 2020.

244 Speaking at a conference, she said: Jeff Bercovici and Sara James, "Memo Pad: Win-Tour of Duty," *WWD*, March 7, 2006.

244 Yet, even with that $200,000 . . . "she's done so much for you that of course you're going to: Interview with Jack McCollough and Lazaro Hernandez.

245 Designer Isaac Mizrahi enjoyed Anna's support . . . "my years as a couturier were waning": Isaac Mizrahi, *IM: A Memoir* (New York: Flatiron Books, 2019), iBook, 473–74.

246 Mizrahi added, "For such a glamorous business": Eric Wilson, "Check, Please," *WWD*, October 18, 2004.

246 Zang Toi received Anna's support . . . then walked off with her bodyguard: Interview with Zang Toi, October 6, 2020.

246 The next month he was profiled in a story: "New Faces," *Vogue*, March 1990.

Chapter 22: Big Vogue

249 to function as the GM for the entire industry: Background interview.

249 She helped John Galliano . . . setting him up to helm LVMH-owned Givenchy: Amy M. Spindler, "Galliano Is Named Designer for House of Givenchy," *New York Times*, July 12, 1995.

249 recommended Marc Jacobs to design Louis Vuitton: Cathy Horyn, "Citizen Anna," *New York Times*, February 1, 2007.

249 Anna started calling her empire "Big Vogue": Lee Wallick, "Media: Magazines: The Wintour Collection," *Guardian*, May 9, 2005.

250 Anna had asked Amy Astley to create prototypes: Essay by Amy Astley provided to author, July 21, 2021.

250 When she was working on the test issues . . . for that *Teen Vogue* book: Interview with Aimee Cho, October 16, 2020.

250 Astley described her vision . . . to make the magazine very "you": Essay by Amy Astley.

250 *Teen Vogue* was tested a handful of times . . . the competing *Cosmo Girl*: Lisa Lockwood, "Memo Pad: *Teen Vogue*'s Future," *WWD*, April 5, 2020; Jacob Bernstein, "*Teen Vogue* to Become Bimonthly," *WWD*, June 7, 2002.

250 Critiques of the issues were: Bernstein, "Teen Vogue to Become Bimonthly."

250 Bee Shaffer, who . . . didn't have a strong interest in fashion: "Bee Shaffer on What Life Is Like as Anna Wintour's Daughter—*Teen Vogue*," YouTube, May 6, 2014, https://www.youtube.com/watch?v=0gM0nEWxhf4.

250 Astley told the *New York Observer*: Sridhar Pappu, "As Blix Unloads, News Comes Back to U.N. Bureaus; 'It's to a point where I almost can't write about it anymore. If people don't understand it, I don't know what else to do?', Maggie Farley, *The Los Angeles Times*, on covering the Iraq story from the U.N.," *New York Observer*, February 3, 2003.

250 Bee first attended the Met Gala in 2004: "Bee Shaffer on What Life Is Like as Anna Wintour's Daughter," YouTube.

250 Charles Churchward, *Vogue*'s design director . . "that takes a toll": Interview with Charles Churchward, June 4, 2020.

251 Anna poured more energy: Interview with Aimee Cho.

251 But Astley saw the digital future coming: Essay by Amy Astley.

251 she probably didn't expect her cochair Tom Ford . . . "It's just not going to happen": Interview with Tom Ford, October 22, 2020.

251 Anna was also particular about food . . . gum from their mouths the night of the party: Interview with Stephanie Winston Wolkoff, May 1, 2021, and text messages to author from Winston Wolkoff, May 2, 2021.

252 Anna was also always concerned: Text message from Stephanie Winston Wolkoff, September 13, 2021; and background interview.

252 If a guest, in Anna's eyes: Background interview.

252 Anna, who was "militant" about the party . . . because it's free styling: Interview with Stephanie Winston Wolkoff.

252 "everybody went crazy" . . . "I must have looked really uncomfortable": Interview with Andrew Bolton, December 15, 2020.

252 Publishers like Florio could sell so much advertising . . . sold to a men's brand: Interview with background source.

253 Their success got Newhouse thinking . . . weren't quite doing: Interviews with Tom Florio, August 12, 2020, and April 19, 2021.

253 *Men's Vogue*, Newhouse and Fielden thought . . . no question whose magazine it was: Interview with background source.

253 Anna discussed *Men's Vogue* with Shelby Bryan: Interview with Shelby Bryan, July 21, 2021.

253 Anna ran *Men's Vogue* the same way she ran *Vogue* . . . and piece of clothing that appeared: Interviews with two background sources.

253 she became less and less hands-on . . . he was a straight man: Background interview.

253 "She adored Jay. She likes the boys": Interview with Laurie Jones, December 5, 2020.

253 For Anna, *Men's Vogue* wasn't just a business opportunity: Interviews with Laurie Jones and background source.

253 It was a departure . . . a weightier journalistic approach to topics like politics: Background interview.

254 Anna and Fielden knew from the beginning . . . cutting-edge men's fashion didn't have broad appeal: Background interviews with three sources.

254 The *Men's Vogue* reader was "somebody who's very comfortable": Interview with Tom Florio, April 19, 2021.

254 "With George Clooney on the cover . . . a dead quail or pheasant or whatever: "Just in Time for Thursgay Styles: *Men's Vogue*," Gawker.com, August 18, 2005, https://gawker.com/118022%2Fjust-in-time-for-thursgay-styles-mens-vogue.

254 At the end of the day on September 8, 2005 . . . tucking her chin toward her collarbones: Background interview.

255 Lauer opened by posing the question, "Will men care?" . . . "this is fashion for men like yourself, Matt": "Anna Wintour and Jay Fielden Discuss Their New Magazine, *Men's Vogue*," *Today*, NBC, September 9, 2005.

255 It was the kind of thing she probably would never say fifteen years later . . .

she probably felt she had no choice: Interviews with several background sources.

255   Anna did occasionally express concern . . . "too gay": Background interview with source who heard comments.

255   tended to prefer women appearing in shoots: Background interviews with three sources.

255   while some were quick to see her as homophobic . . . to uphold that perspective: Background interviews with three sources.

256   It made for splashy headlines . . . two men, Dick Page and James Gibbs, kissing: Amy Odell, "*Men's Vogue* Refused to Publish Marc Jacobs Ad Starring Gay Couple," NYmag.com, September 2, 2009, https://www.thecut .com/2009/09/mens_vogue_refused_to_publish.html.

256   the magazine did well: Background interview.

256   In 2007, Fielden had booked . . . wanted them to play by her rules: Background interview.

256   Plus, *Men's Vogue*: Background interviews with three sources.

256   Anna knew it was important . . . "Black people don't sell": Background interview.

257   The company had provided . . . who her audience would respond to: Background interviews with two sources.

257   Harvey Weinstein himself kept tabs . . . "You're definitely influencing my work and my life": Email from Harvey Weinstein to Anna Wintour, September 23, 2007, provided to author by background source.

257   She reduced the Wilson/Anderson: Ben Widdicombe, "Gatecrasher. It's a Bad 'Zine, Man!" *New York Daily News*, January 10, 2008.

257   Some saw it as a power move: Background interview.

257   Anna continued to do . . . And her overtures worked: Interviews with two background sources.

257   news broke that Meryl Streep would play Miranda Priestly: Amy DiLuna, "Meryl Takes on a Wintour's Tale," *New York Daily News*, May 3, 2005.

257   Director David Frankel was adamant . . . take pictures of Anna's office in order to replicate it: Interview with David Frankel, July 8, 2020.

258   Right after Streep signed on . . . "She seemed delighted and told me not to hesitate": Isaac Mizrahi, *IM: A Memoir* (New York: Flatiron Books, 2019), iBook, 472.

258   Frankel found other designers . . . then mysteriously bailed: Interview with David Frankel.

258   Gisele Bündchen . . . after clearing the appearance with *Vogue*: Interview with Aline Brosh McKenna, July 14, 2020.

258   Many people in the fashion industry . . . "the one place she had no influence": Interview with David Frankel.

259   Anna got to attend a special screening: "Movie Maven," *WWD*, May 25, 2006.

259   Anna had a seat at the end of the row: Email from William Norwich, July 19, 2021.

259   Bee . . . said, "Mom, they really got you": Interview with David Frankel, July 8, 2020.

259   After the credits, Anna slipped out: Email from William Norwich, May 25, 2021.

259   *Vogue Living*, which would launch before the end of the year: Sara James, "Memo Pad: At Home with Hamish," *WWD*, March 27, 2006.

259   This was never her goal: Interview with Anne McNally, May 6, 2021.

Chapter 23: The Crash

260   Originally, R. J. Cutler, fascinated by an article in *New York* . . . "The days I wore my made-to-order Charvet clothes, it was a different Anna": Interview with R. J. Cutler, September 29, 2020.

261   Cutler's crew was able . . . "because you'll lose": *The September Issue*, directed by R. J. Cutler (2009; New York; A&E Indie Films and Actual Reality Pictures).

262   "They were driving me mad . . . I hated it": Interview with Grace Coddington, December 19, 2020.

262   During filming at the couture shows . . . "her frequent refusals of access": Interview with R. J. Cutler.

262   At one point, cameras focused, a worried Tom Florio . . . She agreed, and told him to move forward: Interview with Tom Florio, August 12, 2020.

263   *Vogue*'s advertisers responded well . . . driving a hundred additional pages of advertising into the magazine: "More on Women's Beauty/Fashion Magazines: (1) *Vogue*'s Newest 'Connection' Is 'ShopVogue.TV,'" *Media Industry Newsletter*, July 30, 2007.

263   As Florio was raking in ad bookings . . . "we just put out the biggest issue in history": Interview with Tom Florio.

263   Indeed, the September 2007 was . . . the biggest in the history of monthly consumer magazines: Maria Aspan, "The Web Way to Magazine Ad Sales," *New York Times*, August 21, 2007, https://www.nytimes.com/2007/08/21/business/media/21adco.html.

263   "You should all be congratulating him" . . . Florio's program stood: Interview with Tom Florio.

264   There was no question that being a *Vogue* brand had value . . . "which was one of the death knells of my brand": Interviews with Scott Sternberg, August 14 and 21, 2020.

264   Indeed, in 2015, he announced: Irina Aleksander, "Sweatpants Forever," *New York Times*, August 6, 2020.

265   After William McComb was named CEO of Liz Claiborne . . . so he had called Anna: Interview with William McComb, June 11, 2019.

265   Anna suggested he talk to Liz Claiborne: Cathy Horyn, "The Fashion

Designer Narciso Rodriguez Finds a Savior with Help from His Friends,"
New York Times, May 7, 2007.

265 Anna took McComb to db Bistro Moderne . . . control of his brand, as
Anna hoped: Interview with William McComb.

266 McComb rang her up again when Isaac Mizrahi's five-year deal: Ibid.

266 The Target line sold as much as $300 million each year: Eric Wilson and
Michael Barbaro, "Isaac Mizrahi Leaves Target to Revamp Liz Claiborne,"
New York Times, January 16, 2008.

266 it wasn't the best deal . . . which was, he added, "kind of the point of it":
Interview with William McComb.

266 When her assistant Aimee Cho left *Vogue* . . . which was a coup for her
line: Interview with Aimee Cho, October 16, 2020.

267 Because *Vogue* was so plugged into fashion companies . . . "controlling your
costs at that company was revolutionary": Interview with Tom Florio.

267 rising to $1:60: "Euro Breaches $1.60 as ECB Warns of Possible Rate Rise,"
New York Times, April 22, 2008, https://www.nytimes.com/2008/04/22
/business/worldbusiness/22iht-22euro.12230841.html.

267 Doing her part, Anna sent: Interview with Laurie Jones, May 20, 2021.

267 Talley said his salary was cut by $50,000: Interview with André Leon Tal-
ley, April 10, 2021.

267 as Laurie Jones remembered it, the cut was due to: Interview with Laurie
Jones.

268 As a result, *Vogue* . . . made a profit in 2008: Interview with Tom Florio.

268 "the Shape Issue" . . . "dedicated to fashion and fitness for all": Anna Wintour, "Editor's Letter: Pro Active," *Vogue*, April 2008.

268 Bündchen was young . . . and had no idea who Clooney was: Interview
with Tonne Goodman, June 10, 2021.

268 Bündchen's reputation of being good . . . on high-fashion shoots: Interview
with Charles Churchward, June 4, 2020.

268 The shoot took place in Cleveland . . . James was a total pro: Interview with
Charles Churchward.

268 *Vogue*'s senior editors warned Anna . . . "we'd have all gone crazy": Interview with Laurie Jones, December 5, 2020.

269 ESPN columnist Jemele Hill wrote: Jemele Hill, "LeBron Should Be More
Careful with His Image," ESPN.com, March 21, 2008, https://www.espn
.com/espn/page2/story?page=hill/080320.

269 It wasn't the sort of thing that would deeply trouble Si Newhouse either:
Background interview.

269 And around the office, *Vogue* staffers mostly didn't understand: Interviews
with Sonya Mooney, August 25, 2020, and Charles Churchward.

269 That summer in Paris . . . "Because it didn't even register on the radar of
anyone": Interview with Sonya Mooney.

269 The *Men's Vogue* team had a bad feeling: Interviews with two background
sources.

269 Things had certainly started well . . . expected a loss: Background interview.

270   A fashion feature shoot: Background interview

270   But it was now clear . . . "Advertising is going dark": Background interview.

270   Meanwhile, the magazine was meant to be putting together a benefit . . . "your magazine has been shut down": Interview with Bonnie Morrison, July 17, 2020.

270   Once the *Men's Vogue* staff . . . with visible tears in her eyes: Interviews with two background sources present in the meeting.

270   *Men's Vogue* hadn't lost nearly as much: Background interview with source familiar with Condé Nast financials.

270   *Portfolio*, which was closed a few months later: David Carr, "*Portfolio* Magazine Shut, a Victim of Recession," *New York Times*, August 27, 2009.

270   Condé Nast lost 30 percent of its revenue: Background interview with source familiar with Condé Nast financials.

271   The next day . . . with no place for him after that, [Fielden] left the company: Background interview.

271   Anna told a sympathetic friend, "I've moved on": Interview with Bonnie Morrison.

271   *Vogue*'s total circulation fell 6 percent and newsstand sales fell 15 percent: Stephanie D. Smith and Miles Socha, "Memo Pad: You're Either In or You're Out," *WWD*, December 3, 2008.

271   *Teen Vogue* had found an unexpectedly great promotional vehicle: Interview with Lisa Love, October 20, 2020.

271   But by the end of 2008, *Vogue Living*: Stephanie D. Smith, "Memo Pad: No Home," *WWD*, July 1, 2008.

272   Newhouse dismissed the reports as "the silliest rumor I've ever heard": Smith and Socha, "Memo Pad: You're Either In or You're Out."

272   there was never a possibility, as far as executives knew: Background interview.

272   Her annoyance was evidenced that fall . . . "Just go away": Charlotte Cowles, "In Which We Offend Anna Wintour and She Shoos Us Away," NYmag.com, November 21, 2008, https://www.thecut.com/2008/11/in_which_we_offend_anna_wintou.html.

Chapter 24: Politics and Pain

273   The day of the premiere . . . "That's an exhibit": Interviews with R. J. Cutler, September 29, 2020, and Amanda Lundberg, August 20, 2020.

273   Months earlier, at the end of the editing process: Interview with R. J. Cutler.

273   Anna missed the screening . . . television critic Joan Juliet Buck: Background interview.

273   Afterward, Anna had notes . . . and their work together: Interview with R. J. Cutler.

274   Anna said that maybe it was time . . . "the movie Anna Wintour doesn't want you to see": Background interview.

274 Tom Florio had no misgivings: Interview with Tom Florio, August 12, 2020.

274 Still, underneath seemed to be a distinguishable tartness: Background interview.

274 Anna laughed when Coddington said . . . "It's your film anyway": Interview with Grace Coddington, December 19, 2020.

274 What she and Florio needed . . . to get people to come into them: Interview with Tom Florio, August 12, 2020.

275 Anna approved the ideas . . . "That's not big enough": Interview with Bonnie Morrison, June 24, 2020; Stephanie Winston Wolkoff text message to author.

275 "It's like, do you expect us to get U2 to play?": Interview with Bonnie Morrison, June 24, 2020.

275 Anna began her night . . . (Bird, a store in Brooklyn): Sarah Spellings, "Remembering the Messiest Night in Fashion," NYmag.com, September 11, 2019, https://www.thecut.com/2019/09/remembering-fashions -night-out-2009-10-years-later.html.

275 As it turned out, the problem . . . Condé Nast declining to provide a reason: Valeriya Safronova, "Why Fashion's Night Out Faltered," *New York Times*, September 3, 2014, https://www.nytimes.com/2014/09/04/fash ion/why-fashions-night-out-faltered.html.

276 In the *New York Times*, however: Manohla Dargis, "The Cameras Zoom In on Fashion's Empress," *New York Times*, August 27, 2009.

276 The film also put Tonne Goodman in an awkward spot: Interview with Tonne Goodman, June 10, 2021.

276 Anna decided she wanted an interview with Asma al-Assad . . . "No one's going to notice your piece anyway": Joan Juliet Buck, *The Price of Illusion* (New York: Simon & Schuster, 2017), iBook, 941–44.

277 It described Asma al-Assad . . . "97 percent of the vote": Joan Juliet Buck, "A Rose in the Desert," *Vogue*, March 2011.

277 one who killed thousands of civilians: Max Fisher, "The Only Remaining Online Copy of *Vogue*'s Asma al-Assad Profile," *Atlantic*, January 3, 2012, https://www.theatlantic.com/international/archive/2012/01/the-only -remaining-online-

277 Laurie Jones said she told Anna they shouldn't run the story . . . and didn't operate quickly: Interview with Laurie Jones, December 5, 2020.

277 the photos were still what decided what ran: Background interview.

277 Almost as soon as the story went online . . . her contract was canceled: Buck, *The Price of Illusion*, 946–47.

278 After the story ran, Anna never called Buck: Background interview.

278 Laurie Jones, who had worked for Anna for twenty years . . . "It was just too much after all that": Interview with Laurie Jones.

278 On July 5, 2011, Anna attended[Lagerfeld's] couture show . . . thanking him for all his help: Interviews with André Leon Talley, March 20 and April 10, 2021.

280   "I don't want to give myself credit": Interview with Shelby Bryan, July 21, 2021.

280   Anna had hoped to feature Clinton . . . "This is America, not Saudi Arabia": Anna Wintour, "Editor's Letter: Pretty Powerful," *Vogue*, February 2008.

280   In June 2008, after Obama . . . dinner with her at Calvin Klein's house: "Stylish Stampede," PageSix.com, June 13, 2008, https://pagesix.com /2008/06/13/stylish-stampede/.

281   In September 2008, Anna [hosted] . . . with proceeds going toward the campaign: Kristi Ellis, "Fashion's Favorite Son: Executives, Designers Pony Up Cash for Obama," *WWD*, October 21, 2008; "For Obama, the Devil Wears Pra-duh," The Caucus (blog), *New York Times*, August 13, 2008, https://thecaucus.blogs.nytimes.com/2008/08/13/for-obama-the-devil -wears-pra-duh/.

281   The collections were Anna's brainchild . . . hardest-working, lowest-main-tenance fund-raisers: Interviews with two background sources.

281   The campaign saw her as . . . made it easy for the campaign: Background interview.

281   giving *Vogue* a full day with her [Michele]: Interview with Tonne Goodman.

281   She called Tom and asked him to host: Interview with Tom Ford, October 22, 2020.

281   When Obama's campaign needed money that year . . . because it was Clinton's only ask: Background interview with source close to the campaign.

282   Lasry never became ambassador: Donovan Slack, "Report: Lasry Drops Out after Ties to Gambling Ring Questioned," Politico, April 26, 2013, https://www.politico.com/blogs/politico44/2013/04/report-lasry-drops -out-after-ties-to-gambling-ring-questioned-162710.

282   Anna seemed to have no problem with the news: Background interview.

282   Nor was it obvious to her bosses: Background interview.

283   Anna had hinted: Background interview.

283   Anna hadn't said anything about the promotion: Interview with Anne McNally, May 6, 2021.

Chapter 25: Anna Wintour, Artistic Director

284   In late 2012, Si Newhouse, now eighty-five . . . "one of the most powerful women in magazine publishing": Eric Wilson, "Condé Nast Adds to Job of Longtime *Vogue* Editor," *New York Times*, March 12, 2013.

284   Anna said she saw the role as: Wilson, "Condé Nast Adds to Job."

285   *Vanity Fair* editor-in-chief Graydon Carter didn't let his editors . . . appeared to ice others out: Background interview.

285   *Men's Vogue* and *GQ*'s rivalry: Background interview.

285   But Newhouse, though he clearly: Interviews with two background sources.

285   Anna, Graydon Carter, and *New Yorker* editor-in-chief David Remnick . . . outweighed concern over potential pitfalls: Background interview.

286   In 2010, Condé Nast had cut budgets . . . by about 25 percent: Stephanie
       Clifford, "Cuts Meet a Culture of Spending at Condé Nast," *New York
       Times*, September 27, 2009.

286   By the end of 2012, news leaked . . . including the *New Yorker*: Keith Kelly,
       "Condé Budget Cuts of 5% on 2013 Agenda," *New York Post*, October 5,
       2012.

286   Anna bought the neighboring six-acre lot: "Anna Wintour Snaps Up
       Waterfront Property Next to Her 62-Acre Long Island Estate 'to Pre-
       vent Anyone Else from Doing So,'" *Daily Mail*, July 16, 2013, https://www
       .dailymail.co.uk/femail/article-2364153/Anna-Wintour-snaps-water
       front-property-62-acre-Long-Island-estate-prevent-doing-so.html.

286   Her compound now comprised . . . "but definitely is in her home life":
       Interviews with Lisa Love, October 20, 2020, and May 25, 2021.

286   Anna liked to start her weekend days . . . to find plants that needed fixing:
       Interview with Miranda Brooks, May 7, 2021.

287   For meals, Anna's chef . . . all served family-style: Interviews with André
       Leon Talley, April 10, 2021, and Lisa Love.

287   Brooks has tried to convince Anna: Interview with Miranda Brooks.

287   In fact, her go-to lunch . . . from the nearby Palm restaurant: Background
       interviews with two sources.

287   Lunches and dinners . . . around thirty people: Interviews with André
       Leon Talley and background source.

287   those who don't manage to slip away . . . as Anna has done: Interview with
       Lisa Love.

287   After dinner, the guests might move . . . slips away before everyone else: Inter-
       view with Jack McCollough and Lazaro Hernandez, November 18, 2020.

287   Anna, who loves to dance: Stephanie Winston Wolkoff text message to
       author, May 2, 2021.

287   Each summer, she held Camp Mastic . . . "she likes to party": Interview
       with Lisa Love.

287   She seemed to remain bemused . . . as a joke for all her guests: Background
       interview.

287   eighteen years after she bought the house . . . "It's *highly* looked after to get
       that appearance": Interview with Miranda Brooks.

288   [West], who had been friends with Anna for years: Background interview.

288   Anna said to Grace Coddington . . . "That would be fantastic": Interview
       with Grace Coddington, May 17, 2021.

288   Anna and West discussed face-to-face: Background interview.

288   When she finally went [to the gala] for the first time . . . "give in to what
       culture, what people want": Interview with Stephanie Winston Wolkoff,
       May 1, 2021.

288   "[They] were part of the conversation . . . our audiences would be hor-
       rified": Anna Wintour, "Introduction," *Anna Wintour Teaches Creativity
       and Leadership*, MasterClass, https://www.masterclass.com/classes/anna
       -wintour-teaches-creativity-and-leadership/chapters/introduction.

288 She knew she had to keep the entire thing secret . . . until Kardashian showed up for her fittings: Interview with Grace Coddington.

289 "All the designers were super-excited": Interview with Hamish Bowles, December 2, 2020.

289 *Vogue* staff knew something was up . . . the Duchess of Cambridge: Interview with Mark Holgate, July 15, 2021.

289 Anna told Coddington and Bowles to wear disguises . . . put on dark glasses: Interview with Grace Coddington.

289 In the art department . . . "I want you to write another letter": Interview with Mark Holgate.

289 The hashtag #boycottvogue trended on Twitter: Hannah Marriott, "Why Kim Kardashian Deserves to Be on the Cover of *Vogue*," *Guardian*, March 24, 2014, https://www.theguardian.com/fashion/2014/mar/24/why-kim-kardashian-deserves-to-be-on-the-cover-of-vogue.

290 It wasn't Coddington's favorite set of pictures: Interview with Grace Coddington.

290 Holgate had been to many fashion shows . . . remaining, as it usually does, behind the scenes: Interview with Mark Holgate.

291 Brandon Holley, who edited the shopping magazine *Lucky* . . . a 20 percent decline in 2012: Keith Kelly, "Anna Gets *Lucky* and *Brides* Altar-ation Jobs," *New York Post*, April 5, 2013.

291 Holley, who had the support of the executive team . . . to improve the print product: Background interview.

291 Anna was primarily concerned with magazines' visuals: Interviews with two background sources.

291 But she soon became involved . . . Chen was appointed *Lucky*'s new editor-in-chief: Erik Maza, "Eva Chen to Succeed Brandon Holley at *Lucky*," *WWD*, June 18, 2013.

291 Anna wanted her own people in these editor-in-chief jobs: Background interview.

291 but Bob Sauerberg . . . said . . . "we made the decisions together": Interview with Bob Sauerberg, July 13, 2021.

291 *Lucky* wasn't the only publication . . . with this approach, Anna had erred: Background interviews.

292 Employees felt a similar drain on the originality: Interviews with three background sources.

292 *Lucky* merged with online retailer BeachMint: David Yi, "Lucky Magazine Shuts Down Once and For All, Here's Why It Failed," Mashable.com, November 3, 2015, https://mashable.com/archive/lucky-magazine-layoffs#4MLY4jBilgqu.

292 *Self* eliminated its print edition: Todd Spangler, "Glamour to Cease Publishing Regular Print Mag in Condé Nast's Latest Digital Shift," *Variety*, November 28, 2018, https://variety.com/2018/biz/news/glamour-ceases-print-magagazine-conde-nast-1203033464/.

292 waking up as early as four thirty: Anna Wintour, "Getting Work Done and

Anna's Management Tips," *Anna Wintour Teaches Creativity and Leadership*, MasterClass, https://www.masterclass.com/classes/anna-wintour-teaches-creativity-and-leadership/chapters/getting-the-work-done-anna-s-management-tips.

292   and asking her *Vogue* staff to schedule meetings: Interviews with Hamish Bowles and Mark Holgate.

292   "There was really no change at all" . . . alongside a drained Bowles: Interview with Hamish Bowles.

293   *Vanity Fair* editor-in-chief Graydon Carter . . . that feeling was gone: Background interviews.

293   Anna's Editorial Task Force meetings: Described in interviews with several former Condé Nast employees.

294   her son, Charlie, married his college sweetheart: Mark Guiducci and Eaddy Kiernan, "Elizabeth Cordry and Charlie Shaffer's Wedding in Mastic Beach," Vogue.com, July 7, 2014, https://www.vogue.com/article/elizabeth-cordry-charlie-shaffer-wedding-in-mastic-beach-new-york.

294   "I'm here because I'm so impressed" . . . said the first lady: Nancy Chilton, "First Lady Michelle Obama Opens the Costume Institute's Anna Wintour Costume Center," MetMuseum.org, https://www.metmuseum.org/blogs/now-at-the-met/2014/anna-wintour-costume-center-ribbon-cutting.

294   The remodeled center . . . a donation from the billionaire Tisch family: "Lizzie and Jonathan Tisch Make $10 Million Gift to Launch the Renovation of the Metropolitan Museum's Costume Institute," MetMuseum.org, January 11, 2011, https://www.metmuseum.org/press/news/2011/lizzie-and-jonathan-tisch-make-10-million-gift-to-launch-the-renovation-of-the-metropolitan-museums-costume-institute.

294   "I'm here today because of Anna" . . . Calvin Klein, Ralph Lauren: Ray A. Smith, "Michelle Obama Cuts the Ribbon for New Anna Wintour Costume Center," *Wall Street Journal*, May 5, 2014, https://www.wsj.com/articles/BL-SEB-81096.

294   She added that "fashion isn't an exclusive club": Krissah Thompson, "Michelle Obama and Anna Wintour's Mutual Admiration Society," *Washington Post*, May 5, 2014, https://www.washingtonpost.com/news/arts-and-entertainment/wp/2014/05/05/michelle-obama-and-anna-wintours-mutual-admiration-society/.

294   This sort of recognition . . . [Anna] really wanted as her legacy: Interviews with Grace Coddington, December 19, 2020, and William Norwich, December 16, 2020.

294   a different side of Anna came out that morning: Interview with Andrew Bolton, December 15, 2020.

294   Anna hadn't really had eyes and ears at Style.com . . . easily able to sell ads on Vogue.com: Interviews with several background sources.

294   Anna had signed off on letting her go: Background interview.

295   But by the summer of 2013 . . . since it was being managed outside the company: Interviews with two background sources.

295 Understanding how to run digital media . . . "that just doesn't get me what I need to do": Interview with Bob Sauerberg.

296 Anna, aware that her site wasn't competitive . . . to five million [unique visitors] in under two years: Interviews with two background sources.

296 the site had never made money: Interviews with three background sources familiar with the financials.

296 based on that . . . pitched Condé Nast's corporate executives . . . exactly what she didn't want at this point: Background interviews with two sources familiar with the discussions.

296 Some saw this takeover . . . to keep them happy: Interviews with several background sources.

297 When she flew to London . . . "Kids love looking at the things they missed," Blanks said: Interview with background source familiar with the discussion.

297 The disconnect was one of many . . . feedback from Anna's people on what they were doing: Background interview.

298 [Jonathan Newhouse] was cooking up an idea . . . not buying Net-a-Porter: Background interview.

298 valued in March of 2015 at $775 million: Kristin Tice Studeman, "Net-a-Porter and Yoox Are Officially Merging," NYmag.com, March 31, 2015, https://www.thecut.com/2015/03/net-a-porter-and-yoox-are-officially-merging.html.

298 In one meeting presenting the new site: Background interview.

298 One day in early 2015 . . . brand and URL for its store: Background interview.

298 Embracing the new endeavor, Anna joined Sauerberg: Interview with Bob Sauerberg.

298 If there was no Style.com brand . . . and in media more broadly: Background interview.

Chapter 26: Changes

299 *Teen Vogue* was on a winning streak . . . the magazine wasn't profitable: Background interview.

299 Amy Astley . . . shifted the head count to her web staff whenever she could: Background interviews with two sources familiar with her thinking.

299 But her magazine had a big problem . . . or getting their first job: Background interview.

300 So Astley and her publisher . . . diverse and inclusive storytelling: Interviews with two background sources.

300 "play[ed] a major role in a progressive sea change": Elaine Welteroth, "Introducing Our August Cover Stars: The Three New Faces of Fashion You Need to Know," *Teen Vogue*, July 7, 2015, https://www.teenvogue.com/story/teen-vogue-august-2015-cover-models.

300 "favorite *Teen Vogue* cover ever": Essay by Amy Astley provided to author, July 21, 2021.

300 Anna had always been involved . . . not other sections like beauty: Interviews with two background sources.

300 She also always knew who was advertising . . . biggest and most reliable revenue drivers: Background interview.

300 Phillip Picardi was twenty-two years old . . . "this game is over": Interview with Phillip Picardi, August 10, 2020.

301 Over the course of a year . . . Wagenheim was let go: Background interview.

301 Astley told her team the news through tears: Background interview.

301 Picardi was too . . . And Picardi still didn't know what was going on: Interview with Phillip Picardi.

302 The next six months at *Teen Vogue* . . . the mood was not cheerful: Background interview.

302 Anna always sat at the head of the table . . . "What do you think?": Background interviews with two sources who were there.

302 This was something Anna did often: Interviews with two background sources.

302 Back when she was overseeing *Men's Vogue* . . . "they won't respect me": Interview with Bonnie Morrison, June 24, 2020.

303 What was Astley's team supposed to say . . . keep reporting to Astley: Background interviews with two sources who were there.

303 The Vogue.com team . . . Blanks was among those who went elsewhere: Interviews with several background sources.

303 But Vogue.com, with our without Style.com's best talent . . . cameos of herself in Vogue.com videos: Background interview.

303 she appeared with Ben Stiller and Owen Wilson: "Anna Wintour Talks Runway Walks with Derek Zoolander and Hansel Backstage at Valentino," Vogue.com, March 10, 2015, https://www.vogue.com/video/watch/fashion-week-anna-wintour-talks-runway-walks-with-derek-zoolander-and-hansel-backstage-at-valentino.

303 Part of the reason *Vogue*'s access to celebrities . . . they were now selling tons of advertising against the content: Background interview.

304 *Vogue*'s sales team hadn't been allowed to monetize the party: Interview with Tom Florio, August 12, 2020.

304 Aurora James applied to the CFDA/*Vogue* Fashion Fund . . . "being disguised as being progressive: Interview with Aurora James, November 24, 2020.

305 In 2013, she partnered with Vera Wang: Laurie Brookins, "Anna Wintour, Vera Wang Team Up for Youth Anxiety Center," *The Hollywood Reporter*, June 19, 2018, https://www.hollywoodreporter.com/lifestyle/style/anna-wintour-vera-wang-tory-burch-celebrate-motherhood-at-youth-anxiety-center-benefit-1121380/.

305 "You might have to decide" . . . Anna could have steered her away from: Interview with Aurora James.

306 Tory Burch recalled emailing her . . . for which Anna sends a list of names: Interview with Tory Burch, May 6, 2021.

306 But Anna also lobbied for James . . . "she really fought for it": Interview with Aurora James.

306 In late January 2016 came an announcement . . . doing everything more cheaply: Lauren Sherman, "Grace Coddington to Step Down as Creative Director of American Vogue," BusinessofFashion.com, January 20, 2016, https://www.businessoffashion.com/articles/news-analysis/bof-exclusive -grace-coddington-to-step-down-as-creative-director-of-american-vogue.

306 Anna wanted to change the way Coddington works . . . "I don't know any-body else that could do what she does": Interview with Grace Coddington, December 19, 2020.

307 In May 2016, Anna called Phillip Picardi . . . Astley, was becoming editor-in-chief of *Architectural Digest*: Interview with Phillip Picardi.

307 the appointment was more of the result of Astley being proactive: Interview with Bob Sauerberg, July 13, 2021.

308 a $10,000 raise: Elaine Welteroth, *More Than Enough: Claiming Space for Who You Are (No Matter What They Say)* (New York: Viking, 2019), 227.

308 repairs to the HVAC system: Background interview.

308 "You're the editor" . . . Anna "does not discuss money": Elaine Welteroth, *More Than Enough*, 228.

308 Anna may have thought . . . the whole thing felt confusing: Interviews with three background sources.

308 And to at least one colleague . . . had set up a fight club: Background interview.

308 Alexander Liberman, who admitted: Dodie Kazanjian and Calvin Tom-kins, *Alex* (New York: Knopf, 1993), 316.

308 the most diverse generation in history: Richard Fry and Kim Parker, "Early Benchmarks Show 'Post-Millennials' on Track to Be Most Diverse, Best-Educated Generation Yet," Pew Research Center, November 15, 2018, https://www.pewresearch.org/social-trends/2018/11/15/early-benchmarks -show-post-millennials-on-track-to-be-most-diverse-best-educated -generation-yet/.

309 Welteroth wrote in her memoir: Welteroth, *More Than Enough*, 231

309 As soon as Welteroth got back to the *Teen Vogue* floor . . . about *Teen Vogue*'s new triumvirate: Welteroth, *More Than Enough*, 229, and back-ground interview.

309 Welteroth felt . . . "if I were a White man": Welteroth, *More Than Enough*, 229.

309 being called into Anna's office because of her "tone": Background interview.

309 Anna came through the art department . . . *Teen Vogue*'s left-leaning politi-cal coverage: Background interviews with two sources.

310 TeenVogue.com published the story that would go viral: Lauren Duca, "Donald Trump Is Gaslighting America," TeenVogue.com, December 10, 2016, https://www.teenvogue.com/story/donald-trump-is-gaslighting -america.

310   "It was a scathing piece": Katie Mettler, "In 'Scorched-Earth' Op-Ed, a
       Teen Vogue Writer Says Trump Is 'Gaslighting America,'" *Washington Post*,
       December 12, 2016, https://www.washingtonpost.com/news/morning
       -mix/wp/2016/12/12/in-scorched-earth-op-ed-a-teen-vogue-writer-says
       -trump-is-gaslighting-america/.

310   Picardi and Welteroth went on *The Daily Show*: "Elaine Welteroth & Phil-
       lip Picardi - How Teen Vogue Has Grown Up | The Daily Show," *The
       Daily Show with Trevor Noah*, YouTube, August 26, 2018, https://www
       .youtube.com/watch?v=eCg8OMVGeT4.

310   Dan Rather became a fan: Sophie Gilbert, "*Teen Vogue*'s Political Coverage
       Isn't Surprising," *The Atlantic*, December 12, 2016, https://www.theatlantic
       .com/entertainment/archive/2016/12/teen-vogue-politics/510374/.

310   She thought Picardi . . . at a time when print was dying: Background inter-
       view.

310   Web traffic went from . . . print subscriptions tripled: Welteroth, *More
       Than Enough*, 264.

310   Though it didn't get the same recognition . . . one of the first outlets to
       interview her: Interview with Sally Singer, January 14, 2021.

311   Bob Sauerberg put Anna in charge of it. . . "move the company forward in
       that regard": Interview with Bob Sauerberg, July 13, 2021.

311   The council brought employees . . . on a set schedule: Background inter-
       view.

311   When one staff member came to her . . . "We need to move on": Interview
       with background source with knowledge of the discussion.

311   A year into her job, Welteroth . . . Anna gave her everything she asked for:
       Welteroth, *More Than Enough*, 265.

312   As much as she had come to despise Trump, she felt the need to invite him
       to the building: Interviews with several background sources familiar with
       her thinking.

312   Graydon Carter, whose needling of Trump . . . "I don't have to work with
       him": Background interview.

312   she bothered issuing a statement: Email from background source to author.

312   comments she was reported to have [made]: Samantha Cooney, "Anna
       Wintour Met with Donald Trump after Apologizing for Criticism,"
       Time.com, December 14, 2016, https://time.com/4602146/anna-wintour
       -donald-trump-apology/.

312   Anna had agreed for the meeting to be off the record: Background inter-
       view.

312   Graydon Carter sat in the meeting with a scowl: Photo seen by author in
       FaceTime call with Stephanie Winston Wolkoff, May 1, 2021.

312   But the other editors-in-chief in the room seemed horrified: Background
       interview.

312   Trump advisor Kellyanne Conway: Background interview.

312   Carter then wrote: Graydon Carter, "A Pillar of Ignorance and Certitude,"
       Vanity Fair, March 2017.

312   Anna was free to go on James Corden's *Late Late Show* and say: Hilary Weaver, "Donald Trump Is No Longer Welcome at the Met Gala," Vanity Fair.com, October 26, 2017, https://www.vanityfair.com/style/2017/10/donald-trump-is-not-invited-to-met-gala.

313   a creature of habit, she often simply fell back on . . . you may as well not even apply: Background interviews with two sources.

313   "Anna wants to fill that assistant spot": Background interview.

313   One editor, determined to expand the scope . . . proving she fit into the *Vogue* world: Background interview.

313   previously appearing in the September 2007 issue: William Norwich, "American Beauties," *Vogue*, September 2007.

313   Staff at *Vogue* observed that those . . . similar preferential treatment: Background interviews with four sources.

313   When new photographers also wanted to work . . . diversity was fine up to a point: Background interview.

314   not that Anna ever explained: Background interviews with two sources.

314   Another person who worked: Background interview.

314   Her staff had previously encouraged: Background interviews with two sources.

314   Often her Post-its: Background interviews with three sources.

314   This is one reason images in *Vogue* . . . before she saw the pictures: Background interviews with two sources.

314   She once asked her photo department . . . to retouch the fat around a baby's neck: Background interview.

314   In one meeting about beauty . . . "she's looking quite rough these days": Background interview with source present in the meeting.

314   personally self-conscious: Interviews with two background sources.

314   Paltrow had not one visible wrinkle: Molly Creeden, "Face Time," *Vogue*, February 2016.

314   Anna was treated like a monarch . . . unless she first talked to you: Interviews with at least five background sources.

315   Anna had the idea to dress Karlie Kloss . . . a *Vogue* favorite: Interviews with two background sources.

315   *Vogue* had done this sort of thing before . . . Frida Kahlo in the July 2012 issue: Background interview.

315   In the July 2007 "Escapes" . . . (the photos cost money and would run): Background interview.

315   But staff at *Vogue* knew: Background interviews with two sources.

315   They decided not to post it on Vogue.com: Background interview.

315   After Kloss tweeted: Background interviews with two sources.

315   The Asian American Journalists Association reach out: Email from AAJA provided to author by background source.

315   a representative from *Vogue* . . . recommendations went ignored: Background interview.

315 it wasn't clear that Anna . . . surprisingly tone-deaf by 2017: Background interview.

315 model Gigi Hadid appeared in a fashion spread: Photography by Greg Harris, "Kicking It," *Vogue*, November 2017, https://www.vogue.com/slideshow/gigi-hadid-athleisure-trend-vogue-november-2017-issue.

316 That year marked a personal milestone: Nicole Sands, "Anna Wintour Welcomes Granddaughter Caroline," People.com, March 31, 2017, https://people.com/parents/anna-wintour-welcomes-granddaughter-caroline/.

316 Months later when Caroline was crawling . . . and change her diapers: Interview with Anne McNally, May 6, 2021.

316 a second granddaughter, Ella: Erica Temptesta, "'Watch Out World': Anna Wintour's Son and Daughter-in-Law Welcome a Baby Girl Named Ella Shaffer, Making the *Vogue* Editor a Grandmother-of-Two," *Daily Mail*, February 5, 2019, https://www.dailymail.co.uk/femail/article-6671631/Anna-Wintours-son-daughter-law-welcome-baby-girl-named-Ella-Shaffer.html.

316 It's not like the kids know . . . "She is still Anna": Interview with Anne McNally, May 6, 2021.

316 Around this time, Phillip Picardi became frustrated . . . "someone to say no to you every step of the way": Interview with Phillip Picardi.

317 "There are certain editors . . . need rather more of my attention": Interview with David Hare, October 27, 2020.

317 Anna eventually heard that Picardi . . . almost no way for Picardi to know: Interview with Phillip Picardi.

317 losses that would eventually total more than $120 million: Edmund Lee and Sapna Maheshwari, "Facing Losses, Condé Nast Plans to Put Three Magazines Up for Sale," *New York Times*, August 1, 2018.

317 Some loss was expected . . . the total caught executives off guard: Background interview with source familiar with company's financials.

317 Finally, Anna took off her sunglasses . . . let the salespeople finish the call: Interview with Phillip Picardi.

318 Sauerberg said he didn't demand . . . "It's not like launching a *Portfolio*": Interview with Bob Sauerberg.

318 Condé Nast was making headlines . . . announced she was also departing: Katherine Rosman, "How to Quit a Magazine, by Cindi Leive," *New York Times*, September 14, 2017, https://www.nytimes.com/2017/09/14/fashion/cindi-leive-glamour.html.

318 Circumventing his boss, Carter told only . . . which served multiple titles: Background interview.

318 In 2018, the company's newer star editors: Amanda Arnold, "*Teen Vogue* Editor-in-Chief Elaine Welteroth is Leaving Condé Nast," NYMag.com, January 11, 2018, https://www.thecut.com/2018/01/teen-vogue-eic-elaine-welteroth-is-leaving-cond-nast.html; Opheli Garcia Lawler, "*Teen Vogue* Head Phillip Picardi Is Leaving Condé Nast," NYMag.com, August 23,

2018, https://www.thecut.com/2018/08/teen-vogue-head-phillip-picardi -leaves-cond-nast.html.

319 Remnick helped Sauerberg . . . "into the company, and into the industry": Interview with Bob Sauerberg.

319 other friends find her much more regal . . . though she still has a twinkle in her eye: Background interview.

319 André Leon Talley wrote in his memoir: André Leon Talley, *The Chiffon Trenches* (New York: Ballantine, 2020), iBook, 457.

319 Anna viewed tennis star Serena Williams: Email to author from Anna Wintour's spokesperson, October 1, 2020.

319 It's a distinction Williams affords to Anna too . . . has never played tennis with Anna: Interview with Serena Williams, November 7, 2020.

320 On Tuesday, February 20, 2018 . . . right next to Anna: Holly Ellyatt, "Queen Shocks Fashion World, Joins *Vogue*'s Anna Wintour on the Front Row at London Fashion Week," CNBC.com, February 21, 2018, https:// www.cnbc.com/2018/02/21/queen-surprises-london-fashion-week -with-anna-wintour.html.

320 The Queen was there to honor Quinn: Brooke Bobb, "Queen Elizabeth– Favorite Richard Quinn Has Updated One of England's Most Iconic Prints," Vogue.com, June 29, 2018, https://www.vogue.com/article/richard -quinn-liberty-london-queen-elizabeth.

320 Anna had previously interacted with the Queen . . . on the pink Chanel suit: "*Vogue* Editor Anna Wintour Made a Dame at Palace Ceremony," BBC.co.uk, May 5, 2017, https://www.bbc.com/news/entertainment-arts -39817660.

320 "how long we've both been": Anna Wintour, interview by Tina Brown, Women in the World Conference, New York, April 12, 2019.

320 a rare Anna-approved cameo: Background interview.

320 Anna was also amused by it . . . "she's not remotely blasé": Interview with David Hare, October 27, 2020.

321 In 2018, *Vogue*'s creative digital director . . . didn't want the series to be *about* Anna: Interview with Sally Singer, January 14, 2021.

321 It was also to connect "non-*Vogue*" people: Interviews with Sally Singer and background source.

321 Other Condé Nast brands were making videos . . . had her eye on the bot- tom line: Background interview.

322 She insisted she not be filmed with dark chocolate: Background interview with source familiar with the sponsorship discussions.

Chapter 27: The Met Gala

323 the Anna Wintour Holiday: Background interview.

323 On Monday, May 7, 2018, Anna arrived first: Interview with Lisa Love, October 20, 2020.

323 rumors that she would leave Condé Nast: Emily Smith, Ian Mohr, and Oli Coleman, "Is Anna Wintour Out at *Vogue?" New York Post*, April 2, 2018.

324 Bee's wedding, like her brother's: Sarah Spellings, "Finally, We Know More about Anna Wintour's Daughter's Wedding," The Cut, July 10, 2018, https://www.thecut.com/2018/07/details-wedding-bee-shaffer-francesco -carrozzini.html.

324 a mighty thirty-foot-high floral replica: "Met Gala 2018," BizBash.com, May 24, 2018, https://www.bizbash.com/home/media-galler/13359400 /met-gala-2018.

324 Anna was *happy* . . . their zipper had broken and had to be fixed: Interview with Lisa Love, October 20, 2020.

324 Beneath Anna in the basement . . . then photographed in the dresses: Background interviews with several sources.

324 for Anna' most senior fashion editors to approve: Text message from Stephanie Winston Wolkoff to author, July 21, 2021.

324 At dinner, where everything had been thought of . . . Kardashian physically couldn't sit: Interview with Lisa Love.

325 Some would argue it also grew in sheer profligacy: Background interviews with two sources.

325 every decision she made was about . . . more money for the museum: Background interviews with several sources.

325 In 2008, tables could be purchased . . . and tickets $30,000: Met Gala document containing financial figures, provided to author by background source.

325 As soon as the gala finished . . . every four to six weeks: Interview with Andrew Bolton and Nancy Chilton, December 15, 2020.

325 The planning process was a tug-of-war . . . and simply erect Katy Perry's stage in front of it: Background interviews with two sources.

326 *Vogue* invited two hundred guests . . . "it can't come out of the *Vogue* budget: Interview with Lisa Love.

326 Though celebrities never paid . . . a donation to the Costume Institute: Interview with Lisa Love, October 6, 2020, and text message from Stephanie Winston Wolkoff to author, May 2, 2021.

326 There was the year Karl Lagerfeld attended: Background interview.

326 George and Amal Clooney . . . to touch up hair and makeup: Interviews with two background sources.

326 For the biggest stars . . . for *China: Through the Looking Glass*: Background interview.

326 When the Chinese government didn't want to send items . . . successfully convincing them to make the loans: Interview with Shelby Bryan, July 21, 2021.

327 While the cost and extravagance have gone up . . . for a haul of $12 million: Met Gala document containing financial figures, provided to author by background source.

327 "For the costume industry": Interview with Kimberly Chrisman-Campbell, July 28, 2020.

327 "The only thing about the Met . . . I'm not going to make a costume": Interview with Tom Ford, October 22, 2020.

327 But Anna loved the over-the-top looks: Interview with Lisa Love.

328 On October 5, 2017, the *New York Times*: Jodi Kantor and Megan Twohey, "Harvey Weinstein Paid Off Sexual Harassment Accusers for Decades," *New York Times*, October 5, 2017, https://www.nytimes.com/2017/10/05 /us/harvey-weinstein-harassment-allegations.html.

328 followed five days later: Ronan Farrow, "From Aggressive Overtures to Sexual Assault: Harvey Weinstein's Accusers Tell Their Stories," *New Yorker*, October 10, 2017, https://www.newyorker.com/news/news-desk /from-aggressive-overtures-to-sexual-assault-harvey-weinsteins-accusers -tell-their-stories.

328 Someone working closely with Anna: Background interview.

328 she and Weinstein seemed to have a relationship: Background interviews with two sources.

328 This was why Anna repeatedly made the allowance . . . the Jimmy Choo cofounder: Background interview.

328 Anna had to be talked out of having lunch with Weinstein: Background interview with source familiar with her thinking.

328 it took a full eight days . . . to appear in the paper: Vanessa Friedman, Jacob Bernstein, and Matthew Schneier, "Fashion Breaks Its Silence on Harvey Weinstein Scandal," *New York Times*, October 13, 2017, https://www .nytimes.com/2017/10/13/style/harvey-weinstein-marchesa-georgina -chapman-anna-wintour.html.

328 Before she issued that statement . . . for more than a decade: Background interview.

328 On *The Late Show with Stephen Colbert*: Dave Quinn, "Anna Wintour Calls Scarlett Johansson Wearing Marchesa to Met Gala 'Great Gesture of Support,'" People.com, May 10, 2018, https://people.com/style/anna-wintour -praises-scarlett-johansson-for-wearing-marchesa-to-met-gala.

328 Chapman's profile in the June 2018 issue: Anna Wintour, "Editor's Letter: Georgina Chapman Breaks Her Silence," *Vogue*, June 2018.

329 she was the one who called Parsons to ask if Galliano: Email to author from background source familiar with the discussion.

329 The school was prepared . . . after a wave of backlash: Julia Talanova and Lorenzo Ferrigno, "Parsons Cancels Designer John Galliano's Class," CNN.com, May 8, 2013, https://www.cnn.com/2013/05/08/us/new-york -parsons-class/index.html.

329 "This is not a designer with Galliano-level talent": Stella Bugbee, "Who Is Anna Wintour Asking Us to Forgive in Her Editor's Letter?" NYMag .com, May 11, 2018, https://www.thecut.com/2018/05/anna-wintour -asks-us-to-forgive-in-her-editors-letter.html.

329 *Vogue*'s favored photographers: Jacob Bernstein, Matthew Schneier, and Vanessa Friedman, "Male Models Say Mario Testino and Bruce Weber Sexually Exploited Them," *New York Times*, January 13, 2018.

329 Anna announced . . . *Vogue* would stop working with them right away: Vanessa Friedman, "Condé Nast Crafts Rules to Protect Models from Harassment," *New York Times*, January 13, 2018.

329 Patrick Demarchelier was the next: Jenn Abelson and Sacha Pfeiffer, "Modeling's Glamour Hides Web of Abuse," *Boston Globe*, February 16, 2018.

329 Tonne Goodman, still one of Anna's top editors . . . "as heartbroken as we were": Interview with Tonne Goodman, June 10, 2021.

330 Helena Suric, who worked as *Vogue*'s bookings editor . . . "it was a huge things": Interview with Helena Suric, October 30, 2020.

330 Many of the Post-it notes . . . how models looked too thin: Background interview.

330 "I have literally argued with her" . . . "how models shouldn't be too thin": Interview with Helena Suric, October 30, 2020.

331 came up with the Code of Conduct . . . approved by Condé Nast: Anna Wintour, "Anna Wintour Responds to Mario Testino and Bruce Weber Sexual Misconduct Allegations," Vogue.com, January 13, 2018, https://www.vogue.com/article/anna-wintour-responds-mario-testino-bruce-weber-sexual-misconduct-allegations.

331 Casting director James Scully . . . "It could have come back to haunt them": Interview with James Scully, August 4, 2020.

331 When Beyoncé insisted . . . *Vogue* suggested twenty-three-year-old Tyler Mitchell: Interview with background source familiar with the discussion.

331 Anna attended wearing a cape of feathers by Chanel: Veronica Rocha and Meg Wagner, "Anna Wintour Hits the Red Carpet in Pink Feather Look," CNN, May 6, 2019, https://www.cnn.com/entertainment/live-news/met-gala-2019/h_442f13c3703d6d14df1840766d63e899.

332 Burberry had announced: Imran Amed, "Burberry Stops Destroying Product and Bans Real Fur," Business of Fashion, September 6, 2018, https://www.businessoffashion.com/articles/news-analysis/burberry-stops-destroying-product-and-bans-real-fur.

332 around that time that Anna had decided . . . the profits going to charity: Background interview.

332 It was the first time in all her years hosting . . . Anna, a devoted theatergoer, loved it: Interview with Lisa Love, October 25, 2020.

332 Anna's impatience can be evident . . . less than an hour after they start: Interview with David Hare, October 27, 2020.

332 "We were trying to think of people": Interview with Andrew Bolton, December 15, 2020.

Epilogue: The Pandemic

333 Anna reportedly sent the message to her team: Ben Smith, "Anna Wintour Made Condé Nast the Embodiment of Boomer Excess. Can It Change to Meet This Crisis?" *New York Times*, April 26, 2020.

333 Smith said Anna was concerned . . . retailers had gone home without placing orders: Interview with Virginia Smith, October 27, 2020.

333 In March, when the US was going into lockdown . . . their staff's salaries, just survive: Interview with Tom Ford, October 22, 2020.

334 Ralph Lauren donated . . . was disbursed to 128 recipients: "A Common Thread," CFDA.com, https://cfda.com/programs/designers/cfdavogue -fashion-fund.

334 Aurora James, the Brother Vellies designer . . . from A Common Thread: Interview with Aurora James, November 25, 2020.

334 a 20 percent pay cut: Edmund Lee and Vanessa Friedman, "Pay Cuts Come to Condé Nast, the Glossy Publisher of *Vogue* and *Vanity Fair*," *New York Times*, April 13, 2020, https://www.nytimes.com/2020/04/13/busi ness/media/conde-nast-coronavirus-layoffs.html.

334 working from home, wearing track pants: Anna Wintour, "Anna Wintour Introduces *Vogue* Global Conversations," Vogue.com, April 13, 2020, https://www.vogue.com/article/anna-wintour-introduces-vogue-global -conversations.

334 taking up jogging, and . . . blueberry muffins: Anna Wintour, "My Dream of Re-Emergence," Vogue.com, April 27, 2020, https://www.vogue.com /article/anna-wintour-re-emergence-dream.

334 Instead of having racks . . . instead of actual clothes: Interview with Virginia Smith.

334 which disproportionately affected BIPOC Americans: William F. Marshall III, "Coronavirus Infection by Race: What's Behind the Health Disparities?" Mayo Clinic, August 13, 2020, https://www.mayoclinic.org /diseases-conditions/coronavirus/expert-answers/coronavirus-infection -by-race/faq-20488802.

334 "The need for change should fall": Anna Wintour, "Joe Biden Should Choose a Woman of Color to Be His Vice President—and He Should Do It Now," Vogue.com, May 31, 2020, https://www.vogue.com/article /joe-biden-vice-president-woman-of-color.

335 First came upheaval [at] Refinery29: Katie Robertson, "Refinery29 Editor Resigns after Former Employees Describe 'Toxic Culture,'" *New York Times*, June 8, 2020.

335 Then came a staff uprising at *Bon Appétit*: Jenny G. Zhang, "New Report Details Pervasive Culture of Racism at *Bon Appétit*: 'Nowhere Have I Ever Felt More Isolated,'" Eater.com, June 10, 2020.

335 Anna's strategy to get ahead . . . make the problem go away, and move on: Background interview.

335 she sent her staff an email—quickly leaked: Sara Nathan, "Anna Wintour

Admits to 'Hurtful or Intolerant' Behavior at *Vogue*," PageSix.com, June 9, 2020, https://pagesix.com/2020/06/09/anna-wintour-admits-to-hurtful-and-intolerant-behavior-at-vogue/.

335 Less than a week later, the *New York Times*: Ginia Bellafante, "Can Anna Wintour Survive the Social Justice Movement?" *New York Times*, June 11, 2020.

335 Anna emailed Aurora James . . . "Could the pledge translate to the publishing industry?": Interview with Aurora James, November 25, 2020; conversation with Casteel recalled by James corroborated by a representative for Casteel.

336 "the highest-ranking Black man in the history of fashion journalism": André Leon Talley, *The Chiffon Trenches* (New York: Ballantine, 2020), iBook, 208.

336 On the press tour . . . "gets in the way of her white privilege": Edmund Lee, "The White Issue: Has Anna Wintour's Diversity Push Come Too Late?" *New York Times*, October 24, 2020.

337 Anna was hurt . . . and those in her inner circle were flummoxed: Interviews with several friends.

337 "Simple human kindness": Talley, *The Chiffon Trenches*, 448.

337 Yet Anna . . . had been exceedingly kind: Interviews with Laurie Jones, December 5, 2020, and May 20, 2021, and Anne McNally, May 6, 2021.

337 When she became concerned about his weight: Talley, *The Chiffon Trenches*, 375–76; interview with Laurie Jones, May 20, 2021.

337 Talley fell out of her social circle . . . "She has no time for me": Interview with André Leon Talley, March 20, 2021.

337 Talley's book further fueled . . . "doing the work": Lee, "The White Issue."

338 Anna's actions toward Talley were never vindictive: Interview with Laurie Jones.

338 though they had broken up much earlier: Interview with Shelby Bryan, July 13, 2021.

338 another story about Anna on October 24: Lee, "The White Issue."

339 Weathering the negative press . . . hasn't been easy for Anna: Interviews with David Hare, October 27, 2020, and Lisa Love, October 20, 2020.

339 "I think her concern is": Interview with William Norwich, December 16, 2020.

339 Anna approached Whembley Sewell . . . to Sewell to run along with *Them*: Interview with Whembley Sewell, December 7, 2020.

340 Sewell wasn't an editor-in-chief for long: Emilia Petrarca, "The Devil Wears Allbirds," NYMag.com, September 1, 2021, https://www.thecut.com/2021/09/silicon-valley-fashion-editors.html.

340 New York congresswoman Alexandria Ocasio-Cortez . . . "TAX THE RICH" in red on the back: Jessica Testa, "A.O.C.'s Met Gala Designer Explains Her 'Tax the Rich' Dress," *New York Times*, September 16, 2021.

340 "A.O.C. wanted to get glammed up": Maureen Dowd, "Never Com-

plain, Never Explain," *New York Times*, September 18, 2021, https://www
.nytimes.com/2021/09/18/opinion/elizabeth-holmes-AOC-dress.html.

341   "If you get frozen be her . . . It's that cold": Interview with Lisa Love.

341   "If you're trying to climb a social ladder": Interview with Aurora James.

341   She ended the disastrous year of 2020 . . . including the *New Yorker* and every
international title: Kerry Flynn, "Anna Wintour Has Long Reigned Supreme
at Condé Nast. Now It's Official," CNN.com, December 15, 2020, https://
www.cnn.com/2020/12/15/media/anna-wintour-conde-nast-promotion/index
.html.

341   The same was painfully not true of Alexi McCammond: Kerry Flynn,
"*Teen Vogue*'s New Editor Out of a Job after Backlash over Old Tweets,"
CNN.com, March 20, 2021, https://www.cnn.com/2021/03/18/media
/alexi-mccammond-teen-vogue-out/index.html.

341   Her phone call is all it takes to get a brand to sponsor: Interviews with Lisa
Love and Andrew Bolton, December 15, 2020.

342   Anna surely has a plan: Interview with Lisa Love

342   being paid for her advice instead of giving it away for free: Interview with
Anne McNally, May 6, 2021.

Index

About the Author

Amy Odell is a fashion and culture journalist. Her work has appeared in *New York* magazine, *The Economist*'s *1843*, *Time*, *Cosmopolitan*, and numerous other publications. She previously authored the essay collection *Tales from the Back Row*. *Anna* is her first biography. She lives in Westchester, New York, with her husband and two children.